A History of the Burmah Oil Company
Volume II: 1924–66

T. A. B. CORLEY

A History of the Burmah Oil Company
Volume II: 1924–66

HEINEMANN : LONDON

William Heinemann Ltd
Michelin House, 81 Fulham Road, London sw3 6rb

LONDON   MELBOURNE   AUCKLAND

First published 1988
© The Burmah Oil Company 1988

British Library Cataloguing in Publication Data
Corley, T. A. B. (Thomas Anthony Buchanan) *1923–*
A history of the Burmah Oil Company
Vol. 2, 1924–66
1. Great Britain. Petroleum industries.
Burmah Oil Company to 1987
I. Title
338.7'6223382'0941

ISBN 0 434 01807 4

Typeset by Hewer Text Composition Services, Edinburgh
Printed and bound in Great Britain by
Mackays of Chatham

'Truly there is a tide in the affairs of men; but there is no gulf-stream setting forever in one direction.'

James Russell Lowell,
*Among My Books, New England
Two Centuries Ago* (1887)
[See Chapter VII, p. 219 below.]

Contents

List of Illustrations

ix

Author's Note

In the course of researching the present volume, I have been privileged to meet or correspond with many people who have been able to contribute to the narrative, either directly or as background. It is not possible here to mention them all by name. I do, however, ask them to accept my sincere gratitude.

In particular, my thanks are due to John Maltby, Chairman of Burmah Oil, for his lively interest and help throughout. Three former chairmen, the late William Eadie, Hamish Lumsden and Sir Alastair Down, gave me the opportunity of talking to them and benefiting from their first-hand knowledge of events. Of the retired directors Stanley Churchfield, the late John Drysdale, Bill Maclachlan, Keith Wilson, and especially Jack Strain and Bob Tainsh, have all provided expert assistance, as have the following former managers; Richard Dixon, Michael Cooke, Michael Hastings, Brian Jones, Cecil Maxwell-Lefroy, Graham Robertson, Tom Simmonds and Ken Stringer. Peter Perry has kindly compiled the Index.

As former Secretary of The Burmah Oil Society, Tony Gowan has been tireless in providing information from his own experience and in suggesting members of the Society who might usefully be approached. I am grateful also to his successor, Arthur Colman. Eileen Murphy of the London Office has once again been a constant source of help. Lady (Norah) Roper and Mrs Norman S. (Nancie) Swan, and from outside the company Sir Eric Berthoud and the late Leslie Forster, all made available to me documentary evidence of great value.

Four people, above all, have contributed to good effect their particular talents and expertise. James Alexander, Head of Public Affairs, has dealt most efficiently with the administrative side of the project. John Harvey, retired Director of Public Affairs, has once again put his long experience of the company's history and of national politics at my disposal, and helped materially with reading and commenting on files and successive drafts. Bridget Stockford has applied her skills both as the Burmah Group Archivist and as an economic historian to dealing with all my queries as they arose, and has assisted me in many other ways, while Kay Mann has word-processed and amended draft after draft with great cheerfulness and efficiency. The willing help of so many people has truly made this a co-operative effort. Except in the quest for accuracy, no one has suggested that I should delete – and perhaps more importantly, add – anything to my drafting, so that it remains an independent work. I therefore take full responsibility for both the facts and the opinions expressed.

Although I have made every effort to put all figures on a consistent basis, they should be regarded as orders of magnitude rather than correct down to the last digit. This is because the financial underpinning of successive phases of the company's progress has been less thorough than I should have liked as for the most part I have had to rely on figures published in the annual reports. Such data (e.g. country-by-country) as have survived in the internal memoranda I have studied have been patchy in places and in certain instances not easily reconcilable with subsequent data.

A further problem, familiar to all researchers into oil history, is that the measures of gallon, barrel and ton vary from one source of information to the next, the precise definition often not being given. For the sake of simplicity, the barrel is here taken to be 40, and the long ton 250, imperial gallons, and questions of variations between individual products are ignored. It seemed more important to convey clear orders of magnitude rather than provide lengthy discussions on very technical matters.

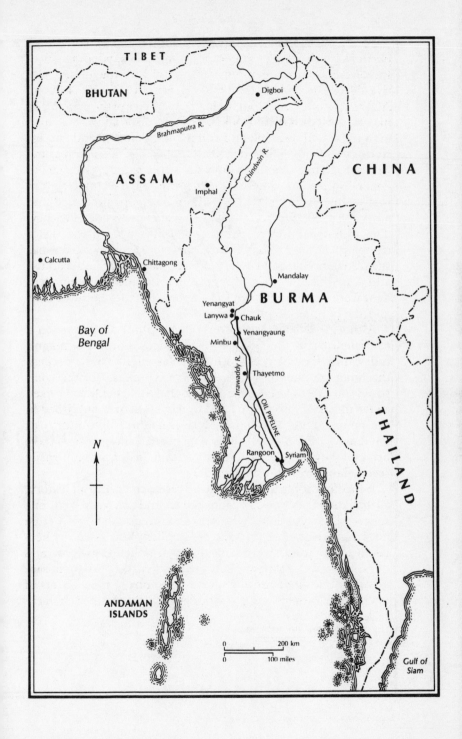

TIBET

BHUTAN

Digboi

Brahmaputra R.

ASSAM

CHINA

Imphal

Chindwin R.

Calcutta

Chittagong

Mandalay

BURMA

Bay of
Bengal

Yenangyat
Lanywa   Chauk
Yenangyaung
Minbu

Irrawaddy R.

Thayetmo

OIL PIPELINE

THAILAND

N

Rangoon   Syriam

ANDAMAN
ISLANDS

0   200 km
0   100 miles

Gulf of
Siam

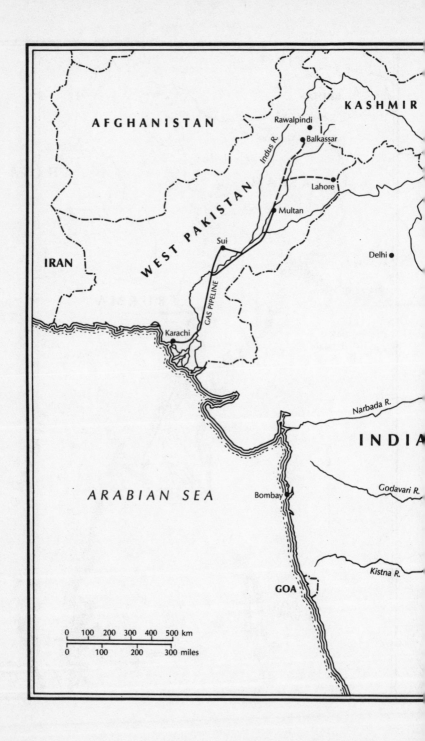

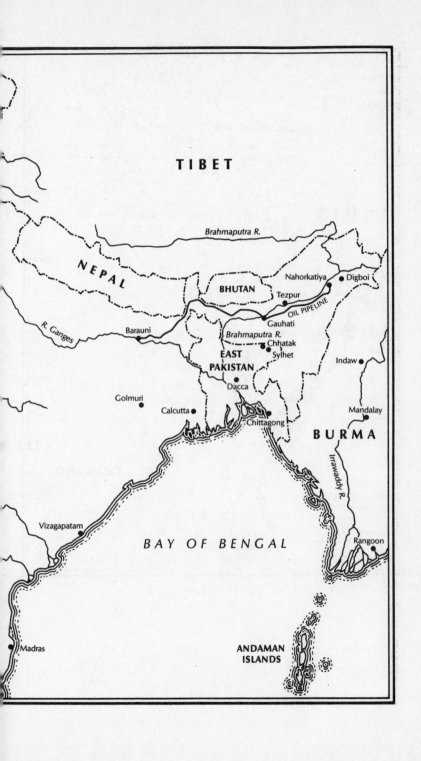

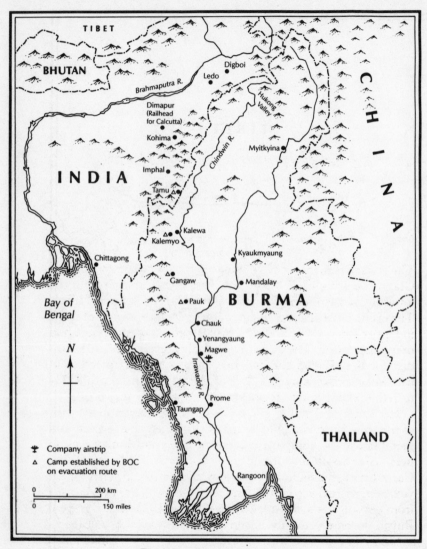

Denial and evacuation 1942

INTRODUCTION[1]

The Burmah Oil Company
1886–1924*

Origins

The establishment of The Burmah Oil Company Ltd in
Glasgow during 1886, with £120,000 capital, sprang from the
foresight of two men, David S. Cargill and Kirkman Finlay.
The crude oil deposits developed by the company were situated
in Upper Burma where King Thibaw and his predecessors had
previously ruled. Their capricious variations in prices demanded for the oil and the practice of delaying shipments had
frustrated earlier attempts by British entrepreneurs profitably
to refine and market oil products in Burma.

However, in 1874 Cargill, a Glasgow merchant and director
of the then Rangoon Oil Company, travelled to Rangoon and
met Finlay, the company's agent on the spot. Finlay was so
persuasive about the long-term prospects for Burmese oil that
Cargill in 1876 bought up the ailing enterprise and ran it for ten
years on his own account. He spent in all £100,000, which came
from earnings in some investments he had in Ceylon; yet from
Burma he received only meagre returns.

Cargill's patience was rewarded when in 1886 the British
annexed Upper Burma after the third Anglo-Burmese war.
The whole of Burma became a province of the Indian empire,

---

* This Introduction outlines some of the themes of Volume I of this History.
Further particulars are given in 'Strategic Factors in the Growth of a
Multinational Enterprise: The Burmah Oil Company 1886–1928' in M. C.
Casson (ed.) *The Growth of International Business* (1983) pp. 214–35.

and its new government granted him a number of oil conces-sions. He could then carry out some much-needed investment, financed with the new company's capital as this was called up. He bought equipment for the first-ever machine drilling in Burma, the initial producing well being completed in 1889. He had more up-to-date techniques introduced in the Rangoon refinery. In addition to wax, required for candles in Burma and also shipped as far afield as Britain, the main finished product was kerosene, a cheap variety refined for local use. Small quantities of heavier fractions were sold as lubricants and as fuel oil. Since the major use of oil was for illumination, the light fractions were burnt off as being apparently of little commercial use.

Developments to 1905

The new company grew steadily, at first making little mark in the world of oil. Cargill as chairman and Finlay as managing director pursued a conservative financial policy, heavily under-valuing assets. By 1901 its issued ordinary share capital totalled no more than £200,000, although that year's refinery throughput was over 750,000 barrels. To overhaul its financial structure and make borrowing easier for future expansion, in 1902 the company was put into liquidation and a new Burmah Oil Company was immediately formed, with a greatly en-hanced capital of £1.5 million.

This more realistic corporate structure came just when the company was entering a phase of challenge from outside. It had by then effectively saturated the kerosene market in Burma, and was beginning to ship large quantities to mainland India. Its agent there was the Calcutta mercantile house of Shaw Wallace & Co., whose principal in London, C. W. Wallace, became increasingly involved in the affairs of Burmah Oil. Wallace was made a director of the company in 1902. However, this entry into India – one of the most extensive single markets for kerosene in the world – attracted the hostility of the existing suppliers, namely Royal Dutch and Shell (through their joint marketing subsidiary the Asiatic Petroleum Company) and the American giant, Standard Oil. These giants strove to knock Burmah Oil out by a prolonged price war.

Partly through the support of the local Indian and Burmese governments, which refused to grant these rivals licences to undertake their own production in Burma itself, the company successfully beat off this assault. In 1905 it concluded with Asiatic a kerosene agreement, later extended to other products. To keep the market stable, the company arranged to sell its excess production to its rivals, although not at particularly remunerative rates. However, it insisted – much to the chagrin of Asiatic – on setting a maximum price for the kerosene it sold in the Indian empire.

Burmah Oil's struggle with rivals over India coincided with the demise of the first generation of its entrepreneurs. In 1903 Finlay died and David Cargill became terminally ill; he died the following year. David Cargill's son John, in his mid-thirties, unexpectedly found himself thrust into the sole direction of the company, being elected chairman in 1904. John Cargill had hitherto lived in the shadow of his formidable and tenacious father, and remained a somewhat diffident man; his qualities included dedication, high principle and sturdy commonsense. He was well advised not only by Wallace but also by Sir Boverton Redwood, the respected oil analyst, who had been consultant to Burmah Oil since 1893.

An issue of high policy arose in 1903, when the Admiralty asked the company for a long-term contract to supply fuel oil. Now that the first oil-burning British warships were being laid down, it was looking for a reliable source of fuel; Burmah Oil was the only oil producer of any note in the whole of the British empire. In 1905 an agreement was signed. A war clause provided for an annual supply of up to 100,000 tons in the event of hostilities. So far from gaining any financial benefit, the company was consistently out of pocket on the deal, as the Admiralty declined to reimburse the expense of installing fuel oil manufacturing plant or storage costs.

What this agreement did lead to was something of far greater moment: a request by the Admiralty that the company should assume the managerial and financial burden of prospecting for oil in Persia. The British holder of the concession there, W. K. D'Arcy, was running short of funds and on the brink of selling out to foreign capitalists; Whitehall's fear was that, as southern Persia was considered to be in the British sphere of influence, such a sale would gravely harm national economic and strategic interests. If the concessions turned out to be productive, that country would therefore become a secure source of fuel oil, far nearer to the West than was Rangoon. In 1905 the Burmah Oil directors agreed to provide the necessary resources and, if successful there, to launch a new company to work the deposits.

Further developments in these years involved production and refining in Burma. On the one hand, the company was at last able to use light fractions by turning them into petrol, just when motor vehicles were appearing in the East, and better quality kerosene. On the other hand, by 1905 it was having to accept that, despite very extensive prospecting outside the proven oilfields in Burma, there seemed little chance of discovering worthwhile new fields there, so that reserves existed for perhaps no more than three or four decades' use. That limitation effectively dampened any prospect of spectacular new growth in the province.

Product Agreements and Diversification 1905–20

After 1905, much of Burmah Oil's entrepreneurial effort was taken up with operating the product agreements with Asiatic. Standard Oil tacitly accepted the framework of the agreements and reached secret verbal 'understandings' with the parties concerned, imprecise enough not to breach the US anti-trust laws. In 1909 and 1910–11 Standard Oil did wage two price wars with Burmah Oil and Asiatic, in disputes over market shares, but then settled down to a prolonged period of more or less willing acceptance of its market share.

Burmah Oil's London office had been manned on an *ad hoc* basis ever since Finlay's death. Wallace and his deputy from Shaw Wallace & Co., Charles (later Lord) Greenway, were among those who undertook day-to-day liaison with Asiatic. Then in 1912 two men joined the London office from Burma. The senior was (Sir) Campbell Kirkman Finlay, son of the late managing director and himself until lately the company's general manager in Rangoon, and the junior was Robert I. Watson. When Finlay joined the army in 1914, Watson took over the London office, and remained there until his retirement at the end of 1947. Watson's character and remarkable career will be discussed in Chapter I and subsequent chapters.

Much effort from 1905 onwards had to go into Persia as well, Wallace becoming increasingly involved with the venture there. After nearly £400,000 had been spent, in 1908 the drilling team being financed by Burmah Oil discovered oil at Masjid-i-Sulaiman in southern Persia. That turned out to be the largest known oil deposit in the world to date, and the forerunner of many other discoveries throughout the Middle East. Burmah Oil then established in 1909 a 97 per cent-owned subsidiary, the Anglo-Persian Oil Company, which in 1935 was renamed Anglo-Iranian and in 1954 the British Petroleum Company. The other 3 per cent was held by the Canadian magnate Lord Strathcona, who became that company's chairman. Wallace was the vice-chairman and Greenway managing director. Two other Burmah Oil directors, including Cargill, were made non-executive directors; Finlay joined them in 1912.

The very extensive oil strike in Persia did not for some years provide Burmah Oil with a source of revenue. No ordinary dividend was paid by Anglo-Persian before 1917, and in the meantime Burmah Oil had to advance the money for the preference dividends. The considerable extra outlay on a pipeline and on the refinery which was constructed on the Persian gulf at Abadan, and difficulties over finding markets for all the products – which (apart from fuel oil) until 1922 had to be sold unprofitably through Shell – led to Cargill's refusal in 1912 to advance any more money to the subsidiary. Greenway thereupon approached the Admiralty for financial help.

The fortunate coincidence that Anglo-Persian could supply fuel oil – from a part of the world subject to Britain's influence – but was short of cash, and that the First Lord of the Admiralty, Winston Churchill, needed fuel oil for his warships and might persuade the Chancellor of the Exchequer, and ultimately Parliament, to make an investment, led to two agreements being concluded in 1914. The British government secured from Burmah Oil a majority shareholding in Anglo-Persian, Burmah Oil's stake falling to just under 32 per cent. At the same time, the Admiralty signed a very large-scale fuel oil contract with Anglo-Persian.

The First World War of 1914 to 1918 affected the company's operations mainly in the East. Burmah Oil had to provide both fuel oil – although not on the wartime scale contemplated in the Admiralty's agreement of 1905 – and the maximum possible quantity of kerosene when Asiatic and Standard Oil curtailed shipments to India in 1917. It also exported petrol to various theatres of war, including East Africa and Mesopotamia.

Watson, by then fully in charge of the London office, also served on government bodies concerned with the allocation of oil products in Britain. Then in 1915 Shell devised a plan for a British-controlled oil combine, by a merger with Burmah Oil. Since Shell was 60 per cent Dutch-owned, that merger would have given the combine a majority British stake. Burmah Oil shareholders were expected to benefit financially from Shell's world-wide activities. Much negotiation, but no conclusive results, occurred before 1920.

New Strategy 1920–4

In 1920 R. I. Watson was appointed Burmah Oil's managing director, a post he had effectively held for several years. His strategy will be related in Chapter I below. However, two aspects may be mentioned here, namely diversification and agreements with other companies.

As to diversification, in 1921 he acquired the Assam Oil Company, one of the two producers of any consequence in mainland India, but inefficient as a result of being under-financed and poorly managed. Its subsequent history is narrated below.

From 1920 onwards, together with Sir Robert Waley Cohen of Shell, he vigorously sought to persuade the British government to accept the merger of Burmah Oil not only with Shell but also with Anglo-Persian, by then necessary as a British counterweight to the relatively larger Dutch interests in Shell. The merger scheme was opposed by Anglo-Persian, the Admiralty, and many sections of British public opinion hostile to an oil trust. Not until 1924 was it finally turned down by the first Labour government, although earlier on Conservative ministers had seemed willing to see the government holdings of

Anglo-Persian shares sold to the private sector, an integral part of the scheme. How Watson, after this rebuff, strove to secure as many merger-type advantages as possible will be described below.

Thus, after nearly forty years Burmah Oil had by 1924 become a company of some consequence, although still very much smaller than the giants. It had an issued capital of £9 million ordinary and preference shares, and total assets of more than £15 million. The Rangoon refinery had a throughput of just under 5 million barrels, compared with less than 50,000 barrels in 1886. Net profit was up from £8,000 to £2.25 million in 1924. The present volume will narrate the company's further progress in the following forty years or so to 1966.

Notes

1 Since Volume I was published, entries for the following have appeared in David J. Jeremy (ed.), *Dictionary of Business Biography*, 5 vols., 1984–6 (henceforth *DBB*): Sir John Cargill, William K. D'Arcy, Charles (Lord) Greenway, Sir T. Boverton Redwood, Charles W. Wallace and Robert I. Watson. David S. Cargill, Sir John Cargill and R. I. Watson have entries in Anthony Slaven and Sydney Checkland (eds), *Dictionary of Scottish Business Biography 1860–1960 I: The Staple Industries*, Aberdeen, 1986.

CHAPTER I

Watson at the Summit
1924–38

In this period, the Burmah Oil Company was of greater consequence in the oil affairs of Britain and the world than ever before or since. Its influence owed nothing to the physical size of the company or the geographical spread of its operations, however. In size, as Table 1 shows, it was minute compared with its main rivals. Geographically, since its foundation in 1886, its direct sphere of operations had been in Burma, and India. It also had a significant, if indirect, involvement in Persia, but made no claim to be in the same league as the global leaders of the oil industry.

TABLE 1
Leading world oil firms, 1939
(by issued capital: £ Million equivalent)

Standard Oil of New Jersey (Esso/Exxon)	143.5
Royal Dutch-Shell	104.1
Socony-Vacuum Oil Company (Mobil)	101.6
Standard Oil of Indiana (Amoco)	81.6
Standard Oil of California (Socal/Chevron)	81.0
Texas Corporation (Texaco)	58.1
Gulf Oil Corporation	48.5
Anglo-Iranian Oil Company (BP)	32.8
The Burmah Oil Company	17.7

Source: W. E. Skinner, *The Oil and Petroleum Year Book* (1940)

Burmah Oil's relative insignificance can be illustrated in another way. In 1939 world oil output was 1,819 million barrels (of 40 imperial gallons); of that the Indian subcontinent and Burma contributed about 8.4 million barrels, or just under half of one per cent. While dominant in the Indian market, the company was virtually unheard of elsewhere, except in oil circles. The head office of this Scottish-registered company was in Glasgow, and the chairman was Sir John Cargill Bt., the 72-year-old son of the founder David Cargill. Well known and respected as he was in Glasgow's rather inward-looking mercantile community, Sir John seldom sought to make his mark elsewhere. The only noteworthy feature of this reclusive company appeared to be its antiquated name, recalling how the province where it operated had been spelt in the Victorian heyday of the 1880s.

Burmah Oil was in reality run from London, where Cargill's highly industrious and resolute fellow-Scottish managing director worked in the office suite on the first floor of Britannic House in Finsbury Circus. Robert Irving Watson, aged 61 in 1939, was slight, dapper and bald. Awkward in adult social company, but completely at ease with children and animals, he lived mainly for his work. He had gone through the mill for ten years in the company's then managing agency in Rangoon, Finlay Fleming & Co. He was a voracious reader and a copious annotator of documents, much given to dictating complex and stylistically involved letters and memoranda on every conceivable aspect of the company's work or on oil matters generally. Since his handwriting was notoriously difficult to read, his secretary was much in demand as the only person capable of deciphering the comments which he scrawled, usually in pencil, across many of the papers coming before him. His photographic memory and legal training made it almost impossible to trip him up over points of detail.

At the same time he had a broad vision, both for his company and for the progress of the oil industry in general. It was the latter which gave Burmah Oil its disproportionate standing on the international scene. However, the way in which he reorganised the company from top to toe illustrates his creative gifts, and that achievement must be described first. Burmah Oil had been much in need of an overhaul after years of comparative inertia and the fallow period of the First World War. As managing director since 1920, he had initially concentrated on making operations in the East more cost-effective.

In Burma, therefore, he had sharply improved the efficiency of both drilling and refining. His scheme to bring electricity to the oilfields eliminated wasteful drilling and pumping by steam engines, thus saving both money and none-too-plentiful oil resources. The reconstruction of the technically obsolescent Rangoon refineries on a single site, with up-to-date machinery, had drastically cut costs there. On the subcontinent of India, he had in 1921 acquired the long-established but run-down Assam Oil Company. Since then he had poured into it over £1 million as well as managerial and technical effort, thereby gradually converting it into a more modern integrated enterprise. By 1936 it had entirely repaid the loans and was earning profits, and throughput from its reconstructed refinery at Digboi was over twelve times the 1920 figure and equivalent to almost a third of Burmah Oil's own throughput at that time.

As important in a different way was the Tinplate Company of India, established by Watson in 1918 as a joint venture with the Indian-owned Tata Iron and Steel Company, to provide economic production of tinplate for kerosene and petrol cans, and other oil containers. Tinplate imports into India had therefore been substantially reduced, and in 1934 the Tinplate Company was for the first time paying ordinary dividends. Before long the two indigenous companies were to find themselves vital contributors to wartime needs in the subcontinent.

These reforms in the East were just a prelude to Watson's further step of imposing effective head-office control over every aspect of work there. In 1920 the company's structure had been virtually unaltered since the 1880s, with the managing agents in Rangoon administering all affairs in Burma and India on behalf of the directors in Britain. In local command was a general manager for the East who, like his office assistants from whose ranks he had risen, had originally been recruited by the company at home. From 1929 to 1936 that post was held by Kenneth Harper, an employee since 1913. Harper's long managerial experience had been widened by his service on India's Council of State in Delhi, by attendance in 1931–2 at

the Burma round-table conference in London – as representative of the local Europeans – to work towards giving the
province self-rule, and then in 1933 as a delegate from Burma to
the joint parliamentary committee on Indian constitutional
reform. Three years later he was knighted for his public services
and came home to join the London office. In 1937 he became a
Burmah Oil director. His successor in Rangoon was Harold
Roper, a former rowing blue who had won the MC in the First
World War.

The main oilfields were in Upper Burma, over 300 miles
north of Rangoon, and connected by a pipeline with the
refinery there (see illustration). As was shown in Volume 1, the
American drillers, under their own fields managers, had from
the outset been adept at maintaining a remarkable degree of
independence from authority. The resident fields agent, an
office man charged with imposing company control on operations there, and subject to the general manager in Rangoon,

Pipeline from oilfields to Rangoon, on the river Irrawaddy near Syriam.

had never had an easy time. The geologists, whose work was mainly in the fields or outlying areas considered to be worth prospecting, were based at Rangoon. In Calcutta were a company general manager for India and also the headquarters of the sub-agents there, Shaw Wallace & Co. Watson therefore had to send instructions or information to, or to consult, these and other centres: a process he branded as 'dilatory, duplicating, expensive and unsatisfactory'.

His efforts to change all that were helped by rapidly improving communications. For very pressing business, cables could be sent; otherwise correspondence went by surface mail, via Bombay, which took about twenty-one days from office to office. When in 1933 Imperial Airways inaugurated a weekly service between London and Rangoon, Watson with characteristic parsimony laid down that the air mail letters were to be used only in absolute emergencies. During the 1920s he decreed London to be the main centre of company operations. He had the plant, stores and engineering department moved down from Glasgow; the accounts department followed rather later, in 1941. From 1936 onwards nearly all board meetings were held in London.

After 1924 he arranged to deal with oilfields affairs directly. He sought to weaken the American influence in the fields by beginning to train both British and Burmese drillers and by making the fields more subject to office direction. The chief geologist and his staff were transferred to the oilfields and thus away from the control of Finlay Fleming & Co. On refinery matters Watson and his London-based advisory chemist, Andrew Campbell, corresponded directly with the works manager and his staff. Part of the more detailed accounting function in Burma was delegated from the Rangoon office to the separate centres: oilfields, refining and so on. Similarly, he dealt from London with prospecting in India and the affairs of Assam Oil.

Hence the only major functions to remain the direct responsibility of the managing agents were the local co-ordination of accounts and the marketing of the refined products. Yet these agents still had a vital advisory and information-disseminating task, as Watson explained in 1925:

As far as possible, each unit of the company's organisation is to be made self-supporting and placed in direct touch and communication with the head office in London, as regards the details of its internal working. The connecting link [for implementing head office policy] will continue to be the managing agents in Rangoon who, whilst not interfering in the details of the administration of each unit, will continue to hold a watching brief for the company, advising where necessary and maintaining a contact for the exchange of ideas and suggestions between the various units.

The web, with most strands leading back to the London office, was not intended to enforce rigid lines of command; Watson, for all his strong ideas, was not a dictator. In contrast with, say, Shell which required its agencies across the world to comply automatically with head-office instructions, Watson expected his senior people to express their views on the basis of local knowledge. The general manager in Rangoon who, after all, came out of the same stable of assistants as he had, could write on terms of relative informality – although, in the last resort, Watson's word was paramount. Watson summed up the relationship thus:

> It has been my deliberate policy to encourage all our men in every sphere and position to think beyond their immediate 'last' and never be deterred from this by any fear that they may be 'butting in' to waters beyond their depth or outwith their responsibilities, so long as they have, or think they have, any contribution to make to the welfare of the 'machine' as a whole.

Being only human, he had a few favoured managers overseas whose judgement he particularly trusted, and to whom he permitted considerable freedom as to what they could say.

At the same time, he was conscious that the managing agency system, indispensable when voyages under sail had taken months, had become entirely outdated in an era of far more speedy communications. The events of 1928, in which the agency of Finlay Fleming & Co. was terminated and a branch office created, and Shaw Wallace & Co.'s agency in Calcutta was replaced by a joint marketing company with Shell for India, will be narrated below. He remained steadfastly impervious to the poignant laments of traditionally-minded older colleagues who sorely regretted the severing of old ties, and he went resolutely ahead with these changes.

In a real sense, therefore, Watson was both the architect and master builder of the Burmah Oil Company in this era.[1] He not only created a structure more appropriate to the second quarter of the twentieth century than the former semi-detached system but also, by prodigious expenditure of effort, painstakingly supervised every stage of its construction.

His overall design was simple. Burmah Oil was not, and at that period could not aspire to be, a world-scale major oil enterprise. The relatively limited amount the company could do, it did well. Of the 8.4 million barrels produced during 1939 in the Indian subcontinent, mentioned above, about two-thirds came from Burmah Oil, say 5.6 million barrels. Just over 800,000 barrels of products were consumed in Burma; apart from a little paraffin wax exported to Britain, the rest was marketed in India. The smaller rival companies in the province, such as the British Burmah Petroleum Company and the Indo-Burma Petroleum Company, between them produced about one million barrels and their product marketing was, through arrangements that had been made over the years, undertaken by or with the agreement of Burmah Oil. No less than 53 per cent of the kerosene and 40 per cent of the motor spirit used in India came from Burma.

Some further indigenous production on the subcontinent was provided by Assam Oil and by the Attock Oil Company, an independent producer and refiner operating in the Punjab. After a number of unprofitable years, the latter had in 1934 accepted a loan from Burmah Oil, which acquired in return a special shareholding in the company. These two Indian-based companies produced nearly 2 million barrels between them, supplying 18 per cent of mainland India's kerosene and 18 per cent of its motor spirit. Thus Watson was benevolently fostering a network of interacting market relations between Burmah Oil and the principal producers in the Indian empire.

He had already built up a highly efficient statistical department in his London office. That showed that by 1933 the company had 3077 wells in Burma, with an average yield of only 4.8 barrels a day. Thus at that time its total output was no greater than the amount that one single well could produce in Persia or the newer fields of Iraq. In consequence, costs greatly exceeded those in Persia. Because of the limited yield and the need to use pumps, expenses of production were nearly six times those of Persia while the cost of refining and transporting by pipelines were three times as much. Although the relatively short sea trip to India economised on freight charges, aggregate costs were still nearly three times those of Persia. However, that disparity was offset by the more favourable returns, once again over three times those of Persia, from Burmese oil which yielded relatively greater fractions of the more valuable products such as petrol and wax.

While by world standards Burmah Oil was a moderate-sized company, it ranked among the giants in relation to British manufacturing firms of the day.* Although its employees in Britain numbered no more than a few hundred, over 40,000 were directly employed abroad: nearly 32,000 of these in the fields and at the refinery, and 7,500 in installations such as those at Calcutta and Bombay. Only five British industrial firms had larger workforces.

Never, then, could a multinational company of that size have been so completely dominated by one man as Burmah Oil was by Watson in this era. Early in 1939 his deputy managing director, Gilbert C. Whigham, portrayed the extent of his control in a reply to Roper, who had complained from Rangoon about some delay or other in passing on information, as follows:

> I would mention that in this office practically all the correspondence is seen by [Watson], and he is therefore completely *au fait* with what is going on in each and every department and the correspondence that it is conducting. He sees practically all the inward correspondence before it is replied to and himself makes such comments as he considers necessary.
>
> The correspondence, as you can well imagine, is very voluminous at times and it is no light task to peruse it, but in a business with so many interests, connections and ramifications as ours, it is

---

* In terms of market valuation of the total issued capital on the stock exchange, the company in 1930 was worth about £35 million, and therefore fell between Guinness, the seventh largest British manufacturing company (£43 million), and Dunlop Rubber (£28 million).[2] However, in contrast with such companies, almost all of Burmah Oil's assets were held abroad.

impossible to bear the responsibility for its conduct without thus keeping in touch with all departments, for what may appear unimportant to a junior may, with his wider knowledge and greater experience, appear important to him.

In this all-embracing devotion to the company's affairs Watson was entirely at one with his chairman, Sir John Cargill, a deeply diffident and pessimistic man who had reluctantly taken over the chairmanship at the age of 37 on his father's death, and who had willingly seen the reins of real power pass to Watson. Involved as he was with civic affairs in Glasgow, with outside directorships of Scottish companies, with his family interests in department stores and tea plantations in Ceylon, Cargill by the 1930s played a somewhat passive role in policy-making within the Burmah Oil Company.

He still readily performed his tasks with effect on formal occasions such as annual general meetings, and presided genially at board meetings – with Watson at his side – even after they were held in London from 1936 onwards. To be sure, travelling down to London filled his careworn spirit with gloom for a day or two beforehand: when war broke out in 1939, he was mightily relieved when Watson assured him that he need no longer come down because of wartime transport difficulties. He thereafter met the directors as a body only when they convened in Glasgow each year shortly before the annual general meeting. In 1929 his wife had been taken ill and died suddenly during a visit to London. Cargill was hastily summoned south and it was Watson who broke the news of her death to him at Euston. He afterwards became even more withdrawn, consoled by his many friends and by his only child Allison who lived not far away at Loretto school near Edinburgh, where her husband was headmaster. Sir John's only brother to become a director, David W. T. Cargill, died childless in 1939.

No one could have been more attentive, although necessarily from a distance, than was Watson. He kept his chairman fully informed about what was going on, without saddling him with the onus of making any agonising decisions, and helped him over any domestic or legal problem that happened to arise.[3]

Enjoying as he did the total trust of his chairman, and having a largely reconstructed company behind him, Watson could

confidently hold his own in the wider world of oil where
Burmah Oil's standing was proportionally greater than its size.
What was the explanation of this disproportionate status?
Above all, it was the discovery of oil in Persia and the
company's subsequent part in the formation of the Anglo-
Persian Oil Company, as well as its close involvement in
Anglo-Persian's early growth. Burmah Oil had not enjoyed any
such advantage of a diversified asset base in the 1890s when its
growing output first allowed it to sell its products extensively in
mainland India, and it had come up against powerful rivals
there such as Standard Oil, Royal Dutch, and Shell. Being the
largest single market for oil in the eastern hemisphere outside
Europe, India was a country well worth fighting over. The two
last-named competitors became even more of a threat when
they merged their eastern marketing activities into the Asiatic
Petroleum Company in 1903, presided over by the Dutch-born
managing director Henri Deterding, and then merged completely in 1907 as Royal Dutch-Shell.

Despite intense competition from these rivals, Burmah Oil
successfully built up a market for its kerosene and other
products, helped by the government of India's tariff of some 14
per cent on imported kerosene. It was also helped by official
rejections of efforts by both Standard Oil and Shell to obtain
concessions in Burma itself. Shell was then regarded by the
Burmah Oil directors as the main rival, with Deterding
apparently aiming to make his company the dominant oil
company in the eastern hemisphere, as Standard Oil then was
in the West. After a very debilitating price war in 1903–5,
Burmah Oil had perforce to conclude a kerosene marketing
agreement with Asiatic. However, it was able to safeguard the
consumer from some of the exploitation caused by the agreement's restrictive terms: it voluntarily introduced a maximum
price limit for the kerosene it marketed under its own name,
mainly a cheap discoloured brand bought by the poor in
Burma and India. That maximum price undertaking helped to
keep down oil prices in those markets; during the 1930s it
covered directly a third of the trade carried on there by the
company and its associates, and it endured until 1942. After a
period of intermittent warfare to 1911, Standard Oil broadly
accepted the price terms and share of the market tacitly left to it

as a result of the agreement between Burmah Oil and Asiatic, the more easily done because its own kerosene was of superior quality, being relatively colourless. A further price war, to be described later, broke out in the late 1920s.

Relations between the directors of Burmah Oil and those of Shell in London remained correct but distant until Watson joined the London office from Rangoon in 1912 and began to undertake liaison work with the Shell director (Sir) Robert Waley Cohen over the kerosene and other product agreements. The two men often indulged in stand-up rows of heroic dimensions, but were clearly made for each other, rapidly building up a deep mutual regard and even affection. In 1919 Watson took the initiative and proposed a kerosene pool agreement to comprise Shell, Burmah Oil and the smaller companies in the province. For the first time the indigenous producers would be allowed to turn out as much as they chose, and Shell duly conceded priority to the marketing of those products in the Indian subcontinent.

Having won this vital safeguard for his company's markets, Watson was able to organise an appropriate level of production. The wells in Burma were high-cost small producers with short expectancy of life; in the absence of further major discoveries, the province's oil seemed likely to run out within perhaps as little as two decades. His strategy was therefore to avoid as far as possible uncertainty in the product markets by keeping refinery throughput stable. Quite remarkably, from 1923 – when the reconstruction was completed – until 1938 the total annual throughput never varied more than $1\frac{1}{2}$ per cent either way from 5 million barrels. He then fixed the level of crude production at the fields so as to keep the refinery appropriately supplied. That example of oil conservation, so different from the profligacy of producers in such countries as the US, promised to give the wells a correspondingly longer life, enhanced by the sharp reduction in oil used for fields operations as a result of electrification: the power generating station was run on casing-head gas from the wells, which would otherwise have had to be wastefully burnt off.

A threat which could badly disrupt Watson's careful plans for stabilising the oil market in India would be any attempt by other companies to enter that market. One potentially disruptive force was the company, mentioned above, that had grown to twice the size of Burmah Oil: the Anglo-Persian Oil Company. To be sure, Burmah Oil had a very special if hardly straightforward connection with Anglo-Persian, having established the latter in 1909 after the oil strike at Masjid-i-Sulaiman.

Why had Burmah Oil not insisted on handling the Persian operations entirely within its own corporate structure? One reason was that the terms of the Shah's original concession in 1901 had specified that an entirely new company should be set up if oil were to be discovered in Persia. Moreover, Burmah Oil was run on a very thin layer of top management: of the four executive directors in office between 1909 and 1912, only one worked full-time on the company's affairs, and there was not even a managing director between 1903 and 1920. Of the Burmah Oil directors who did count – and the non-executive directors counted for little – some were old Burma hands, having earlier served in Finlay Fleming & Co., but some were old India hands, since by default various partners from Shaw Wallace & Co. had been drawn into the directorate.

When Anglo-Persian was set up in 1909, the Burma element tended to stay put and the old India hands to move over to the new company. The most durable of the latter was Charles (later Lord) Greenway, chairman of Anglo-Persian from 1914 until 1927. This broad splitting of interests was to become of great moment: whereas Burmah Oil was preoccupied with safeguarding its product markets in the Indian empire, Anglo-Persian began to look further afield.

A major issue of concern to Burmah Oil was the ever increasing volume of kerosene turned out by Abadan as a by-product of Anglo-Persian's fuel oil contract for the Admiralty. In 1922 that company's marketing agreement with Shell terminated, and shortly before then Burmah Oil arranged with Anglo-Persian that neither would trespass on the other's markets. Although clearly designed by Watson to deny the latter an outlet in India, that allowed Anglo-Persian to export variable but relatively small amounts of kerosene to the subcontinent over the new few years. Not until 1928, as will be shown subsequently, did he provide greater access for Persian kerosene to the Indian consumer, as part of a wider settlement between the interested companies.

From the outset, Anglo-Persian's top managers had demonstrated that they were not to be overawed by their major shareholders. Although between 1923 and 1956 Burmah Oil had a 26½ per cent voting stake and at least two directors on the Anglo-Persian board – Watson being a member from 1918 to 1947, over matters of strategy the inter-corporate relationship became more that of two affiliates rather than that of parent and subsidiary. To be sure, much consultation at the personal level took place, helped by the two companies being accommodated on different floors of the London office blocks henceforth referred to as Britannic House.

In this unique inter-corporate relationship, a further worry surfaced in the summer of 1925. That was that a government appointee would take over the chairmanship of and gravely weaken Burmah Oil's influence in Anglo-Persian. Greenway, approaching his seventieth year, declared his wish to retire in a year or so, and Whitehall was clearly determined to influence the choice of his successor. Three years previously, Cargill and Watson had vainly resisted an attempt by Stanley Baldwin, President of the Board of Trade, to have Sir John Cadman[4] made a managing director (See Vol. I p. 282). In August 1925 Winston Churchill, as Chancellor of the Exchequer, wrote to the senior government director, laying down the official view that Cadman should at once be made deputy chairman, with the reversion of the chairmanship on Greenway's eventual retirement.[5]

As an act of courtesy, Churchill also informed Cargill, as chairman of Anglo-Persian's second largest shareholding entity, that he was 'instructing the government directors' to make this proposal. Greatly upset, Cargill protested that under the terms of the previous accords the government had surrendered any right to 'force its views on the [Anglo-Persian Oil] company' over so purely commercial a matter as board appointments. He also objected to the possibility of Cadman being joint chairman and managing director, since 'the chairman should not interfere in details and the daily running of the business': a principle, he complacently added, 'on which I have carried on the business of the Burmah Oil Company'. Back came a conciliatory letter from Churchill; he declared he had done no more than propose the line which the government directors should take when the chairmanship issue came before the board. 'Meanwhile', he concluded with a Churchillian flourish, 'I will see that the argument of principle which you set forth is fully weighed and balanced.'

To be sure, a number of years had passed since Cargill had had to write such an important outside communication off his own bat; however, his constant mentor Watson had been absent on holiday, and on returning judiciously awarded his chairman only moderate marks for this unaided effort. Cargill, he suggested, should have been more forthright in condemning dictation by government, both on principle and because of officialdom's lack of understanding of all the considerations involved. He also asked around for any background information he could obtain. From Greenway he learnt the circumstances of the latter's appointment as chairman in 1914 (see Vol. I p.198), when the vice-chairman C. W. Wallace had acted on a suggestion – no more – from the Admiralty.

Watson also gained the impression that there had been some 'intriguing' on the Anglo-Persian executive to leave clear for Cadman the route to the top, and that government ministers had been 'used' to that end. Burmah Oil's reliable ally on that board, John D. Stewart, chairman of the managing committee, had recently suffered a breakdown in health and the pro-Cadman directors were blocking the succession to Stewart's key post of another friend of Burmah Oil, H. E. Nichols. In the event Nichols had won the chairmanship of the managing committee and – according to Watson – the Cadmanites then induced Churchill to promote their candidate through the votes of the government directors.

To checkmate these alleged moves, Watson sought to promote Cargill's candidature for the Anglo-Persian chairmanship. Watson thought he could secure the necessary majority on the board, in which case the government would have to acquiesce. 'Then we should carry on otherwise largely as at present, with a management committee and Nichols as its chairman', he suggested to Cargill. 'With this organisation – and Charles Greenway definitely out of special authority – we should be able to control the future and the man', presumably Cadman.

Whether this was a genuine proposal, or one aired merely to flatter the diffident Cargill, it is impossible to guess. Certainly the structure of Anglo-Persian sorely needed a radical over-haul: even Watson, had he become the power behind that throne, would have had his work cut out to impose the necessary organisational changes, in addition to his highly onerous work in Burmah. Whatever Cargill's response, within days the issue was settled otherwise. On 29 September 1925 Anglo-Persian's board elected Cadman to the deputy chair-manship and made him chairman-designate. Stewart resigned but, perhaps as a *quid pro quo* to the Burmah Oil side, Gilbert Whigham was appointed in his place as director.

Watson, for all his forceful and sometimes acerbic tempera-ment, was not one to harbour grudges, and after Greenway retired in March 1927, unstintingly helped Cadman to find his feet as chairman. That was the very time when Anglo-Persian, through the magnitude of its output and geographical range of activities, was establishing itself as a force in the world of oil. Simultaneously, a fundamental change was about to take place in corporate inter-relationships within the industry as a whole. Cut-throat competition leading to price wars would gradually give way to unprecedented measures of collaboration. The current declining demand for products, combined with recent significant oil discoveries, notably in the Middle East, left collaboration as the only alternative to damaging anarchy.

Shortly after Greenway's retirement, Watson suffered a riding accident, apparently being thrown from his horse. He was briefly in a nursing home, and then had to wear a special boot for some months, but on the whole felt that he had 'got through pretty cheaply'. In view of his achievements in the decades to come, it is interesting to speculate on what would have happened to the company had he been killed. The progress of oil affairs generally might have been somewhat different as well. His sheer intellectual force and knowledge of every branch of the subject made him an ideal counsellor of those with broader responsibilities. In Anglo-Persian he en-couraged Cadman to repair the previously strained relationship with Shell. Greenway and Cohen had never hit it off: now, however, the former was safely out of the way and Cohen was withdrawing from executive responsibilities, so that the less abrasive Deterding was the chief negotiator for Shell.

Watson also objected to Anglo-Persian's dissipation of its marketing strength by selling its products through insignificant national corporate outlets, in his view of little consequence, rather than exploring ways of co-operating downstream with the majors which he termed 'the real holders of power'. In mid-July 1927 he was present at a crucial meeting between Cadman and Deterding, from which emerged plans for a joint marketing company, owned half each by Anglo-Persian and Shell – the Consolidated Petroleum Company Ltd – for the joint distribution of oil products in an area stretching from Syria and Palestine to Egypt and the Red Sea ports, down to East Africa, and South Africa, then across the Indian Ocean to Madagascar, Reunion, Mauritius and Ceylon.[6]

The next major step by Watson was to plan a similar joint organisation with Shell in India. That owed its genesis to Watson's practice of spending the quiet weeks round Christmas and the new year at the Suvretta House Hotel in the Swiss resort of St Moritz. Deterding used to stay at a nearby chalet, and the two men had ample opportunity, in between skiing and skating, to talk things over at leisure. The kerosene pool agreement of 1919 in India had been highly advantageous for Burmah Oil, but at Shell's expense. By 1926/7 Burmah Oil and other indigenous producers were providing 65 per cent of India's kerosene needs. Shell's contribution had fallen to 4 per cent compared with 16 per cent in 1919/20 and, as will be seen later, was coming under further pressure from outside rivals. In September 1927 the Burmah Oil board approved arrangements for a Burmah-Shell joint company to be set up in India.

To indicate how difficult it was for Watson to please both major companies at the same time, news of these arrangements caused some consternation among Anglo-Persian's top management, already resentful at the way in which he had largely kept Persian kerosene out of India. One director of Anglo-Persian went so far as to assert that the arrangements effectively lifted the restrictions on his company actively competing with Burmah Oil in the subcontinent, once the latter's share of the market had dropped below 75 per cent. In the end, wiser counsel prevailed and, as we shall see, Anglo-Persian was included in the agreement.[7] At the beginning of 1928 the Burmah-Shell Oil Storage and Distributing Company of India began its operations, with each side owning 50 per cent of the assets. It marketed throughout the subcontinent, apart from two 'reserved areas', that in Assam – supplied by Assam Oil – and that in Chittagong and its environs, supplied by Burmah Oil.

Six agreements, A to F, set out the provisions in full detail. Burmah-Shell was required to purchase all its oil supplies from the two parent companies, Burmah Oil's indigenous oil having the prior claim, after which Shell could import the balance. However, Shell undertook to give 50 per cent of its import rights to Anglo-Persian. Thus if Burmah-Shell required 300 units and Burmah Oil could provide 200 from its indigenous production, Shell and Anglo-Persian would import 50 each. If, however, Burmah Oil had no more than 20 units, then Anglo-Persian would have a one-third right of supply, providing 100 to Shell's 100. To make up the 80 shortfall, Burmah Oil would buy 40 each directly from the two companies.

As to the price charged, each consigning company would receive from Burmah-Shell the full proceeds received from sales less all charges incurred, a rental on installations and a commission on these sales, which varied between products. As a consignor, each company would furnish its own share of working capital for excise duties, rail freights and debtors. In return for the exceptionally favourable position enjoyed by its indigenous oil, Burmah Oil undertook not to market directly in other parts of the world, but to consign any surplus oil to Shell and to Anglo-Persian in equal quantities. Anglo-Persian too, had what was undoubtedly a lucrative share of a market from which it had earlier been largely excluded.

For Watson, this was in many ways the most noteworthy achievement of his life. In India, Shell was now very much the junior partner, totally confined within the indigenous principle. Why, then, did the canny Deterding agree to it? He doubtless felt that his company would enjoy economies of distribution and marketing, with duplication eliminated; there was also the symbolic advantage that in the current depressed economic climate – which could well deteriorate further – the two companies would be working in concert rather than against each other. The arrangement was to last for twenty years in the first instance, rather than the six months of previous accords. Moreover, Deterding seems to have looked on this and the Consolidated deal as necessary preludes to a similar one with rivals further east, including those in China.

The headquarters of Burmah-Shell were to be in Calcutta, but it took much acrimonious correspondence with Shell before Watson, as the major supplier of oil products to the subcontinent, won the right to establish the London office in Britannic House. The acting general manager in London, an ex-Shell man, was shown into a room there by Watson himself; it was completely bare. Soon after his being left alone, a young secretary appeared, her arms full of the accumulated mail from India, and dumped it on the floor. There he sat, opening the envelopes and trying to decide which departments in his respective companies he needed to approach to find the answers to the queries raised, while waiting for furniture and a telephone to be installed.[8]

To help cement relations with Shell, in May 1928 Watson secured the agreement of the Burmah Oil board to the purchase of some 800,000 ordinary shares of the (British) Shell Transport and Trading Company: these were bought that September for just under £4.2 million, and were largely paid for by a £4 million $5\frac{1}{2}$ per cent debenture issue. The number of Shell shares was made up to one million in January 1929 when a share issue took place. Also in 1928 Watson was elected to the board of Shell Transport and Trading. He was thereafter a director and significant shareholder in the two oil giants wholly or partly based in Britain.

He appreciated all too well the signal value of the Burmah-Shell agreement, which he described a few years later as the sheet-anchor of Burmah Oil's position. While it must never be surrendered, he felt it should equally never be ruthlessly used. 'Privileges such as we enjoy carry obligations', he told Harper in Rangoon. Yet he had also provided that the unprecedented degree of control Burmah Oil now held over the lucrative Indian market would be safeguarded even after the company's life as a producer had come to an end. It looked as if a time would come when oil in the province of Burma ran out: one agreement granted the company the right not only to obtain oil from outside – which really meant from Anglo-Persian – should indigenous supplies no longer be available, but also to dispose of its 50 per cent stake in Burmah-Shell to Anglo-Persian, provided that Burmah Oil still held an interest in the latter company.

The timing of the *rapprochements* owed a great deal to an external threat posed by the Standard Oil Company of New York, known as Socony. That company exported American kerosene into India, by the mid-1920s contributing a quarter of the subcontinent's total requirements. Then in 1927 it prepared to import kerosene from Soviet Russia. Before 1917 many producing fields in Russia had been owned by Royal Dutch-Shell, but were then expropriated by the Soviets. Deterding had bargained hard for compensation, but without success. Socony then signed a three-year contract with the Soviet authorities to buy, at very low prices, kerosene for shipment to India; Russia at that time badly needed foreign currency to finance the purchase of capital goods from the West.

In July 1927 Deterding warned Watson that the first shipments of Russian oil would shortly be reaching Indian ports. Watson at once offered total support in fending off that threat. He also induced Shell to allow Anglo-Persian to join the kerosene pool – effectively at Shell's expense – as a *quid pro quo* for its support. Even more unexpectedly, Deterding agreed to compensate pool members for any losses they might incur during the forthcoming price war. The rate of compensation was to vary according to the price paid in China, a market unaffected by the current dispute, to the extent of half the difference between the level of prices in India and in China.

That September, just before the arrival of Russian shipments in Bombay, Shell and Burmah Oil simultaneously cut the prices of its brands by 40–50 per cent, varying in different parts of India: cuts which Socony matched. The indigenous companies then strove to enlist the help of the government of India. In December Burmah Oil, British Burmah, Indo-Burma, Assam Oil and Attock Oil requested Delhi either to ban

Russian oil imports outright or to increase tariffs on all imported kerosene so as to offset the price cuts.

At first it looked as if Delhi might respond positively by helping the companies in one way or the other. However, no official action was taken until March 1928, when the petition was referred to the Indian Tariff Board. That board set up an enquiry to establish whether the interests of the Indian people would be served by introducing a penal tariff against the dumping of oil.[9] Moreover, what should be the appropriate level of kerosene prices at Indian ports, and how far were current prices below that level? Burmah Oil and its Assam Oil subsidiary made it clear that they were not applying for tougher protection, unlike their smaller and more vulnerable rivals, but would be pleased to participate in the enquiry.

Unfortunately, the hearings of the Tariff Board enquiry did not go as Watson had hoped. The company's spokesman was William A. Gray, the general manager for the East. A man of donnish background (his father was master of Jesus College, Cambridge), he lacked the forcefulness and the ready wit to present his case really effectively. In any event, his brief had been gravely weakened by Watson's refusal to plead for a tariff increase. Gray was soon afterwards succeeded by Kenneth Harper and returned to London, where he did well in dealing with technical matters, although no technician himself. He became a director in 1937.

The Tariff Board's majority report of June 1928 (signed by an Indian and a British Indian Civil Service man) accepted that dumping of Soviet oil had taken place, but pointed out that the worst of the price war was now over. Besides, the indigenous companies could be expected to have been stimulated to greater economies by their recent hardships. Those views were accepted by Delhi. However, the enquiry's chairman, an Indian who produced a very hard-hitting minority report, went so far as to assert that 'all petroleum products are being sold in India at exorbitant prices owing to the oil business being in the hands of the oil trust'. In justification, he rejected the companies' current practice of using the Gulf (of Mexico) as the datum for pricing. Instead he took the price at which Soviet kerosene could be delivered to Indian ports, even though that was at a bargain basement level fixed by the Russian authorities for non-commercial ends. The minority report finally made a serious charge against the petitioners, of having shown 'a lack of candour amounting almost to *mala fides*'. This was because Deterding's compensation proposal had been kept secret and had only slipped out during the cross-examination of witnesses. In fact, no compensation was ever paid since prices did not fall significantly below the level in China.

Watson at once challenged the Tariff Board findings in a 5000-word public statement. That dismissed out of hand the assertions of the chairman's minority report on the grounds of special pleading. As to using the delivered cost of Soviet oil as the basis of calculating the true cost of Indian kerosene, he argued that 'normally, with 70 or more per cent of the world's production, the American market *au fond* determines the selling price of petroleum products just as India fixes the world's price for jute'. He also emphasised – as his general manager had failed to do during the enquiry – that Burmah Oil's maximum price for kerosene had not been altered in the company's favour since 1905. That, Watson claimed, had saved the poorer Indian consumer the equivalent of about £3 million a year since the kerosene pool had been formed in 1919.

He did not adequately answer a wider issue which the enquiry had stirred up. In the 1890s, Burmah Oil had itself broken into the Indian kerosene market, then dominated by Standard Oil and Royal Dutch, and had thereby benefitted local buyers by forcing down price levels. Now the company was resisting the entry of imported kerosene – admittedly of contested ownership – which once again would have benefitted local people. Enjoying the market power it did in India, Burmah Oil might perhaps itself have accepted lower prices there.

Price reductions would have meant lower profits, and it is not easy with hindsight to suggest what a more reasonable profit level would have been. Perhaps the most satisfactory yardstick is net profit per barrel of oil refined. In historical terms, between the wars that figure was undoubtedly quite high. After 1921 there were two refineries, at Digboi as well as Syriam, but the Digboi throughput in the 1920s is not known. From 1930 to 1936, the average figure was the equivalent, in decimal currency, of 33.1p. That compared with the average from 1889 to 1914 inclusive of 16.6p, when the company had only the Burmese refinery. The post-war figures, if reduced to pre-1914 prices so as to allow for subsequent inflation, would have averaged 22.3p.

Watson would doubtless have argued that the higher figure in real terms reflected his contribution in raising the company's revenue and in reducing costs. At any rate, the outside solutions advocated in the minority report were for the encouragement of crude oil imports into India and the construction of refineries on the subcontinent, preferably near the port of Bombay. Not until the early 1950s, after independence, did Burmah-Shell in fact build a refinery there.

It needs to be stressed that the agreements actually signed in 1928 to set up Burmah-Shell and Consolidated Petroleum – the Anglo-Persian and Shell joint venture mentioned earlier – were fundamentally intended to secure large savings in the capital and working costs of distribution by eliminating unnecessary duplication of services, thereby benefitting customers and companies alike. These were not the only far-reaching oil agreements of 1928. That September Deterding invited Walter Teagle, president of Standard Oil Company of New Jersey, and Cadman to Achnacarry House, a Scottish hunting lodge in Inverness-shire, ostensibly to enjoy some grouse shooting. In fact, they secretly hammered out an accord, entitled the Pool Association but subsequently known as the 'As-Is' agreement.[10]

'As-Is' involved the parties' acceptance that future market shares would relate to existing volumes of business, and that costly ocean freights would be reduced by drawing supplies from the areas of production nearest to the consumer. Unless marketing and distribution costs were reduced by such means, oil product prices would remain unduly high and hence limit the market. On the production side, the parties hoped that wasteful competition arising from, say, the development by various rival firms of the same production facilities would be curbed by the pooling efforts. As Watson often remarked in the next few years, 'Achnacarry was always distribution', and could thus be seen as comparable with the Burmah-Shell and Consolidated Petroleum agreements of the same year.

Not unexpectedly, some critics branded the Pool Association

as a blatant device for artificially raising the industry's profits at the expense of consumers. The accord's defenders denied this and took a longer-term view that it was a means of husbanding a valuable resource. Conservation would follow from its provisions, and the consumer would enjoy a long-run security of supply without having to bear the cost of short-sighted production methods and unnecessarily expensive distribution methods. As a corollary to these other arrangements, the Red Line agreement of July 1928 was intended to ensure international co-operation in locating and developing new oilfields in Turkey, Syria, Lebanon, Iraq and Saudi Arabia. The companies with stakes in the Turkish Petroleum Company (see Vol. I, Chapter XIII) were the signatories. These included Anglo-Persian and Shell, so that Watson was indirectly involved.

In the early months of Burmah-Shell's operations, the price war in India ebbed and flowed; but soon all parties appeared willing to seek a settlement of the quarrel. During June 1928 representatives of Burmah Oil, Anglo-Persian, Socony and Shell met in London. Some very tough bargaining took place, and Watson later claimed to have hit on the formula which finally led to an accord. That fixed Socony's share of the Indian kerosene market according to aggregate sales there in 1926, the last normal year, with adjustment up or down depending on subsequent higher or lower aggregate sales. There were similar provisions for petrol. The accord was to run for ten years, so as to give Anglo–Persian and Shell time to adjust performance to its terms.

To Watson's dismay, Socony was soon reported to be deeply unhappy about the accord, and by the end of the year was said to be on the point of repudiating it. The chairman, Herbert Pratt, demanded a revision of the arrangment, one which would award his company a fixed 26 per cent of India's kerosene trade, regardless of the impact on other parties. Having been nominated as chief negotiator for the European companies, Watson sent such a blunt cable in reply to this demand that Pratt at once backed down.

However, in the last six months of 1928, Socony shipped no less than one million gallons of excess kerosene to India over

and above the 60 million gallons permitted under the agreement. Early in 1929 Harper, mindful of the Indian Tariff
Board's recent refusal to help local producers, commented
glumly, 'Unfortunately the Indian front must be even more
attractive to the Standard than before, now they know that the
indigenous industry cannot rely on the government of India to
preserve it from extinction.' Certainly the price cuts seemed to
be hurting those local companies and also Shell more than they
hurt Socony. That May Deterding persuaded a very reluctant
Watson to offer Socony a sweetener in the form of an increased
share of the subcontinent's petrol trade; yet that offer induced
no change of heart among the Americans.

A meeting was held in London during July 1929 of representatives of the main US companies participating in the Committee of the American Export Association, together with representatives of Shell, Anglo-Persian and Burmah Oil. Although
the object was to discuss the implementation of the Achnacarry
principles, it failed to end the stalemate with Socony. According to Watson, that conference showed a 'good spirit of give and
take' and a lively appreciation of one another's problems,
although no general break-through could be expected as long
as some US producers and marketers refused to come into line.
As two Socony directors were present, Watson took the
opportunity to float some ideas for settling the problem of
excess trading. The Socony directors found his proposals
'sensible', but once they were back in the US they sent
counter-proposals which Watson could only reject; the influence of their implacable president Charles Meyer seemed
too strong for progress to be made. Watson acknowledged to
Rangoon the tight-rope he was walking. 'I have sought to play
for time and try to hold our friends from any action which could
be construed as sufficient ground for Socony finally denouncing
the June 1928 agreement', he wrote.

Deterding was a most difficult ally to rein back, especially
when he learnt that during 1929 Socony had shipped no fewer
than 6.6 million gallons of excess kerosene. In January 1930 he
went to New York and attempted to have it out with the Socony
people, but to no effect; when Watson later met him in St
Moritz, Sir Henri's patience was reported to be very sorely
tried. Herein lay the sharp contrast between the two men. The

volatile Deterding, famed for the daring of his bold *coups*, became edgy and apprehensive in any long drawn-out war of attrition. That was precisely the kind of situation in which the dour and pertinacious Watson came into his own. In the current unsettled state of oil affairs, world-wide as well as in India, he just hung on, keeping discussion alive – more, he admitted, in the hope that better times would eventually come than through conviction that what he termed the 'big idea', of a comprehensive understanding with the Americans, could be brought off.

That November Watson spelt out his basic philosophy to his managers in Rangoon. He commended some remarks lately made by Hugo Loudon, chairman of Royal Dutch, who attributed the oil industry's current troubles in general to a seemingly irreconcilable struggle between producers and distributors. Many of the former had made real sacrifices by accepting falls in price and restrictions on output, and greatly resented the latters' failure to resolve their mutual differences. That, said Watson, explained the industry's problems in the short run; however, long-term stabilisation could be achieved only if overall demand and supply became matched on a permanent basis. If not, then no scheme could possibly work because each participant would 'strain to secure for himself such business as may be offering'. Hence, in the existing state of basic instability, Socony with its source of cheap Russian oil would continue to give trouble.

That errant company's excess kerosene for 1930, although below the 1929 record total, was still unacceptably high at over 4.5 million gallons. Watson sent a strong letter of protest to Meyer, but received no satisfactory reply. Meanwhile, Deterding was all for some exemplary price cuts. Watson successfully countered that move by arguing that prices had already fallen because of the excess supplies and that the Socony people were 'cowards'; thus the best tactic would be to 'show a firm front' and announce a refusal to sacrifice further market shares.

Cowards or not, the Socony directors still gave no sign of budging, and in May 1931 even Watson had run out of excuses to hold back Deterding's insistence on really tough action. He did press the point that driving down prices further would hit the smaller indigenous companies unduly hard, and would make relations with the governments in Delhi and Rangoon even more 'delicate' than they already were. When in mid-year Socony announced merger plans with the New York-based Vacuum Oil company, which sold the Mobil brand of motor oil in India, Watson hoped that the moderate outlook of the latter's directors would help to make the new combine anxious for peace. Deterding, after a study of the Socony results for 1930, wondered if the lower declared trading profits, on top of what appeared to have been some creative accounting, would encourage that company to be less intransigent. In July 1931 there was a false dawn, with Socony allowing Indian prices to rise, and Watson seeking to 'nudge them back' towards the pre-1927 levels by following up the increases. Then prices collapsed again, and the lengthy contest with this vexatious company was overtaken by the eruption of the worst economic crisis that Britain, and indeed the world, had ever known.

The events of the troubled summer of 1931 were followed by Watson with his customary hard-headed and sceptical comments. In August Britain suffered a catastrophic run on the pound, and before the end of the month the Labour cabinet resigned, having failed to agree some drastic economy measures to restore international confidence in sterling, to be succeeded by a National government. Watson profoundly hoped that the latter would honour its promises to maintain a rigorous policy of retrenchment – indeed, the same kinds of economy measures he had remorselessly urged on his eastern staff writ very large. Early in September J. B. A. Kessler, managing director of Royal Dutch, published a plan for international co-operation in the oil industry involving drastic reductions in output and a strategy of conserving oil on a world scale. He uttered the unpalatable truth that in the current crisis, all the industry's troubles were caused by over-production, by a patchy regard for conservation in the US and by growing competition, especially from countries such as Romania.[11]

Kessler's plan, proposing as it did a remedy to a depressed industry, evoked quite a stir round the world. But who would be bold enough to take an initiative which might collapse in ignominy? Watson and Deterding were resolved to do what they could. The following month, after Britain had gone off the gold standard they jointly persuaded the other oil companies active in the country, namely Jersey Standard's subsidiary the Anglo-American Oil Company, Anglo-Persian, Burmah Oil – which sold some wax in the British market, Canadian and Mexican Eagle, and Shell, to sign a joint manifesto. That gave a pledge of the closest possible co-operation, and in particular of not increasing the prices of petroleum products just because of the recent appreciation of the dollar, now that sterling was free to float downwards.[12] Watson told his Rangoon managers that once the British companies had agreed to sign, the American affiliates based in London reluctantly followed suit. The manifesto, he hoped, would both help to inspire confidence in sterling and hold back inflation in Britain.

Perhaps as important, Watson foresaw two longer-term beneficial consequences of the manifesto. The first was that US and French interests would be brought to the conference table in order to promote internationally agreed measures to combat the depression; in fact, nearly five years were to pass before tripartite talks with Britain took place even on such fundamental topics as stabilising exchange rates. The second possible outcome, according to Watson, might be more permanent and closer arrangements 'between at least one or more of the parties concerned'. Sure enough, later that month Anglo-Persian and Shell agreed in principle for their marketing organisations in Britain to be merged. The new combine, Shell-Mex and BP Ltd, was registered in November 1931.

Although excess kerosene sales had fallen in 1931 to a more acceptable 800,000 gallons after the excise duty in India on oil products had been raised by 25 per cent that September, the problem of Socony in India rumbled on. By January 1932 Watson felt that kerosene prices there had sunk to the lowest tolerable point. He had suffered the chagrin of seeing Burmah Oil's profits halved in the past few years compared with 1921; yet, having hung on tenaciously for so long, he was resolved on complete victory over Socony. That company was known to be suffering financially in most markets of the world, as well as India, where its representatives were said to be 'completely fed up' with the unremunerative prices. Meyer was on the point of resignation, and the more accommodating Vacuum directors, notably Charles Arnott, now Socony-Vacuum's president, were gaining the upper hand on the combine's board. Watson categorically refused to accept a *de facto* cessation of hostilities, by a gradual rise in prices, without Socony-Vacuum's formal recognition of its obligations under the 1928 agreement.

Then in May Watson, William Fraser – deputy chairman of Anglo-Persian[13] – and Kessler attended a conference in New York on Russian oil, presided over by Arnott. Despite the urgency imposed by the world economic crisis, US oil interests had been unable to accept the Kessler plan as a basis of discussion, since any concerted proposals to restrict output there would fall foul of the American anti-trust laws. Even so, the New York discussions were to pave the way for what Watson so greatly looked forward to: namely a world confer-ence on oil conservation. The hands of the US delegates were further tied by a failure of Congress to put through bills permitting joint corporate action in the interest of oil conserva-tion; however, since representatives at the conference accounted between them for 80 per cent of the world's export markets, the mere fact that they were jointly tackling problems of common concern was a good omen. Watson had no particular ambition to be hob-nobbing on equal terms with the *crème de la crème* of the world oil industry, but in this era scarcely any important international petroleum conference would have been complete without this unassuming but resourceful man of the lofty cranium, never stumped for an idea or a salient fact.

The conference failed in its main objective: to reach an agreement with Soviet delegates over Russian oil exports. However, Watson was content that the Americans had accepted a general understanding to uphold the principles of Achnacarry on the basis of market shares in 1931. A more tangible result he achieved from his six weeks' absence in New York was an agreement with Socony-Vacuum which he had personally drafted and which was signed on 3 June 1932 to replace the 1928 accord. It was to be for five years rather than the former ten. While it did not insist on the indigenous principle in kerosene, that principle was accepted for petrol. Once again a formula was laid down for Socony-Vacuum's share of the Indian kerosene market, allowing both for increases and for falls in the market; that company pledged itself to work as closely as possible to the agreed quota. It was also prepared to be excluded from the fuel market and to limit its trade in lubricants and wax. That July an international conference was held in Paris to try to settle the problem of the incursion of Romanian oil into various markets. Although India was not involved, Watson attended, and once again the basis of settlement was the Achnacarry 'As-Is' principle.

After his return from Paris, Watson was under no illusion that despite recent progress, the world's oil problems had been anywhere near overcome. He acknowledged the signal benefits of greatly improved relations between American and European oil interests. Yet, as he floridly put it to Rangoon, the structure of agreements and understandings 'is built on the shifting and dangerous sands of artificial restriction and is all the time under the fire of declining demand. There can be nothing but continued uncertainty and difficulties with such foundations.'

In the aftermath of the 1932 settlement in the US, Watson had a strange tiff with Shell. The two companies, together with Anglo-Persian, had earlier agreed that Socony would be expected to compensate them for their lost earnings on the excess kerosene Socony had poured into India since 1928; at the same time, they would allow Socony an extended period in which to pay. Striving in New York to bring about a settlement as quickly as possible, Watson let Socony off its compensation payments. Shell, in the person of Frederick Godber, its director, estimated the value of that forgone claim to be nearly £200,000, and declared that as Watson had not carried out what he had been mandated to do, Burmah Oil should be expected to pay the bill.

Watson did what he had done so successfully during earlier rows with Cohen. He composed a 13-page memorandum, with ample appendices, which exhaustively dealt with every conceivable aspect of the issue. In conclusion, he proved to his own – if not to the other side's – satisfaction that, so far from Shell and Anglo-Persian having suffered financially, they were handsomely in pocket. The two companies notionally had in hand the oil they would otherwise have despatched to India, all 18 million gallons of it, which at the current improved prices could have been sold and given them the net benefit of £160,000. The bewildered Godber could only reply that he really found it rather difficult to understand the relevance of all those 'suppositious' figures, and that he had envisaged, when putting forward the claim, that it would be dealt with by 'calm personal discussion' and not in such a bureaucratic way.

Watson then met Deterding face to face over this question and convinced him that there was effectively nothing between them, since the supposed points of difference had all been ironed out in the New York settlement anyway. No more was heard about the financial claim. Watson now felt that everything was so well in hand that he could depart for a cold-weather trip to India and Burma; as it happened, it was to be his last. He left in November and returned in March 1933.

He was thus away for the important negotiations which hammered out the heads of agreement for oil distribution in December 1932. These laid down the general guidelines on which local cartel arrangements were to be based. For the next eighteen months or so, during the nadir of the world depression, the principal companies involved strove hard to avoid cut-throat competition. The US remained the main culprit, with independent producers – particularly those exploiting the new East Texas field – unloading large quantities of oil on to the market, secure behind the anti-trust legislation. US oil prices in consequence plummeted; the Romanians in particular were also making trouble, thus jeopardising the fragile network of world oil accords.

Relief came after the inauguration of Franklin D. Roosevelt as the American president early in 1933, fired with a resolve to overturn outdated ideas in the interests of getting the US and the world economies moving again. That summer the National Recovery Act permitted a code of fair competition for the petroleum industry; in plainer terms, accepting cartel prices in Texas and later for exports shipped from the Gulf of Mexico.

Burmah Oil's performance in India was improving also. The share of total demand provided by US and Russian kerosene fell from an average of nearly 30 per cent in 1930–2 to 20 per cent in 1932–4. The company's gross profits in these years were far from buoyant; yet without Watson's tough economy measures and efforts to stabilise the industry, they might have been far worse, as Table 2 shows.

TABLE 2

Burmah Oil – Gross profits 1929–34 (£ millions)

	Trading Profits	Interest	Total
1929	3.0	1.2	4.2
1930	2.1	1.4	3.5
1931	1.6	1.0	2.6
1932	1.1	1.1	2.2
1933	1.4	1.2	2.6
1934	1.4	0.8	2.2

By the beginning of 1934 the tone of Watson's correspondence suggested that he had become less overwhelmed with
day-to-day preoccupations. The government of India, in
anticipation of constitutional change in Burma, was sending an
official to inspect the province's oil industry and to seek a
balanced view between the lobbying of the companies concerned and the fierce criticism of some indigenous politicians
and consumer interests. Watson instructed Harper to see that
all the information required should be provided, on a confidential basis, so as to secure the official's 'reasonable sympathy and
reasoned support'. He went on,

> We have now got them interested: let us make the most and best of
> our opportunities. . . . We have nothing to hide: on the contrary, we
> have a great deal to be proud of in the work we have done not only
> to consolidate the indigenous industry but [also] to protect it, as we
> have so far succeeded in doing, against some of the most powerfully
> organised potential competition, while at the same time recognis-
> ing our responsibilities to the state itself and to the consumer.

Watson took a more objective line than did Sir John Cargill,
who a few years before had declared – in another of his unaided
efforts – to a former lieutenant-governor of Burma that in
twenty-seven years as chairman he had constantly felt
aggrieved and hurt at the biased way in which the governments
of India and Burma invariably treated the company. Apart
from the 'single striking instance' of Curzon's resolute action to

prevent the Standard Oil Company from gaining a foothold with concessions in Burma and thereby to safeguard the company from extinction (see Vol. I pp.65 ff.), Sir John continued,

> the attitude of both the governments of India and Burma towards the company had, generally speaking, been either unsympathetic, unhelpful and [sic] in many instances definitely antagonistic, and always prepared to help and encourage opposition to the company – in a number of cases engineered by unscrupulous company promoters who lined their pockets at the expense of the general public and without doing the slightest good – and in fact in many cases harm – to the indigenous oil industry of Burma.

The improved situation did not mean, however, that a permanent balance between output and gradually improving demand had been achieved. On the contrary, further challenges to world stability in oil were building up with new production coming on stream in the Middle East, notably from Iraq and Bahrain. The latter state, in the Persian Gulf, could well pose a grave threat to Burmah Oil in the Indian market.

As recently as 1926, when offered the concession in Bahrain, Watson and his colleagues had turned it down, preferring to concentrate their operational energies on the Indian empire which they thoroughly understood. Anglo-Persian, far better placed to work on a Middle Eastern concession, had likewise shown no interest, since its experts were not convinced that oil could be found there. In 1933 the Admiralty pressed hard for the concession to go to Burmah Oil as a *quid pro quo* for Anglo-Persian and the American Mellon group's Gulf Oil Corporation having been given favourable treatment in neighbouring Kuwait.[14]

In the event, the Bahrain concession went to the California Texas Oil Company, known as Caltex, a joint subsidiary of the California Standard and of the Texas Company. By 1939 the efforts of Caltex had made Bahrain into the world's fifteenth largest oil-producing country, turning out more crude than the province of Burma, and much more cheaply. When oil from Bahrain began to arrive in India during 1937, Watson succeeded in accommodating its sale there along Achnacarry lines, with remarkably little fuss. His task was made the easier since Russia, for defence reasons, was heavily scaling down its petroleum exports to the subcontinent.

In April 1934, delegates from the major American oil companies came over to London to meet representatives of Anglo-Persian and Shell, partly to tie up what Watson called the 'loose ends' of Achnacarry and investigate possible means of extending its provisions, and partly to plan concerted action to make way for the fresh Middle Eastern sources of supply. 'I am afraid I am going to be hauled into all this', Watson wrote to Rangoon in mock annoyance, 'but intend, as far as possible, confining the time I give to it to participation in the discussions and consideration of wider and tighter application and not in cleaning up the past.'

The upshot of that London meeting was a draft Memorandum of Principles, ratified in June, which carried further than previous accords the two-tier system of controlling oil distribution. The upper tier – to which Watson evidently restricted his efforts – was concerned with clarifying the general principles set out at Achnacarry, while the second tier applied those principles to local marketing agreements throughout the world, giving recognition to differing circumstances in each country. For some reason, that memorandum was never taken beyond the draft stage, but its intentions remained intact until shortly before the outbreak of war in 1939.

Watson in his mid-fifties had thus become an elder statesman of the oil industry. In April 1934 his extraordinary personal reputation was demonstrated when he was asked by Fraser of Anglo-Persian and Kessler of Royal Dutch-Shell to arbitrate over certain terms in a disputed petrol contract between the two companies. He accepted the task with great reluctance; however, having been briefed by both sides on a Monday, by the Thursday he had arrived at his decision. Characteristically, he discovered along the way that there was more to the dispute than met the eye.

On Anglo-Persian's board he still made his presence felt, especially when he was concerned that government was interfering too much. When a matter cropped up about that company's construction of a pipeline through Palestine to the Mediterranean, and the Admiralty demanded certain conditions which Cadman as chairman could not guarantee to get through his board, one of the government directors privately explained the reasons to the Secretary of the Admiralty. On many occasions, he stated, a section of the board, headed by the Burmah Oil directors, 'is definitely hostile to the government connection with the Anglo-Persian Company, and always gives trouble when it suspects that official pressure is being applied to influence the board's actions'. That assumed hostility may have cost Watson an honour such as a knighthood which he seemed to deserve so greatly.

By 1935, when a new crisis afflicted the oil companies, Watson had become a veteran of petroleum diplomacy at the highest level. He had worked tirelessly over the central issue of how to regulate supply in conditions of sagging demand. This fresh problem had oddly similar dimensions. In October of that year, Italy invaded Abyssinia; the League of Nations council agreed to impose financial and other immediate sanctions on the aggressor, and proposed to extend sanctions to oil and other strategic products as soon as the interested countries agreed.[15].

However, it proved exceedingly difficult to implement this agreement. With ministers divided, the British cabinet on 2 December consented to support oil sanctions, but refused to take the initiative; it would, however, follow other governments if they embarked on the first step. Those other governments, and especially France, seemed equally wobbly. Hence top officials exerted pressure on the oil companies, in particular Anglo-Persian and Shell, to take the resolute action from which their political masters shrank. At Downing Street the cabinet had been told of Cadman's informed opinion that it would be impossible to secure a voluntary embargo among US corporations which feared anti-trust measures. Many American oil producers were small independent ones, and Washington had no constitutional powers to prevent sanctions-busting by such devices as shipping oil direct to Italy, or chartering tankers for that purpose.

The British oil companies' stance was that, while they had marketing and other interests in Italy – which could well risk expropriation if they did impose an embargo – they were willing to accept any political decision that was positive and firm. What they were not prepared to do in the circumstances was to have their arms twisted into making voluntary restrictions. With good intentions all round but no stomach for decisive action, the matter drifted on over the new year. Some outside party was bound to suspect the good faith of the oil companies, and early in January 1936 the Labour pacifist peer Lord Ponsonby of Shulbrede wrote a letter to *The Times*, asserting among other things,

> I understand on good authority, that the arrangements made by the oil interests to ensure that a flow of oil shall pass through the gaps in the encirclement of Italy, whatever attempt may be made to stop them, are complete.

Three days later, Watson wrote to *The Times* a robust reply, as follows:

> Speaking with some little knowledge of these 'oil interests' and of how they regard and discharge their responsibilities, I can say with confidence that his lordship's and his authority's suggestion that they would get behind with the object of defeating either this or any other constitutional veto by their respective governments is as baseless as it is insulting.[16]

That Watson should have been chosen to make this authoritative disclaimer is of some interest. Over and above his repute in oil circles, he was the only person to be a director of both Anglo-Persian and Shell, and he could speak with special conviction because as a Burmah Oil man he had no direct involvement in Italian markets. Although Ponsonby subsequently came back in *The Times* on certain other issues raised in his original letter, he did not attempt to defend his assertion.

As Watson passed his sixtieth birthday in 1938, he seriously contemplated retirement. However, the approach of war seems to have deterred him. After the Munich crisis that September had led to a speeding up of preparatory measures, Watson was asked to become chairman-designate of a wartime regulating agency for oil products, the Petroleum Board. Having served on its predecessor in the previous conflict, he had no desire to become involved in such onerous work again. In any case, he felt that his own company needed him more. The easy-going Whigham, although a seasoned business man, was at 62 perhaps not up to facing the wartime burden of the managing directorship with Cargill as chairman. As matters worked out, it was Watson who bore the brunt of the company's travail when war erupted in the Far East and swiftly destroyed all that had been achieved, with so much effort, in Burma over so many decades.

Notes

1 A phrase used in a tribute, *The Times*, 5 February 1948.

2 L. Hannah, *The Rise of the Corporate Economy*, 2nd edn, 1976, p. 102.

3 For a libel case brought against Cargill, over which Watson gave much help and legal advice, see *The Times*, 25 April 1936.

4 R. W. Ferrier, 'John, First Lord, Cadman', *DBB* I, pp. 558–64; an entry is also in *Dictionary of National Biography 1941–50*, 1959, pp. 126–8.

5 For an account from Anglo-Persian's viewpoint see R. W. Ferrier, *The History of the British Petroleum Company I: The Developing Years 1901–32*, 1982, pp. 333ff.

6 ibid., pp. 510ff.

7 ibid., p. 511.

8 *Burmah Shell of Pakistan Monthly News Review: 1968 Supplement*, 'Forty Years of Burmah-Shell' pp. 3–4. M. S. Patwardhan – a former employee and later chairman of Burmah-Shell of India – gives an attractively written sketch of that firm's history in *Oil and Other Multinationals in India*, Bombay, 1986.

9 The main source is Indian Tariff Board, *Report Regarding the Grant of Protection to the Oil Industry*, and *Oral Evidence Recorded during the Enquiry*, Government of India, Calcutta, 1928–9.

10 All evidence so far published on the Achnacarry agreement of 1928 has been recycled from US Senate Select Committee on Small Business, *The International Petroleum Cartel* Washington DC, 1952, pp. 199ff., 268ff. Disappointingly, the authoritative volume by H. M. Larson, E. M. Knowlton and C. S. Popple, *History of Standard Oil Company (New Jersey) 1927–50: New Horizons*, New York, 1971, pp. 308–14 adds little to our knowledge of the agreement, but outlines some of the later international discussions to 1939. See also H. F. Williamson *et al.*, *The American Petroleum Industry: The Age of Energy 1899–1959*, Evanston, 1963, pp. 527ff., 736ff.

11 *Petroleum Times* XXVI, 5 September 1931, pp. 299ff.

12 Ibid., 3 October 1931, p. 450.

13 For Fraser (subsequently chairman of his company and a director of Burmah Oil) see R. W. Ferrier, 'William Milligan Fraser, First Lord Strathalmond', *DBB* II, pp. 423–7; see also entry in *Dictionary of National Biography 1961–70*, 1981, pp. 395–7. For Fraser's background in Scottish shale oil see *Scottish Dictionary of Business Biography* I, pp. 35–6.

14 H. V. F. Winstone and Z. Freeth, *Kuwait, Prospect and Reality*, 1972, p. 149. This reference has not been traced in the Public Record Office (henceforth PRO).

15 For the ditherings of the great powers over oil sanctions against Italy see W. N. Medlicott, D. Dakin and M. E. Lambert (eds), *Documents on British Foreign Policy 1919–39 Second Series XV*, 1976, esp. pp. 36off. (cabinet meeting) and pp. 332ff. (memoranda submitted to cabinet).

16 *The Times*, 10 January 1936. Ponsonby's letters are in ibid. 7 and 13 January.

CHAPTER II

Constitutional Changes and War 1937–41

No developments in the East were of greater political significance to Burmah Oil than the constitutional changes in Burma and India after 1918. Before and during the First World War, Burma had been no more than an outlying and partly neglected province of the Indian empire. The lieutenant-governor ruled through a nominated legislative council, only half its members being non-Europeans; that council was subject to an official veto. Then in 1923 a system of dyarchy, dividing power between official and elected representatives, was introduced: an apparently limited step, but one that a civil servant in Burma described as 'the parting of the ways'.[1] Some Burmese ministers were appointed, accountable to an elected parliament, and local government similarly became subject to elections.

Watson took a reasonably benign view of these developments, but favoured the principle of good and stable administration rather than the over-emphasis on self-determination for the local peoples. A vital connected issue was Burma's future relationship with India, which had in 1917 been promised responsible government within the British empire. Ten years later the Simon commission was set up to consider India's political future, and there was for the first time a practical possibility that Burma could be separated from its powerful neighbour. In 1928 the general manager in Rangoon, William A. Gray, wrote home that he expected conditions in India over the next few decades to be 'chaotic', with any considerable advance towards self-government leading to bad government or alternatively unrest in the absence of political advance. He added,

> In Burma, on the other hand, it is my belief that, in the event of separation, within a short space of time we should have a number of Burmans drawing large salaries in high posts and doing no work, and British secretaries actually carrying out the work of administration.

The pessimistic Sir John Cargill, who saw the correspondence, minuted 'I agree absolutely!'

Also in 1928, Watson and Whigham were both of the opinion that it would be more constructive 'to assure good government in both India and Burma and then to consider what would be best in the economic interests of Burma'. On broad grounds, therefore, their view was that it would be a misguided policy for the province to go for separation, but in any case the Burmese would not be easy to manage; whether constitutionally separated or not, Burma's politics would be influenced by events in India and other countries seeking self-determination.

Watson further believed that the province would find its prospective share of India's national debt and defence burden so onerous that it might be better served by remaining within the Indian empire. He was interested to learn that the governor of Burma, Sir Harcourt Butler, having called for full data on the 'profit and loss' of a complete break from India, privately doubted if Burma would benefit financially from the step. Watson therefore advocated internal home rule for the province, with favourable treatment being given on questions of defence and credit.

By mid-1931, the round-table conferences on constitutional reform in India were taking place, and opinion in Burma seemed to favour some federal scheme within the Indian empire; that was the message that emerged from the Burmese elections of 1932. Watson, on the other hand, by then felt that the province should go for complete separation under its own constitution, but with all the economic advantages of federalism secured by trade and other agreements. One highly desirable condition, vital to the company, would be that Burmese oil products should enjoy tariff-free importation into India. Although

Watson was convinced that the Burmese would not be able to run their own country unaided in the foreseeable future, and similarly saw no early prospect of their being appointed to senior posts in the company, he had already arranged for the more advanced training of Burmese drillers. When Harper wrote home that Burmanisation in the company was likely to be negligible, except possibly in junior technical jobs, Watson agreed when Cargill minuted 'Yes!'

Regrettably, the correspondence with Rangoon has been lost for the two years between the passing of the Government of Burma Act by the British parliament in 1935 and Burma's formal split from India in April 1937. Burma remained under the governor, who reported directly to the Secretary of State for India and Burma. Watson was apparently working hard behind the scenes to make sure that there should be a lengthy interim period before fiscal arrangements between Burma and India should be changed in any way. An official Order in Council shortly afterwards prohibited both countries from altering unilaterally their current tariff arrangements for three years from that date.

In a special issue of *The Times* dated 20 April 1937, to commemorate Burma's separation day, Watson stressed the importance, there and in India, 'of preserving unimpaired the indigenous resources of oil', which were of the utmost economic and strategic value to both countries alike, and the undesirability of either government taking measures which would encourage foreign competitors to jeopardise the industry's effective working. Such steps were by no means impossible. Burma now had a prime minister and cabinet, with two chambers, the lower one being all-elected; the governor was responsible only for foreign affairs, defence and currency matters. It was noteworthy that Burmese men received the vote at 18, something not granted in Britain until 1969, and women at 21, subject to a literacy test. Ministers were thus in charge and had fairly wide powers over home affairs, including those for oil.

These far-reaching constitutional reforms in Burma did nothing to halt a growing tide of unrest there, even among the company's employees. The riots of the early 1930s, chiefly directed against Indians, were confined to Rangoon and did not affect the company directly; yet they proved a political turning-point, in promoting the formation of a new Burmese party, the Thakins, an intensely anti-British group set on working for outright independence. They sought to provoke, or at least prolong, the strike which erupted at Chauk in January 1938. That arose out of a minor incident, ineptly handled, when a workman was dismissed and later reinstated on the same day. The 3,000 men who then struck there were later joined by another 3,000 from Yenangyaung. They demanded monthly instead of daily payment, and paid holidays for 53 days in the year: the company had recently increased the paid leave allowance from 3 to 17 days, far more generous than that given to workers elsewhere in the Indian empire and even in Britain at that time. Watson refused to consider these demands, and Roper asked the government of Burma to set up a court of enquiry under the Trade Disputes Act, which was done.

The main organiser of the strike was the 22-year-old Aung San, native of a village in the oilfields area. He came of traditionally anti-British stock, his grandfather, a local mayor, having been killed fighting on the Burmese side during the war of 1885. In the course of the strike, Burmah Oil's labour and welfare offices were physically attacked, despite most employees' acceptance of their efficiency and standards of service. The strike gradually petered out as a sporadic return to work took place. The court of enquiry adjudicated that the other oil companies should raise their conditions of work to those offered by Burmah Oil, but the Thakins were plainly wishing to prolong unrest for political reasons.

A further strike erupted in 1939. A number of strikers marched to the capital, where they proceeded to block all the entrances to the company's Rangoon office by lying down on the pavement and road. Burmese women provocatively removed their sandals, shaking them at the staff looking discreetly out of the windows, and raised their lungis, or full-length skirts, to the knees and danced around.

Since at the end of office hours the crowd made no effort to disperse, the staff inside were clearly anxious that the female employees, all Burmese or Anglo-Burmese, should get out unharmed. One assistant therefore stationed himself at the office entrance, one gingerly stepped over the bodies to the edge

of the mob, and one managed to find a foothold in the middle.
They then picked up the girls one by one and swung them so
that the next man could catch them; once free of the mob – in
the words of the account – they 'legged it fast for home'. The
Burmese press made much of the incident, with headlines such
as 'British Officers Abusing Local Girls', but there was no
adverse reaction from the crowd.

Output at the fields was not much affected by the strikes. In
1938 the total for all companies was down by just over 4 per
cent, with Burmah Oil's loss slightly greater at 4.8 per cent;
then the 1939 figure recovered almost exactly to that for 1937.
In any case, Watson was able to keep refinery throughput
steady in 1938 because of the abundant stocks being held at
Syriam. The strike at Digboi, from the spring of 1939 until
September, was more serious, markedly reducing its flow of oil
products: refinery throughput was down from just over 1.6
million to 1.26 million barrels between 1938 and 1939. Hence
Syriam produced an equivalent extra amount of output – 5.4
million barrels as against 5.07 million barrels – to make up for
this shortfall.

The Second World War became possible, and perhaps inevitable, from the early 1930s onwards, with the rise to power of
Hitler in Germany and the increasingly militaristic stance of
imperial Japan. In Whitehall, serious defence preparations
remained frozen as long as the 'ten year rule'* was officially in
force. Once it had lapsed, the whole of the British government's
war planning machinery began to take on momentum.

In this planning for the possibility of war, Burmah Oil had a
minor but distinctive part. A generation earlier, in 1905, the
Committee of Imperial Defence had, at the time when the
Royal Navy was beginning to change from coal to fuel oil,
emphasised to government departments the immense strategic

---

* This was a decision of the Cabinet Committee on Finance in 1919 that the
armed services should plan on the assumption that no major war was
anticipated over the next ten years. The 'rule' was renewed from year to year
until the early 1930s but does not seem ever to have been abolished as such. In
March 1932 the Committee of Imperial Defence recommended abandonment, and in 1933 the cabinet – following Japanese attacks on northern China
– embarked on some purely defensive measures, notably building up
Singapore and other Far Eastern bases. None for Burma was included.

importance of the Burmese oilfields, then the only worthwhile sources of oil in the British empire. Also in 1905, Burmah Oil had concluded the financially unremunerative fuel oil contract with the Admiralty, mentioned in the Introduction.

Thereafter other companies, in particular Anglo-Persian (in 1935 renamed Anglo-Iranian), had helped to satisfy in abundance the navy's growing fuel oil needs. Burmah Oil's fuel oil contract was still operative, but in name only: as Burmese crude was light and waxy, fuel oil was not the most convenient product for it to make. With the Admiralty's consent, therefore, it used Anglo-Iranian's refinery at Abadan to provide such fuel oil as the navy needed under its contract. By 1939 the Admiralty was on the point of cancelling the 1905 contract altogether, but on the outbreak of war that September it instead agreed to suspend drawing any fuel oil supplies from Rangoon, so as to allow alternative products to be turned out for the government of India and other essential customers.

Here the geographical location of Burma and the characteristics of its oil happily coincided. Geographically, the province was benefitting from the advent of the air age. As R. I. Watson pointed out in the article he wrote for *The Times* special number in April 1937, Burma was on one of the main air routes of the world, connecting Europe and the Far East. Rangoon airport was a key staging post, giving the colony both a commercial and a strategic role of great significance. Moreover, Burmah Oil's aviation spirit was of an almost uniquely high octane value, although at that time it produced only a limited amount for local use.

In 1932, once the ten-year rule began to be reconsidered, the Committee of Imperial Defence's interdepartmental sub-committee for petroleum supplies, named the Oil Board, started actively planning for oil availability in any future war. Reporting to the Oil Board was the secret Principal Supply Officers' Committee (India), on which the Burmah-Shell manager in Calcutta served *ex officio*. Its task was to forecast wartime supply and demand for oil products throughout the Indian empire.

Two years later, that body asked Watson how far Burmah Oil would be able to help out in the event of war. Not unexpectedly, heading the committee's list of requirements was aviation spirit, since air power would be crucial in any future conflict. To be sure, the Royal Dutch-Shell refineries in Borneo and Sumatra turned out large quantities of that product; yet planning would have to take account of the possibility that Japan would overrun those installations. An alternative source in the eastern hemisphere was Abadan, but that refinery was then technically unable to produce aviation spirit to the required specification. That left Burma, held to be secure behind the fifteen-inch guns of Singapore and its own natural defences to the east.

Watson at once put in hand a typically thorough investigation. It showed the main limiting factor, as ever, to be that of tankers, the next being the capacity of the company's pipeline from the oilfields to Rangoon; that could handle a maximum of 7.5 million barrels a year, over 50 per cent above the existing refinery throughput. The Syriam refinery, thoroughly reorganised along modern lines by Watson a decade before – with ample spare capacity to allow for breakdowns and maintenance – could comfortably process a substantial extra amount of crude. In the oilfields a survey revealed that, given six months' notice, a number of promising but so far undrilled exploration areas, especially in the rich Chauk field, could be brought into production.

Since, during that six months, oil stocks would have to be run down so as to keep the refinery at increased throughput levels, Watson arranged to build up stocks. He ordered additional storage tanks, to hold 625,000 barrels, equivalent to a month's capacity running. The company's representatives then had prolonged discussions with the principal supply officers to work out the most useful mix of refined products to meet the wartime requirements of the army, air force and civilian customers; the navy would rely on Abadan. Since the precise circumstances of war could not of course be foreseen, the company furnished a schedule of alternative combinations of products from which the principal supply officers could choose if and when the time arrived.

From September 1937 onwards Watson arranged for a series of geological reviews to be carried out, with results that became significant after war had been declared. A major engineering task about this time was the reclamation of a large stretch of the

Irrawaddy river bed on the east bank at Chauk, by using dredged sand behind a long retaining wall. That allowed wells to be drilled into certain parts of the oilfield lying under the river. Indo-Burma had been the first to prove the extension of the field under the Irrawaddy, and had built a retaining wall on the west bank during 1925–6. Watson also arranged for new machinery to be installed at the pumping stations, as well as a radio link to permit instant communications.

In the short run, therefore, Watson was very confident of being able to meet the authorities' likely defence needs. However, the long-term oil prospects throughout the Indian empire remained problematical, whether in peace or war. As always in the risky oil business, there were pluses and minuses. Thanks to extensions and improvements, Assam Oil had increased its refinery throughput by nearly 25 per cent between 1931 and 1934, from 1.3 million to 1.6 million barrels (compared with Burmah Oil's 5 million barrels in 1934). That higher level was maintained until 1942, except in 1939 when the lengthy labour dispute at Digboi reduced the year's throughput to 1.26 million barrels, as explained above.

On the west side of India, in the Punjab, the independent Attock Oil Company had increasingly close ties with Burmah Oil, which marketed that company's refined products and also supplied it with debenture finance (see Chapter I): Burmah Oil's geological staff also helped Attock Oil's geologists to locate some deep test wells. An important find at Dhulian began to be productive in 1937, and trebled Attock Oil's output from just over 250,000 barrels that year to nearly 760,000 barrels in 1939. On the debit side, in 1933 Burmah Oil's field at Badarpur, opened up as recently as 1915, became exhausted and had to be abandoned, having overall cost more than it had yielded in revenue. In 1938/9 Burmah Oil and the other indigenous Burmese companies, together with Assam Oil and Attock Oil, were between them meeting just over half of India's total consumption of refined products, contributing 35, 11 and 4 per cent respectively.

To add to the company's problems, foreign oil companies were also anxious to carry out tests in India. Since the early 1900s the government of India's policy had been to exclude all

such companies; the recent constitutional changes were beginning to erode that safeguard, since Delhi was transferring to
provincial governments the authority to grant oil prospecting
licences as well as operating leases. In 1935, the year when
India's constitutional changes took place, British Controlled
Oilfields Ltd, a Canadian company which was producing in
Trinidad, Ecuador and Venezuela, proposed to apply for
concessions in the Indian states; however, the directors later
lost interest. Two years later a newly-formed company, Indian
Oil Concessions Ltd, was registered in Calcutta. The majority
stake belonged to the Indian merchants Andrew Yule & Co.,
but a 45 per cent interest was held by Caltex, which – as
Chapter I showed – was building up a market in India for its
Bahrain oil, and which would be providing the geological staff.
It soon acquired a concession for the whole of a Punjabi state,
and was known to be negotiating for others.

Watson lost no time in planning his counter-measures. His
principal aide here was one of the ablest of the company's
senior staff in the East: W. E. V. Abraham, then chief geologist
in Burma. Like many of those unfortunates burdened with
acronymic initials, Abraham had a ready-made nickname:
Weva – pronounced Weaver – and it is as Weva that he will
henceforth be named in the present narrative. He was a
perceptive Ulsterman, with a liking for informality. Then in his
early forties, he had lived a very active life in Burma since his
first appointment there in 1920. Not only did he keep Watson
fully briefed on geological matters, revealing to him the steadily
increasing life expectancy of the established fields, but he also
found time to command the Upper Burma battalion of the
Burma Auxiliary Force as a lieutenant-colonel. He played as
hard as he worked, believing in the virtue of taking time off for
leisure pursuits, his favourite being polo. He was somewhat
unusual among early geologists in being as interested in
production methods and in ways of securing more economic
output as he was in purely technical questions. This searching
interest and general 'get-up-and-go' attitude was particularly
congenial to the American drillers and managers in the fields
who dubbed him 'the nozzle man'.

Watson treated him with fatherly indulgence. Not only
were his reports lucidly written and replete with all the

information that even Watson could ask for, but he also did not shrink from making comments on wider and often very sensitive issues. When he briefly visited Persia in 1934, he perceived the need for relations between Anglo-Persian and the government there to be as friendly as possible, since this relationship was likely to become crucial for that company in ten or twenty years' time – as indeed it turned out. At the personal level, he found that hostility on the Persian side was often matched by a dislike of Persians by many of that company's European employees. He felt that these antagonisms could be eased by the British freely giving disinterested advice and help in many directions outside oil. Watson sent the report to William Fraser, deputy chairman of Anglo-Persian, explaining that he deliberately sought to encourage his own men to state their views (quoted in Chapter I) and he offered Weva's presentation of 'these pictures as they have appeared to him in the hope that we may find something in his canvas that may be helpful or suggestive or both'. The dour Fraser's reply would have been interesting, but appears not to have survived in the Burmah Oil archives.

In 1937 Weva was not above wangling for himself a trip home to represent his battalion at the coronation of George VI that May, even inducing someone to hold his horse in Tothill Street, close to Westminster Abbey, while he popped in and climbed up to a vantage point where for ten minutes or so he had a grandstand view of the ceremony. When that August, after some leave, he reported to Watson in the London office, he was told that he was to come home and work there. His private reaction was one of profound regret: 'No more polo; no more evenings at the club before changing for dinner.'[2] At Britannic House he joined, and often lunched with, a colleague also recently returned from Burma. That was a former assistant with Finlay Fleming & Co., Hubert Ashton, the Cambridge cricketing blue who was a son of the aged but still serving director H. S. Ashton.

In London, a major task of Weva's was to head an investigation into the prospects of discovering oilfields beneath the vast alluvial deposits in the river basins of the Indus, Ganges, Brahmaputra and Irrawaddy, to select areas for exploration and then to negotiate concessions in the selected areas. By early 1939 Weva had secured prospecting licences in the state of Tripura, near Calcutta, and was actively bidding for licences in Sind and the Punjab.

This exploration was to be carried out jointly with Shell and Anglo-Iranian. Those companies' geologists had gone to see Thomas Dewhurst, Burmah Oil's chief geologist in London, and proposed this move, saying that if he declined, they would seek to go ahead on their own. They agreed to provide the extra staff needed to cope with their potentially very extensive programme. This led to an influx of British, Dutch, Swiss and other geologists with international experience; in consequence, the company's thinking on exploration techniques was radically altered by this co-operation with its two rivals.

Weva was less successful in Burma itself, where licensing was now regulated by the Burmese ministers concerned. The Minister of Commerce and Industry in Rangoon felt strongly that any as yet untapped natural resources should remain so and not be exploited by capitalists from overseas. He refused Weva's application for an exploration licence over an area of more than 35,000 square miles, nearly 14 per cent of Burma's total area. Eventually local ministers compromised by offering the company a guarantee of priority, thus putting it at the head of the queue; Roper as general manager in Rangoon had difficulty in convincing the dissatisfied Watson that nothing more could be expected for the time being. However, Watson soon became reconciled to what he had been offered, and candidly explained to his board that he had primarily sought to make sure that, so far as could be determined, no potentially oil-bearing areas in India and Burma were left which might 'excite the interest of third parties'. He had in mind the North American exploration companies, which he feared would not have the same regard for conservation as Burmah Oil had shown.

Unfortunately, while relations with the authorities in Rangoon remained good, the India Office still harboured its long-standing hostility towards the company. In September 1939 an official declared to his opposite number in the Petroleum Department that the directors 'seem to admit with a good deal of candour that they are in the Indian exploration business largely or mainly to keep other people out'. This rather vague assertion overlooked the facts that Anglo-Iranian and Shell had proposed the scheme in the first place and were active partners with Burmah Oil in the exploration.

That official's Petroleum Department colleague dissociated himself from this rather extreme view, stating, 'I have never been quite able to understand the attitude of the India Office in this matter, because similar views have been expressed on other occasions.'[3] The Petroleum Department was to prove a good friend to the company during the war, but the inimical attitude of the India and the Burma Offices persisted until their extinction in 1947–8 when the two countries achieved independence.

Over and above concerns about exploration, in May 1939 Weva had two worries. The first was the industrial tension in Burma and India, mentioned earlier, at a time when expansion was vital. Second, drilling and pumping equipment had to be ordered if potential wartime requirements of aviation spirit, already pledged to the authorities, were to be met. Output in both Burma and India was in fact increased on the outbreak of war with Germany, and the equipment earlier ordered began to arrive in 1940. A further pre-war concern was to make sure that the oil tanks for storage at Syriam were camouflaged in case of air attack. Watson gave permission for this to be done, but insisted on the bill being sent to the government of Burma. The necessary work was carried out during the summer of 1939. Three weeks after the declaration of war, an RAF aircraft made a reconnaissance of Syriam and reported that the storage tanks had been satisfactorily disguised.

One organisational change which took place at this time was to split up operations in the East between seven subsidiary companies. This was done partly to accommodate the separation of Burma from India and partly for tax reasons. The seven subsidiaries, set up in 1939, dealt respectively with Burma concessions, India concessions, pipelines, refineries, Burma trading, India trading and tankers.[4] The local governments raised no objections to existing licences and leases being transferred to the relevant concessions' subsidiaries. The new organisation was inevitably referred to as Snow White and the Seven Dwarfs, because the immensely popular Walt Disney cartoon film had recently appeared.

When war came in September 1939, there was not the same wealth of talent among Burmah Oil's executive directors as there had been in August 1914. Now, apart from Watson – for Cargill was not to attend a London board meeting again – there were his able deputy Gilbert Whigham, Sir Kenneth Harper, formerly general manager in Rangoon who concentrated on staff matters, and William A. Gray on the technical side. None of these were particularly 'yes-men', but clearly the word of Watson prevailed. There were some non-executive directors, such as the former Indian civil servant Sir Louis Kershaw, but their function was purely advisory. After D. W. T. Cargill's death in September 1939, Sir William Fraser of Anglo-Iranian joined the board in a non-executive capacity.

From the outbreak of war, Watson continued to co-operate fully with the authorities. To be sure, this often involved time-consuming bureaucratic wrangles. Weva asked the central and provincial governments in India to allow prospecting work to be suspended, without the company suffering a penalty. He requested the India Office to take up the matter with Delhi, which pointed out that it no longer had authority over prospecting but would do its best to persuade individual provinces. Eventually, after a prodigious amount of correspondence, most provinces agreed. There were also long drawn-out discussions about imposing price control over refined products, which Watson readily accepted in principle. However, remembering the unsatisfactory enforcement attempts in the First World War, he was privately sceptical about their effectiveness.

The company was equally keen to help the war effort in Burma. Roper took steps to extend the operations of the company's workshops there by going on to 24-hour working. This substantially economised in the use of its own equipment, as it learnt to use scrap materials to an extent never before achieved, even between 1914 and 1918. It also arranged to carry out repair work for the armed forces. Unfortunately, that led to a shortage of skilled labour, which was to some extent met from the trained lads coming out of the company's trade school. Although by 1940 nearly all the emergency drilling and production equipment had arrived safely in Burma, it was not put into use straight away, but was held in readiness to await the planned increase in output.

The tanker M. V. *Yenangyaung* (with anti-aircraft gun) during the Second World War.

The declaration of war led to the exodus of many businesses from London. Britannic House was left partly empty when Anglo-Iranian was evacuated to Llandarcy in South Wales, although the sturdiness of the building made its basement very popular as an air raid shelter. One function which could not be moved was that of Burmah-Shell, which the authorities had made the main programming unit for all bulk imports into India for its own use and for US companies such as Standard-Vacuum (Stanvac) and the California-Texas Oil Company (Caltex). It was thus the link between the Petroleum Board's overseas supply committee and India, where the Cooper-Lawson committee sat to allocate the supplies: Guy Cooper, knighted in 1941, was the general manager of Burmah-Shell in India.

Since this liaison work required the transmission of highly confidential data – for the enemy would have welcomed knowledge of oil stock levels and tanker sailings – there had to be a secure method of exchanging information. Early in the war Cooper's personal assistant in Calcutta received a secret coded cable from home, which read, 'Have you a bible in your office?' A separate communication revealed the reason for this odd enquiry. The London office was to use biblical phrases for composing and deciphering coded messages in the 'one-time' letter pad system, said to be unbreakable. The letter pads themselves were sent out from Britain under military security; the Calcutta office, on receiving them, was instructed to cable back, 'Level here.' Unfortunately, a telegraphist misread the message as, 'Laval here.' The censor at once alerted officials and a brief but intensive flap occurred: the collaborator Pierre Laval was the French premier in the Vichy government, and it would indeed have caused a sensation had he turned up in India. This error was soon put right and, for the rest of the war, a copy of the bible was one of the most frequently consulted works in the personal assistant's bookcase.[5]

The other immovable object in Britannic House was R. I. Watson, who not only declared that he had no intention of going but also took charge of the building's fire precautions. The staff that remained was divided into fire-watching parties, each of which slept on the premises every tenth night. A heavily sandbagged shelter was constructed on the flat section of the roof, which gave an excellent field of vision, both for fire-bombs and also to view the heavy bombing that from 1940 onwards became routine in the metropolis.

Watson's skill in reconciling humanity with the call of duty was shown when one of his staff lost his only son in action. Remote as he seemed, Watson always insisted on being told of any troubles affecting his people; when the bereaved man's next spell of fire-watching came round, he was not excused so that he could be with his wife – for that might have weakened London's defences! Instead, she was invited to come along too. Even though Britannic House was never hit, there were some bad moments, especially when Moorgate station was bombed. Yet there were also lighter occasions. At Christmas 1943 the 46-year-old accountant William Eadie, recently brought home from Burmah-Shell in India to transfer the accounts department from Glasgow to London, composed a ditty, which began,

> Section A of the BOC
>   Is down for duty two-nine-three.
> Two-nine-three on Xmas night.
>   Is indeed a sorry plight.

This offering accompanied the menu for the Christmas dinner, which included such delicacies as stirrup-pump soup, haggis *de l'intérieure*, block-buster pudding and *gâteau au sultana d'Irak* – obviously an austerity version of Christmas cake. Eadie was far abler as an accountant than as a versifier, and when the Burmah-Shell general manager in London died suddenly in 1944, he took over for a time until a successor could be brought back from India.

One member of the Burmah Oil staff was not a fire-watcher. That was Weva, who had before the war joined the Territorials in London and had his own defence duties to perform. Watson had not objected to his 'playing about' (as he had put it) but solemnly warned him that his presence in the office was vital and that there was absolutely no question of his going back full-time into uniform. Weva might perhaps have accepted this, however reluctantly, as Ashton – who like Roper had won the MC in the first war – had to do. However, the surrender of France and the Dunkirk evacuation swiftly changed his mind, and he engineered a demand for his services by the War Office, even though he would have to start afresh as a second lieutenant. Only after much remonstation would Watson let him go. Having first of all served in the War Office, in 1941 Weva was sent to the Middle East, where he was eventually restored to the rank of lieutenant-colonel in the planning section of GHQ.

His rare combination of oil expertise, negotiating skill and intellectual curiosity allowed him to hold his own in whatever company, however exalted. He seems to have hobnobbed with almost everyone of any consequence in the war, up to but not including Winston Churchill. As Neville Gass, of Anglo-Iranian, wrote with a touch of envy to Watson in mid-1942, 'I can think of no one who has been more successful in having a really good war. He is always full of good cheer and seems continually to have a roving commission that must be full of interest.' On the long voyage via the Cape to the Middle East, he spent his time reading H. A. L. Fisher's *History of Europe*, going over each chapter in his mind after first having read it.[6]

The energy with which the company was assisting the war effort contrasted piquantly with the comparative torpor among official circles in Burma. In 1939 the local forces comprised four regular and two territorial Burma Army Battalions, together with units of the largely European-manned Burma Auxiliary Force. This establishment was primarily meant for internal security duties, and was expanded in 1940–41 and a Burma Navy and Air Force were added. However, the defence of Burma from external threat received a low priority in London, partly because the supreme military authority kept changing. Until 1937, it came under the Commander-in-Chief, India; it was then made directly responsible to the chiefs of staff in London who, in November 1940, transferred it to the Far East command in Singapore. One positive decision taken at this time was to re-open the Burma road to China. Not until December 1941, after the outbreak of war in the east, did Burma revert for defence purposes to India, where it clearly belonged. With a shortage of equipment, and with no anti-aircraft guns, Burma was correctly described as 'practically without the means of defending herself'.[7]

Although Burmah Oil's wartime activities soon settled down into a routine, Watson did not let up on assisting the authorities in any way he could. In 1940, when uncertainties over oil supplies were causing concern, he ordered further quantities of drilling and pumping equipment from Britain: enough to increase crude output by about 50 per cent, if and when the emergency programme had to be put into effect. That July he gave instructions to open up a potentially prolific reserve area in Chauk. A number of wells there were drilled down to the oil sands so that, by a process of 'bullet-perforation', they could be made to flow at a moment's notice and provide 800,000 extra barrels a year, with another 700,000 barrels available without further drilling; say 25 per cent more production.

In August 1940 Roper was able to write confidentially to Watson, in a letter conveyed by safe hand. This revealed that a comprehensive defence scheme by the Burmese authorities, drafted as early as the beginning of 1938, had still been largely on paper at the outbreak of war in Europe in 1939 and had advanced very little since then. Admittedly, Burma on its own could not afford the cost of ambitious defence measures and, until the fall of France in June 1940 made Indo-China vulnerable to Japanese incursions, felt itself perfectly secure.

Concern mounted when Japan signed a military and economic pact with Germany and Italy in August 1940, by which time many people blamed the lack of drive on the governor himself.

Since 1936, Sir Archibald Cochrane had served as the first governor of Burma not to have come from the Indian Civil Service. He was an ex-naval man and a former MP. An unnamed 'senior personage' described Cochrane's rule to Roper as a 'tragedy'. On the political side, his unbending quarterback manner had denied to the Burmese ministers an opportunity of meeting him except on a formal basis. They never felt able to talk to him freely, let alone to exchange ideas that would have broadened both sides' views. As to defence, he had failed to give a lead in pushing through effective measures. Even after Dunkirk, he had done little apart from requiring all European males to undertake military training.

At Christmas 1940 a new governor for Burma was named. He was Sir Reginald Dorman-Smith; for a change, a relative youngster of only 41. He has been described as dramatically good-looking, immaculate and pipe-smoking: a man who had enjoyed a distinguished career of sheltered achievement.[8] A member of the Anglo-Irish ascendancy, he had served as a subaltern in the Indian army, but since then had tended to go into jobs at the top; he therefore lacked the ripe judgement, tinged with a healthy scepticism, which able men tend to gain by observing over a lengthy period the failings of their superiors. As an agriculturalist, he had been president of the National Farmers' Union and, as an MP, he had early in 1939 been appointed by Neville Chamberlain – without first having held junior office – as Minister of Agriculture and Fisheries.

He had done tolerably well as a minister. His sagacious measure in April 1939 to build up stocks of tractors and fertilisers, and to grant subsidies for ploughing grassland, showed that he was capable of giving a much needed jolt to inertia among officials and the farming community alike. Similarly, his launching of what became the 'dig for victory' campaign that August was a sensible precautionary step.[9] However, like most ministers in his department, he had been by no means popular among farmers, least of all after having been the NFU's lobbyist-in-chief before his appointment as minister. Some time later, when Burma was in agony, a journalist out there unkindly recalled a time – probably in 1939 – when Dorman-Smith had addressed a gathering of highly dissatisfied and angry farmers from Lincolnshire. Attempting to mollify them without having anything tangible to offer, he had answered their complaints by pointing out that, after all, when one put a bull into a field with a herd of cows, one could not expect to see immediate results. 'No,' yelled one irate farmer, 'but if the bull was any good, you could certainly expect to see smiles on the faces of the cows!'

Dorman-Smith did not survive the ministerial purge of May 1940 after Winston Churchill's arrival at 10 Downing Street. Doubtless, however, the fact that he had learnt to cope with argumentative British farmers led to his being considered suitable to deal with no less argumentative Burmese ministers. He had moreover already shown a willingness to take far-sighted measures in preparation for the all-out conflict to come. At the very least his informality, and reliance on personal contact in seeking to understand the other man's point of view, made a welcome change from the rigid offhandedness of Cochrane. The world, it was widely said, was at his feet; had things turned out differently in Burma, he might have been on the first rung of a distinguished proconsular career. In February 1941 Watson, Whigham and Harper had a short briefing interview with him at the Burma Office. Watson commented to Roper on his 'attractive and easy manner and good appearance', and said that he seemed to be a 'good mixer'.

The governor-designate certainly took his job seriously. Before setting off by sea, he had sought the views of British intelligence about the likelihood of a Japanese attack on Burma. These were obtained from the Far East Combined Bureau in Singapore, a joint services organisation for intelligence.[10] The emphatic reply was that such an attack would definitely not take place, since it would bring the might of the United States down on Japan. If the Japanese were foolish enough to start a war, they would almost certainly strike against Indo-China, Thailand and the oil-bearing territories of the East Indies. Even in this unlikely eventuality, Burma's natural defences to the east, of almost impenetrable mountains and forests, would rule out the slightest chance of a successful invasion.

By the middle of 1941, intelligence chiefs in London were beginning to contemplate the possibility of Japan's eventual entry into the war. However, they regarded it as equally possible that any Japanese attack would be aimed first at Russia, already gravely weakened by the German invasion. They continued to declare that Burma would be in no danger whatever. Dorman-Smith later felt deeply betrayed by this assessment, conveying as it did a false reassurance that was to cost the province dear: hence a bitter remark he made to the Secretary of State for Burma, L. S. Amery, in January 1942, regarding 'the falsification of all our intelligence reports from Singapore about Japan coming into the war.'[11]

Even allowing for these bland forecasts, he was surprised on his arrival in April 1941 to find an almost complete lack of urgency about preparing for war, and he at once sought to provide a vigorous lead from the top. As a politician he knew only too well the precariousness of his balancing act: on the one hand to maintain an imperturbable exterior so as to sustain morale and minimise panic, and on the other to galvanise the complacent administrators into improving the totally inadequate defences. Civil defence was virtually non-existent, with Rangoon estimated to be out of range of any Japanese aircraft. At his request, a civil defence expert was sent out from Britain to advise on steps to protect both people and vital installations such as those at Syriam, which needed more than just camouflage to furnish an adequate safeguard.

The political dimension to his task was excessively tricky. The prime minister of Burma at that time was U Saw, whom his predecessor, Ba Maw, later dubbed as possessing great energy, but with some good qualities 'corrupted by a demon-like personal ambition uncurbed by either a clear political faith or a conscience'.[12] Dorman-Smith was resolved to establish a good relationship with him; fortunately, despite at first glance having so little in common, they hit it off remarkably well. On the other side were the British commercial representatives in Burma, including those of the oil companies. They had for years been showing understandable concern over the safeguarding of their own interests under the new constitution. They seem quickly to have gained confidence in him and to feel that he was more understanding than his predecessor. By mid-1941, then, Dorman-Smith had launched himself into what promised to be a constructive governorship.

Burmah-Shell in India had meanwhile been undertaking essential if unspectacular work, similar to Burmah Oil's contribution there during the First World War. It sought, for instance, to make sure that available supplies of oil products were distributed as fairly as possible. Rival companies such as Stanvac and Caltex co-operated to the full with Burmah-Shell's overseeing of their imports, even though the United States was then neutral. After that country's entry into the war, in May 1942 those companies formally joined the Cooper-Lawson committee, which allocated oil products and gave technical advice to the government of India.

More specific contributions by Burmah-Shell varied in successive phases of the war. Until 1941, forces' requirements of oil in India were not much above pre-war levels, although that year Burmah-Shell fulfilled an urgent order for the export of petrol in tins for the Middle East. When supplies began to be needed for Russia, routed via Persia, all the oil companies in India helped to build up refuelling points for the flow of lorries on that route. For instance, they provided fifty complete kerbside pump units, as well as spare parts and bulk petrol lorries to keep these units supplied with petrol. Tankers conveyed all this equipment to Abadan, the final shipment leaving from Bombay in April 1942. Tinmaking plant was also required, so that petrol could be packed in Persia and transported to Russia by road.

Since 1939, Watson had worked as hard as at any time during his life, without a break. Until well into his forties, he had scarcely known a day's illness; subsequently his main time off sick had been after his riding accident of 1927. However, now that he had passed his sixtieth year, the stress of wartime existence, over and above his very close supervision of company affairs, was catching up on his health. Living out in rural Berkshire, he was able at least to escape most of the night bombings on London, but on one occasion when he insisted on coming into the office despite being unwell, Ashton arranged for him to be picked up by hired car from Paddington. Watson was so irate at this extravagance that no one dared to repeat the arrangement.

In the exceptionally hot summer of 1941, he complained of a 'touch of the sun', which was followed by a chill, and he was forced to take to his bed. A week later he attempted to return to work, but was at last persuaded to go for a month's holiday. On 1 August he departed, no doubt to his beloved Scotland. Judging by his later correspondence with Roper, the two matters that he pondered over most during his leave were who would pay for protecting installations in the East against possible air attack, and what the political prospects appeared to be for both India and Burma. As to the protective measures, Burma was not rich in tax revenue and the company could easily have met the expenses itself. However, Watson felt as a matter of principle that the government should pay.

It was India's political future that worried him most of all, because of the hostility between Hindus and Moslems. While he accepted that the British authorities had given very explicit pledges on ultimate self-government, so that there was no question of the clock being set back, this sectarian conflict could well lead to a temporary stopping of the clock. Burma, on the other hand, had no comparable communal issue. On grounds both of what the United States and the other wartime allies expected, and of plain logic, he was therefore convinced that it must be allowed in due course to attain its aspirations; but not yet.

As it happened, in mid-August Churchill and Roosevelt made a declaration, as part of the Atlantic Charter, on the right of all peoples of the world to choose their own form of government. Roper enquired of Watson if this would modify earlier distinctly cautious declarations made about Burma: 'Not at all,' Watson replied. His reasoning was that a decisive victory in the war would give Britain such commanding prestige that neither India nor Burma would wish, or could afford, to be other than members of the Commonwealth. The less sanguine Roper suggested the alternative possibility that, as the danger from external foes receded, there could be a greater likelihood of the British empire falling apart. More immediately, Watson instructed Roper to see that Burmah-Shell in India and the company itself in Burma should both redouble their efforts to encourage support for 'the war and the empire'. Although not much given to aphorisms, he did on this occasion deliver himself of one:

> Generosity and keeping one's word is the best policy between men and the greatest political wisdom between peoples.

In fact, the Atlantic Charter had repercussions in Burma itself. Clement Attlee, on behalf of the British war cabinet, gave his assurance that the declaration applied to the British empire as well as to the rest of the world. Churchill, on the other hand, was not willing to make more tangible promises until the war had been won. Burmese ministers became so dissatisfied with the lack of movement in London that in the summer of 1941 U Saw and one of his colleagues, encouraged by Dorman-Smith, asked if they could visit London for discussions. 'Certainly let an invitation be sent,' minuted Churchill to Amery, 'provided that in general you see U Saw.'[13] But *he* saw U Saw as well, once again declining to give any firm promise that Burma could look forward to early independence. On his way home, U Saw secretly made contact with the Japanese ambassador in Lisbon and then gave his support to Japan as soon as Burma was invaded. British intelligence had picked up the contact, however, and U Saw was interned until 1945.

A number of events continued at this time to edge the supreme ruling group in Japan inextricably towards war: among others, worsening relations with the United States, which imposed a trade embargo in mid-1941, the weakness of Britain as its military and naval losses mounted that year, and the German invasion of Russia in June which seemed to foreshadow a Soviet collapse. The Russian conflict had brought a new – originally Chinese – phrase into the English language, the 'scorched earth' policy of denying to the enemy any worthwhile assets in conquered territory. In July J. R. Case, local manager of British Burmah, complained to Dorman-Smith during a visit by the governor to the oilfields, that no official guidance had been given on any scorched-earth plans so as to ensure the effective denial of the Burmese oil industry to an invading army. The word 'denial' was then used, and will be used below, in the sense of deliberately destroying or wrecking material resources as so to prevent their effective use by an enemy.

The General Officer Commanding in Burma, Lieutenant-General D. K. McLeod, soon afterwards wrote to the warden of the oilfields – a civil servant, Robin McGuire – stating that any instructions needed would be issued in good time, with the military actually carrying out the demolition. That reply greatly worried Burmah Oil's fields manager, John Dalgleish, who raised with his superintendent engineer, Marr Grieve, the question of possible denial. They then brought into the discussions a few senior technical managers, but as Grieve had responsibility for fire-fighting and was also chief ARP warden, he was clearly the one who should draw up plans. So secret were their deliberations that scorched earth was referred to as 'molten mutti' or mud. Dalgleish then confidentially approached the other companies, who readily promised their aid.

No doubt Roper was kept fully informed. On broader developments, he had since Dunkirk in May 1940 been regularly briefed on a confidential basis by senior army officers in Rangoon. Having fought in the First World War, he must have been able to read the signs. Even so, he had to be careful about what he said in correspondence home, since letters went by open mail which could have fallen into enemy hands and were in any case censored. He therefore chose to say that it was very unlikely that scorched earth would ever be seen in the province. 'If the Japanese should come to Burma,' he wrote to Watson in August, 'we are in a far better condition to meet them than we were six months ago.'

Dorman-Smith, anxious to see economies in scarce technical manpower at a time when maximum production was required, suggested that the province's three main oil companies should help by amalgamating their activities. That was not one of his happier interventions. Roper, recalling the past hostility of the authorities both in Delhi and Rangoon towards any moves in the direction of monopoly, declined the suggestion on behalf of his and the other companies. Meanwhile, as the threat from Japan intensified that autumn, the correspondence between Watson and Roper gave no indication of any undue concern on the part of either. On 5 December Roper wrote that the

Japanese were in a tight corner, but a peaceful solution was more probable than war. Two days later, on the lazy Sunday morning of 7 December, the totally unexpected attack on Pearl Harbor propelled the United States into the war: as Watson observed to Roper on the 11th, the world was quite clearly unprepared for that treacherous act of aggression by Japan.

The sinking of the British capital ships *Prince of Wales* and *Repulse* on 10 December was for Churchill – as for his fellow countrymen – one of the worst direct shocks of the whole war. Yet the significance of that disaster seemed surprisingly lost on Watson: he recalled the official news of the battle of Jutland in 1916, when the exaggeration of the British as against the German losses had caused a severe initial jolt. In reality, however, the long-term consequence of Jutland was that the German high seas fleet never ventured out again to fight whereas the material, let alone the moral, effect of the 1941 sinkings was to lay open the whole of the Far East to the Japanese. Roper, too, writing on the 12th, and reporting that both the oilfields had had air-raid warnings which had turned out to be false alarms, continued, 'The army in Burma is so strong that it should be able to resist any enemy force likely to come their way.' By the time that letter had reached London, the Japanese forces had moved so rapidly on so many fronts that Watson was able to minute with the benefit of hindsight, 'So they said in Malaya!'

Only a day later, on 13 December, the British evacuated Victoria Point, the southernmost tip of Burma, and by the 18th the Japanese had occupied the airfield there, thus cutting air communications between India and Malaya. Dorman-Smith had made a broadcast on 8 December which had encouraged complacency but now, all too aware of the panic that could arise once people in Burma realised that the enemy was poised for an attack there, he went as far as he could by declaring publicly, 'We should prepare both our ways of life and our minds for a long and bitter struggle.' On the 19th Roper did no more than acknowledge Watson's permission to erect a protective brick screen for part of the Syriam plant and for other installations.

Then on the 23rd and again on Christmas Day Rangoon was bombed. In the absence of anti-aircraft guns or barrage balloons, horrible casualties and panic occurred among the Burmese and Indians, and services in the capital were brought virtually to a standstill. 'Frankly,' a dismayed Dorman-Smith informed Amery, 'I did not expect this situation to arise to such a pronounced degree.' But Watson had now at long last woken up to the likely fate of Burma, and of the oil enterprise there that had filled his life for the past forty years. On 24 December his letter to Roper mentioned the governor of Burma's declaration that there was no question of evacuating Rangoon. What, he asked, about the wives and children? Moreover, he went on,

> we have known nothing of any 'scorched earth' plans for the petroleum industry which the authorities may have, should the necessity arise. This, of course, must be for their decision, and one can but hope that the occasion for anything of the sort will never require to be faced. If it should, however, you will co-operate to the fullest extent after receipt of authoritative intimation in writing to you of such decision.

This unconditional readiness to accept without demur any written denial instructions was the more noteworthy in that, when Singapore was on the brink of disaster the following February some British, Australian and Indian commercial interests appealed to local or home governments against the demolition of their assets and even obstructed the efforts of the denial teams.[14] At no time did Watson ever consider going down that path. What did concern him was there should be a guarantee of adequate compensation for any such measures. In the event, wrangles over compensation were destined to throw their long shadow over Burmah Oil's future for the best part of a generation.

Unknown to Watson, Amery as Secretary of State had cabled to Dorman-Smith on 20 December, 'I presume a scheme exists for putting the oil refineries and the Burmah Oil pipeline out of action in case of necessity, and taking other action to deny oil resources to the enemy.' Dorman-Smith did not reply until the 31st, when he admitted that there was no such scheme: 'as expected', a Burma Office man reported sardonically to the Petroleum Department.[15]

On the 28th the governor's counsellor on defence, Sir John Wise, had called together at Rangoon army headquarters the local managers of the three oil companies to prepare demolition schemes. The Indo-Burma representative asked if destruction was to be total, or whether it would be enough to immobilise the installations for, say, nine months. Wise said he would have to consult London. Roper then reported that Shell had made a detailed study of demolition techniques; he had in fact learnt about this from the ex-chief geologist of Anglo-Iranian, who had passed through Rangoon in the previous August and had been impressed with the thoroughness of preparations made in Iraq and in the Dutch East Indies. Roper asked for a copy of the Shell study to be obtained from London, so that he and the other company general managers could draw on it in preparing their own plans. Meanwhile, they were confident that they could put in hand at short notice a simpler and less drastic scheme that would ensure denial for nine to twelve months. Dorman-Smith agreed with the military authorities that the responsibility for putting denial measures into operation must rest with the General Officer Commanding in Burma.

So, as the year 1941 died unmourned by the free world and 1942 was ushered in, Burmah Oil was on the brink of what could well be a catastrophe. Watson had agreed in principle to denial – should it unfortunately prove necessary – but stressed the need for adequate compensation. Urgent talks were going on in Burma about how best to implement a demolition scheme, and all agreed that the military must have the final say about giving orders. Yet the precise plans for denial actually to be put into effect were the upshot of decisions taken thousands of miles away: not in the Burmah Oil boardroom nor by the oil company representatives concerned nor by the governor nor by the military in the province. A man from Shell, Leslie Forster, would shortly be descending on Burma.

Notes

1 G. E. Harvey, *British Rule in Burma*, 1946, p. 73. This volume provides a good account of constitutional (and other) developments to 1942.
2 Sir W. Abraham (Weva), *Time Off for War: The Recollections of a Wartime Staff Officer*, privately printed, 1982, p. 2.
3 PRO POWE 33/456, correspondence between Croft (India Office) and Starling (Petroleum Department) 25 September and 14 October 1939.

4 The reason for setting up the subsidiaries is explained in the Annual Report for 1939 and in Cargill's statement at the annual general meeting, 7 June 1940.

5 *Burmah-Shell of Pakistan Monthly News Review: 1968 Supplement* pp. 4, 9, 12.

6 Abraham, *Time Off*, p. 12.

7 S. W. Kirby, *The War Against Japan History of the Second World War: UK Military Series, II: India's Most Dangerous Hour* HMSO, 1958, p. 9. See also Chapter III, footnote 1.

8 Tim Carew, *The Longest Retreat: The Burma Campaign 1942*, 1969, pp. 10–11.

9 K. A. H. Murray, *Agriculture* (History of the Second World War: UK Civil Series), HMSO, 1955, pp. 57, 73, 245. An important account of Dorman-Smith's time as governor of Burma, based on his private papers, is M. Collis, *Last and First in Burma 1941–1948*, 1956. These private papers are now in India Office Records (IOR), MSS Eur E 215.

10 F. H. Hinsley, *British Intelligence in the Second World War II*, 1981, pp. 75–7.

11 IOR, MSS Eur E 215 I fo. 8.

12 Ba Maw, *Breakthrough in Burma*, Yale, 1968, p. 52.

13 W. S. Churchill, *The Second World War III: The Grand Alliance*, 1950, p. 727.

14 Kirkby, *War against Japan* I, pp. 408–9.

15 IOR, M/3/980, Amery to Dorman-Smith 20 December 1941. This file continues the denial story until the repercussions of the Forster report at the end of 1942 (see Chapter IV below).

CHAPTER III

Denial and Evacuation 1942[1]

The harrowing events in Burma of January to April 1942, when the British forces were routed by the advancing Japanese, have been frequently and variously described over the years. Books and articles relate the military campaigns and the devastating consequences of war for official and civilian life in the country. Yet despite the essential contribution it made in so many different ways, no full account has been published of Burmah Oil's role in these events. Three main questions, above all, dominate the present account. First, what assistance did the company give to the defence forces? How precisely did it help these forces to resist, and later to withdraw and live to fight another day? Second, how did it set about denying its militarily valuable assets to an oil-hungry enemy? What efforts did the denial schemes involved, and how complete was the destruction? Third, how true was the contemporary impression, recently revived, that Europeans carefully planned evacuation for themselves and their families from Burma, and to a lesser extent for Anglo-Burmese and Anglo-Indians, but largely abandoned the Indians to their fate?

At the beginning of 1942, many people were all too aware that Burma was under grave threat, with the Japanese poised to press home their attack; the defensive strength in the country was all too fragile because of inadequate manpower and equipment, and Rangoon was almost totally disorganised after the recent air raids. For the Burmah Oil managers on the spot, these dangers proved a spur to even more intense activity, especially after 27 December 1941 when Watson in London had cabled Roper with instructions to place the Syriam refinery and the topping plants at the oilfields on maximum throughput. Military and civilian oil needs in Burma were on the increase, and exports to India had also to be maintained for as long as possible. Although port labour at Rangoon had largely disappeared, oil products destined for India could still be pumped into such tankers as Britain's Ministry of War Transport was able to provide.

The company at once increased its refinery throughput from 5 million to around 5.8 million barrels a year and arranged a mix of products appropriate to the country's current needs. These included petrol for cars, army lorries and tanks; some aviation petrol for the relatively few allied aircraft still left in Burma; lubricants, to replace those previously imported from the United States; jute batching oil, to treat the jute required to satisfy the enormous wartime need for sandbags; and finally asphalt, for the emergency construction of roads and the surfacing of airfield runways.

At Syriam, the company's manifold ancillary facilities were also at full stretch. The tin-making plants there and at Dunneedaw were turning out the annual equivalent of 900,000 forty or twenty-gallon drums, many to be filled with lubricating oil for army and civilian use. The research chemists were kept busy on scores of practical problems: for instance, devising the most suitable type of kerosene for army cookers, and a cheap insecticide base, comparable with Standard Oil of New Jersey's celebrated Flit, for the use of the army, which was suffering almost as many losses from disease as at the hands of the enemy; products were needed to provide smoke-screens, and toluene for the explosive TNT. The refinery engineers and construction staff helped the military with the building of offices, living quarters and installation for the infantry, RAF and anti-aircraft forces, and with the provision of water supplies. The Syriam staff further equipped and kept its existing Air Raid Precautions organisation in a high state of readiness, complete with a bomb disposal squad and regular anti-sabotage patrols. The refinery's own fire service was expanded, and the plant and oil stores were given additional blast and splinter-proof protection against air attack.

These preparations were all the more remarkable in that a quarter of the company's European staff – 75 out of 302 then in the country – had already been released for full-time national service. They also demonstrate how vital were oil products of all kinds in complex and technically advanced warfare. Aided by British Burmah at Thilawa and Indo-Burma at Seikkyi, such efforts were an earnest of the oil companies' determination to put right in Burma the deficiencies in *matériel* resulting from years of official neglect of defence preparations, in Britain, India and Burma alike.

There was not, in the event, to be a static campaign in southern Burma. Instead, within a week or so of advancing across the Burmese frontier on 15 January, the Japanese captured the two airfields of Mergui and Tavoy along the Tenasserim coast and were threatening Moulmein. Since they were by then within striking distance of Rangoon itself, Lieutenant-General Thomas Hutton, commander in Burma under General Wavell and a highly able administrator, ordered on 22 January that no less than three-quarters of the military stores in Rangoon, some 14,000 tons in all, should be loaded up and transported north to Mandalay.[2] This huge operation, transported both by rail and by a fleet of Irrawaddy Flotilla Company vessels, was scheduled to be completed in a month. Otherwise, the British forces in their subsequent withdrawal north would have lacked essential supplies in what was to be the longest retreat in the nation's history, and might therefore have been completely overwhelmed.

Roper and his staff had since December been striving to persuade the army to lay down adequate stocks of petrol in Upper Burma, in case Rangoon had to be evacuated. As senior officers would not agree to this suggestion, he arranged on his own responsibility – without receiving any firm commitment concerning payment – for 16,000 barrels of motor spirit and 8,000 barrels of aviation spirit to be packaged in drums and despatched north. The Irrawaddy Flotilla Company, although preoccupied with its commitment to transport the military stores, managed to provide crude oil flats, on which the drums were towed upstream. As Dorman-Smith subsequently admitted, without this reserve of petrol the withdrawal of the army and of the civil authorities would have been gravely hampered. The company was then given the task of maintaining the central reserve depot at Mandalay, which included the civil government's stocks of petrol, kerosene and lubricants.

It was becoming more and more unlikely that the company would for much longer be able to rely on Syriam for refined products; facilities for topping the crude – that is, taking out the lightest fractions for petrol – would therefore have to be extended at the oilfields. Even before the outbreak of war against Japan, managers had taken steps to increase refining at the fields, as some supplies were being transported by river into China; moreover, local refining avoided the unnecessary use of river-craft for carrying products all the way from Rangoon to Upper Burma.

In January 1942 Roper discussed with the military an ambitious scheme for constructing a substantial refinery at the fields, to produce a wide range of products. Both the speed of the Japanese advance and increasing shortages of non-European labour frustrated these plans. Instead, improvised arrangements were at once made at the fields, for example by adapting available equipment. At the height of this period, just before the fields were evacuated and demolitions had begun, the equivalent of 430,000 barrels a year of motor spirit was being produced by all three companies, mainly at Chauk, but some also at Yenangyaung and Minbu. Since Roper calculated that the total consumption by the British and Chinese armies and the civilian population was then about 300,000 barrels a year, there would be enough in hand against possible further needs. Moreover, both Burmah Oil at Chauk and Indo-Burma at Lanywa had extra plant under construction which would in due course double output. Had the military line been held against the enemy, the British forces would have been more than well equipped with the modern equivalent of the sinews of war.

Many other services were provided by the company's oilfields organisation. The workshops and motor repair shops undertook countless jobs for the army, air force and civil defence, for the losses by bombing, captures by the Japanese

and appalling road surfaces made the maintenance of road-
worthy vehicles all the more essential. The construction
department erected huts for troops, the telegraph department
provided technical advice to the signallers, apparatus –
including seven wireless transmitting sets – and labour, while
other departments contributed surveying instruments and
X-ray outfits. About 3,000 tons of company stores were handed
over to the Royal Engineers and loaded on to flats for them;
moreover, the company's hospitals, supplemented by private
donations, gave beds, sheets, pillows and the like for military
medical units.

The company's airstrip near the oilfields at Magwe became
an RAF base, and every help was given to the government's
Public Works Department to erect buildings, and provide
water and electrical power there. In the company workshops, a
radio locator salvaged from Rangoon was converted into a
mobile unit, capable of being carried on a truck. Damaged
tanks were repaired in the Singu workshops, which also
armour-plated the sides of six patrol launches for use by the
Royal Marines.

All these highly constructive labours were an essential prelude
to the other two main episodes at this sorry time: denial and
evacuation. From the beginning of January 1942 Roper was
busy with contingency plans to arrange for certain categories of
people to leave the country. Here the government in Rangoon
was not giving the practical help needed. The civil defence
expert, already requested by Dorman-Smith, arrived from
home about this time, and soon gained the esteem of the
governor for declaring, on the basis of recent experience in
Britain, that any bombing of Burma would quickly arouse the
loyalty and patriotism of all races there. The Japanese air
attacks on Rangoon, and the mass exodus that followed, proved
the hollowness of that view. Roper had already been working
out, with his opposite number in the Bombay Burmah Trading
Corporation, an evacuation scheme for dependants and employees who could be spared. The appointment of a commissioner for civil evacuation, John S. Vorley of the forestry
service, in December 1941 transferred all such schemes to
official hands.

As many as 15,000 Indians were said to have headed north after the air raids, but were persuaded to return, to be accommodated in camps such as that on the Rangoon racecourse. Although many skilled workers had fled from the refineries, throughput was somehow maintained for the time being. When early in January Dorman-Smith pressed Roper to encourage the recruitment of women into the army, mainly to take over clerical jobs, Roper's sharp response was that it was far more urgent to seek guidance on getting women and children to safety from Rangoon and the oilfields. Having received all too little guidance, he was alarmed when the military in Rangoon warned him on 12 January that the capital could well be blockaded by sea and also undergo even heavier bombing than hitherto. Hence all non-essential personnel should be encouraged to leave the country. Roper at once made his own transport arrangements for British dependants of company employees.

After having booked passages for them in a steamer about to return in convoy to Calcutta, Roper was dismayed by their stubborn refusal to go by that route. On the inward journey two ships in the convoy had been sunk by Japanese submarines, and the dependants chose to face the hardships of a trek into northern Burma rather than the submarine menace. Early in February, after Moulmein had been captured by the Japanese, the evacuees began to arrive in the oilfields, hoping to fly on to India by Chinese Airways, together with the dependants there whom Dalgleish as fields manager was urging to leave. However, company representatives who approached the airline found that the pilots were refusing to fly to India under wartime conditions, and a month's frustrating delay then ensued.

On 9 February the Japanese army command ordered an advance towards Rangoon and also a thrust to the north of the capital as a prelude to an attack on both Yenangyaung and Mandalay. The prizes of capturing the refinery and the oilfields intact were so well understood that despite overwhelming air power, the Japanese never bombed any of the oil installations, only one or two adjacent buildings such as staff bungalows being damaged. By 24 February they were across the Sittang river, where the bridge was unfortunately blown with many

British and Indian troops on the wrong side: this was the last real obstacle to Rangoon.

Roper was extremely concerned because, although about 70,000 Indians had already been evacuated by sea, the likely capture of Rangoon could well put that option in jeopardy for the future. Given the continuing absence of official evacuation plans, he therefore needed to take an initiative of his own. The terrain by land into India was so rough that no proper road into India had ever been constructed, even though the army authorities had been persistently urging this on the politicians since 1937. Travellers had habitually gone by sea, usually between Calcutta and Rangoon. Early in February, therefore, Roper despatched two company men, Robert Adamson and James Webster, armed with a Public Works Department gazetteer, on what they called a 'scouting expedition', to plot a possible evacuation route north. Even though they were accompanied by eight skilled drivers, fitters and other technicians, the sheer discomfort and even physical danger convinced them that, as the route then stood, only grown men could undertake the journey. With some improvements, however, it might be managed by sturdy women and older children, but certainly not by the delicate or those under eight years.

They identified a rough bullock cart track from Yenangyat to Tamu, near the Indo-Burmese border, a distance of about 340 miles. The frequent *chaungs*, or dry river beds, rocks and tree roots were likely to inflict great damage on tyres and springs. Moreover, the fine choking dust underfoot penetrated every chink in the cars and made it difficult to breathe even with wetted handkerchiefs over mouths and noses. Witnesses later agreed that motoring through the dust was like ploughing through a heavy sea, with waves being thrown over the bonnet and windscreen. From Tamu a mountain range of 6–8,000 feet had to be crossed, and in the absence of a road, that stretch would need to be covered on foot.

On the basis of this report, Burmah Oil set up camps at Pauk, Gangaw, Kalemyo and Tamu, distances of 50, 140, 230 and 340 miles respectively from the oilfields. Sleeping quarters, cookhouses and toilet facilities had to be improvised, as well as bamboo shelters as protection from the elements. Convoys with European drivers brought stocks of tinned goods and other

Yenangyaung field in the 1930s
(Compare Plate 11 in Volume 1)

Chauk field pre-1934 (Note rigs standing in river Irrawaddy)

Oilfields dispute, 1939. March of strikers to Rangoon

Imperial Airways proving flight to India, with improved aircraft-fuelling lorry.
Delhi, 1927
(Compare Plate 29 in Volume 1. Inflatable tyres have replaced solid tyres)

Sir John T. Cargill, Bart., chairman
1904–43

Nyounghla Club, at oilfields, Christmas morning 1932 (Second row from front, Weva is fourth from left, with C. W. Armstrong on his left. Far right in that row are G. W. Lepper, with glasses, and Marr Grieve)

Robert I. Watson and friends. Managing director 1920–47, chairman 1943–47

Yenan House (Burmah Oil's Rangoon office) dressed overall c. 1929 (Note 'BOC' flag, of red, white and blue, flown by company tankers from 1898 to the 1960s)

provisions to the camps from Mandalay and Rangoon. Some geologists and other oilfields staff were detailed to try to improve the track to India, by supervising the clearance of boulders and the filling in of the *chaungs* with branches of trees. Arrangements were made to hand over cars to the military at Tamu, before the arduous climb through the mountain pass began.

In mid-February Dalgleish briefed the heads of department at the oilfields on possible evacuation measures. Every consideration must be given to non-Europeans, which meant Indians and those of mixed race, since most Burmese would be able to disperse to their home localities. He also placed Walter T. Watts, a senior manager at the fields, in charge of evacuation. On the 19th Watts held a series of meetings with groups of European and non-European senior employees at Chauk and Yenangyaung, setting out the various alternative routes by sea, air and land. While the company would do everything it could, evacuation would be 'no picnic' for women and children; the women would have to fend for themselves both *en route* and on reaching India. It annoyed him when the following day the Director of Civil Aviation in Burma arrived at Yenangyaung, charged by the governor to arrange an airlift, and at once declared that it would be quite impossible officially to charter any planes, something which Watts had been vainly striving to do privately for weeks. When he refused to appeal to his opposite number in India, Watts wore him down by argument, and even drafted the cable which he then agreed to send.

A fleet of separately chartered aircraft began to arrive on 21 February, for the evacuation of women and children. Watts's task was complicated by priority in other planes being given to Indian Civil Service families and by the refusal of the RAF to provide transport for any more families. Other organisations whose dependants were thus displaced then appealed to Burmah Oil. The planes' destination was Chittagong where, perhaps inevitably in these circumstances, the company organisation to deal with refugees left much to be desired. The journey to Calcutta was then completed by rail, an excruciatingly uncomfortable one, with overcrowded carriages, no suitable food and little water. On their arrival the Burmah-

Shell organisation spared no effort to give them immediate assistance, arrange accommodation in the crowded city and disperse them to hill stations or elsewhere.

From the beginning of March onwards a fairly regular air shuttle service operated out of Magwe. The main airlift, involving 650 passengers, was completed successfully. Then an administrative bungle at Chittagong and the bombing of Magwe on 21 March brought the airlift to an end, so that those still waiting had to be sent off overland.

On 20 February, the army gave Roper orders to shut down the refineries and ancillary operations. The government of Burma thereafter took over responsibility for oil production in the country, as well as for crude stocks and evacuation expenses. The cost from February to April 1942 was £915,000, later refunded to the three companies, of which Burmah Oil's share was £656,000. Roper had already been pressing Vorley to ensure that the non-essential refinery staffs and their dependants, numbering 4–5,000, should be evacuated rather be left in the Rangoon camps. Tragically, amid all the confusion, the last boat was allowed to sail without passengers, and on the 21st Vorley issued five days' rations of food and advised them to set off north. As the railway stations were already swarming with people, most of them took to the road.

Despite all his other preoccupations, Roper was also aware that the company's assets might well have to be destroyed. Chapter II referred to the meeting of 28 December 1941 to discuss a limited scheme of demolition. By chance, a far more thorough-going scheme arose out of the encounter of two senior oilmen on 31 December, far away in Teheran. Eric Berthoud, a former Anglo-Iranian manager then employed by the Petroleum Department in London, met Leslie Forster, a civil engineer working for Shell.[3] Forster had considerable experience of oilfield demolition work. He was in fact on his way home from the Caucasus, where he had led a delegation of British experts who were advising the Russians on the possible denial of their oilfields, at a time when the German front was only a few hundred miles away.

Berthoud relayed to Forster official concern, especially in the Petroleum Department, that the oilfields and refineries in the

East might fall into enemy hands, considering how desperate the Japanese were for oil. He asked if Forster would be prepared to go to Burma and give technical advice on the spot. Forster readily agreed. Berthoud at once cabled to Maurice Bridgeman, a senior official of the Petroleum Department, who obtained the consent of Shell in London. Some bureaucratic delays followed; not until 24 January did Forster, then in Cairo, receive his instructions. He was to leave for Burma immediately, to advise the governor on oil denial.

Forster envisaged that his mission would be similar to the one he had undertaken the previous year to Palestine, Iraq and Iran, then feared to be under threat from a German invasion of the Middle East. In each country he had reviewed with an expert eye the respective denial schemes already prepared by the British, and had recommended improvements where needed. To his subsequent chagrin, he travelled very light to Burma, as it never crossed his mind that he would be remaining so as personally to supervise the work of demolition there. For one thing, two engineers who had successfully blown up the oil installations in Sarawak were officially stated to be on their way to Burma. Whatever may have happened to them, they failed to arrive.

Meanwhile, Watson was unhappy that the government of Burma's war risk insurance scheme omitted to provide cover for any damage to oil installations there. He appealed to the Burma Office; however, given the chaotic situation in Burma itself, the reply was that no action could be taken at that late hour. All he could do was to tell Roper to secure written instructions from the competent authorities for any scorched-earth action that became necessary.

Forster flew into Rangoon on the evening of 3 February. When he entered Government House the next morning, he was shaken by the contrast between the all too visible signs of war and civil collapse in the capital – especially the deserted streets and boarded-up shops – and the imperturbable atmosphere in the governor's suite. Although the Japanese had already fought their way to Moulmein and were poised to make an all-out thrust against Rangoon, Dorman-Smith's amiable, relaxed and almost carefree manner grated on the single-minded and war-hardened Forster, who could only conclude that he himself was being tolerated there simply to pacify the bureaucrats in England. The governor soon passed him on to General Hutton and to the major-general in charge of admistration, Eric Goddard.

As it happened, Hutton had only the previous day issued preparatory orders about the need for putting out of action any installations that might be of value to the enemy's war effort. Forster found these two generals keen, alert, intelligent and very anxious to help in any way, despite their totally inadequate resources. Shortly afterwards Roper arrived and took charge of him. They crossed to Syriam to meet the refinery manager and also Captain W. D. Scott, who had been seconded from the Royal Engineers to carry out the actual demolitions.[4] Roper was not involved directly in the next stage, for he had plenty of other tasks. He was busy arranging for the emergency topping plant and all the ancillary equipment to be despatched to the oilfields and put into working order there as quickly as possible. He assumed, as Forster did himself, that the latter was merely a technical adviser who would be here today and gone tomorrow.

Forster, accompanied by Scott, at once began a rapid survey of Syriam, the British Burmah refinery at Thilawa, that of Indo-Burma at Seikkyi, and the nearby Admiralty fuel oil bunkering station. By then he had found the earlier partial plans to be totally impracticable. He therefore called a meeting of the senior staff of the four installations for the next morning: as he later put it, 'I then went off by myself to do some quiet thinking.'

The outcome of his solitary deliberations caused a stir among the next day's gathering of staff. In a few masterly strokes he set out the tactics to be followed. Above all, it must be a quick job: no more than two hours should be allowed from the issuing of instructions – the D (denial) signal, as it was to be known – for actual demolition and withdrawal to take place. Considerations of time, safety of personnel and the shortage of explosives allowed only the most essential targets to be tackled.

Getting right down to basics, he reminded them that, once crude oil had left the mouth of a well, three items of equipment were absolutely vital to its ultimate conversion into usable products: pumps to draw out the oil, pipelines to transport it and tanks to store it, whether in crude or refined form. Since refineries contained too many pipes for all of them to be permanently wrecked, he would concentrate on the two other categories of pumps and storage tanks. Their denial would besides prevent the enemy from shipping crude oil to alternative refineries elsewhere in the East.

Having previously made an extensive study of incendiary devices at the Special Operations Executive office in Cairo, he knew that storage tanks could be easily destroyed by fire, especially as Burmese crude was notably light in composition. Pumps not required for handling products for the army and other local use would be dismantled and thrown into the river. All designs and specifications, catalogues and insurance inventories, which might help the enemy to start up refining again, were to be brought together in a convenient place ready to be soaked in kerosene and burnt when the signal was given.

This was in truth a far more ambitious scheme than anything earlier contemplated, and Forster situated himself at Syriam, the guest of the assistant manager there, Mr Henry, a taciturn but hospitable Scot. Every second or third day he crossed to Rangoon in order to brief the governor or his staff and the Army command. Whereas Dorman-Smith appeared still to be out of touch with reality, the military took the point: once they were fully satisfied with his professional competence, they backed him to the hilt.

If complete rather than partial demolition were to be required, then it was well that plans had been brought as far forward as they had. The Shell directors in London, Forster's employers, were agitating for him to be recalled, claiming that his absence was hampering work of substantial importance to their company. However, Berthoud strongly recommended that he should be instructed to remain in Burma for as long as necessary, and the people in Whitehall overruled Shell. This was a fortunate move, as on 6 February the Burma Office told Bridgeman at the Petroleum Department that a denial scheme must be prepared for the oilfields as well.

Watson was in the meantime keeping up pressure in Whitehall over compensation for what he called scorched-earth losses. The Petroleum Department referred him to the Burma

Office, and Amery as Secretary of State minuted confidentially that on certain conditions – such as if resumption of operations eventually became feasible, and if compensation were not forthcoming from any other source – 'we shall no doubt if necessary have to promise replacement after the war of destroyed property'. Having settled the compensation issue to his own satisfaction, on 20 February Amery cabled to Dorman-Smith, 'Denial plans should be as complete as possible without reference to any post-war implications.'

By then military events in Burma had deterioriated with startling rapidity. As recently as 17 February, when Forster had sought official sanction for preparatory work at the refineries to involve systematic dismantling and removal of surplus machinery and equipment, so as to shorten the time needed for a complete denial, the governor had (according to Forster) 'laughed quite heartily' at what he saw as this defeatist attitude. Forster was not to be put off. Almost immediately, the military had to seek permission from London for the refineries to be shut down and for evacuation of their staffs to begin. The shut-down took place on the 20th. The only work still permitted was the despatch of such refined products as could be handled by the remaining labour, reinforced by some troops lent for the purpose. A small 'last-ditch' team, headed by Roper, moved into the office. Roper or his representative had to attend a daily meeting with the army, and the party maintained a 24-hour telephone watch in shifts in case of urgent orders. Perhaps the most courageous of the whole team were the six Anglo-Burmese girls, ex-employees of the Rangoon Telephone Company, who manned the office switchboard through which the order for destruction would have to be passed.

It was a time of acute tension for Roper's party, all of whom well understood the risks of Japanese pre-emptive strikes either from the sea or by parachute drops from the air. Forster considered that the military protection of the refineries was adequate against such assaults. However, later accounts make it clear that the defending forces were frighteningly sparse and ill-equipped. It has never been satisfactorily explained why the Japanese did not make greater efforts to capture the refineries – and later on the oilfields – intact.

At the end of the war in 1945, Bill Maclachlan, a former

assistant in Rangoon who was later a general manager in both India and Pakistan, and later still rose to the Burmah Oil board (See Chapters XI and XII) was Senior Intelligence Officer of XII Army.[5] This was a new force with its headquarters in Rangoon now that Slim's XIV Army headquarters had moved to India. During Maclachlan's interrogation of captured Japanese generals, he asked why they had not advanced straight down the road to Rangoon and taken the oil installations, rather than making a flanking movement round the west side of the city. The generals' answer was that they very well understood the necessity of reaching Rangoon before denial of the installations took place, but they simply did not have the men available to force a way through. The small detachment sent to outflank the road, in the hope of getting to Rangoon quickly, failed in its objective.

On 19 February, Forster had set off on his first visit to the oilfields in Upper Burma. On the way, he inspected the pipeline's pumping stations and next day gave orders that the pipeline should be made inoperative by being filled with water. At the fields Forster encountered a novel pattern of existence which was not at all to his liking. In his memoirs he asserted that, elsewhere in the world, the atmosphere of oil companies was 'free and easy and completely democratic'. Yet Burmah Oil appeared to him to have uniquely separated its British staff into what he described as a small élite group of public school-educated office managers, who made no effort to master the technical side of their work, and a larger but less highly esteemed group of engineers, production men and mechanics – a distinction in his eyes comparable with that between 'gentlemen' and 'players' in English cricket at that time.

As Syriam was entirely composed of technical staff, he had not noticed the distinction there. At Yenangyaung, on the other hand, the management houses and residences of the warden and other high government officials were concentrated on the high ground near the east bank of the Irrawaddy, and it was in the fields manager's bungalow, as the guest of Dalgleish, that he subsequently claimed to have encountered such a distinction for the first time. Dalgleish held a small dinner party to introduce him, and although Forster – according to his later account – tried to steer the conversation away from trivialities towards urgent denial questions, he found but little interest. Even when the BBC radio news gave a delayed account of the fall of Singapore on 15 February and his own immediate thought was 'Now the Japs will really be able to turn the heat on Burma', the others seemed to show no real concern.

Undoubtedly, there was a gulf here between the lean, hard and ruthless Forster who exemplified the post-Dunkirk Briton, and men who – apart from veterans of the First World War – had no personal knowledge of the unrelenting demands of a total war. The latter may have felt that, at the initial meeting, they could relax and get to know the newcomer on a social footing. That proved to be difficult, as his single-mindedness amounted almost to obsession. There were, both then and later, only half-friendly arguments about whether technical or office men should be in charge. It was felt that he rather 'laid down the law' on this and other subjects, without allowing others to have their say.

One of his fellow guests that first night had been Marr Grieve, the superintendent engineer at the fields who in 1941 had been placed in charge of the technical side of any denial programme (see Chapter II). A quiet and knowledgeable Scot, Grieve by great good fortune was very happy to work as Forster's assistant, translating his overall plans into detailed programmes of work; clearly any personality clash at that level would have severely hampered the whole operation. A voracious reader, Grieve had for years been fascinated by the social and industrial scene in Soviet Russia; a topic in which Forster happened to be equally knowledgeable. Grieve was not of course in any way subversive, but over the years he had endured a great deal of mild chaff from many of his peers. Consequently, he made 'no secret of his utter contempt and dislike for the management group and the civil authorities', as the approving Forster was to put it. This accidental circumstance, of minor importance in normal times, was exacerbated by Forster's constant practice of giving instructions without referring to higher authority. On denial matters, the chain of command had been precisely laid down to avoid confusion: orders would come from the military to the District Commissioner and to the warden of the oilfields, and then on to Forster.

The significance of these differences of opinion and tempera-
ment were to become plain later on. Forster recorded that he
allowed the first formal denial meeting of staff at the fields to
be chaired by the warden, principally so that the latter
should feel 'important and involved'; not until twenty years
later did he learn that a chain of command had actually
existed. Meanwhile, he was gratified to achieve at that
meeting the same kind of awed respect among technical staff
which he had obtained at the refineries. To make sure that
the Japanese would be unable to start up drilling again, he
gave instructions that all major and vital items of drilling
equipment were to be brought to some central point. As soon
as news came through that Rangoon had been lost to the
enemy, the equipment should be cut up with oxy-acetylene
torches. The large machine shops and generator floor of the
power station were to have low brick walls built in the
doorways, and piping installed, so that they could be flooded
with oil and set ablaze at short notice.

In the fields about 3,000 wells with very small levels of
production were to be destroyed immediately, while the more
prolific ones were to be kept going for the requirements of the
army. All those with medium yields were to be prepared for
rapid destruction by cement plugs being placed at the bottom
of each. Once the D order came, a small explosive charge would
sever the tubing in the well, which on impact with the plug
would become twisted beyond repair. Steel junk would then be
dropped on top of this tangled mess. The oil storage tanks
would also have to be prepared for destruction.

On 28 February, Forster heard that the army had given an E
preparatory warning notice for the refineries, and he arranged
to return to Rangoon. His journey by air on 1 March was in the
company of General Wavell, the supreme commander, and
General Hutton. As it happened, Hutton was on the brink of
being relieved of his command in Burma. Winston Churchill,
alive to widespread charges that the military reverses there
were due to shortcomings at the top, appointed in his stead an
officer more experienced in warfare, Lieutenant-General Sir
Harold Alexander, who had won a golden reputation during
the Dunkirk evacuation and was currently General Officer in
charge of Britain's Southern Command. By the end of February

Alexander had arrived at GHQ Cairo. At that time Weva was a lieutenant-colonel on the staff of the Commander-in-Chief there, General Claude Auchinleck. Weva put the idea into Auchinleck's mind that some suitably qualified staff officer should accompany Alexander to Rangoon to furnish him with specialist advice, and later to bring back to Cairo first-hand news of what conditions were really like in Burma. No prizes are needed for guessing who Weva had in mind for this interesting assignment, and he was duly detailed to go.[6] A full if tactful account which Weva later sent to Watson provides a valuable contemporary picture of events.

Alexander, while perhaps not the greatest strategist among army commanders, had the inestimable advantage of being a lucky general; above all he was a realist as well as possessing courage of the highest order. Conversing on the journey with Weva, who was able to brief him with authority on the country and the people, he remarked that the only hope of saving Burma was to take the offensive, but he could only decide where and how after he had been able to assess the chances following his arrival. However, when Alexander met Wavell during a stop-over in India on 3 March, Wavell declared that, with Singapore now lost, Britain's position in the Far East critically depended on Rangoon being held. Every effort must therefore be made to halt the Japanese advance.

Armed with these instructions Alexander arrived in Rangoon on 5 March, to what has justly been called 'one of the most unpromising commands in the history of British arms';[7] he had yet to discover how very unpromising it was to prove. During an overnight stop near the oilfields, the industrious Weva, who never let pass an opportunity to seek professional information on the spot, made a brief visit to Dalgleish's office. There he discovered what no one outside Burma had been able to tell him; how much throughput the topping plant would actually achieve now that Syriam was closed down. It turned out to be 375,000 barrels a year: comfortably above Roper's estimate of the country's total requirements. Materially speaking, Burma's defence now depended on as much motor spirit as possible being provided.

On the afternoon of the 5th, while Alexander was busy on a briefing session by the military experts, Weva slipped out to visit Roper and other senior managers in the Rangoon office. Described by Weva in truly Pepysian terms as 'reasonably cheerful, considering the circumstances', Roper disclosed that communications were by then so bad that he was no longer in any real sense general manager in the East. His only means of contact with the outer world was through the company's telegraph to the fields. He had therefore instructed Dalgleish as fields manager to take full administrative responsibility there, now that Rangoon was cut off.

At a time of year when temperatures were rising continuously, the 'last ditch' denial staff at Syriam were standing by in conditions of some suspense, as the D signal was being postponed until General Alexander had completed his assessment of the chances of saving Rangoon. The 'last-ditchers' were also in much discomfort, since they had neither electric fans nor lights. To Weva, Rangoon was a most extraordinary spectacle, being no longer its usual bustling self but a deserted city although the water supply, electric light and fire brigade services were then still functioning. He drove over to the senior managers' residential complex at Greenbank: to his astonishment, he found everything much as normal, but without a soul in the houses or compound. The last manager to leave, C. W. Armstrong, had employed a mixed team of Burmese and Indian servants, who insisted on remaining with him, and on washing and drying up the dishes before their departure. Walking up to the house he had occupied as chief geologist, Weva entered and took out of the sitting-room refrigerator a soda-water.[8] 'One had the feeling that it must all have been a bad dream, out of which one would suddenly waken,' he later told Watson. That feeling, he added, persisted at intervals all the time he was in Burma. On 17 March he returned to Cairo. 'I'm glad I went,' he concluded his account, 'if only to see my old friends again.'

Weva was extremely candid about the Burmese war in his secret report to General Auchinleck, pointing out that

> The fundamental reason for the loss of Rangoon was a failure to appreciate quickly that as soon as Singapore ceased to be of value to us as a naval base (which was after the first week or two of the Jap[anese] war), the holding of Singapore became very much less important than the holding of Rangoon and Burma. Had this been

appreciated, it would not have been possible for troops to have been poured into Singapore at the expense of Burma (especially 18th Division).

General Auchinleck minuted, 'Right!'

According to Weva, a contributory factor to the loss was the Burma command's inability to understand that the holding of Rangoon was fundamental to the effective protection of Upper Burma. Its implicit thinking – never put on paper in so many words – had been to try to stop the enemy wherever it could, but be prepared to retreat in good order, so as to form a defensive line further north. (The evacuation of supplies northwards by Hutton's orders had clearly been part of that strategy). Wavell's attempt, at the beginning of March, to cancel orders for abandoning Rangoon therefore came far too late, and Alexander's well-meaning attempt to hold the capital almost led to the bulk of his forces being lost. 'Had this same determination and clear reading of the position been there two or three months earlier, Rangoon would almost certainly still be in our hands,' Weva declared, and concluded that Alexander had an impossible task in trying to hold Upper Burma if the Japanese were able to use the port of Rangoon.[9]

Once he discovered that Rangoon could not be saved, on 7 March Alexander took the irrevocable decision that the capital would have to be evacuated and the demolitions carried out. That day the military command issued the D signal and the denial was ordered. However, no smoke, fires or explosions were permitted until 2 p.m., so as not to arouse enemy suspicions. Civil authority had already disintegrated in the capital: the police were disbanded, inmates of gaols and mental hospitals had been set free, and groups of marauders were roaming the city streets. Forster alerted the refineries and also the oilfields, with cabled instructions by prearranged codes, to start cutting up the drilling equipment.

Sunday, 7 March in Rangoon turned out to be a glorious spring day, fine and sunny and with a light breeze from the south: the kind of rest-day morning when the company's staff would normally have been looking forward to consuming their beer and pink gins on the verandahs of the club or of one another's bungalows, and the Burmese would have been out strolling in their hundreds. But club, residences and promenades alike were devoid of people, and the denial team at Syriam, having carried out their allotted preparatory tasks, showed the stress they were under by keeping busy on private little denial jobs, of small value in themselves but giving them something with which to occupy themselves.

They had been so well drilled that precisely at 2 p.m. they were at their stations, ready to begin denial operations. The major task was to open the tank drain valves and let a large pool of oil accumulate round each tank before delayed action charges were set off. These charges were ignited by what were known as 'gadgets'. Wooden boxes some 18 inches square and 9 inches high were packed with jute, in the middle of which was an 8-ounce bottle filled with some sulphuric acid and then topped up with petrol. The bottle was tightly sealed with a cork which contained a small explosive capsule made of plastic. On the order being given, the bottle would be turned upside down and the valve on the storage tank opened up so that the oil would run out inside the bund or earth ramp surrounding the tank. The operator would then withdraw to a safe distance. In about ten or fifteen minutes' time, the acid would eat through the plastic capsule and set off an explosion; the jute would catch fire and ignite the oil from the tank. Very soon the fire would badly buckle the steel plates and the tanks would be rendered unusable. Forster found himself with nothing to do except to greet and congratulate each party of men as, their tasks completed, they made their way to their rendezvous. As he wrote in his memoirs,

> It was a spectacular sight as tremendous fires commenced spouting up all over the place, creating huge amounts of black smoke. Away in the distance, I could see the smoke columns beginning to rise over each of the other two refineries and the [Admiralty] bunkering station. From time to time a tank would blow up, with the characteristic mushroom-shaped cloud which later came to be associated with the atom bomb.[10]

Although his team ran appalling risks, particularly of explosions going off prematurely, remarkably there were no casualties, but all became filthy from dirt and oily smuts. Then they drove down to the jetty in a convoy of about forty cars and trucks. There they lined up the vehicles and put a charge under each bonnet. Scott at once connected them all up to one fuse and immobilised them.

Most of the party were picked up by launch and ferried to the British India cargo boat *Fultala*, standing by with two other ships, the *Henri Janson* and the *Alipore*, to sail for Calcutta. Each man had his own rations and about a gallon of water. Forster and Scott were taken by another launch across to Rangoon docks on the other side of the river, as they had planned to travel by road to the oilfields for more preparatory work on the demolitions there. At the landing-place they were told that the Japanese had already cut the road to the north of the capital; they at once re-embarked and their launch set off down river after the evacuation steamer. On the way they observed a party of men busy dynamiting the legs of the huge dockside cranes, so as to topple them into the water and prevent the enemy from securing ships alongside. Otherwise Rangoon appeared to be completely deserted.

By then it was about 6 p.m., and a pall of black smoke, completely engulfing the refineries, darkened the late afternoon sky. An RAF reconnaissance plane high over the capital estimated the smoke to be solid for nearly four miles up. In the refineries themselves, the heat generated by the sea of flame beneath the smoke was so intense that a huge quantity of the heavier fractions was being carried into the upper air; later it condensed and fell like rain. Luckily for Forster and Scott, their launch managed to locate the *Fultala* in the gloom and they embarked. The boat was very full, with over two hundred people on board. Most were Indians, either in the Burmese forces or oil company employees.

As the vessels got under way, convoyed by a Royal Navy sloop, and slowly steamed past the three refineries and the bunkering depot, those on board had a grandstand view of what was reckoned to be the largest man-made conflagration the world had ever seen up to that time. The light breeze, still blowing from the south, kept the heavy pall of smoke off the foreshore, to display what Forster called 'a magnificent but tragic sight'. In the gathering darkness, the whole sky was lurid with the glare of the inferno. According to later reconnaissance reports, the installations continued to burn for seven or eight weeks, well into May.

All the denial party were by then dog-tired and indescribably grubby. Two of them, having carried out Forster's instruction to cement off the under-water pipeline from the Rangoon side to Syriam, were plastered with half-set concrete and had to strip and be hosed down on a corner of the crowded desk. As there were no passenger cabins, the women on board were accommodated in the dining saloon, the telephonists having been joined by the hospital matron, some Burmese nurses and the Syriam works manager's secretary. The company paid for them to be provided with three meals a day. A nurse had to be called out to help the doctors when a Burmah Oil man, who had arranged a plank over an open hatch to provide room for him to stretch out, rolled over into the hatch in his sleep and broke his leg. The telephone girls received no official decorations for their valour, but Roper was gratified to learn later that they found very good jobs in Calcutta.

Forster, having been on his feet continuously for more than forty hours, stretched out on a hatch cover and slept until the middle of the next morning. After that, he subsequently recalled, 'the time passed uneventfully without a cloud – or more important, an enemy aircraft or warship – to be seen.' That was providential, as lifeboats or floats would have been enough for only a fraction of those on board. In between pondering over the extraordinary events of the past few weeks, he kept his mind active by exercising it on some totally irrelevant puzzles. Why, for instance, did Rudyard Kipling make so many geographical errors in his poem 'Mandalay'? Considering the number of years Kipling had lived in the East, had he carried poetic licence too far? The Irrawaddy River almost certainly contained no flying fish; there was no bay on the 'road' across which the dawn could be seen coming up like thunder, or indeed in any other way, from China; and at Moulmein the old pagoda, and all other erections, looked westward to the sea and not eastward. Having omitted to discuss the last-named weighty problem with any old Burma hand, he would not have known that the pagoda in question stood on the Rangoon river front at Botatoung, just where it ran eastward before turning south towards the open sea. Sadly, it was bombed to destruction by the RAF when it was being used as an observation post by the Japanese.

Nearly five days of enforced idleness built up Forster's strength wonderfully, and as soon as the boat reached Calcutta on 12 March, he made for army headquarters to convince the senior officers there that he had personal orders from General Alexander to return to Burma with all speed. Air passages were at once arranged for himself and Captain Scott. An army plane flew them to the airfield at Magwe, and they were taken to Yenangyaung. There he was furious to hear that the instruction he had sent on 7 March to the fields had been disregarded. That was the one to carry out preliminary work such as cutting up drilling equipment. Dalgleish, having received the instruction, was forbidden to act on it by McGuire, the warden, on the grounds that it was he who should issue any demolition orders. Ignoring McGuire completely, Forster proceeded to call together the fields denial team and told them to carry out his instruction as quickly as possible. An open conflict sooner or later between Forster and the warden now seemed inevitable.

Roper, who had also played his part in the Syriam denial and travelled to Calcutta in the *Fultala*, received a cable from Dorman-Smith on 15 March asking him to take an RAF plane back to Burma and report to Government House at Maymyo, where the governor was in residence after being evacuated from Rangoon. On arrival Roper was told of his appointment as director of the petroleum industry for Burma, an official post to co-ordinate all the companies' remaining work there. He protested that as Burmah Oil's general manager for the East, he had responsibilities in India as well as over such matters as evacuation and could not possibly hold the post. Instead, therefore, that function was divided between two of his senior men from the Rangoon office: C. W. (Willie) Armstrong, who was made controller of the petroleum industry for Burma, on the production side, and John A. Drysdale, who became controller of petroleum products, responsible for their distribution.

As to denial, Forster had unilaterally assumed executive authority for all planning and organisation because, as he later said, it was the only way to get anything done. In practice, there were so many different aspects of work to attend to that the central denial committee – which appears to have got on tolerably well together despite some underlying tensions – adopted the cherished Whitehall practice of setting up *ad hoc* committees, so that life turned itself into what Dalgleish later called 'an almost continuous series of meetings, by day and by night, frequently disturbed by and interspersed with interviews and official visitors'. One night no fewer than three separate meetings were taking place in his bungalow, with a fourth outside on the lawn, where the local or subordinate commanders, who headed the various 'platoons' of denial workers, were briefed and consulted. Gradually, as the procedures were ironed out, discussions became more formalised, and each team member came to understand the overall strategy and his own part in that strategy.

On 2 April, when the Japanese were a hundred miles north of Rangoon, General Alexander visited Yenangyaung and met a select group of senior oil company managers to brief them on the military situation. It was quickly noticed that he was having to rely on a sketch map torn out of a transport timetable, and someone slipped out to the company's geological office to provide him with as many excellent maps as he needed. Two days later Forster travelled with Alexander for discussions at Burma GHQ, which had also moved north to Maymyo. Fully reviewing the denial plans, to which they gave their approval, they agreed that it was still essential to continue producing and refining at the fields for military petrol needs.

On 9 April Forster met for the first time Lieutenant-General William Slim, who had lately assumed command of the two divisions and brigade known as Burcorps, then operating in the relatively unpopulated dry zone of Upper Burma.[11] Slim laid down that as the Japanese advance had been so rapid, the advance notice for denial must be reduced from three days to one day. Forster put in hand further demolitions, for instance of some pumping equipment on the outlying tank farms. Then, on the 14th, he received the expected E signal from Slim to undertake the first phase of the destruction. That involved completely shutting-down all installations and laying explosive charges, ready to be set off when the final signal was received. The following day Slim visited the fields and personally

authorised the total destruction of all remaining installations at
Yenangyaung except the power station; that was to be saved for
the time being, as the Chauk field – still producing for the army
– could not operate without it. Forster felt much pride in having
completed the whole work within the 24-hour timetable that
Slim had set him. All personnel were then evacuated north to
Chauk.

It was after weeks of unremitting labour and stress that
tempers had begun to fray. As recently as the 14th Dalgleish's
bungalow had been destroyed by a Japanese bomb, killing his
Indian butler; Forster had been absent, and Dalgleish and a
colleague had taken refuge in a slit trench close by, but the
incident shook them all up at an already tense time. Other
denial workers found themselves similarly unnerved; one group
of three or four, temporarily sharing a bungalow and pooling
their remaining resources, found themselves bickering, not
entirely in jest, over how to eke out the last pegs of whisky and
tinned Christmas puddings.

As news arrived of the inexorable Japanese advance, in
which the road to Thittabwe had been cut, the power station
there was blown up at midnight on the 16th/17th. On the 18th,
according to Forster, the warden confronted him and forbade
him to carry out any further denial work without specific
authority from himself; approval would not be forthcoming
unless Forster gave an assurance that the authorities had
undertaken to compensate the oil companies in full for their
losses. He also asked to see Forster's written orders from the
British government, which of course did not exist. Forster
brushed aside this intervention as the height of absurdity when
so much – including the power station – had already been
immobilised. If the warden and others attempted any further to
block the completion of the denial plans, Forster said he would
shoot them with his Colt .38 revolver. The warden decided not
to argue, and departed.

The warden and other witnesses later claimed that Forster
had over-dramatised a clash of wills that had undoubtedly
taken place, and had never really understood the vital importance of having a clear line of command. The underlying fear in
the warden's and the managers' minds was that if by some fluke
the Japanese attack were to come to a halt, millions of pounds'

worth of resources would have been unnecessarily sacrificed. On the same day, however, reports came through that the enemy was advancing up the west bank of the Irrawaddy river. The fierce battle of Yenangyaung, at its height on 18/19 April during which the British 1st Burma Division was virtually wiped out as a fighting force, took place all too near to the fields. Having received instructions from the army therefore, Forster gave the signal for the first stage of demolitions at Chauk to take place.

The preparations and the denial itself occurred in conditions of intense heat, for in the dry zone of Upper Burma daytime temperatures could rise to as high as 46°C, or 115°F. A soldier, fighting there, later put it graphically, 'From seven in the morning until seven at night the sun beat down with a ferocity I do not recall even in Arabia – it simply blazed. There was little shade and the flies were a torment.'[12] For the 'last-ditchers', engaged on demolition, a further hazard was that metal exposed to the sun could seriously burn the unwary who touched it. What was subsequently remembered above all was the almost intolerable artificial as well as natural heat. Every producing well had been set on fire and, as the wind was blowing in their direction, the denial team received the full impact. A quite unreal factor, as later described, was 'the intense breathless silence when one stopped for a moment; the smoke pall seemed to absorb all noise'. As the team was totally exhausted by the end of that gruelling day, it was a relief to them that on the 19th – a Sunday – more hopeful news came from the front, which allowed them to take a little rest and to inspect the damage so as to confirm that an effective job had been done. Then at 3.30 p.m. that day the D order was given for final demolition. The teams then left Chauk for the north and the arduous journey to India.

No satisfactory narrative could or will ever be written on the evacuation of British, Indian and mixed-race civilians from Burma, across the inhospitable terrain to India, in those early months of 1942. What can certainly be said is that it was one of the great migrations of history, with no fewer than 400,000 men, women and children involved. Almost exactly 300,000 are believed to have gone overland, while 67,000 reached

Calcutta by sea from Burmese ports, to be cared for by the
Evacuees Reception Committee there.[13] Others did not need to
seek the committee's help, but many must have died on the
way.

All those who later wrote of their experiences – as company
employees did at Watson's request – agreed that they encountered a whole range of human behaviour, from the most heroic
self-sacrifice to appalling selfishness. On the debit side, Dorman-Smith set a poor example by evacuating some of his
domestic pets to India; by contrast, many company and other
staff had the harrowing task of personally destroying much-
loved animals which had often been their companions for many
years.[14] One man on the trek north was astonished to see
the governor's Indian bearer striding past the throngs of
refugees carrying his master's pet monkey on his shoulder; the
monkey survived the journey but perished soon after reaching
Calcutta.[15] Some able-bodied men forced their way on to
evacuation planes and thus deprived sick or wounded people of
seats. Some – even, it was said, company employees – who had
omitted to bring cigarettes, liquor or bedding, thought little of
stealing from the bags of colleagues when their backs were
turned.

However, most of those who had to walk all or part of the
journey merely kept on with doggedness, behaving neither as
heroes nor as villains. One put it succinctly and accurately:

> Our thoughts as we passed through these almost inaccessible
> places moved in an uneasy triangle between supplies, sickness and
> mileage. . . . We had to cover a certain distance in a certain time or
> supplies would not suffice. Sickness was not considered from a
> selfish standpoint so much as the embarrassment it would impose
> on others. . . . There was no turning back if anyone fell sick nor
> spare food to permit delay.

Those who undoubtedly came off worst over evacuation
were the Indians, and a great oil company which employed
almost 10,000 of that race in Burma must be judged by the
efforts it made to assist them in their hour of need.[16] Before an
account is given of these efforts, Table 3 tabulates the figures
which Roper included in his evacuation report at the beginning
of 1943.

TABLE 3
Indian employees of Burmah Oil evacuated, 1942

	Indians on payroll (approx.)	Number arrived in India	Percentage of arrivals
Syriam	3700	2860	77
Dunneedaw	1500	1285	86
Yenangyaung	2500	1355	54
Chauk	1550	1035	66
Pipeline, depots etc	550	115	21
	9800	6650	67

By far the highest proportion saved came from the refineries. The less essential workers were ferried across to Rangoon, and from there most of them apparently went to Prome, where they turned west to Taungup near the coast and took passage to Calcutta. Those who stayed on to the end were later evacuated by the *Fultala* and her sister ship on 7 March; company officials spent the voyage making nominal lists of employees on board. To be sure, the above figures tell us nothing about families; Watson always allowed four or five dependants per non-European employee, so that the fates of up to 50,000 Indian people may well have been involved.

For those at the fields, the real anxiety began after Rangoon was evacuated on 20 February, and the roads north through Yenangyaung became congested with refugees. For four days the traffic passing through the town never stopped; as reported at the time, 'the sight of the motor vehicles of all descriptions and ages packed tight with men, women and children, belongings and furniture was a pathetic one which was disturbing' to onlookers and to the oilfields workers who relied on hearsay.

Dalgleish's appointment of Watts in mid-February as the company's evacuation co-ordinator was mentioned earlier. A committee was set up to keep employees informed of arrangements, laid down in order of priority, which was not based on racial criteria but on company and humanitarian needs, as well as those of the defence forces and civilian consumers in Burma. The families of all races came first, followed by non-essential male Indians; personnel remaining behind for denial operations; last came records, equipment and essential stores. When the Indians at the fields declared that they must leave in order to take their families to safety, unless an evacuation scheme was immediately organised, Watts at once asked the warden of the oilfields to order up enough river steamers and flats for the purpose. The warden readily took up the matter with higher authority, which at once vetoed the plan. Watts then insisted that supplies of petrol and other products would come to a halt because the Indians who manned the topping plants and ancillary machinery would simply desert with their families.

This threat was successful, and steamers and flats were moored in conspicuous positions at Nyaunghla and Chauk, to reassure the Indian workers and their dependants. The warden took responsibility for provisioning the vessels with fourteen days' rations – rice, dhal, salt and cooking oil – and fuel, while the company undertook such tasks as supplying wood fuel for cooking on board and the issuing of tickets. It also paid advances of wages to married employees to help finance the evacuation of their dependants. Four doctors, two sisters and their orderlies inoculated all would-be passengers against cholera, no one being admitted on board unless the ticket bore an inoculation certificate on the back.

The oil companies' labour offices were well versed in all the needs of the Indian community, as shown by the list of rules they drew up. Notices had to be produced in the various dialects, a male escort was detailed for every five women and children – later misinterpreted as allowing too high a proportion of men to travel, an Indian doctor was placed in overall charge of passengers in each vessel and elders were appointed to supervise the issue of rations, enforce discipline and see that lights and fires were effectively screened. After permission was given on 13 April, three separate sailings took place, each calling at Lanywa and Yenangyat; they carried between 3,000 and 3,250 from Nyaunghla and 2,300 from Chauk.

The system of evacuating Indians from the fields broke down when government would not allow the vessels to proceed further than Kyaukmyaung, north of Mandalay, where it had set up a transit camp. From then on, the oil companies' responsibility for refugees ceased. In its wisdom, government had laid down that Europeans would be evacuated via Kalewa and Tamu, while the Indians would go on from Kyaukmyaung. The warden of the oilfields tried hard to convince the officials concerned that the Indians must be kept on the move; otherwise they would risk being captured by the Japanese, who would gladly use their skills. The government, anxious to prevent congestion on the various routes, refused.

Although some Indians were able to hire bullock carts to take them on, the fatal delay meant that when the monsoon struck early in May and the dusty tracks then became waterlogged, most of them were caught on the journey. An entirely neglected source, the evacuation report by J. S. Vorley, the commissioner of civil evacuation – said to have been suppressed because of its critical nature but in fact openly available in the India Office archives – gave two reasons for the civil authorities' failure in this regard: they had little idea of the military situation (but neither did the military themselves most of the time), and they were not flexible enough to make the transition from a peacetime to a wartime attitude of mind.

> To be unpleasantly candid [Vorley wrote], the experiences in Rangoon and Mandalay proved again what has so frequently been proved in Europe in recent years, namely that for successful administration in the war, active and comparatively young brains and intellects are essential.

Yet his final summing-up was far from harsh:

> There were cowards of all races, there were mistakes innumerable, but the history of the evacuation in Burma when it is known will, I think, be a tale of courage, devotion to duty and self-sacrifice which will be above all criticisms.[17]

Vorley's figures of numbers evacuated and of casualties are on record, and need not be given in detail here. He reckoned that, to the end of May, when his report concluded, no fewer than 331,000 had been evacuated from Burma, and casualties were only some 6,500, or less than 2 per cent of the total. That was far from being the final death-toll, estimated at anywhere between

10,000 and 50,000. Sheer fatigue and disease claimed many of the women and children and the old; some struggled on but died soon after reaching safety. The senior Burmah Oil employees in their reports, while wishing that they themselves had been able to do more, often bitterly reflected upon failure of the government of Burma to pay adequate attention to evacuation matters. To be sure, some government officials involved had given devoted service to evacuees in their particular areas, but their hands had been tied by blinkered governmental policies – or by the absence of policies.

Looking back on the denial and evacuation, there were certain piquant ironies, as there had been in the 1885 war before Upper Burma was incorporated into the British empire. First, many of the earlier preparations that the company had so willingly undertaken at the behest of government had proved useless. The reserve wells at Chauk, brought at great expense into instant readiness, were destroyed without a drop of oil being raised from them. The plans to turn out vast quantities of aviation spirit, as the major supplier for the British forces in the Far East, were overtaken by the speed of the Japanese advance, and it was plentiful oil products for vehicles that the authorities had then mainly needed. The machinery and equipment ordered from Britain to facilitate the maximum output and refining of products were never brought into service: the boxes so carefully stored were opened only so that the contents could be smashed up.

The second irony was that, although a thorough demolition of the oil production and refining installations had taken place, the Japanese were still able to find ways of making oil products for essential purposes, as Chapter V will show. A third irony was that the hostilities of 1942 brought no lasting benefit to anyone, except perhaps in an indirect way to the inhabitants of Burma itself. The Japanese were a few years later turned out of the country quite as ignominiously as the British had been; but only a year or two after they had regained control at such a high cost of lives and material goods, the British granted independence to Burma. Even if Watson were in the future to carry out his resolve to undertake the arduous and expensive task of rebuilding his oil enterprise in Burma, he must by May of 1942 have sensed that a new and even less compliant political atmosphere would lie ahead than had prevailed in the years of British rule.

Notes

1 Many accounts have been written about the disastrous Burma campaign of 1941–2. The official history, Kirby, *War against Japan*, has been supplemented – but not supplanted – by H. P. Willmott's admirable but brief Chapter 12, 'From Victoria Point to Yenangyaung' in *Empires in the Balance: Japanese and Allied Pacific Strategies to April 1942*, 1982, pp. 398–434. L. Allen, *Burma: The Longest War 1941–45*, 1984, has the advantage of having fully consulted the Japanese sources. J. Lunt, *A Hell of a Licking: The Retreat from Burma 1941–2*, 1986, is a well-balanced and first-hand account. The company's papers on denial and the subsequent legal case are in IOR, MSS Eur F 156.

2 Kirby, *War against Japan* II, p. 33.

3 I am very grateful to the late Leslie Forster for permission to quote from Chapter 8 'Burma' of his unpublished memoirs, a primary source for the denial episode. See also Sir E. Berthoud, *An Unexpected Life: Memoirs 1900–80*, privately printed, 1980, pp. 107ff.

4 For Scott's article, 'How We Blew Up Burmah Oil' see *Sunday Telegraph*, 14 February 1965.

5 The contemporary account by W. P. G. Maclachlan, then in the Burma Rifles, of evacuation to India is 'Burma Journey' I: *National Review* 120, June 1943, and II and III in ibid.121, July and August 1943.

6 Abraham, *Time Off*, p. 25.

7 Anon., 'The Burmah Oil Affair', *Harvard Law Review* 79, 1965–6, p. 614. Reservations about Alexander's intellectual capacity as a commander are in Allen, *Burma: The Longest War*, p, 50.

8 Abraham, *Time Off*, p. 25.

9 PRO WO 106/2659, 'Diary of Lt. Col. W. E. V. Abraham, Liaison Officer for Mideast' 9 March 1942 and 'Conclusions Based on Visits to Burma and India' 17 March 1942. Lunt, *A Hell of a Licking*, who quotes this judgment (pp. 84–5) doubts whether a clearer appreciation of the factors involved would have made much difference to the course of the campaign: ibid. p. 85.

10 IOR, M/3[P]/821. R. Dorman-Smith, *Report on the Burma Campaign 1941–42*, Simla, November 1943, Appendix V, Report on Civil Evacuation (by Professor B. R. Pearn) gives an equally evocative description of the scene, quoted in Kirby, *War against Japan* p. 95. cf. Collis, *Last and First*, p. 116.

11 Sir W. Slim, *Defeat into Victory*, 1956, is a primary source. His description of the denial at Yenangyaung is on pp. 61–2.

12 Lunt, *A Hell of a Licking*, p. 207.

13 This information is from Pearn's Appendix to Dorman-Smith, *Report* (see note 10 above).

14 Collis, *Last and First*, pp. 117, 132, 151–2, 166.

15 A. R. Tainsh, *And Some Fell by the Wayside: An Account of the North Burma Evacuation*, Calcutta, 1948, p. 14.

16 See H. Tinker, 'A Forgotten Long March: The Indian Exodus from Burma, 1942', *Journal of South-East Asian Studies* VI, March 1975, pp. 1–15. This misleadingly describes the first motor convoys in March 1942, 'mainly to carry the European and Eurasian employees of the Burma [sic] Oil Company' as an 'apparent policy of racial discrimination' (p. 7). It also incorrectly states that J. S. Vorley's report (see note 17 below) 'is missing from the records ... and appears to have been suppressed'. p. 7n.

17 IOR, M/3/955, J. S. Vorley, 'Report on the Work of the Department of Civil Evacuation and Welfare in Burma December 1941–31 May 1942', p. 48A. This balanced conclusion was echoed by Dorman-Smith, *Report* Part IV, Chapter 8, p. 140.

CHAPTER IV

Towards Reconstruction
1942–5

The man most prostrated by the melancholy events of 1942 in Burma was undoubtedly Sir John Cargill, the Burmah Oil chairman. A lifelong worrier, he had already had more than enough to make him terribly anxious about the rapidly spreading war. The only surviving letter of his in this period was one to a close colleague early that year. 'If you want to see the grounds why I take such an alarmist view of the whole position in the East and the Far East', he wrote, 'get the *National Review* for January.' Admiral Thursfield's gloomy article 'War in the Pacific', he said, 'might quite easily have been written by me!' Mercifully, time has erased all evidence of his total anguish over the destruction – however unavoidable – of everything in Burma that his father and he had painstakingly built up since the 1870s.

Watson was equally moved by the recent occurrences, but reacted somewhat differently. In the absence of letters or cables, his main source of up-to-date news from Burma was by then *The Times*. On 10 March 1942, it had merely reported a pall of smoke hanging over Rangoon, attributed to fires caused by saboteurs. Then on the 11th it confirmed that the 'valuable oil refineries' at and near Syriam had been destroyed. He at once cabled, via Chittagong, a message:

It is difficult for me, and for so many of us, to take philosophically this miserable interruption – for one still clings to the hope that it may be no more – of so much which has occupied all our energies for so long, and which we can legitimately claim has been of such value in so many ways to so many; but to hope for rehabilitation of it sooner or later does help.

By 16 April his fears were concentrated on the fields, where he felt the chances of halting the Japanese to be slender. 'Your anxieties, like our own here,' he wrote to Roper, 'for all in the fields must be acute. I can again only wish you well through these unpleasant conditions.' He also commented on Roper's earlier letters that had shown up 'in an almost tragically illuminating way' what appeared to have been a complete lack of official appreciation, by the army as well as the local government, of how grave the Japanese threat had been and how unprepared the province generally was for all-out war. Then a telegram from Roper 'somewhere in Burma' confirmed his worst apprehensions that the oilfields could not be saved, and his comments were movingly laconic:

So ends for the time being all our labours in Burma. What a subject for tears it all is!

There were two reasons why these events were causing him so much mental agony, over and above the human tragedy and the material losses, the latter all the more painful because self-administered. The first was that, in common with Sherlock Holmes, he had a mind like a racing engine, which tore itself to pieces when not connected up to the workload for which it was built. For four decades he had toiled to keep up with the weekly flow of correspondence and daily cables, and those from Burma were now abruptly halted. Not until 11 May, when back in Calcutta after his road trek out of Burma, could Roper write at length and deal with Watson's repeated earlier complaints about being kept short of information. He had had to be discreet when mail was subject to strict censorship, and reliable information had in any case been hard to come by when official appreciations of the Japanese menace had been so far removed from reality. Watson did not receive this letter until July: there may have been some cabled messages before then, but in wartime conditions little of substance could be communicated by that route.

The second reason for his distress of mind was that his son

Neil, an assistant in the Rangoon office, was not among those reported as having safely arrived in India. Not until some months afterwards did he hear that Neil Watson had contracted diphtheria during the evacuation, then as often as not a fatal disease. The son had pulled through but his recuperation had been delayed by complications. Mercifully he made a full recovery in due course.

There was one way in which Watson could occupy his hyperactive mind. On 11 March, the day of *The Times'* report on the oil refineries' destruction, he wrote to Geoffrey Lloyd, the Minister for Petroleum, requesting the government to lay down immediate plans for replacing the company's properties already denied or to be denied – for the oilfields had yet to be overrun. Would it therefore grant priority to manufacture of the equipment needed for rehabilitation? Not surprisingly, at the very time when British troops were still being bundled out of lower Burma, and huge problems of defending the Indian subcontinent were building up, this was the last matter that the government was concerned to discuss. Reconstruction in the abstract was all very well, but practical steps of that kind could certainly not then be contemplated, and perhaps not for years to come.[1]

Undeterred by this official indifference at home, Watson set his staffs in London and in the East to work on detailed studies of reconstruction in all its aspects. He needed to have informed data and ideas by him, just in case the authorities should wish to talk. No less vital, it kept the nucleus of experts on their toes even though it produced no immediate practical benefit: much as the journalists of a newspaper on strike will continue to produce copy that has very little chance of being printed. By the end of March an engineer in head office had put together some preliminary thoughts on future refining strategy in Burma. A revolutionary new idea was that he expected all companies there to have one joint refinery, in the interests of economy. Having considered, but rejected, the alternative of the refinery being located up-country near the oilfields, the engineer concluded that Rangoon, as the country's major port and commercial centre, was still the most logical site.

On 14 April – a few days before the destruction of Chauk and

Lanywa and thus at a time when the company was about to be deprived of its last oilfields in Burma – Percy Evans, the chief geologist in London, cabled to Roper in Calcutta (who had in fact already returned to Burma) about the geological work that must be put in hand without delay. Once they were no longer required in the Burmese fields, most of the geologists should be released for military service; four however were to be kept on, to undertake an investigation of the company's post-war geological reserves. 'Many important future decisions', Evans added, were 'hanging on' these researches. The four geologists would also propose the most economic means of production. Although Evans accepted that reconstruction could not be planned quickly, an overall framework would be required within which the company could work out more detailed questions such as the type and capacity of the new refinery.

By 1 June, C. A. Sansom, then senior geologist for Burma, had produced Burma Rehabilitation Note No. 1, which sketched a 'plan of work' for restoring the oilfields. The first priority was to compile up-to-date maps showing the latest known level of production of each well. From these maps they would seek to choose the wells that were most worth reconditioning. Drilling expenses would be calculated, so as to draw up an estimate of probable future direct costs per foot, and of speeds per string of rotary and cable-tool drills field by field. A rough picture would gradually be assembled of the most economic levels of production in each of the main fields. Nine Burma Rehabilitation Notes were compiled before the end of 1942; one related an interesting discussion with Royal Dutch-Shell geologists about problems encountered after lengthy shut-downs of wells, derived from experience in Romania, California and elsewhere.

Comments by Watson on another of these notes further illustrated his overall strategy for reconstruction in Burma. These comments were made to W. A. Gray, the executive director concerned with such questions. To Watson, the first crucial factor was how much crude oil in the country was ultimately recoverable; taken with the annual economic rate of extraction, that provided the basis for determining the nature and extent of operations in both the oilfields and the refinery – not forgetting, in a typical Watson afterthought, the 'frills'.

Once these operations had been costed, an annual charge for amortising capital would have to be added, over whatever period seemed most economic. An aggregate oilfields cost for drilling and producing would be supplemented by pipeline and refining costs, to give a 'whole ultimate resources' cost, which would have to be compared with historical data. He summed up as follows:

> If we are to aim at starting again – as soon as possible, as near as circumstances permit – at where we left off, we *must* be able to justify doing so by some such approach as this. The alternative would be that we start much as we did in 1886 and build up only very gradually as we saw our way clear in oil and profit from it, and *that* we cannot contemplate in the quite different circumstances of our acquired knowledge in these more than fifty years.

As a check on these projections G. W. Lepper, Sansom's predecessor as senior geologist who was currently working for the Petroleum Department, produced for Watson a note on the more practical aspects of oilfields rehabilitation. Plans should be made in stages for each section of the main drilling and production services, and appropriate back-up facilities provided. For each stage, all preliminary design and procurement work would have to be completed, so that when instructions were received to go ahead, the equipment manufacturers could at once put the appropriate orders in hand. The first stages of the plan would clearly involve providing for the earliest possible output of oil products to supply the British occupation troops. That need should encourage officials in Whitehall to issue manufacturing permits and to sanction the necessary shipping arrangements as quickly as possible.

Lepper was not afraid to raise some tricky questions. First, would the company want to go in for full electrification again, or would the 'possible insecurity of tenure' (because the installations might in due course be expropriated if Burma became independent) modify the overall criterion from maximum fuel economy to one of lower capital expenditure? Secondly, would it be wise to work to the old standards of 'sound' oilfield development, which had stressed care and conservation? On the first point, Watson minuted, 'We must take the risk of incurring high capital spending now as before', and on the second, 'In principle, yes.'

Roper from Calcutta felt that a separate word of caution would not be out of place. 'We are impressed by the energy with which you have at once taken up rehabilitation, but I fear that the volume of new [crude oil] production to be expected would not justify the large amount of drilling plant or such a large refinery to maintain production for a sufficiently long time', he wrote to Watson. In his view too much attention was being paid to the tactics and not enough to the overall strategy. Watson's only response was to urge Roper to use this 'breathing space' to sort out other matters such as determining the wage rates for Burmese and Indian labour, job by job.

The upheavals of war had quite unexpectedly turned indigenous Indian oil production into something of key importance to the subcontinent, now in the front line with the Japanese close to its eastern borders. The two main companies, Assam Oil and Attock Oil, between them produced just over 2 million barrels of crude, as against output of 7 million barrels in Burma during 1941.

Despite considerable efforts, Attock Oil's production fell by more than half from 0.87 million barrels in 1941 to 0.41 million in 1944 and 0.32 million in 1945. Assam Oil succeeded in increasing refinery throughput from 1.65 million barrels in 1941 to 1.83 million in 1943 and 2.08 million in 1944, after which it tailed off to 1.7 million barrels in 1945. The importance of Digboi to the Indian economy can be seen from its being given more anti-aircraft guns than any other location in the subcontinent. As in Burma, employees aided the war effort in many different ways, for instance helping with the construction of a nearby airfield and laying a petrol pipeline, later supplemented by bulk tank installations.

The summer of 1942 was a tense time at Digboi, with the Japanese poised near the frontier with India. Children and most of the women were evacuated, and as Digboi was on the route from Myitkyina, through the Hukong valley in northern Burma and the Pangsau pass inside India, no fewer than 500 Europeans and 10,000 Indians were reported at the beginning of May to have set off along that route. The onset of the monsoon two weeks later made it extremely difficult to follow the almost completely washed-away path through the jungle and to ford the swollen and fast-running rivers: John S. Vorley in his evacuation report estimated the casualties as 10 per cent of the 20,000 or so who trekked that way, but they must almost certainly have been appreciably higher. The managers of the tea-gardens in Assam gave much assistance in setting up and manning camps. Similarly, the local staffs at Digboi did what they could to help the refugees who reached that far, by then at the end of their endurance; as at Yenangyaung, the painful sight of those refugees passing through inevitably hit morale there. On the other hand, the arrival of Burmah Oil employees who could be used there strengthened the facilities that Digboi could provide to India's war effort. Fortunately, the carefully prepared denial programme never had to be put into effect.

In May 1942 the Petroleum Department called in the London representatives of the companies involved and asked them to prepare a crash programme for stepping up output in India. Gray attended for Burmah Oil, and the significance of the meeting was highlighted by the presence of Sir William Fraser, chairman of Anglo-Iranian since Cadman's death a year before. Gray promised to ensure that Assam Oil would give every possible assistance. However, he had to explain the difficulties now that Digboi itself was under threat from the Japanese and in the throes of devising its own denial programme, so that Indian labour there was very nervous. The meeting concluded that it was a top priority for Assam Oil and Attock Oil to be helped with extra plant and equipment from sources in India, Iran or Bahrain, in that order. The Petroleum Department promised to find out what might be obtained from the United States as well. Despite considerable efforts, however, by 1944 those companies' joint level of production was no higher than that for 1941, as shown above.

Hence India had to rely very heavily on imported oil products. As had been the case in Burma, the most vital product was petrol. Digboi was able to make more petrol when it received a cracking plant; even so, between 1942 and 1945 no less than 90 per cent of petrol needs had to be imported; even more inconveniently, it had to come in on the west coast and be transported overland to the theatre of war in the east. As early as February 1942 Burmah-Shell at Bombay arranged with the

Indian railway authorities to run special trains of tank wagons at high speed across India to Calcutta. This commendable enterprise still could not deliver the enormous quantities required, as available rolling stock was insufficient. The Indian defence department therefore authorised the construction of a six-inch pipeline, originally intended to run 800 miles to Allahabad, more than half-way to Calcutta; however, shortage of pipe restricted it to 270 miles, as far as Bhuswal on the eastern border of Bombay province. Burmah-Shell undertook the construction itself, using Burmah Oil technical staff who were rounded up from other jobs they had taken. The pipeline was in operation by June 1943.

A major problem, arising out of the war, exercised Watson at this time. How could Burmah Oil honour its commitment to provide oil to Indian consumers under the Burmah-Shell agreement, now that its main source of supply had been cut off? Had the oil run out through natural exhaustion, the company would have suffered certain penalties, but Watson insisted that it was unreasonable to be penalised as a result of an act of war. Only a week after denial at Syriam, he opened the attack on Frederick Godber, managing director of Shell. A voluminous correspondence followed: Godber pointed out that Shell, too, had suffered grievously from the loss of its installations in the Far East. Having made a practice of spreading its risks as widely as possible, his company should not now have to subsidise those which had chosen not to diversify. Eventually, Watson wore him down to a compromise, which Anglo-Iranian accepted as well: Burmah Oil was allowed to import, from any source, up to two-thirds of Burmah-Shell's requirements of petrol and kerosene which it could not provide from its own production. Watson had therefore upheld the important principle, underlying the 1928 agreement, of indigenous preference.

He also drafted on behalf of the three companies involved a 'Joint Statement of Aims', each promising not to take advantage of wartime circumstances to do one another down, and declaring that each would help the others after the war to re-establish their pre-1939 trading positions. These negotiations are noteworthy, not merely for the benefits they conferred on Burmah Oil, but also as illustrating that Watson at 63 had lost none of his formidable power of persuasion and skill in deploying legalistic arguments, nor his established reputation in the British oil industry generally. He was able to buy in the supplies for Burmah-Shell, on advantageous terms, from Anglo-Iranian and from Caltex in Bahrain. With Burma for the moment out of the running, the Middle East was having to provide many of the oil products required in India.

For a good eighteen months from mid-1942 onwards, Watson was much exercised with the repercussions of Forster's report to the Petroleum Department in London, on 'Denial of the Oil Industry in Burma'.[2] Although all his papers had been destroyed in the bombing of Dalgleish's bungalow, Forster had in between times at Yenangyaung drafted the section on the refineries' denial; when he showed it to Roper, it was free of personal criticisms. Back in Cairo that May, one and a half stones lighter and badly in need of a complete rest, he was under intense official pressure to complete his report. Too exhausted to care whether or not he hurt people's feelings, at the last moment he rewrote the Introduction, which contained the following passage:

> The most serious difficulty [in the task of preparing for denial] was however the quality of most of the senior and executive staff of the oil companies, who completely failed to give a lead or to set an energetic example to the other employees. The civil authorities also displayed a regrettable inability to adjust their outlook to a realistic appreciation of emergency conditions and to the necessity for swift and decisive action, even up to 24 hours before the final demolition of the last oilfields. This state of mind was the principal reason for [my] prolonging the visit, so as to be certain that the technical staff should have the fullest support.

In his 'acknowledgements and recommendations' he very pointedly thanked all the staffs of British Burmah and Indo-Burma, but only the technical staff of Burmah Oil. Roper was, however, given a Class II commendation, as follows:

> His interest in the schemes and cheerful sharing of hard physical work and privations set a high standard which was greatly appreciated and did much to encourage many of his staff.

This report was fairly extensively circulated around GHQ India. On being told of the criticisms, Roper at once saw the Director of Military Operations – apparently responsible for distributing the document – and vigorously refuted them. Then Forster's main assistant within the company, Marr Grieve, told the press in an interview that Dalgleish and other office managers had scuttled from the oilfields prematurely before the demolitions were complete; that was an untruth which was easily disproved. 'What good to anybody or to the war effort the airing of all this can do,' Roper commented to Watson, 'I cannot imagine.' Meanwhile the Petroleum Department found itself embroiled in the kind of protracted correspondence at which Watson was such a master; its civil servants would only allow him to peruse the report in the department itself. It took a series of strong remonstrations before he was given extracts of all those parts that concerned the company.

Officials in the Burma Office, veterans of quite a few lengthy tussles with the tenacious Watson, minuted internally, 'We will leave the Petroleum Department to deal unaided with the trouble they have created for themselves', and advised that department to limit itself to formal acknowledgements to any future letters from Burmah Oil. As usually happened, Watson had the last word. In his considered reply, he sought to 'set in proper perspective' Forster's accusations that Burmah Oil's senior office staff had shown apathy and failed to give a stronger lead during the denial. 'It was clearly no apathy at all', he riposted, 'but careful deliberation as to the best reconciling of two essential but mutually conflicting duties', the other being the production and supply of oil products at the government's behest. The permanent secretary of the department accepted his views.

Forster also wrote to Sir Stafford Cripps, the Lord Privy Seal, lately returned from his mission to India, criticising the government because 'very few' of the 8,000 skilled refinery and oilfields workers had reached India. How Cripps replied to these incorrect allegations is not known. The Petroleum Department received a copy of an intercepted letter by Roper, stating, 'No other concern did more for the Indian staff than we did.' That remark did not deter an assistant secretary in the Burma Office from minuting, 'It seems to be the case that very few European employees of the oil companies failed to get away and that they did not delay their departure to assist the Indian employees.'[3] Such criticism omitted to take note of Roper's remark in the same letter, that most of the Indian employees had in the respective periods of evacuation activity been handed over to the government of Burma – as indeed the company had been instructed to do.

The number of arrivals had risen by mid-1943, according to Watson in his report to the Burmah Oil annual general meeting that September. Those contacted in India by the company's labour staff now stood at 7,200 but, he continued, 'unhappily, 72 of these had died since reaching India and reported deaths of a further 185 were still being investigated'. No information was given about dependants. J. R. Case, the oilfields manager of British Burmah, later said that a high proportion of his company's Indian employees had died; he blamed that on the failure to provide suitable transport, camps and a water supply *en route*, 'and the even more culpable lack of medical attention'. According to Case, about 35 per cent of the men who made the trek and up to 70 per cent of the women and children died after they had actually completed the journey, as a result of malaria or sheer exhaustion; the percentages could be challenged, but the causes of death can be confirmed from other sources.

Watson was meanwhile urging Roper to arrange for medical examinations and, where necessary, treatment for all evacuated employees who had suffered hardship likely to leave permanent scars. Suitable care at that stage could well prevent or minimise subsequent chronic ill-health. He learnt that a number had had serious health breakdowns, and he commented to Roper that it was a scandal that 'these poor fellows should [immediately after reaching India and often in precarious states of health] have been so left to their own resources or to the far from tender and efficient services of incompetent and inadequate hospitals, while both the employers and relations were kept completely ignorant of where they were or what had happened to them.' He recalled the severe but well-deserved criticisms levelled, for the same reasons, at the Indian authorities responsible for a similar 'mishandling' of the sick in Mesopotamia during the First World War.

By the end of 1942, debates within the company about the alleged shortcomings of senior office management had been widened by the arrival of written accounts by employees on denial and evacuation. Watson had encouraged them to speak freely, not only about the conduct of the civil and military authorities and the Burmese but also about any weaknesses they saw in the company's organisation at that time, especially in the fields. One or two managers were not afraid to speak their minds and to make contributions to what in effect became an 'audit of empire'. A senior technical man at the fields, Blagrave Deane, gave his view that British soldiers and airmen had scarcely seen the point of fighting for a Burma whose inhabitants did not want British rule and which was almost certain to become independent after the end of the war. Instances of retaliation or treachery had only hardened feelings of hostility towards the Burmese. On the European civilians in the country, the manager was equally forthright:

> Unfortunately there is a fairly large section amongst the European personnel who are completely oblivious of the benefits they have enjoyed from Burma and its people, and instead of trying to grasp the pleasure, so easily derived by cultivating a knowledge of the country and an interest in its people, they make no effort to conceal their hatred of both. . . . It is to be hoped [that] by care in choice of new personnel, and good example in leadership, efforts will be made to eradicate this failing.
>
> Many wives are bad offenders; instead of playing the part of emissaries of kindness and goodwill, they cause a further gulf between ourselves and the country and add to our unpopularity and jealousy by extravagant ostentation and arrogant deportment, which often goes grotesquely with their petty meanness. The Americans are liked and admired far above the British; natural and generous, they were understood. Prestige is not created by people who cannot mix with dignity and generosity.

Watson's reply tactfully suggested that some of these criticisms owed their origin to 'inadequate knowledge of all the circumstances'.

The fields superintendent at Yenangyaung, J. A. Butlin, wrote at length on what he regarded as the weaknesses in the company's organisation there 'and how the new organisation should be built up to obtain the greatest efficiency coupled with the most economical running.' Almost every paragraph of his sixteen-page note was commented on by one or other executive director, so seriously were his remarks taken at head office. One matter, on which he admitted he had earlier been influenced by Forster, was the impossibility of anyone except an office assistant in Burmah Oil rising to an administrative post, so that 'the company may be losing first-class brainpower and ability'. (Watson minuted that Weva had so risen, but conceded that he was so far the sole exception.)

Butlin stated that he had for years made a practice of taking out in turn junior members of the office staff over the fields, but all too often the young men had not shown the least interest in the tour, 'apart from a pleasant chat', thereby showing themselves 'obviously unfitted or unsuited for their jobs'. (Those who were keen to learn, often found it an uphill struggle. One was told by an American driller, 'Say, why don't you go to bed with the catalog and figure it all out there?') In times of stress, Butlin argued, the company could be successfully administered by heads of technical departments, 'but the same cannot be said of the administration being able to run the technical departments, without the heads.' (Watson saw no specific criticism of the company in this statement that did not apply equally to British industry as a whole.)

Butlin therefore suggested that only candidates with engineering degrees should be recruited to the company, so that technically trained men would in time take over both the administrative and the technical top posts – although outstanding men without degrees should also be considered. That system would automatically do away with a 'privileged class' of employees who enjoyed better amenities – in housing, furniture, furnishing and the number of servants – than technical men, who had often given many years of dedicated and successful service to the company. 'Another thing which had caused a lot of friction and bad feeling in the past was the fact that fish knives and forks were a stores issue to office staff and geologists but not to drillers and engineers.' He claimed that none of this segregation or discrimination existed in Royal Dutch-Shell; an allegation to which the Burmah Oil directors demurred, as Shell technical managers were frequently stationed off the fields and therefore not immediately accessible.

At the end of 1943 Watson received an equally hard-hitting memorandum from John Drysdale who, having lately held the responsible emergency post of controller of petroleum products in Burma, could scarcely be accused of having imperfect knowledge. Drysdale, possessing one of the most original minds in the company at this time, had since the denial thought much about what the company's future in Burma should be; piecemeal changes in the existing structure would not be good enough, since what was necessary was to 'build anew'. He foresaw that after Burma had been freed from Japanese occupation, a popularly elected government would come into power, leading to a clash between nationalist feeling and the rights of property.

In the Burmese oil sector, Drysdale continued, there were two features locally regarded as objectionable by the indigenous population. These were the presence of foreign technicians and management, and the existence of a foreign and absentee ownership and directorate. Three interacting 'difficulties' would thus confront Burmah Oil after the war: nationalistic feeling in the country, labour troubles, and government actions hostile to the company. He carefully analysed each of these difficulties; for instance, with labour, the company must find some way of identifying itself more specifically with the lives and feelings of indigenous workers, and vice versa. He therefore recommended that 'something like' a Burma Oil Industries Ltd should be set up in Rangoon, in which there should be a government stake, since no private Burmese capital was likely to be forthcoming. That firm would have two classes of shares, ordinary and employees' shares. The board would sit in Burma, possibly with a government nominee as one of its members. There would be two operations directors, one for production and one for refining and marketing, and a public relations and personnel director. Only the chairman and/or managing director would be in correspondence with the oil interests in Britain.

Drysdale also discussed what he saw as the low morale of the great majority of British employees in Burma, who (in his view) displayed the same symptoms of harbouring largely imaginary grievances as did Burmese labour. Although their terms of employment were as good as or better than anyone else's there, they were in the main a 'discontented lot'. His remedy was that pay, bonuses and the provident fund should be restructured so as to provide a permanent and concrete interest in the company's activities. Other measures could also be taken, which would incidentally save much money. For example, office staff lived in 'ridiculously expensive individual housing' with an absurdly high outlay on servants. 'My servants' bill in Rangoon over a period of ten years would have sufficed to buy a house of my own and several acres of garden.' Hence blocks of air-conditioned flats should be built; the occupants would be better contented because they would be encouraged to mix more widely among themselves and at the clubs. The company would also save money if it owned and ran a transport pool both for business and for pleasure. Racially segregated bars and clubs should be banned; apart from the principle of the thing, 'many Burmese both male and female make much better company than many of our [British] staff and wives.'

A strong personnel office would also operate a promotion system which would allow more technical men to be advanced to senior management posts. A Burmanisation programme was of course essential, but was being held back by the current inadequate standards of school and university education in Burma. The company should therefore encourage the government of Burma to send boys to be educated in Britain; also a considerable number of Burmese boys and girls needed to be sent to British, Commonwealth and/or American schools at the age of 14. For indigenous employees as a whole the 'curse of improvidence' worried him, and he suggested that the company should establish a co-operative bank, to make loans at reasonable rates to employees on the security of their provident funds, hence cutting out the money-lenders whose grip was so powerful on so many of them.

Unusually, Watson made few comments on Drysdale's paper, except to point out at the beginning that he himself was currently preoccupied with even more fundamental considerations, such as the value and extent of the oil deposits, without which no organisation would exist at all in Burma. As Roper was about to come home for consultation, he arranged to discuss the paper verbally on his arrival, and no further written reactions are to be found. Few of Drysdale's radical proposals were put into effect; even if they had been, perhaps the very fast pace of development in Burma between 1945 and 1947 would have overtaken many of them. But Drysdale was clearly a man marked for promotion, and in 1946 he was brought back to the London office.

The object of any audit is to give a balanced account of whatever is being surveyed, and the three reports quoted above – by able, articulate, but in their different ways all critical, employees, one influenced by many conversations with Forster – should properly be set alongside others which reflect a broader spread of views. Were the majority of British expatriates in Burma, and especially company staff, self-centred and blinkered in their attitudes to life in the host country? Was the alleged gulf between office and technical staff a harmful canker in the body corporate?

On the first question, many expatriate company employees took relatively little interest in the country and its people: an attitude perhaps fostered by the pre-1939 terms of service, which contained no provision for local leave. Even so, there were many who, often in the course of their company jobs, did travel widely in what was then a very attractive and generally peaceful country, and had friendly contacts with local people, whether employees or others.

One office assistant, disillusioned with the Indian houseboys whose ministrations so throughly insulated them from the country, engaged in their place Burmese – who were otherwise employed only as bearers – and through them came to know and understand the people, much to the company's benefit when he later became a senior manager in Rangoon after independence. Another, whose service in the army and in CAS (B) – see Chapter V below – modified his earlier if subconscious public-school feelings of racial superiority and paternalism, became a thorough Burmaphile when he married the locally-born daughter of British parents, and together they mixed freely with all sorts and conditions. The company encouraged the learning of Burmese and other local languages, paying good rewards for success in government examinations; however, few progressed to an advanced stage where they were really fluent in the language. After 1945, however, Burmese language courses were laid down for newcomers, and wives were encouraged to participate as well and to sit the examinations. By then, racial attitudes in the country had changed quite markedly.

Why was there a general failure of the races before 1939 to mix on the social level? Since many employees spent a considerable amount of their leisure time in sports, one of them has pointed out that excluding the Burmese from British clubs deprived them of the opportunity of playing golf and tennis together. While cricket and rugby were of little interest to them, the Burmese were passionately fond of soccer, and a league programme of matches between departments roused the spectators to such partisan frenzy that games had sometimes to be suspended until passions had simmered down. Here both races played together, and observers later recognised that more might have been done to foster mixed sporting tournaments of this kind, which undoubtedly helped to alleviate the feelings of discontent never far from the surface. In the oilfields, one contributory reason was that although management tried hard to ensure that all races were admitted as appropriate to the main clubs in Yenangyaung and Chauk, which were subsidised by the company (see Vol. I p.158), such efforts were frustrated by the more long-service and die-hard expatriate club committee members.

The magistrate and chronicler of life in pre-1939 Burma, Maurice Collis, believed that 'merchants' had by the nature of their business few direct dealings with Burmese, and therefore little opportunity to strike up friendships.[4] A senior company wife was overheard to say, 'Yes, the Burmans are all right, but what can one do with them?' presumably because their natural reserve in unfamiliar surroundings was not immediately thawed by the rather distant affability which is the normal reaction of practised British hostesses to strangers. Thus subconscious attitudes rather than deliberate policies seem to have prevented racial barriers from being dismantled.

On the question of the gulf between office management and technical staff, many of the latter at the oilfields were undoubtedly dissatisfied with the concept of non-technicians in overall charge, even though that was a common arrangement in many large companies, and did produce in Burmah Oil a good number of able senior managers and even chief representatives. However, dissatisfaction in the oilfields was exacerbated by some less competent managers and by the autocratic regime of certain long-entrenched heads of major departments

– otherwise known as the 'barons' – in the absence of an overall technical operations manager. It was said that each departmental head was adept at detecting and stopping any infringement of his sovereignty either by another department or by the (non-technical) fields agent or his staff.

The rigid departmental system was blamed for the outbreak of strikes at the fields in 1938–9, but disappeared forever when war engulfed Burma. Watson's reforms at the fields after 1945 brought in what a later manager called 'an age of colourless conformity to a card-indexed pattern of mind and action governed by "dos" and "don'ts" and "what will the next man think?"' In retrospect the golden age of larger-than-life characters had made up in entertainment value what it had lost in over-compartmentalisation.

In Britannic House, Watson, Whigham and Harper annotated Gray's note on this topic and then reacted in writing to one another's comments, until the reader can almost hear the men carrying on a four-way debate. When Gray defended the existing office supremacy over technical men with the time-honoured phrase, 'We do not keep a dog and then do all the barking ourselves', Watson queried, 'Are we not dealing here with complaints by the dog that he is not allowed to bark?' The restriction of fish knives and forks to the élite seemed to Gray rather petty, perhaps 'a relic of the old days when some of our Americans [amended by Watson to 'men'] would not have known what they were meant for'. Harper dismissed complaints about cutlery as 'significant of the narrow outlook some men acquire'.

Although Watson had kept his own staffs busy on reconstruction work, even his great energy and persistence had little galvanising effect on the bureaucrats in Whitehall. Having endured four months of total official silence, in July 1942 he proposed to the Petroleum Department that he should be permitted to order production and refining plant immediately, for shipment at the earliest possible opportunity to a safe place as near to Burma as possible. That plant would then be forwarded and installed 'the moment we can get back – just behind our advancing army', he suggested. Once again, no answer. In mid-August he wrote formally to the secretaries of both the Petroleum Department (by then part of the newly created Ministry of Fuel and Power) and the Department of Overseas Trade, setting out this proposal in some detail.

In fact, totally different plans were in the wind. After consulting with Bridgeman of the Petroleum Department, who then happened to be in Calcutta, the Commander-in-Chief in India, Lord Wavell, proposed that same August to set up an oil reconstruction unit for Burma, composed of production and refining experts who knew the country well. In Burmah Oil's London office, Gray had been appointed co-ordinator. At the end of September he put forward two alternative plans. Scheme A would permit a reasonably high level of production within three months by new wells being drilled in the potentially highly productive field of Chauk. Scheme B, on the other hand, would secure small quantities more quickly by the restoration of existing wells. The former would require portable drilling and topping equipment to be held in readiness near the Indian border. As most equipment could be obtained only from the United States, and as substantial delays were inevitable, orders would have to be placed as soon as possible. Gray emphasised that both plans depended also on building up a nucleus of trained Burmese drillers and other technicians.

By December, specifications of the necessary equipment had been sent to India and to the British procurement office in Washington. Watson feared lest there might be a prolonged delay until officialdom had been able to translate those specifications into firm orders for manufacturers. In fact officialdom needed an authoritative personage, respected in military as well as civilian circles, to fit these requirements into an overall programme. The choice not surprisingly fell on Weva, still serving on the staff at GHQ Cairo. Having for months energetically fended off all attempts by higher authority to enmesh him in the oil side of the army's work, he now found himself (as he said) 'in real danger' when the War Office signal arrived, ordering him to London where he was to master-mind arrangements for heading a party of oil experts back to Burma on its eventual liberation. 'This was by no means my idea of fun,' he later admitted.[5] He had joined the army to see the world, not to sit around and wait perhaps for years on end, with infrequent bouts of active training to provide some diversion.

As usual with Weva, higher authority duly co-operated. The War Office was informed that he could not be spared indefinitely from his current duties, which included striving to reduce the inflated size of the Cairo headquarters staff. However, he could be released for a few weeks to draw up an informed report on how best the Burma oilfields rehabilitation should be organised, and recommend suitable personnel. He was soon on his way to Delhi. There, using to the full his skill for assembling a team of diligent and effective men and for exploiting his high-powered contacts to cut through red tape, he rapidly had the skeleton of a scheme worked out. C. W. Armstrong, who had been very active in the denial of the oilfields and was currently in the Indian army, was designated as the future leader. Having summarised his findings in a long signal to the War Office, Weva thankfully left Delhi for Cairo. In fact, Armstrong stayed long enough to lick the unit into shape, and then went to a more important job in the oil directorate of GHQ, India.

Another familiar name to become involved was that of Leslie Forster. In September 1942 Eric Berthoud, then an assistant secretary in the Petroleum Department, proposed him as a government representative on the technical side, to draw up in London an agreed plan with Burmah Oil, British Burmah and Indo-Burma and then go to India to act as a 'dispassionate civilian adviser' to the reconstruction unit. His superiors in the Petroleum Department jibbed at this idea, as they feared that Forster's earlier criticisms of Burmah Oil's non-technical staff in Burma had reduced his potential value as leader of a team in which the company would perforce be represented.[6]

In any case, by March 1943 the American authorities were coming round to the view that it would be preferable to build up the production of the oilfields in Assam to the maximum capacity of the Digboi refinery, and to construct a pipeline from there in support of the operations in Burma. Since there was no military advantage in using scarce resources for projects of no immediate use to the country's oil requirements, they argued that the rehabilitation of the Burmese fields should be abandoned for the time being. Forster, by then a member of the British Petroleum Mission in Washington, remained a useful adviser so long as he could be kept clear of involvement in

Burmah Oil's affairs. He forcefully argued that it would be impossible to rehabilitate oil production in Burma quickly enough to help military operational needs during the country's reconquest; he therefore agreed that the pipeline project – further discussed below – should take priority.

Despite this shift in thinking on the other side of the Atlantic, the British authorities continued to plan on the basis of the rehabilitation scheme. By May 1943 this had been agreed in outline by both the War Office in London and the Commander-in-Chief, India. Weva had worked on the assumption that there would be a gradual transition from the emergency military operations into civilian rehabilitation. Watson raised powerful arguments against this notion, which he felt would help to scupper his campaign for compensation over denial. So strong were his feelings that he imposed a ban on the discussion of Scheme A in company correspondence, even internally, since – he declared – that was solely a matter for the military authorities. The company, on the other hand, should concentrate on rehabilitation proper, which could not possibly start until after the military period had ended.

In July the requisition for the equipment needed was in the hands of the American army engineers in Washington. The personnel required would be 'combed out' from their wartime service. The reconstruction unit would concentrate on Chauk, as being potentially the most productive field in Burma.

In May 1943 R. I. Watson became chairman of Burmah Oil, when Cargill retired owing to poor health and advancing age. Many in the outside world assumed that he had held that post for years; he now combined it with the managing directorship. Notwithstanding the Americans' alternative plans, in the early summer he kept himself very active discussing Schemes A and B. Various members of Burmah Oil's staff came home to consult with the London office. Forster in Washington was busy drafting suggestions on how he saw Scheme A being carried out. Then in August 1943 an Anglo-American summit meeting was held in Quebec. Among other decisions made by the combined chiefs of staff was one that two pipelines should be built for carrying oil into northern Burma. The more important pipeline was to be from Calcutta north and then east to a tank farm near Digboi; that was put in hand immediately and completed in a few months, top priority being given to it. From there it went south-east, towards the border with China, to carry supplies to that country as well as Burma itself. The other pipeline, from the port of Chittagong to near Digboi, was also planned but not started until November 1944.

These two pipeline schemes, pursued with all the vigour that the United States authorities could command with their vast war potential, effectively put paid to any major diversion of resources into equipment for building up oil production in Burma itself for the military. Were that country to be rapidly recaptured by the allies – as indeed it was in due course – only weeks would pass between the oilfields being reoccupied and the liberation of Rangoon, where port facilities could no doubt be restored without delay to bring in oil by sea. Yet work on the planning of Schemes A and B continued until December 1943, when they were finally cancelled. That month Lord Louis Mountbatten, Supreme Allied Commander in South-East Asia, laid down two overriding principles for oil. First, to avoid straining lines of communication in Burma, no rehabilitation work should be undertaken during the campaign itself. Secondly, production at Chauk should be resumed only after Rangoon had been opened to non-military traffic, and oil operations should then be undertaken only by civilian resources.

A severe setback for the oil companies was that all the plant and equipment ordered for Scheme A would no longer be earmarked for Burma. They would therefore have to make their own ordering arrangements for plant, with such assistance as the British government could give in obtaining priority – likely to be somewhat meagre. These arrangements, having been approved by the chiefs of staff in London, were definitive and not subject to modification in any way. Bridgeman and his senior Petroleum Department colleagues drafted a letter to explain matters to Watson, but did not have the heart to send it. Instead, they called him in and personally broke the news as gently as possible.[7] His comments have not survived, but it must have been a nasty blow to him. If the company were to be left on its own by government in future efforts to restore the

Burmese oil industry, would it find itself being cold-shouldered in a similar way over compensation for denial?

Watson had kept the compensation issue firmly in his sights over the two years or so since the denial. He had in his possession certified copies of all relevant documents, notably demolition orders from the civil and military power. Although he had earlier dropped hints about compensation in his correspondence with Whitehall, not until December 1942 did he, and representatives of the other oil companies, receive a summons to the Burma Office, where two middle-ranking officials interviewed them. Dorman-Smith in Simla, when informed of the meeting, thought it a mistake not to have deployed 'bigger Burma [Office] guns' for this clearly crucial discussion.[8] Watson in his turn was unfavourably impressed with the 'dingy and untidy room' in which they met to exchange information and ideas on oil reconstruction and how it should be paid for. 'I can only hope', he told Roper, 'that these men's minds can rise above, and are in no way reflected by, their present surroundings.' To him the symbolism was the more striking as the officials seemed to be 'groping in the dark' over how to go about tackling their problems. The meeting left him feeling depressed and disquieted.

About the only original idea thrown out by these officials was a 'feeler' over possible Burmese state participation in the oil companies. Dorman-Smith had for months been consistently urging this as the only device for heading off friction in Burma after the war. Watson at once blocked the suggestion, ostensibly because it would provoke international complications such as Anglo-Iranian had experienced in certain corners of the globe as a result of being partly state-owned. Instead, he presented a decidedly gloomy scenario of the post-war oil world: perhaps one-third of pre-1942 oil reserves in Burma lost for good through denial, Burma very probably losing tariff protection and also its former geographical freight advantages once the Persian Gulf rather than the Gulf of Mexico was accepted on the basis of pricing; and government over-milking the firms in Burma, as in the past, through high taxes and royalties. The only way of keeping the oil companies there afloat would thus be by adequate financial compensation.

This particular sparring match was resumed in February 1943. Watson was part of a delegation, representing other firms as well as oil companies, to meet L. S. Amery, Secretary of State for India and Burma, to discuss their problems.[9] The last time his and Watson's path had crossed was in 1924: as First Lord, Amery had then helped to overthrow the scheme concocted by Shell Transport & Trading and Burmah Oil to create an all-British oil company by a merger of Burmah Oil with Anglo-Persian and Shell. Sir David Monteath, the Permanent Under-Secretary, later reported to Dorman-Smith about the 'rapid cross-fire' between Amery and Watson, with neither side yielding an inch, so that what might have been a fruitful session turned out to gratify no one.

Monteath was not alone in harbouring suspicions that Watson, not to put too fine a point on it, was turning into a bit of a bore. Watson, for his part, would have retorted that it was justice he was after, and as the parable in the good book expressed it, the aggrieved widow had to pester the unjust judge unmercifully in order to secure her rights: although not a widow, he was still trustee of the many widows and orphans who held Burmah Oil shares. Rather crassly, Monteath commented to Dorman-Smith apropos that February meeting, 'I wish they [the business men] hadn't shareholders to look after the interests of. I'm sure that without that handicap they would be quite easy to handle.'[10] Maybe that was so, but the undeniable truth was they they *did* have shareholders, and were to that extent less amenable to bureaucratic pressures.

After an informal talk with Watson and his colleagues from British Burmah and Indo-Burma in March, Monteath formed the view that they were getting 'a bit sticky and manoeuvring for position'. According to him, their two main worries were whether the British government would grant them sufficient compensation to allow them to restart operations on a scale commensurate with their former size, and whether the political future of Burma would be stable enough to afford them indefinite security of tenure. 'In fact', Monteath continued, 'what they are asking for. . . is a certainty to bet on.' He dismissed them as 'kittle cattle'; that is, difficult customers. On the other hand, Monteath was clearly banking on their resolve to stay in Burma, since he felt there would be plenty of pickings still to be had. 'All we have to do', he confided to Dorman-Smith, 'is to break down their stickiness and disperse their apprehensions without consciously leading them up the garden [path], the end of which no man can see.'[11] This breathtakingly cynical remark well confirms the poverty of ideas in the Burma Office, already discerned by Watson.

Overriding everything in the debate about Burma's post-war affairs was its likely constitutional future. The war cabinet had in August 1942 considered a memorandum by Dorman-Smith which recommended that the British government should provide massive funds for rebuilding Burma. During the reconstruction period – up to five years – there would be direct rule, during which the governor should hold the widest possible consultations with Burmese opinion to see how best to fulfil Whitehall's pledge of complete self-government, and to avoid what he called 'reviving the bad feelings of pre-war Burma'. The cabinet decided to instruct Dorman-Smith to produce detailed studies of reconstruction for Burma: it could go no further because the prime minister, Winston Churchill, resolutely refused to add to existing declarations on self-government. The Chancellor of the Exchequer, Sir Kingsley Wood, was equally cagey on the financial side, saying – as he did when the matter came up again before the war cabinet in April 1943 – only that he would give what assistance he could for restoring destroyed property, but that Burma could not expect preference over others, despite being a British possession.[12]

These discouraging noises from the loftiest political quarters in London did not prevent lively debates from taking place on Burma's future. As Drysdale had privately shown, one of the allegedly bad features of the pre-war set-up, which therefore seemed ripe for reforming proposals, was the dominant position of the British firms there. In October 1942 Amery warned Dorman-Smith that, according to representations made to him – it is not clear by whom – Burmese suspicions of European firms and of the British government's apparent backing of them could well provoke accusations that Whitehall was using the war as a pretext to entrench even further the power wielded by British commerce in Burma.[13]

Predictably, Watson would have none of that. Burmah Oil at least, he argued, could claim an excellent record in the country. His letter of August 1942 to the Department of Overseas Trade had set out the company's impressive contributions both to government revenue in Burma and to public welfare there. In 1940, for instance, it paid over in royalties, duties and taxes about £1.25 million, with a further contribution of over £4.3 million to the revenues of India from imports to the subcontinent. On the welfare side, the company directly employed 17,500 people and provided housing, schools, health services, co-operative stores and provident funds for the benefit of those workers and their dependants: perhaps as many as 100,000 out of 17 million souls in Burma. The total wage bill for Asiatic workers and European and Asiatic supervisory staff topped the £1 million mark, at a time when Burma's net domestic product has been estimated as the equivalent of £66 million.

Watson could also have pointed to the comparatively small amount of local resentment over the company's activities in pre-war Burma. As U Tin Tut, the governor's reconstruction adviser, put it in 1943, 'The exploitation by the Burmah Oil Company of the bulk of the mineral oil resources of Burma has evoked from Burma nationalists no cry beyond that of asking for a more adequate Burmese share of the resulting employment.'[14] People in the country as a whole had next to no interest in how big business was financed; the efforts before 1939 of a Home Rule Party leader to induce them to take up shares in an indigenous oil-refining company had failed abysmally.[15] At the same time, the dividends paid out by Burmah Oil in 1940 – almost entirely to people who lived outside Burma – amounted to over £2.36 million. To be sure, some of the underlying earnings had come from Burmah-Shell or Assam Oil in India and part from investment in Anglo-Iranian and elsewhere. Yet even allowing for that, substantial money derived from the development of Burmese resources was undoubtedly being drained overseas.

The breathing space provided by the Japanese occupation was therefore seen by some as an appropriate one in which to consider how to meet likely Burmese aspirations after the war. The political climate had been radically transformed when the former prime minister Ba Maw and his colleagues, in Japanese-occupied Burma, had issued the Burmese declaration of independence in August 1943. Their resolve was in future to use their own efforts to exploit the province's abundant resources, including oil, with the help of Japanese experts who would provide technical training to the Burmese. The free world knew well that this was frankly a puppet regime, in which there would all too soon be complete disillusionment once independence turned out to be a sham. Yet, to use one of Watson's favourite metaphors, the clock had been put forward, and after the war the most strenuous resistance could be expected should the British authorities make efforts to turn it back.

In the years 1942 to 1944, then, there were some in British circles who pressed for change, and others who felt strongly that the time for change was by no means ripe. The latter included the staff of the Burma Office, paralysed by inertia as well as their Secretary of State's inability to wring a more forward-looking policy out of the prime minister. It seemed to be not only the department's décor that was sorely in need of refurbishment. Its officials thought mainly in terms of tinkering with the 1935 constitution, which had given a measure of self-rule to Burma, without paying regard to the post-1942 realities. Watson appeared to favour caution, and the starkest expression of his thinking to date appeared in a private and confidential note he put to the board in November 1944. For the first time he admitted that his very positive attitude, ever since denial, towards rehabilitation had been partly tactical rather than springing from conviction. Any vacillating on his part, he believed, might have lost Burmah Oil irretrievably the right to future oil concessions and to the priorities over plant, machinery and shipping he had so nearly gained.

In reality, his note continued, he could not make a definitive decision about going back into Burma until he had clear evidence about likely replacement costs and until government was more positive than hitherto about meeting denial claims. He estimated that in the harsher immediate post-war world, trading profits would shrink to perhaps no more than one-eighth of those in 1938–40, at a time when considerable sums would have to be ventured on yet further geological surveys. All in all, therefore, it should not be taken for granted that the company would return to Burma. He might instead have to find less speculative outlets for its funds, or even to put the company into liquidation and distribute the proceeds to shareholders. In short,

> It may be that we have come to the end of the job we specifically set out to do in 1902 [when the company was reconstructed], and it seems opportune, and in any case desirable, that we should carefully review the new situation.

The board accepted the paper; regrettably, the minutes give no particulars of the discussion that must have taken place. This seems to have been the only time when Watson despaired of being able to stay in Burma: his gloomy attitude may have been an opportunist one, or he may genuinely have been suffering from war-weariness, as many were at the outset of the sixth year of war.

Of the senior men anxious for change, the guiding spirit was Dorman-Smith, who endlessly chafed at his servitude as governor-in-exile in an intolerably overcrowded Simla. Having no serious day-to-day decisions to make, he concentrated on reconstruction matters, writing letter after letter to Amery, deploring what he branded as the 'sad lack of imagination within the sombre corridors of the Burma Office', and asking (with no lively hope of an answer), 'Are we going all out to make a first-class job of reconstruction, or are we to be content with a very timid approach?'[16] He strove to induce private businesses to develop positive reconstruction plans, by convening meetings of their representatives in India. Watson allowed Roper to join in these meetings, but only on a personal and informal basis.

At an early meeting with Roper in October 1942, Dorman-Smith discussed with him Burmah Oil's possible role in the post-war world. When the governor asked how far the Burmese would be given a greater managerial part in the company as a whole, Roper was not forthcoming: he saw no reason to suppose that the limited Burmanisation policy, which the company had been pursuing for some years, would be any more effective than previously in bringing Burmese into higher management.

Dorman-Smith continued to exert pressure on Roper and the other oil company representatives. In May 1944 he suggested that, just as they expected the government of Burma to have a coherent policy towards private capital, so private capital should itself have a broader policy towards Burma than simply one of making profits. The initial reactions to that reasonable proposition were encouragingly positive, and most of those concerned openly expressed their willingness actively to encourage Burmese participation in the management of their enterprises. Such statements, the governor replied with no little gratification, would go a long way towards meeting the perfectly legitimate grouses of the Burmese people.[17] Roper appears to have kept silent at the meeting. He knew perfectly well that Watson's existing mood of apprehension gave little hope of Burmah Oil pursuing a radical path in that direction for a while at least.

One question affecting the post-war organisation of Burma's oil industry was both urgent and somewhat delicate. Was there any sense in maintaining three different companies in the country, or had the time come to consider a merger? In the early post-denial months, as shown above, the merits of a single refinery had been discussed, but at no more than the technical level. A year later the suggestion came from Dorman-Smith's reconstruction team for Burma: this was indeed a piquant reversal of the consistent anti-monopoly attitudes which the governments in India and Burma had displayed over the years. It was delicate because the two smaller companies would inevitably feel that their identities would be lost in the giant Burmah Oil.

In November 1943 Watson produced a lengthy memorandum on the possible merger of the three companies. He deployed two powerful arguments: first, merger could be a means of keeping down costs in very difficult post-war conditions. 'It may not be too much to say', he asserted, 'that, without such unification, some considerable portions at least of the Burma [oil] industry have little, if any, hope of economic survival.' Second, a complete merger was the logical culmination of all his efforts to build up marketing agreements, not only with the Shell group in Burmah-Shell, but also with British Burmah, Indo-Burma, Attock Oil, and others. These agreements had been of considerable mutual benefit. The only area of competition remaining between the companies in Burma was the oilfields, 'where we have all chased each other to offset and have all pursued our independent ways in securing concessions.' [Offsetting was the practice of extracting some of what could have been rivals' oil by drilling at the limits of concession blocks.] Merger would end such squabbles and make for more orderly production.

He then opened negotiations with the companies involved; however, matters proceeded slowly. There were all too many problems to settle, a fundamental one being how to agree on valuations to determine the respective merger shares. Not until July 1944 did they decide that 77 per cent should go to Burmah Oil, 17 per cent to Indo-Burma and 6 per cent to British Burmah. Subsequent inter-company discussions revealed that, on the subject of the companies' social amenities for employees, the normally cautious Watson appeared positively liberal compared with others. The Indo-Burma man, for instance, wanted to abolish the labour office (see Vol. I p.151), which dealt with recruitment and the like, as an expensive 'luxury'; in his eyes it had simply engendered suspicion and caused strikes. He also argued that the company's schools should be closed down and education left entirely to the state, while co-operative stores were 'another winner for the strike-monger.' Watson vigorously defended such institutions, many created on his initiative and therefore a source of great personal pride to him. The companies then arranged to set up planning committees to undertake the detailed work that would be required.

Also in July 1944, Watson instructed Roper to request from the government of Burma, still exiled in Simla, formal approval of the proposed merger, and an assurance that all prospecting licences and leases granted to the constituent companies could be freely transferred to the new combine. In September the government replied. It was prepared to welcome a merger in so far as that would promote a more economic development of Burma's oil resources. However, since a complete monopoly would not be permitted, outside interests would be free to apply for future concessions. Nothing was said on such questions as Burmanisation. Watson's correspondence with the Burma Office raised more specialised questions, seeking pledges that a merger would not jeopardise the respective companies' claims for compensation, and that they would not find themselves as a combine having to pay higher taxes in Britain.[18] The war ended before the merger plans had reached any definitive stage.

In the closing months of the war, there was at last some movement on Burma's political future. In November 1944 a group of seven Conservative members of parliament issued an unofficial report, called *Blue-Print for Burma*.[19] They had done a thorough job, consulting nearly all the leading personalities in Britain who had commercial and industrial interests in Burma: whatever evidence Watson submitted has now been lost. Above all, the MPs accepted the need for an unequivocal declaration on full self-government for Burma, even though reconstruction would probably require direct rule for up to six years after liberation. They tacitly recognised that the Burma Office had outlived its usefulness, by advocating the transfer of Burmese affairs in Whitehall to the somewhat more open-minded Dominions Office. Watson could well have been one of those pressing for a further point they made, worded as follows:

> British firms operating in Burma should be entitled to compensation for material loss or damage arising out of the war or the enemy occupation, but full compensation should only be paid to firms that are willing to re-start their operations on a satisfactory basis.

The government of Burma, they continued, would normally be expected to meet that bill but, in accordance with a pledge made in October 1942, the British authorities must stand ready to supplement the resources set aside by the Rangoon government.

The MPs clearly took heed of Dorman-Smith's warnings that Burmese nationalism was a powerful force to be reckoned with, and the voice of a younger Watson in the 1920s, if not in his riper years in the 1940s, can perhaps be heard in the following sentence:

> We are impressed by the opinion of the men with large industrial and business interests in Burma that during the post-war period every effort should be made to carry the goodwill of Burmans in the task of constitution-making, even to the extent of taking political risks.

This report as well as pressure from other notables, such as Mountbatten, led Winston Churchill to agree very grudgingly in December 1944 to set up a cabinet committee that would give serious thought to the future of Burma. During the early months of 1945 – when General Slim was beginning his advance into northern Burma – the war cabinet's India committee, chaired by the deputy prime minister Clement Attlee, considered in great detail possible political steps for Burma that would both ensure stable economic conditions for reconstruction and go some way towards satisfying Burmese aspirations. Dorman-Smith attended a meeting in London held that March; as it happened, a day or so before Mandalay was recaptured. On the question of British firms returning to Burma, he envisaged that, as new resources might not be readily available from other countries, those firms would have to make the fullest use of existing equipment. The Chancellor of the Exchequer, the dour Sir John Anderson, chillingly declared,

> It should be our business to ensure that business firms etc. were not allowed to wait to see what the government were going to do. If they had property in the country [Burma] it was their business to look after it. . . . They must take all steps reasonably open to them to protect their assets, and we on our side must be on guard against any attempt to blackmail us into paying compensation to them, otherwise the firms or individuals concerned would stand back.[20]

His words, uttered in a secret committee, showed him to be the first of many Chancellors who would give little comfort to Burmah Oil over the compensation issue.

The upshot of these and other ministerial deliberations was a White Paper, issued in May 1945, which laid down British government policy towards Burma.[21] It fully accepted that the foundations of the country's economic and social life had been very badly battered by invasion, enemy occupation and then reconquest. Until agriculture and other essential industries that were the country's life-blood had been rebuilt, political reconstruction, including plans for general elections, would not be practicable. The governor would therefore run the country by decree for three years, helped by a mainly official executive council: to be sure, an improvement on the five or six years' period of direct rule earlier recommended.

This blueprint, admirable as it was in many ways, covered

almost every aspect except the one of most direct concern to the Burmese. They had already enjoyed at least nominal independence under the rule of Japan; however illusory that had turned out to be, and however much the economic and social structure had been allowed to decay in the traumatic occupation years, the principle had been won. Precisely as Dorman-Smith had feared, the total absence of clear pledges from Whitehall about control of the country's economic institutions being transferred to Burmese hands could only nourish suspicions that political progress was being deliberately held back until British business had deeply entrenched itself once again. A volatile, and even explosive, situation was therefore building up, and could well be expected to come to a head very shortly after liberation.

Notes

1 The correspondence between Watson and the Petroleum Department can be followed in PRO POWE 33/653–8, 'Burma-Rehabilitation of Oil Industry' March 1942 to May 1945. These six files are indispensable sources both for relations between Burmah Oil (mainly Watson) and the Petroleum Department (in the Ministry of Fuel and Power from June 1942 onwards) and for the twists and turns of Whitehall policy – or absence of policy – until the end of the war in Europe.

2 A full copy of Forster's report is in IOR, M/3/980, 'Denial Scheme'. Reactions to this report are in ibid. and in M/3/796, 'Effect of Denial Schemes', especially report of H. G. Wilkie, ICS, 1942, Chapter 2 on Oil Denial.

3 IOR, M/3/980, comments by Searle and Johnston, Burma Office, 21 October 1942.

4 M. Collis, *Trials in Burma*, Penguin edn 1945, p. 53.

5 Abraham, *Time Off*, p. 38.

6 PRO POWE 33/653 Memo by E. Berthoud (with comment by Sir W. Brown, Secretary Petroleum Department, Ministry of Fuel and Power), 4 September 1942.

7 PRO POWE 33/658, meeting of Bridgeman with Watson, 14 December 1943.

8 IOR, MSS Eur E 215 IV, letter to Amery, 23 February 1943.

9 IOR, M/3/1355, note of deputation to Amery, 17 February 1943.

10 IOR, MSS Eur E 215 III, Monteath to Dorman-Smith, 12 March 1943.

11 Ibid., Monteath to Dorman-Smith, 26 April 1943.

12 H. Tinker (ed.), *Burma: The Struggle for Independence I*, HMSO, 1983, pp. 25–6. This two-part series comprises (mainly official) documents on constitutional relations between Britain and Burma from 1 January 1944 until independence; the first volume closes at 31 August 1946.

13 IOR, MSS Eur E 215 II, Amery to Dorman-Smith 24 October 1942.

14 Tinker, *Burma: Struggle I*, p.30.

15 Indian Statutory Commission XI. *Memoranda Submitted by Government of Burma*, 1930, p. 22.

16 IOR, MSS Eur E 215 VI, Dorman-Smith to Amery, 13 February and 12 March 1944.

17 Ibid., Dorman-Smith to Amery, 30 May 1944.

18 IOR, M/3/1641. 'Contemplated Merger by Burmah Oil Company', correspondence of Roper with government of Burma, 3 April 1944 onwards.

19 Tinker, *Burma: Struggle I*, pp. 70–3.

20 Ibid., pp. 190–1.

21 Command Paper Cmd 6635 (1945), ibid., pp. 262–4.

CHAPTER V

Burma: Liberation and Independence 1945–8

In April 1945 British forces recaptured the Burmese fields. Yenangyaung fell on the 22nd after two days' fighting and with remarkably few allied casualties: three years plus a week after the former demolition of the assets there. The Burma Oilfields Rehabilitation Unit was not far behind the advancing armies. It had left Digboi in mid-March and motored down the road, by then a metalled one, into Burma. Having seen its original reconstruction role down-graded, it was at first purely a reconnaissance party, under the command of an American colonel. Four of his team were Burmah Oil men, one geologist and two engineers among them.

Between 8 April and 4 May they successively carried out surveys of Yenangyat, Chauk and then Yenangyaung. Although of historical rather than immediately practical value, their report was anxiously awaited. How much oil had the Japanese succeeded in raising? Many experts had confidently assumed that denial had been so thorough as to deprive the enemy of any chance to produce very much; yet it turned out that a good deal had been raised. Unable to find any written records, the team had to build up a picture of what had happened from personal observation and the questioning of those on the spot.

The former Burmese employees who met the unit at the fields greeted with derision the idea that the Japanese invaders had known anything about how to work or organise an oilfield. Instead, the Burmese artlessly claimed that it was their own efforts that had been responsible for the output achieved. They had been able with ease to pinpoint the better producing wells, fish junk out of them, assemble production teams and get steam boilers going from among the many scattered around the fields, where necessary cannibalising damaged machines.

The very effective demolition of the power station had ruled out any chance of using electricity, but the already antiquated steam engines for pumping and drilling could be made to work more or less efficiently, with a good deal of improvisation. Burmese noses must have been put out of joint when, from May 1942 onwards, teams of Japanese military oil workers began to move in and undertake the kinds of jobs that were beyond indigenous resources, such as installing pumps to restore a continuous water supply and rebuilding the repair workshops. They also reconditioned a number of topping plants and repaired the pipelines that connected up the various fields. A damaged 2,000KW turbo-alternator at Syriam power station was made to work, and provided a limited amount of electric power for the area.

The Japanese team checked through the main pipeline to Rangoon in August 1943; after draining it of water and making the necessary repairs they operated it spasmodically, on average about one day a month, although crude oil could have been of little use down in the capital with the refineries entirely out of action. Of the sixty storage tanks destroyed at Syriam's tank farm, the Japanese were able to repair only four. The three usable distillation units there were dismantled for shipment outside Burma, and one even ended up in a remote part of the Dutch East Indies. Almost all items of any value from the refineries, even down to firebricks, cork and insulating material for pipes, were crated up. However, the allied naval blockade prevented most of those items from leaving Burma.

The Japanese seem to have achieved maximum production rates in the early months of 1944. From then on, Burmese labour became increasingly disaffected, complaining vociferously of low wages and insufficient food. Allied bombing, too, had caused destruction, particularly of workshops, and disrupted both drilling and longer-term rehabilitation projects in the fields. The most crippling bottlenecks were in transport and in shortages of tins and other containers. Even so, enough crude oil was raised to meet all requirements in Burma for the time being, while no fewer than eleven topping plants turned out motor spirit: so anxious were the Japanese to extract as much petrol as possible from those plants that the octane rating was exceptionally low, causing much mischief to the engines of the vehicles using it, and making frequent overhauls all too necessary.

In 1945, on the eve of the allies' reoccupation, Japanese efforts over denial in the fields were very patchy. Hampered as they were by a shortage of explosives, they also lacked the ingenuity of the 1942 allied demolition teams. They caused some damage by dry-firing boilers and smashing gauges, pumps and other machinery with hammers, but they put out of action different parts of many machines so that it was relatively easy to reassemble a number that worked after a fashion. They also left behind large quantities of crude oil and petrol, making no efforts to drain this off into the ground.[1]

Watson took a wry interest in the rehabilitation unit's findings. Earlier he had wasted much time in unsuccessfully pleading with the authorities to let him see the aerial reconnaissance photographs. But in any case, after reading the denial reports, he had formed the conviction that the Japanese would have been unable to turn out any worthwhile quantities of oil. When one of his oilfields employees came home in about 1944 and had the courage – or foolhardiness – to put the contrary view to Watson, he was told firmly, 'You say the Japanese are producing oil in Burma. We don't believe you.'

In fact, when the rehabilitation unit's report of June 1945 reached Britain in August, its informed calculations were that the Japanese had raised about 2.7 million barrels over the three years of occupation, compared with the 7 million barrels produced in Burma during 1941, and also no less than 4,000 million cubic feet of natural gas, enough to make 4 million gallons of petrol. Watson did not repine at this unexpected news, but cheerfully sent in a bill to the Treasury in London for the cost of the crude oil and gas actually used, which he valued at £2.7 million. The authorities doubted very much whether such a claim was justified and suggested that it should be lodged as part of Japanese reparations; in the event Watson never saw that money.

The company's geologists subsequently reworked the rehabilitation unit's data in the light of their own observations, and estimated that Japanese oil production for each of the occupation years had been roughly as follows (in millions of barrels):

June–December 1942	0.2
1943	0.6
1944	1.2
January–March 1945	0.2
	2.2

This revised total, of which Chauk contributed 1.2 million and Yenangyaung 1.0 million barrels, was some 18 per cent less than the original estimate.

Having completed their report, members of the rehabilitation unit went on to carry out much minor but useful work. They improvised electricity and water supplies for two local civilian hospitals, set up workshops and stores, got some wells producing again and restored to working order topping plants that were still serviceable. They also constructed a roadside filling station, where convoys of petrol lorries could load up each day with supplies. Although only a small percentage of the allies' total oil requirements could then be produced in Burma, at least it effectively contributed to the resources needed in the final months of the war, thus helping to economise on imports and shipping space.

After the First World War, Sir John Cargill had read out in his chairman's address at the 1919 annual general meeting the names of the seven Burmah Oil men – six in the army and one in the navy – who had died on active service. By contrast, no such list was published of casualties in the Second World War. Subsequent researches have shown that twenty-one British members of staff, from the London office or the east, were killed in action or on active service. A further six, plus an American driller, died from other causes during the war.[2] The provident fund accounts of the bachelors killed on active service or by enemy action were passed on to the next of kin, but no gratuities were paid; doubtless any parent who applied to the company was duly helped. Of the married men killed on active service, one had died of heat-stroke during the denial operations and two were torpedoed on the journey to Britain. The widows received an *ex gratia* payment and where necessary their provident fund was topped up to provide a capital sum for the purchase of an appropriate annuity. Those who died in harness were treated no less generously than those killed in action.

No one seems to have chronicled the reopening of the Rangoon office or the early months of its new existence. Although parts of the Burmese capital had been badly damaged, the Merchant Street area, where it was situated, seems to have escaped devastation. However, the office was a shambles, with no furniture or equipment. The files had all been destroyed or removed before the evacuation, and the control of production and refining and the resumption of marketing needed to be organised virtually from scratch.

A new general manager for the East was now in charge. Early in 1945 the newly-knighted Sir Harold Roper had left for home from Calcutta and Paul Lingeman had taken over. Having achieved a distinguished flying record in the First World War, he was later remembered as a quiet and friendly man with first-rate powers of leadership. As the official residence at Greenbank was intact, he shared it on his return with four or five assistants who could not find suitable accommodation elsewhere. This hospitality – at much inconvenience to himself and his family as all the residence's rooms had to be brought into use – earned the criticism of his opposite numbers in other Rangoon firms: the assistants put that criticism down to the latters' guilty consciences at not offering similar facilities to members of their own staffs.

Until well into 1946 the office work was somewhat different from what it had been before 1942, the need for improvisation taking precedence over the application of rules sanctified by long usage. A team of employees was built up in Syriam, but there seemed little chance of refining there for many years to come. The first task was to rebuild housing for the senior staff, after which the clearing of the wreckage could begin; the dockside installations had to be repaired for the bringing in of imported oil products by sea. However, some of the staff were able to begin the preparatory work out of which a new refinery would eventually rise.

At the oilfields, the emergency military administration was in charge, producing 234,000 barrels between May and December 1945, from which the topping plants at Chauk produced 52,000 barrels of motor spirit and 12,000 barrels of kerosene. In March 1946 the companies were allowed to take over again, and were able to plan the building up of output. A large number of wells both in Chauk and later in Yenangyaung were patiently cleared of junk by a few old-time drillers, using ingenious improvised 'fishing' tools. As expected, Chauk was given priority as the most productive field. A new topping plant was set up there, with a maximum annual capacity of 180,000 barrels. Then in April the company resumed distribution throughout Burma, but most of the country received imported products. It looked as if three or four years might well pass before the disrupted and unsettled communications through-out the country, as well as the totally inadequate storage facilities and equipment then available, could be fully re-medied. Meanwhile, the geologists had moved back to resume work that had been necessarily suspended after the outbreak of war.

With the end of hostilities in Europe and Japan, radical changes were beginning to take place in the company's top management in London. In December 1945 the 68-year-old Gilbert Whigham retired as assistant managing director on medical grounds. He remained as director until the end of 1946 and died in 1950. He had been the model lieutenant to Watson: tactful, competent and resourceful. Hubert Ashton also retired in 1945, without having been made a director, to become a Conservative county councillor in Essex and later a member of parliament. He and Roper both sat on the Conservative benches throughout the 1950s, as members for Chelmsford and North Cornwall respectively.

However, earlier that year Weva, since 1944 Major-General W. E. V. Abraham, CBE, had returned, demobilising himself by simply reversing the procedure he had employed to get himself into the army: he declared to his military superiors that Watson could no longer do without him, and was flown home to be released into civilian life more or less on the spot. His routes in and out of the army were made easier by the fact that he never received any military pay. As Burmah Oil continued his salary, he felt it wrong to be remunerated twice over.[3] He was elected to the Burmah Oil board in November 1945. Watson, only one year younger than Whigham and having endured six punishing years of reverses and frustration in war, could not be expected to go on for very much longer. Yet he was keen if possible to see the company through its immediate post-war problems.

Late in July 1945 a Labour government, headed by Clement Attlee as prime minister, took office in Britain. It came in with few more concrete ideas on overall imperial policy than a feeling that, give or take some pockets of exploitation here and there, the British empire was to be cherished as a thing of value. The Lord President of the Council, Herbert Morrison, spoke with affection of the 'jolly old empire', while Ernest Bevin, unexpectedly appointed foreign secretary, had only a year or two earlier confided to Dorman-Smith that he hoped to see the resource-rich and tolerably peaceful Burma become 'a gem of the empire'.[4] Bevin's later privately expressed antipathy towards the policy of scuttle in India and Burma is well known, and his remark to the governor prompts the melancholy reflection of hindsight that Burma was destined within a few years to become the first jewel – if we except the always rather shaky southern Irish emerald – to detach itself completely from the imperial crown. In the whole cabinet, only Attlee and Cripps had ever visited Burma, for a total of sixteen days between them. It was decided at the highest level to continue the coalition policy, based on the White Paper published in May 1945, of working for the re-establishment and mainte-nance of pre-war forms of government in British possessions before contemplating any hand-over to indigenous rule.

The incoming Secretary of State for India and Burma was the veteran ex-agitator Lord Pethick-Lawrence. He had been born as long before as 1871, the same year in which the original Rangoon Oil Company had been established, when Mindon Min ruled at Mandalay, and David Sime Cargill was still a year or two away from his fateful journey of 1873–4 to Rangoon that had led to his involvement in Burmese oil. Amery described his successor to Dorman-Smith rather patronisingly as a 'nice old cup of tea', who was 'not likely to make any difficulties for you'.

To the Bishop of Rangoon, Dorman-Smith acknowledged that he would have liked 'a more adventurous soul' as Secretary of State.[5] However, at least the new man had some slight knowledge of Burmese affairs, gained from attendance at the round-table conference of 1931 on Indian self-determination.

It would have been interesting to have Watson's comments on the appointment of Pethick-Lawrence and on the future of Burma as he saw it in 1945. Unfortunately, the files have not survived. The cabinet's India and Burma Committee, headed by Attlee himself, decided in September 1945 that the oil industry in Burma should not be given priority for financial aid. Other sections of the country's economy, notably agriculture and rice cultivation, were considered to be in far greater need of immediate incentives for rehabilitation. As to the political future of Burma, Dorman-Smith professed himself a worried man. 'All I want to ensure is that His Majesty's Government do not trip up over the Burma hurdle' by prolonging the unpopular military rule there instead of working single-mindedly towards the restoration of a strong and broadly acceptable civilian government. In fact, it was he who was later to stumble and be brought down by events there.

A major problem for all concerned was to foresee the precise political system under which Burma could best operate in the post-liberation years. A military-run Civil Affairs Service (Burma) was set up under the Supreme Allied Commander, South-East Asia, a post held until May 1946 by Lord Louis Mountbatten. That organisation, known as CAS (B), had the twin tasks of restoring law and order in the shattered country and of doing what it could to rehabilitate its economic life by organising supplies of food, especially of rice. However essential for emergency reconstruction work, Dorman-Smith did not believe that the CAS (B) regime would be tolerated by the Burmese people for very long. Even before the Japanese surrender in August he suggested to Pethick-Lawrence the necessity of speeding up the return of civil government, as the only means of returning Burma to a 'road of constitutional advance'.

However, against the advice of senior service commanders –
particularly Mountbatten as Supreme Allied Commander –
Dorman-Smith had civilian government restored as early as
October 1945. He hoped, with the aid of his considerable
charm and carefully nurtured personal contacts, to rally
moderate opinion in Burma behind the policy of holding back
political change while allowing economic reconstruction to
proceed apace. Mountbatten's instinct, on the other hand, was
to seek friendship with elements which had collaborated with
the Japanese but had later come back to the British side:
notably leaders of the Anti-Fascist People's Freedom League,
known as AFPFL. The president of AFPFL was Aung San,
leader of the oilfields strike in 1938–9 and later collaborator
with the Japanese until 1944, when he came over to the allies.
Dorman-Smith both despised and mistrusted Aung San for
what he and those loyal Burmese exiles who had been with him
in Simla regarded as treachery and self-seeking. However,
Mountbatten took the more realistic if opportunistic view, that
Aung San was the only credible representative of the Burmese
with whom he could deal, and that view was eventually to
prevail. Despite Dorman-Smith's wooing of the moderates,
disturbances became more and more widespread, fomented by
people who, in the governor's eyes, were extremists as well as
traitors.

At this time, Burmah Oil had little success with the British
government over resolving financial matters, especially that of
war damage compensation. In March 1946 Dorman-Smith
reported to Pethick-Lawrence that Lingeman as general manager had told him of the company's intention of placing very
extensive orders for equipment, mainly in the United States.
The Burmah Oil directors therefore required as assurance that
the British government would advance them enough cash for
this purpose, while leaving the matter of compensation open for
future discussion.[6]

Pethick-Lawrence at once contacted the Treasury, which
judged that in Britain's current very straitened economic
circumstances, with its overseas financial commitments greatly
outstripping its depleted reserves, government assistance to
Burmah Oil was out of the question. In any case the company

was described as 'quite comfortably off', having already received £656,000 from the British government to repay the expenses of production and other items from February to April 1942, as described in Chapter III. This ministerial decision in Whitehall, affirming that the company could look for no generous treatment on the subject of compensation, was maintained by successive governments under both parties until parliament was finally persuaded to slam the door on the question twenty years later.

How true was it that Burmah Oil was comfortably off, and therefore presumed to be capable of meeting its immediate rehabilitation outlays? In 1941 its gross profit had been just under £4.9 million, of which some £3.5 million had come from its own companies operating in Burma and India, and the remainder from subsidiary companies and investments. By 1946 profits had fallen to £3.1 million; in real terms a drop of almost half as British retail prices rose by about 20 per cent between 1941 and 1946, but still enough to permit a very respectable 12½ per cent ordinary share dividend.

There was in 1946 a fall in direct operating profit from £3.5 million to £560,000, while the contribution of investments and subsidiaries had nearly doubled to almost £2.6 million. Much came from Burmah-Shell, but the steadily growing worldwide activities of Anglo-Iranian and Shell were producing enhanced dividend income from those companies, up from £400,000 in 1941 to £675,000 in 1946. If this trend continued, as it could be expected to do, Burmah Oil might be well on the way to becoming largely an investment company at the expense of its producing and trading functions.

Watson for his part felt very strongly that the company's performance and dividend record had nothing whatever to do with the government's obligations over compensation. When in January 1946 he submitted his claim for the denial in what became known as the Red Book, a 400-page printed volume containing inventories, at original cost, of assets in use at the time of denial, he valued these items at a total of just under £33 million. Even then, he made it clear that he expected to be reimbursed at the appreciably higher replacement cost.

Was he being unrealistic and unreasonable in the claims he was putting in? Many years before in 1930, Sir Charles

Innes – then governor of Burma – had remarked to Hubert Ashton who was then a senior assistant in Rangoon, 'Your Mr Watson is a very clever man, but there are times in life when a little compromise doesn't come amiss.' That remark had been passed back to Watson, who had neatly turned it by responding, 'It seems inherent in the very nature of government that we poor mortals have no opportunity of compromise but must in the end do what we are told.' If he still remembered that riposte, it was all too appropriate now. He found his hand being forced when in February 1946 Arthur Henderson as Under-Secretary of State announced that the government was setting up a claims commission for Burma and other Japanese-occupied countries, to register and assess claims for property lost or destroyed.[7] In June Watson informed Lingeman in Rangoon, 'We and others are of course claiming replacement costs.' Hence the actual sums to be claimed from government would be known only as the assets were replaced and the actual outlay determined. He therefore instructed Lingeman to avoid giving the authorities 'any idea that we are claiming for anything less than rehabilitation costs'.

The Burma Claims Commission knew how to deal with that one. When, in December, Watson met its secretary, J. L. Moffatt, who was about to leave to register claims in Rangoon, Moffatt laid down that all figures should be in the commission's hands by the end of March 1947. Thus the company's claim would have to be at historical cost. Even so, the Burmah Oil people concluded that notwithstanding his 'official mind', Moffatt appeared to be reasonable and anxious to help.

A fundamental weakness at home was that there was no central authority in Whitehall able to focus specifically on Burma's problems. The Secretary of State and his Under-Secretary, Arthur Henderson, as well as the Permanent Secretary Sir David Monteath, were necessarily involved mainly with India, where the British pledge to self-government was bedevilled by the mounting tension between the Hindus and Moslems. The civil servants in the separate Burma Office were as unhelpful as Watson had found them during the war, striving to enforce impossibly restrictive conditions such as an insistence that

Burma's remaining within the Commonwealth was non-negotiable, and subjecting each proposal by Dorman-Smith to minute and normally unconstructive scrutiny.

Not surprisingly, therefore, as 1946 wore on, the political situation in Burma deteriorated inexorably, and fatally for the British. When Dorman-Smith eventually offered Aung San and his AFPFL colleagues some posts on the executive council, they insisted on being given enough posts to give them a dominant position; when the governor would not concede that, they refused to join. From early that year they strove to undermine his administration through a protracted war of nerves, the easier to wage from within because of their plentiful agents and supporters in the various branches of government.

From March 1946 onwards, Pethick-Lawrence was absent heading a cabinet mission to India, in a vain attempt to halt the communal divisions there. Dorman-Smith unsuccessfully invited him to pay a flying visit to Rangoon so as to meet some of the political leaders and learn about events there at first hand. Attlee, who had in fact opposed the Rangoon visit, took overall charge of Burmese questions during the absence of the Secretary of State. A clear-minded man, he became irritated beyond endurance by the governor's lack of decisiveness in dealing with the AFPFL provocations, and by the increasingly incoherent advice he sent back to Whitehall. In June Dorman-Smith was recalled to London and virtually dismissed.[8]

Two months later a new governor, Sir Hubert Rance, arrived. He had been head of CAS (B) from 1945 to 1946 and was therefore familiar with the country. Whitehall, still ultra-cautious in its policy towards Burma despite the sacking of Dorman-Smith, instructed Rance to act within the framework of the May 1945 white paper – although the AFPFL's disruptive tactics had effectively made that document out of date – and certainly to make no promises about future independence. Almost at once Burma was paralysed by a country-wide police strike, followed by other crippling stoppages including some at the oilfields. Rance, with the authorities in London unrealistically passive and his top advisers in Rangoon less than sympathetic, saw that changes would have to take place.

In mid-November Rance put forward some powerful reasons for speeding up the pace of reform in Burma. Aung San, now designated the leader of the Socialist party, was in undisputed control of AFPFL and, since the recent strike, the police and civil servants had transferred their loyalty to him and his party; if the Socialists lost control, they might well desert to the far more hard-line Communists. Direct rule by the British, on the other hand, would require greater numbers of security forces than could, or indeed should, be committed. Hence Aung San and his senior colleagues, already offended because India had received a high-powered British mission – headed by the Secretary of State – whereas they had not, should be invited to London to discuss constitutional proposals. After some hesitation, Rance's suggestion was approved by the cabinet's India and Burma Committee on 26 November, and the Burmese delegation reached London on 9 January 1947.

For Burmah Oil, two matters were of paramount concern. One was that of war damage compensation, and the other was the possible threat of expropriation if and when independence was granted. On war damage, the Burmese delegation made it clear in Whitehall that the British must accept full financial responsibility; Dalton as Chancellor of the Exchequer had, however, already privately informed Pethick-Lawrence that Britain had assumed no such obligation; 'in any case', he added circumspectly, 'we do not yet know the size of the bill or the scale on which it may be possible to pay.' The India and Burma Committee of the cabinet accepted that the recently established War Damage Commission might well assess claims in Burma of as much as £100 million, with Burmah Oil's claim understood to be £50 million. However, the Rangoon government could scarcely be expected to pay compensation to European firms which had destroyed their property on British government orders. Pethick-Lawrence suggested that the two problems of war damage and nationalisation could be agreeably solved if the firms were expropriated by Burma and then given in sterling any compensation payments for which the home government had assumed responsibility. Some committee members felt that the 76-year-old peer was being unduly simplistic, and postponed his suggestion for further consideration – the last that was heard of it.[9]

The hostility of Ernest Bevin to independence for Burma, mentioned earlier, remained as uncompromising as ever. During the Burmese delegation's January visit, he sat next to Aung San at a luncheon but at first had little to say to him. He then turned and observed heartily in his booming voice, 'So we are going to give Burma away to you, are we? Well, you know what they say about the British, they gives something with one 'and, and they takes it back with the other.' As Bevin shook with laughter, Aung San appeared startled and then bewildered, but stayed silent.[10] Bevin could not have known that his Burmese guest, born and brought up in the oilfields area, felt passionately that British companies such as Burmah Oil and Steel Bros were out to swallow up smaller indigenous concerns and believed that these concerns could be made to flourish only by expropriating the Burmah Oils of this world. Any hint, however obviously in jest, that the crafty British might use Burma's economic weakness after independence as an opportunity to feather their own commercial nests, was highly injudicious. Yet Bevin was the only Foreign Secretary since Palmerston who could, and did, get away with such witticisms.

Before the end of January 1947, the delegation had struck a general accord with the British government, known as the Attlee-Aung San agreement. Under its terms, a constituent assembly was proposed and both parties would work together to bring about smooth and rapid progress towards independence. No record exists as to the reactions of Watson and his fellow-directors in London and the managers in Rangoon to these political developments. It is known, however, that the home committee of the Burma Chamber of Commerce, which represented the major businesses with interests in the country, met that month after the agreement was published, and perforce accepted the very far-reaching consequences for their businesses arising from independence: according to the target which AFPFL had set, that was expected to occur by the end of January 1948. A few weeks after the delegation arrived back in Rangoon, Attlee announced that British rule in India would terminate before mid-1948; when Aung San heard this news, he told Rance that 'Burma was now ahead of India in the bid for freedom, and that it was up to Burma to see that she maintained this lead'.[11] In fact, India became independent in August 1947, four and a half months before Burma.

One matter which remained outstanding was the proposal, mentioned in Chapter IV, to merge with the British Burmah and Indo-Burma companies. Despite prodigious amounts of correspondence between the three sets of directors, no concrete amalgamation plan had thus far been agreed, although the physical needs of reconstruction would necessitate their working very closely together. The very fat 'merger' files in the company archives show that until 1954, Burmah Oil was continuously negotiating with British Burmah and Indo-Burma for an outright amalgamation of oil interests in the country. These were gradually overtaken by the joint venture discussions with the government of Burma, so that the three companies concerned would enter the new partnership together. Hence the 'merger' as such never took place; however, Burmah Oil was empowered by the two other companies to negotiate the joint venture agreements, while having to keep the companies informed and obtain their consent to the successive moves. For simplicity, these inter-company consultations are therefore omitted from this account.

However, there was a risk that disclosure of the merger proposals might prejudice the claims, and in February 1947 Watson, Thomas McCreath – the Steel Bros man responsible for Indo-Burma's affairs in Britain, shortly to become a Burmah Oil non-executive director, and a representative of British Burmah, met civil servants of the Burma Office to explain about the intended merger and seek official assurances that the claims would not be prejudiced. The official reply, echoing the Treasury view, was that although Whitehall would not look askance at the merger, the oil companies could scarcely be singled out for special treatment. Watson therefore declared that he would take his case directly to the Treasury. The claim he actually put in, slightly adjusted from the Red Book total, was for approximately £31 million. This was made up as follows: cost of wells (net of oil in the ground) and equipment in the oilfields, £24.5 million; the pipeline about

£500,000, the Syriam refinery nearly £4 million, and stocks of crude oil and products about £2 million.

Although Watson regarded the claim on a historical cost basis as a poor second-best to replacement costs, he clearly expected it to be paid in full, as a debt of honour incurred in return for unstinted co-operation during the war. In fact British governments, acting as guardians of the taxpayer's interests, inevitably tend to look at the wider economic picture when it suits them, and 1947 turned out to be what the Chancellor of the Exchequer, Hugh Dalton, later called the '*annus horrendus*' for Britain.

For Burma, 1947 proved to be horrendous in a very different and more tragic way. On 19 July there occurred an event which as been described as one which 'above all others, has made and marred' that country's subsequent history: the massacre of Aung San and most of his cabinet. He was no more than 31, and seemingly on the threshold of supreme power in Burma. The slaughter was the work of U Saw, who had hoped to take over as prime minister. Instead, he was arrested and later executed; the absurd rumours that British business houses had subsidised this crime were easily disproved. Rance as governor showed a decisiveness which undoubtedly saved Burma from very widespread and perhaps catastrophic violence; he sent for U Nu, president of the recently elected consituent assembly, to take over as prime minister. Rance later judged that Aung San and his murdered associates, had they lived, might have avoided many of Burma's troubles over the succeeding years, as U Nu, although widely respected, did not have the dead man's strength of character.[12] On the other hand, Burmah Oil may well have won a reprieve, since the gentler U Nu did not have the same instinctive animosity towards the oil industry as had the dead leader.

Then in August 1947 an economic crisis erupted in Britain. Ministers, faced with a massive outflow of foreign reserves, were no longer able to honour their obligations, laid down as a condition in the previous year's loan from the United States, over the convertibility of sterling into other currencies. This was described by an authoritative historian as having torn the whole financial credibility of the Labour government into shreds.[13] In the wake of that unnerving crisis, it was Sir

Stafford Cripps who moved into the centre of Britain's political stage, and cut Watson's large denial claim down to a different concept of size.

Cripps had a good working knowledge of Indian and Burmese affairs: he had visited India in 1942 and had thereafter been a member of the war cabinet's India committee. Since Labour's accession to power he had, as shown above, attended the successor India and Burma Committee. The political events which preceded his first meeting with Watson are therefore of some significance. Early in September 1947, when the apparently inept handling of the convertibility question had evoked widespread criticisms that the ministers concerned were not up to their jobs, Cripps boldly requested Attlee to step down as prime minister in favour of Ernest Bevin. This displayed more courage than political nous, for Attlee calmly turned the tables on Cripps by securing an immediate denial from Bevin that he wanted the premiership, and then projecting Cripps upstairs to a newly-created post, that of Minister of Economic Affairs: in effect an overlordship, since he would take charge of both home and overseas economic policy.[14]

On 7 October, Cripps chaired an important meeting with a deputation from the home committee of the Burma Chamber of Commerce, to discuss the negotiations being held in Whitehall with the recently arrived Burma financial mission. Now that independence had been fixed for the beginning of 1948, a commercial agreement had to be hammered out. Cripps stressed that the Burmese mission had shown no anti-British bias, and that if the future independent government of Burma wished to expropriate or nationalise any concern, that government would be prepared to pay equitable compensation. However, Burmese ministers realised that they were short of both financial and technical expertise; thus hasty take-over measures were thought to be highly unlikely.

Watson, on behalf of the Chamber of Commerce as a whole, argued strongly for a provision in the agreement that future disputes on compensation between the government of Burma and any firms affected should be referred to an outside tribunal, preferably the International Court of Justice. Cripps sharply retorted that Burma would be an independent country which would resent anything likely to damage its self-respect. He

added that the mission had already made substantial concessions, and businessmen must be prepared to trust the Burmese
and go into the new regime in a spirit of mutual confidence and
goodwill. As the authoritative historian of Burma's transition
to independent power has commented, 'It was, perhaps,
surprising that many commercial and financial questions
concerning British firms in Burma were postponed for long-
term decision until later', instead of being definitely hammered
out as part of an overall settlement.[15]

Watson was far from happy with this over-trusting attitude,
and when he, Harper and McCreath met the financial mission
two days later, he put on his severest mood. He re-echoed his
sentiments of 1944 in taking a pessimistic view of the future of
Burma's oil industry unless it could discover new producing
areas and oil that was cheaper to raise. Even so, he declared,
the company felt that its duty lay in full commitment to Burma
and in developing the remaining resources there to the best of
its ability. He had therefore drawn up a five-year programme,
which would cost about £14–15 million. He also stressed
Burmah Oil's good record as employer, and its anxiety to bring
Burmese nationals into the top jobs; however, he was concerned that on the administrative side the more promising
candidates tended to be creamed off into the government
service or the legal profession.

He explained how the major oil companies such as Anglo-
Iranian and Shell, which enjoyed access to very low-cost oil,
had pledged themselves by successive agreements to give
Burmah Oil's products priority in the markets of both Burma
and India. The proposed merger with British Burmah and
Indo-Burmah, which had been approved in principle by the
government in Rangoon, would keep these agreements intact;
nationalisation, on the other hand, would automatically bring
them to an end. Even with a tariff advantage, expensive
Burmese oil would be up against, say, Persian oil which was the
cheapest in the world to produce.

When a member of the Burmese financial mission asked him
about a possible joint venture between government and the
Burmese oil companies, he declared that it would be intolerable
for the companies to have only, for instance, a 40 per cent
shareholding while being subject to contractual obligations

with which government as majority shareholders might not agree. With hindsight, it can be seen that Watson's refusal – because of his perfectly legitimate apprehensions about the future – to face the arguments of Dorman-Smith, Drysdale and others about the need to bring in Burmese management and capital, was to add to the problems that Burmah Oil would encounter in the coming decade or more.

These discussions involving the financial mission had studiously disregarded the question of compensation for denial. This was the key financial area where Whitehall had been unable to reach agreement with the Burmese, who categorically refused to accept liability for such compensation. As Dalton reported to Attlee on 11 October, the whole question was to be left undecided for the moment. Dalton believed that the delay could be turned to Britain's advantage: first, it would allow ministers to fit the issue of compensation in Burma into the wider context of compensation for war damage in the Far East generally, and second, the British claimant firms – including Burmah Oil – would be given time to test the validity of these claims in the Burmese courts. If their cases were upheld and the Burmese authorities then repudiated liability, the British government would be in a stronger bargaining position, so that if it had to make a contribution at all, it would be a purely *ex gratia* one. As Dalton put it,

> In the financial settlement I have refrained from cancelling a larger amount than £15 millions of Burma's indebtedness [totalling £52 million], which I might otherwise have been willing to do, against the possibility that we may have later to provide some contribution towards meeting the War Damage claims of British interests.

Attlee said he agreed.[16]

When Watson and Harper, with J. K. Michie, chairman of the home committee of Burma's Chamber of Commerce, met Cripps just over a week later, Cripps largely followed the Dalton line about the Burmese having refused to accept financial responsibility, but being ready to leave the question open for possible 'later adjustment'. Cripps therefore suggested that Watson and others with denial claims should bring friendly test cases against the Rangoon government in the Burmese courts. But, protested Watson, Burma was clearly a bankrupt country. In any case the whole history and logic of the denial operations pointed to responsibility lying clearly with the British government; statements to that effect had already been made in Parliament and in ministerial correspondence.

Cripps replied that Burma with its great rice-growing potential was not expected to remain bankrupt for long, and since there was what he cautiously termed an 'arguable case', it would be sensible to seek a legal judgement in Burma. Were that judgement to go against the plaintiffs, then they could sue the British government. He brushed aside the argument that it was unfair to subject the companies involved to continuing delays over compensation. However, he added, any company that found itself short of funds could call on the Chancellor of the Exchequer for a loan, as had happened in Malaya. He knew he was safe with Burmah Oil at least, since its recently published balance sheet showed that it had £19 million of government securities and other easily realisable assets.

In this meeting Cripps, formerly an eminent barrister, was at his most legalistic. Watson and his colleagues recognised that the advice about a test case was a dodge to put off the day when a British government might have to face up to its obligations, but he did not know of the further Machiavellian twist which Dalton had now given to the issue. In any case, Whitehall's failure to reach agreement on this matter with the Burmese financial mission was due in part to the need for haste; inexperience was also to blame, since this was the first time that independence had been granted to a country with compensation problems over denial. Later, when it came to agreements on self-rule with Sarawak, Brunei and North Borneo, the British government accepted full liability for war damage compensation.

R. I. Watson had had his last brush with the gentlemen in Whitehall. That summer he underwent a serious operation, recuperating in Scotland for a few months, and making plans to step down at the end of 1947. Harper, closely involved in the war damage negotiations, realised that having made representations to Cripps and others, the company had gone as far as it could at that stage. The final legislative arrangements for a hand-over of power were contained in the Burma Independence

Bill, the second House of Commons reading of which was to be held on 5 November. Harper was alarmed to learn that Conservative MPs, whom he had already briefed on the commercial background, were to oppose the bill. He therefore wrote to R. A. Butler, a prominent member of the shadow cabinet and a personal friend, and told him, 'Whatever attractions that line [of outright opposition] may offer from a purely House of Commons point of view, it can do no good in Burma and only merely embarrass our negotiations with the Burmese government', as also those over the all-important commercial treaty. He passed on a telegram from the Burma Chamber of Commerce in Rangoon, pointing out that opposition to the bill was likely to arouse considerable resentment throughout the country.

The second reading was a full-dress debate, with Attlee commending the bill and Churchill eloquently criticising the abandonment of the gradualist approach of the May 1945 white paper, attacking Aung San – since his assassination the unblemished hero of Burma – for having been a traitor and then changing sides, and regretting that no effective provision had been made for British commercial interests in Burma to be safeguarded from arbitrary government actions or be guaranteed compensation. Harper agreed with ministers in believing that the only practical course was to trust the Burmese, and was so much at odds with Churchill's sentiments that he wrote to congratulate two Conservative MPs who made moderate speeches and then voted for the bill. However, the closing days of 1947 were necessarily clouded with apprehension within the company, as the directors in London could not help wondering just how the new regime would react to future events.

They were not the only ones, for the Chiefs of Staff in London feared that civil war would break out and were concerned about the safety of British residents in Burma. They considered stationing a British cruiser within three days' steaming of Rangoon as a precaution. James Bowker, High Commissioner and British ambassador-designate, felt that the Burmese government and armed forces would be perfectly capable of protecting British lives. However, a bizarre tragedy showed up what the governor's secretary later called the 'indiscipline and recklessness' in Rangoon at that time. On the evening of 27 December Lingeman and his wife were sitting with friends on the verandah of the general manager's residence by Inya lake in the Rangoon suburbs, when Mrs Lingeman was shot through the head and died instantly. It turned out to have been a stray bullet, fired at random across the lake by a trigger-happy soldier.[17]

A further death was to occur within a month. Watson, shortly to sever his connections with the company after nearly fifty years, wrote to a crony about his hope that easing up in retirement and the success of his recent operation would enable him to observe for some years yet the company's 'successful emergence from the war's and from the political knocks of recent years which its Burma interests have had to take and are still taking'. After retiring on 31 December he was retained as a consultant, and his comments appeared on letters up to 9 January. A fortnight later he had a massive heart attack at his home at Pangbourne, and died. He was in his seventieth year. Cremation took place at nearby Reading and his ashes were then buried in his native Dumfries.

It would be difficult to overstate Watson's contribution to Burmah Oil's progress over the thirty-five years he spent in the London office. Almost single-handed he had transformed the company from one unit in a network of loose-knit managing agencies into a centralised and fully-fledged multinational company: from 1948 onwards the annual reports started to refer to the Burmah 'group'. Moreover, his personal qualities of intelligence and integrity had earned him a reputation second to none in the British oil scene of his day. These achievements he had won despite the very small percentage of the world's oil resources the company held. To be sure, Burmah Oil had its portfolio of shares in two much larger and more widely diversified oil giants that had access to far cheaper oil. In its current troubles these shares provided an increasing proportion of its profits, but that was not for want of persistent managerial, geological and drilling efforts in Burma, India and – after 1947 – Pakistan.

Burmah Oil's new team was headed by Sir Kenneth Harper, the first of English birth (albeit with Scottish ancestry) to become chairman. As explained in Chapter I, after serving as general manager in Rangoon, he had been in the London office, concentrating first on staff matters but more recently on broader policy issues as well. He had something of the matinée idol about him, having a resemblance to the actor Clive Brook. His character could not have been more different from that of Watson. Gentle, humorous and considerate, in his first address to the London office as chairman he related how his children's young friends held him in special awe because he was known to work in a circus (Finsbury Circus). 'I don't think that you will find me cracking the whip much, or putting people through the hoop', he added. In this kindly spirit, he preferred to call on subordinates in their own offices rather than summon them to the chairman's room, as Watson invariably had. Whereas Watson had paid little attention to regular personal relationships with the London office staff, Harper kept a list of birthdays so that he could offer his greetings on the appropriate date each year.[18] He also introduced an annual staff party, the first one in 1948 consisting of an afternoon river trip on the Thames.

Although he had never been a particularly forceful man, and had for over a decade lived in Watson's immediate shadow, he now found himself chairman and managing director, sharing the latter post with Weva. He looked for high standards from his staff, and the correspondence shows that as he gained confidence, he could be snappish and very determined. In the closing years of his chairmanship, when his managing director and assistant managing director were both qualified accountants and financial questions were looming large, so that many consultations had to be held with the company's auditors, he used to complain half-humorously that there were 'too many accountants round the board'. As the last chairman of Burmah Oil to be a layman, in the sense that he was not trained to any profession in particular, he clearly felt somewhat out of the technical discussions.

Harper joined the Shell board as a non-executive director in Watson's place, and relations with that company remained good. He had already succeeded Whigham as a director of Anglo-Iranian, and it was unfortunate that he did not hit it off with the autocratic Sir William Fraser, who had been a director of Burmah Oil since 1939 and chairman of Anglo-Iranian since 1941. He was to have a deep difference of opinion with Fraser, which soured relations between them from that moment on. Apparently the trouble arose over the failure to give Burmah Oil due credit for having established Anglo-Iranian in publicity material put out by that company in 1951 to mark the fiftieth anniversary of D'Arcy's Persian concession. Harper went so far as to have a four-page leaflet prepared for distribution in June 1951 with the previous year's annual report. That vigorously set out Burmah Oil's pioneering role, refuted the 'picturesque story' that had been put about suggesting that its directors had instructed G. B. Reynolds to abandon the wells at Masjid-i-Sulaiman and claiming that Reynolds had ignored the instruction, going doggedly ahead with his prospecting and striking oil that May (see Volume I pp. 134 ff.). In the end, the leaflet was not issued, but as Fraser was on the Burmah Oil board, the harm had been done. In any case, a malign dispensation had laid down that in periods when the Burmah Oil chairmen had been Scotsmen, those of Anglo–Iranian had been English – except between 1949 and 1956, when the reverse became true. With interlocking directorships and marketing agreements, antipathy at the top could not have been healthy for either company.

One weakness in the organisation of Burmah Oil was that not all functions were even yet housed in London. Although Cargill had been in retirement since 1943, the company secretary still resided in the Glasgow office and did not attend board meetings, so that the books had to shuttle to and fro by registered post – an expensive matter since they weighed up to $8\frac{1}{2}$ lbs. each – and someone in London had to keep minutes. Not until 1949 were those minutes typed and kept in loose-leaf binders, rather than being written by hand in the large minute books. Similarly, the accounts were still drawn up in Rangoon, where a plentiful supply of Scottish accountants resided. Until William Eadie brought the accounts office down to London in 1941, Glasgow's standing instructions to the East had been to send debit or credit notes home for all transactions there; Glasgow then sent back vouchers for precisely the same amounts, with the object – it was explained to Rangoon's bafflement – of clearing the books. Eadie became chief accountant in 1948 and was then able to build up a proper financial system in the London office.

One of Harper's early tasks, in February 1948, was to see that the lawsuits on the denial claims were entered into the local Burmese courts. The sums which the company sought were those of the original claim, plus 50 per cent – presumably to bring them up to replacement cost – plus interest. This made, for Burmah Oil alone, the impressive total of £54.4 million. In May the suits were transferred to Burma's High Court in Rangoon.

On 4 January 1948 the Union of Burma became an independent republic outside the Commonwealth. The new government, headed by U Nu as prime minster, seemed willing from the start to be conciliatory towards the foreign oil companies in its midst. Admittedly, it was reluctant to grant new prospecting licences to non-Burmese applicants but, pending any nationalisation measures that might in due course be taken, allowed existing rights to be maintained. After U Nu had made some rather radical remarks about nationalisation, intended for domestic consumption but alarming to overseas interests, the Minister of Foreign Affairs, U Tin Tut, went so far as to calm Harper's and Weva's fears by telling them in July that his government might be prepared to give an undertaking not to nationalise the oil industry for up to twenty years. However, the Burmah Oil board was uneasy and resolved to seek some definitive assurances.

A letter to be sent by Harper to the government of Burma went through a number of drafts, which had to be agreed with the other two oil companies, since the proposed merger with them had still not been achieved. This stressed the special needs of the oil industry for very considerable capital sums. To enable the outlay on that capital to be recouped, the company requested the Rangoon government to grant it the necessary security from expropriation, and sought a written agreement to that effect. Otherwise the 12,000 oil workers, then employed on rebuilding the Burmese oil industry, might have to be dismissed. The company would of course discuss with Burmese ministers 'any plan whereby at government's expense this unemployment could, temporarily at least, be avoided or lessened'.

Weva tried to persuade the Foreign Office in London to pass

the letter through the British ambassador in Rangoon, in the hope of giving it somewhat greater weight, but the Foreign Office insisted that this would be an empty gesture. In Burma as elsewhere in the world, it pointed out, no government could bind its successor. By then Harper was willing to consider, as Watson would not have done, a partnership with the government, especially if that were the only means of recovering the capital already sunk by the company in Burma. The letter therefore contained a hint that such a partnership might be worth exploring as a prelude to putting up further capital.

The notion of partnership was given a boost by the unfolding of events in Burma itself. Ever since the coming of independence in January, factions hostile to the Union government had striven to mount a determined challenge to its authority. The strike weapon in key industries, which had achieved such spectacular successes in undermining British colonial authority, was used again, to be followed by mutinies among parts of the Burmese army; large tracts of the country were in consequence outside government control. That June, Churchill as leader of the opposition commented gloomily in the House of Commons after certain British non-oil companies had been expropriated: 'as predicted', he declared, 'Burma is descending into a state of anarchy tempered by Communism.'[19] By September the oilfields were cut off by land from the rest of Burma, only air and radio links remaining open, and intermittent skirmishes were even taking place in the villages near Syriam. Lingeman as general manager, in reporting these developments, could only recommend a drastic curtailment of reconstruction work and lay-offs on a substantial scale.

The Burmah Oil board gave its consent to these cut-backs, and at the end of October the oil company managers in Burma told the Rangoon government that, as they could no longer continue repairing the frequent damage done to the pipeline and could not foresee when stability would be restored, all reconstruction would be halted from the end of November. For the future they would simply turn out, from the oilfields' topping plants, whatever quantity of products could be distributed under the prevailing conditions. No further capital would be transferred from Britain unless and until the directors were satisfied that conditions generally were settled and favourable enough to justify new investment.

For once the government of Burma gave a swift reply. In November U Nu asked the companies to submit urgently a plan whereby his government would provide the remaining capital required to complete reconstruction, and in return acquire a corresponding stake in the country's oil industry. Meanwhile, he expected any planned discharges of surplus labour to be postponed. Should his government fail to reach agreement with the oil companies, then it would search energetically for alternative employment for laid-off workers. In accordance with this request, the companies agreed to defer the discharges until the end of December and submitted outline proposals, with notional figures by way of illustration. However, they were privately warned from Whitehall that the government of Burma did not have the resources to put up the capital that was contemplated. No one could have imagined at the time that nearly five years would pass before a joint venture with the Union government was to be formally agreed.

Another matter that dragged on and on was that of compensation for denial. Any judgement from the Burmese courts could well take years to be reached and, as disorder in that country mounted, the Burma Chamber of Commerce's home committee, representing all the plaintiffs, felt that British ministers ought to be lobbied again. It was Ernest Bevin, the Foreign Secretary, who heeded a request which the committee made to him. He wrote to Attlee, suggesting that the prime minister should receive a deputation to discuss war damage compensation. While Bevin acknowledged that the question was 'difficult and complicated', he felt that the companies concerned had shown considerable patience and understanding of the British government's position. 'Certainly', he added, 'the Burmese have not observed the spirit in which the [financial] agreement [of 1947] was signed.'[20]

Three weeks later, Attlee and Cripps, now Chancellor of the Exchequer, agreed to meet a deputation on 29 June 1948. The meeting was unfortunately held at a time of great political tension in Britain, in the middle of a very damaging dock strike, when the Labour government for the first time was having to use emergency powers. Harper was there on the oil companies' behalf, but Michie as chairman of the home committee acted as spokesman. He raised the twin problems of war damage compensation and the threat of nationalisation. Attlee, at his most laconic, at once came back with the pertinent question, 'Are you willing to operate in future in Burma?' That depended, was the reply, on the attitude of the Burmese government, which appeared to be far from encouraging at that time.

Cripps was in an implacable mood, probing relentlessly into how any compensation for denial – which could well further reduce Britain's pitifully inadequate overseas currency reserves – would be used: if to inflate company balances or to give shareholders higher dividends, it was not on. Nor would he be happy if the sums were spent on machinery and equipment which would then be taken over by the government of Burma: 'not a dreadfully attractive set of circumstances for His Majesty's Government', he suggested. He had no time for Harper's submission that the oil industry had, with encouragement from Whitehall, already been advancing money from its own resources in anticipation of compensation payments. He likewise brushed aside the argument that the money in dispute was 'owed to us', riposting, 'That does not matter. There is a lot owed to other people in this country.' Post-war credits for income tax were simply one of many examples.

When the question of equity was raised, Attlee growled, 'There wasn't much equity in the war. You can't get it; that is the trouble.' Cripps rejected the contention that the companies, whatever the eventual outcome of the legal proceedings in Rangoon, would not get a penny out of the Burmese government. However, with Attlee's concurrence, he did agree to consider making an *ex gratia* payment, intended not as compensation but to 'help people get on with their business as regards the future'. In the last resort, if no money were to be provided by the Burmese, 'from our point of view the rest – if I may put it very vulgarly – you can whistle for, because there will not be any more.'[21]

Cripps quoted no figure for the *ex gratia* sum at that stage, but when Michie met him again early in September, he announced it as £10 million tax free, to be divided among all British interests in Burma whose claims had been accepted by the commission. Moreover, if any industry that was nationalised or whose properties had been denied did not receive compensation from the government of Burma, he would be prepared to make loans at a low rate of interest.

Michie later complained vigorously at the paltry size of this sum, but Cripps remained unmoved. Through the Board of Trade he set up the Carter Committee, an independent body headed by the adviser to the Board of Trade on war damage claims. It would allocate the £10 million between the parties concerned. That committee scrutinised Burmah Oil's claim and reduced it to about £17.4 million but, as a *pro rata* proportion of the sum available, the company in the event received only about £4.7 million. This was despite the fact that the oil companies had spent from their own reserves £8 million on rehabilitation in Burma by the end of 1948. However, Cripps and his colleagues made no pretence that the *ex gratia* payment was in satisfaction of, or a substitute for, denial damage claims. The ministers therefore left behind them a sense of outrage among the company's directors, which was to boil over into intermittent acts of lobbying and litigation in the next decade and a half.

Notes

1 PRO POWE 33/659. Memo re Japanese production 14 July 1945.
2 A list is given in *The Burmah Oil Society Newsletter* December 1987. The company's record of honours and awards to staff between 1939 and 1945 is in *ibid* August 1986.
3 Abraham, *Time Off*: foreword by (second) Viscount Slim and pp. 64–5.
4 K. O. Morgan, *Labour in Power 1945–1951*, 1984, p. 193. IOR, MSS Eur E 215 VIII, Dorman-Smith to Pethick-Lawrence, 20 August 1945. This corrects the phraseology in Collis, *Last and First*, pp. 210–11.
5 IOR, MSS Eur E 215 VII, Amery to Dorman-Smith, 18 September 1945; Dorman-Smith to Bishop of Rangoon 5 August 1945.
6 IOR M/4/514, 'Compensation on Burma Oilfields', Dorman-Smith to Pethick-Lawrence, 12 March 1946.
7 Hansard, House of Commons (HC) 419, written answers, pp. 185–8, 18 Feb 1946.

8 The sorry episode of the non-meeting of minds between Attlee and Dorman-Smith can be seen in Tinker, *Burma: Struggle* I, pp. 694ff. This supersedes the brief account in Collis, *Last and First*, pp. 277ff. The falling out of Mountbatten and Dorman-Smith is traced in P. Ziegler, *Mountbatten*, 1985, Chapter 25.

9 Tinker, *Burma: Struggle II*, pp.239, 310–11. This volume covers the period 31 August 1946 to Burma's independence on 4 January 1948.

10 Ibid., pp. 876–7.

11 Ibid., p. 432.

12 Tinker, *The Union of Burma*, 4th edn, 1967, p. 27. Rance's opinion is in Tinker, *Burma: Struggle* II pp. 873–4.

13 Morgan, *Labour in Power*, p. 347.

14 Ibid., pp. 353–4.

15 Tinker, *Burma: Struggle* II, p. xxxv.

16 Ibid. II, pp. 784–5. The meeting of 20 October was partly quoted in Hansard House of Lords (HL) 264, cols 802–3, 25 Mar 1965.

17 Tinker, *Burma: Struggle* II, p. 857.

18 *The Times*, 26 January and 8 February 1961, tribute by W. E. Eadie.

19 Hansard, HC 452, col 658, 17 June 1948.

20 PRO FO 800/441, Bevin papers; Bevin to Attlee, 31 May 1948.

21 This phrase was quoted in Hansard, HC 705, col 1207 3 February 1965.

CHAPTER VI

Towards Joint Venture
1949–54

By early 1949, one year after the establishment of the Union of
Burma, its government was beginning to come to terms with
the reality of administering an independent country. During
the honeymoon period in the first half of 1948 it had introduced
a plethora of nationalisation and social measures; one measure
involved taking the Irrawaddy Flotilla Company into state
ownership. Since Burma was rich in agricultural, mineral and
other products, the new rulers were convinced that once the
country received the full financial returns from that wealth,
instead of seeing them 'drained away' to Britain, India or
elsewhere, Burma could be prosperous as never before.

On the other hand, the relatively conciliatory attitude of the
new regime towards the oil industry was mentioned in Chapter
V. The Burmah Oil directors in London had spoken candidly
to the Burmese authorities about the special needs and
difficulties of oil operations there. As a consequence, U Nu had
agreed to think about taking the less radical path of a joint
venture. However, when the company asked him what share
the government of Burma would wish to acquire, he was unable
to give a precise reply. His country's Treasury was desperately
short of funds, and a stake in oil was only one of the many
contemplated projects that would inevitably require heavy
outlays.

Harper in London knew very well, both from his own people
in Rangoon and from the Foreign Office, of the dilemma facing
U Nu. The Union of Burma's constitution laid down that no

official licences could be granted to any organisation in which the state did not have an interest of at least 60 per cent, while the Burmah Oil directors saw no benefit for anyone in the government's joint-venture share being smaller than one-third. They had calculated the value of the oil properties in Burma as follows:

Value of undestroyed physical assets	£7.0 million
Expenditure on reconstruction, 1945 to end 1948	£6.5 million
Estimated cost of reconstruction still to be undertaken	£10.5 million
	£24.0 million

One third came to £8 million, to which would be added a £1 million share of extra working capital. That totalled £9 million, which the directors would expect the government of Burma to take up. Yet Burma had a budget deficit equivalent to £6 million in 1948/49 and the total central government revenue forecast for 1949/50 was only about £32.5 million.

The government's plan was to borrow the funds from Britain, and at the turn of the year it therefore sent a request to London for a substantial loan, partly for the joint venture and partly to help with balancing the budget. As soon as the loan was granted, it intended to make a payment of £1 million to Burmah Oil as an earnest of its serious intentions, and then pay off to the company the remainder in monthly instalments of £250,000 to £300,000. Harper, during his first trip to the East as chairman, was in Rangoon during January 1949; after some tough bargaining, the government of Burma accepted, subject to certain modifications, some draft heads of agreement on the joint venture. It would in the first instance buy a one-third share.

Later that month, the British cabinet's Economic Policy Committee, headed by Attlee as prime minister, considered the loan application from Rangoon. However, the committee decided that Burma still came well down the priority list of those countries in need of help, and that it could make no firm decision about a loan for the time being. Astonishingly enough, the Burmese government was not told officially until the following December that the loan application would, at best, be seriously delayed. Also in January 1949, Weva passed on some startling news to officials in the Ministry of Fuel and Power.

The company had perforce concluded that Burma's economic future looked too uncertain to justify further capital investment at that stage. Yet the consequences of halting oil rehabilitation could clearly be grave for both the company and the Burmese economy. Burmah Oil would, for instance, incur a £1 million penalty if it did not accept delivery by August of some refining plant on which it held an option. Moreover, the company would have to discharge up to 6,000 employees; that could only lead to serious unrest among the increasingly assertive labour unions, as well as the work-force generally, and sour Burmah Oil's relations with the government in Rangoon.

The directors therefore laid down a deadline of 9 March 1949 for a suspension of investment and the shedding of labour. Officials in Whitehall reacted with speed, inducing them to postpone their programme of sackings for a further month after the date, and hinting that ministers would use the time to consider what could be done in the longer term. On 9 February, the British government agreed to guarantee the company financially against future losses in Burma: that is, to meet the additional expense that could be shown to be directly attributable to its request for postponement. The reason for the guarantee, given confidentially by the Foreign Office, was that Britain's official policy towards South-East Asia was to arrest the spread of communism in the region. The linch-pin in that strategy was a prosperous and truly independent Burma.

To be sure, the world had moved on inexorably since the halcyon pre-1942 era when R. I. Watson had foretold to Roper that a self-governing Burma would be compelled, but at the same time would welcome the opportunity, to maintain very close defence and diplomatic links with Britain, within the cosy protection of the Commonwealth. Now Burma ran its own affairs independently: U Nu often used the simile of his country being 'hemmed in like a tender gourd among the cactus',[2] surrounded as it was by more powerful nations than itself, notably China with its new communist regime. Britain therefore felt an obligation to play a part, however reduced in the austere post-war circumstances, in assisting Burma. An additional factor was Burma's strategic proximity to several Commonwealth countries, one of which – namely Malaya –

was engaged in a long drawn-out battle with its own communist guerrillas. Moreover, Burma was of economic importance in the area, as a significant rice producer and exporter, while the close historical ties and on the whole amicable independence negotiations had ensured a valuable residue of goodwill towards Britain.

Hence the case for assisting Burmah Oil by loans and subsidies was a largely political one, as the Foreign Office admitted in a further briefing to other Whitehall departments. Any move to terminate the guarantee to the company, it declared, would gravely diminish the chances of restoring Burma to the peace and stability that were clearly essential if the loan, requested by the Rangoon government, were to be granted. That declaration did not deter the civil servants in the British Ministry of Fuel and Power from keeping up a barrage of criticism within Whitehall that the guarantee to Burmah Oil was 'totally unjustified' on economic grounds.

This subsidy can nowadays be recognised as an imaginative step to head off a particularly dangerous crisis, and as providing some tangible help at a time when disorder in Burma was spreading across much of the country. Most alarmingly of all, a number of regular battalions had mutinied, to be followed by the Karen regiments which had traditionally been the backbone of the Burmese army. The mutinous Karens were soon besieging Rangoon itself, and the government there survived only by the loyalty of the Chin and Kachin troops, hill warriors from northern Burma, who stood firm until the government could raise and train fresh troops.

Life among the British in Rangoon called forth the usual national phlegm. At Syriam, the strong Scottish influence among the engineers and chemists kept the atmosphere relaxed. Even though the insurgents were only a few miles away, the golfers among them insisted on rushing out on finishing work at 5 p.m., and taking advantage of the brief period of remaining daylight to play as many holes as possible. In Rangoon itself, initial apprehensions were eased when it became clear that the advance of the insurgents was being held, near as the lines of defence were to the capital, and that the sporadic outbreaks of shooting produced few casualties. Perhaps the nearest shave was when a concentrated burst of firing – apparently started by someone accidentally letting off a revolver – led to a spent bullet being fished out of a saucepan of soup in a kitchen at the managers' residences of Britannic Court. The Indian cook was shaken but not stirred. 'Hand not very steady, Sahib', he declared, 'but heart very strong.'

The British tried to keep their lives as normal as possible, some helping to cope with British, American and Indian refugees from Upper Burma who swarmed into Rangoon and for whom camps or individual accommodation had to be arranged. For those going out at night, road-blocks were a common inconvenience, and visits to the club or to friends had to be curtailed so as to be home before the nightly curfew. Some enterprising Burmese even cashed in on the siege by organising bus tours to the defence line. There the tourists could pay two annas to shoot off a rifle at the besiegers; a short burst of automatic fire was rather more expensive.

The government of Burma's financial troubles mounted as the disorder spread. In April Harper pleaded with Treasury officials in London to give the government of Burma a clear 'yes' or 'no' to its request for the loan it so sorely needed, but Whitehall had as yet no answer to make. In fact, it was very energetically seeking to persuade neighbouring Commonwealth countries to join in a programme of financial aid to Burma; by December India, Pakistan and Malaya had promised help and Australia came in during January 1950. The joint aid would comprise a loan to assist with both the budget deficit and expansion of the rice crop. A proposal to lend £6 million was put to and accepted by Rangoon in the early months of 1950. Yet all that Whitehall could do in May 1949 was to hold the line by agreeing to extend indefinitely the guarantee given to Burmah Oil.

Almost incredibly, Attlee's government kept that guarantee a close secret. The Burmah Oil directors were in the circumstances bound to silence, only letting the general manager in Rangoon know personally in the strictest confidence; the Foreign Office likewise notified the British ambassador in Rangoon in conditions of secrecy. Not until August 1949 was the government of Burma, which after all was supposed to be the ultimate beneficiary, informed unofficially; even then no details of the precise arrangements were given. Instead of appearing justifiably indignant, Burmese ministers took the news very well. At Westminster, the House of Commons was not told until almost the end of the financial year in March 1950, when a supplementary budget estimate for the cost had to be put forward: so well could secrets be kept in days when investigative journalists were virtually unknown and state papers were leaked for crates of whisky rather than to score political or ideological points. The far from convincing official reasons given for the secrecy were that premature disclosure would have encouraged unhealthy rumours in both London and Rangoon about Whitehall's future policy towards the Burmese oil industry, and might have helped to scupper Burma's own efforts to reimpose law and order.

The company's British employees at the main oilfields of Chauk and Yenangyaung were about to find themselves at the centre of perhaps the second most traumatic period in the company's entire history to date, eclipsed only by the denial episode of 1942.[3] This second period was to be one of high drama, as well as of constant anxiety, for the diminishing band of expatriate Burmah Oil men, who felt it their duty to remain at almost any cost. They realised only too well that if the last vestige of the British presence had for any reason to be withdrawn from the oilfields as a whole, very serious consequences could well follow for the company. For them physical conditions in the fields were uncomfortable, and at times they even went in fear of their lives.

Late in February 1949 instructions arrived from Rangoon to evacuate wives and children; although for some it was a repetition of what had happened in 1942, the families accepted the inevitable and were taken to Rangoon by RAF flying boat. A few hours later there arrived units of the People's Volunteer Organisation, a guerrilla band pledged to the overthrow of the regime. The first real sign of danger for the company men came when the rebels demanded for themselves the equivalent of £14,000, which was the sum paid monthly to the government in Rangoon for oil royalties and excise duty. The company's aircraft and radio station were surrounded, and only one radio message was permitted to Rangoon; not surprisingly, that was a request to pay out that sum. The general manager, after consulting Burmese ministers, agreed: needless to say, the money had later to be paid all over again to the government of Burma.

The way in which Burmah Oil's managerial staff coped with the insurgents' general behaviour says much about the British character. Ill-trained in the use of arms, these rebels were fairly harmless as long as safety-catches were kept on rifles, and pins in grenades; but fear or anger might well have driven them to some foolhardy actions. The oilfields manager at Chauk, Cecil Maxwell-Lefroy, decided that one way of building up some rapport with them was to instruct them in arms drill, learnt many years before in the Officers' Training Corps at his public school. This drill both helped to gratify the Burmese love of display and to keep the troops occupied.

Thus the British knack of submitting with good nature and even with a degree of humour to the tiresome consequences of *force majeure* clearly warded off much potential trouble. Burmah Oil's general managers in the Indian subcontinent sometimes found relaxed responses similarly useful in times of crisis. The general manager at Karachi at about this time had to refuse some request or other by the local trade union, and in consequence had his effigy burnt. To make sure that he did not miss the fun, the secretary of the union burst into his office and exclaimed, 'Sir, sir, we are burning you on the maidan [the open space in front of the office].' 'So what?' the general manager enquired, without displaying interest. 'But it is so very much like you,' came the excited response. 'You should come and see.' Taking a discreet peep from the side of the window, the general manager agreed it was a good likeness, although privately convinced that any resemblance with the scarecrow-figure being consumed by fire could only be in the eye of the beholder. As he wrote later, 'There was no violence in the occasion – it was a kind of catharsis for frustration, in the main healthy.' At least two other among the company's general managers in the East are known to have been 'victims' of effigy burning about this time.

Negotiations between the Rangoon government and the company over joint venture proceeded intermittently. For the company, Lingeman was the negotiator on the spot until he retired in June 1949; Rupert Carey, son of a former eminent

Burma civil servant, then took over as general manager. Law
and order, so far from improving as the year wore on, markedly
worsened; however, the company strove to keep up, as best it
could, work in the oilfields and the refinery. A programme of
clearing wells was undertaken, and the refinery site was
prepared for eventual reconstruction.

Yet this was merely a continuation of the unreal world that
had existed since 1942. With the oilfields cut off by land from
Rangoon, only limited quantities of products could be turned
out, to feed the very local market still open to the company. As
long as the pipeline was out of action and much of the territory
through which it ran remained in insurgents' hands, a new
refinery at Syriam was inconceivable. Instead Burmah Oil had
to import most of its product requirements. Of the 500,000
barrels of petrol and 250,000 barrels of kerosene consumed in
Burma during 1948, the bulk had come by sea from Abadan.

The Burmese operatives themselves knew that much of what
they did was no better than invented work. The company was
no longer allowed to use the pre-war sanctions of sacking
malefactors or of banning them from the vicinity of refinery or
fields; hence indiscipline, gambling and theft were widespread.
Oil was regularly stolen, and the Burmese found angle-irons
and braces of the old electric pylons that ran from Yenangyaung to Chauk very useful for constructing bedsteads, frames
for bullock cart-wheels and the long knives called *dahs*. Even
where the rehabilitation equipment itself could be protected
from pilfering, it was becoming short in supply. By May 1949
stocks of fields and refinery equipment were very low. About
the only bright spot in this darkening scene was that the
problem of unwanted plant ordered for the refinery, with its £1
million penalty clause, was overcome when it was offered, with
the government of Burma's consent, to Anglo-Iranian. That
company was only too happy to purchase such equipment,
which was still scarce all over the world.

Since the joint-venture negotiations were turning out to be so
protracted, Harper was anxious that Burmese ministers should
detect no sign of weakness on the part of Burmah Oil's
directors. After months of parleying, in July he wrote to Carey,
'We are proceeding only by faith – and because it is at others'
expense – that one day Burma will once again come to its

senses, but it would be as well [if ministers were] not to try our faith too highly.' Should the government of Burma be unwilling to accept reasonable financial terms, he continued, the company must not be expected to reduce its offer below what it had already decided as the irreducible minimum. In such a case, he would reluctantly conclude that ministers in Rangoon were not suitable partners to take into the oil business.

In mid-1949, the company decided to withdraw its six British employees from Yenangyaung. Although that town had fallen into rebel hands the previous February, about the same time as Chauk, the employees had stayed put and had succeeded in persuading the rebels not to harm the fields in any way. In return, however, company managers were forced, with Burmese government approval, to sell their production to the rebels, who also demanded and received protection money in the form of royalty payments. The local trade union leaders took advantage of the rebel occupation to make the workers down tools and then get some discharged men reinstated, with their lost pay made up. It was the third time in eight months that they had wrung concessions out of the company, and the lucrative gains that could be won from direct action were not lost on them.

Although government troops recaptured Yenangyaung in June, the rebels twice unsuccessfully launched a counter-attack. The second time, on 6 July, no fewer than 150 were killed and their bodies laid out on the company's sports ground; the local inhabitants were reported to have flocked out eagerly to gape at and count the corpses. The fighting had been so close to the company office that some shots had actually hit the building, but had fortunately not injured the staff inside. As the rebels still occupied the surrounding countryside, however, they could well renew their attacks on the oilfields at any time.

Carey, alarmed for the safety of the British employees there, at this time sought U Nu's advice on whether or not they should be pulled out. U Nu, realising the serious implications of any British citizens becoming casualties, echoed his concern and advised him to contact the Burmese War Office in Rangoon. It happened that Weva had just dropped in, on one of his regular visits as the company's managing director. He at once flew up to the fields with Carey, under military protection. As fighting seemed very likely to flare up again at or near the Yenangyaung office, he gave instructions for the British staff there to be evacuated, and for 2,000 non-European employees to be discharged, leaving just under 200 to maintain essential services.

On returning to Rangoon, Weva found that U Nu was not available and therefore could not be told of this decision; instead he saw the Foreign Minister, who seems to have failed to grasp the implications of the withdrawal, notably that production at Yenangyaung would be completely halted. Weva also asked the government of Burma not to use the shut-down as a pretext to cancel Burmah Oil's concession there. Although that government later pressed hard for a resumption of the Yenangyaung operations, the company refused as long as the threat from the rebels persisted.

This evacuation episode, which was later the subject of a thorough investigation by an *Ad Hoc* Oilfields Enquiry Committee which the Burmese authorities set up in the autumn,[4] provides a classic case-study of the conflicts between a multinational enterprise and its host government. Each party had its separate objectives and preoccupations. Burmah Oil was concerned about the expense of keeping labour idle, perhaps for years ahead, and about risking the safety of its British employees. The restoration of order was entirely a political matter and therefore outside its competence altogether. The Burmese government, on the other hand, was after the maximum production of oil, since imports were costing very scarce foreign exchange, and it also wanted maximum employment levels, which it regarded as the key to the restoration of order. The more people were actually in real work, the fewer would be roaming about in a volatile state of discontent. By the dismissals it had made, however necessary in the circumstance, the company was undoubtedly building up potential trouble for itself with its hosts in Burma.

While on the same Burmese trip in July 1949, Weva seems to have broached to the Rangoon government the possibility of modifying the joint venture proposal. The company, he suggested, would value its assets in Burma at £15 million,

considerably below the £24 million, but only the amount spent
to date, then standing at £8 million, would be included in the
aggregate sum. This revised figure had almost certainly not
been agreed in advance with the board in London. Weva later
claimed that it had come into his head during a conversation
with U Nu; it had the advantage of being easily divisible into
three. The government's one-third share would thus be around
£5 million.

Yet it was a fairly realistic figure, assuming that the
government of Burma would be prepared to put in its extra
share every time new expenditure was incurred: in the first nine
months of 1949 the company spent no less than £3 million
there. The Burmah Oil board and Whitehall both gave their
blessing to this new basis of negotiation, recognizing the
advantage of greater flexibility than under the old system. By
the beginning of September the overall figure of £15 million was
officially accepted in Rangoon; however, a major condition was
still the provision of a loan by the British government. That
condition remained a worrying one. Should Whitehall refuse
the loan and cause the joint venture to founder, the Burmah Oil
directors could expect no co-operation from the government of
Burma when they began to carry out the further staff reductions that they felt were becoming urgent.

With no progress made over the loan or the joint venture by
late September, the company issued notices discharging 1,400
employees at Chauk and about 2,200 at Syriam. Carey had
already discussed these possible reductions with Burma's
Minister of Foreign Affairs, and in October he and the British
ambassador, James Bowker, met U Nu. Neither meeting was
particularly fruitful: ministers would go no further than a
non-committal recognition of what was being done. Harper
remained hawkish about the dismissals, declaring that he
would not surrender to the Burmese unions and was prepared
to face a show-down, since the company could not be expected
to go on carrying surplus labour on its payroll, whether at its
own or the British government's expense.

At a further meeting with the foreign minister, Bowker
hinted that Whitehall, even if unable to grant a loan, might be
ready to make available some short-term funds to cushion
the effects of the redundancies. However, any aid would

depend on rebel activities ceasing in the oilfields and law and order being restored. He declared bluntly that, if the labour leaders persisted in behaving irresponsibly, they would almost certainly bring about the total collapse of Burma's oil industry.

Hectoring of that kind by the British was all very well, but by then practically all existing industrial installations in the country, including the railways and river traffic, were at a standstill. At the end of October Harper felt that Burma's troubles were building up to some kind of climax. Yet while refusing to invest any more of the company's own capital there, he and his board were prepared to accept U Nu's offer of substantive negotiations on joint venture. When Carey met U Nu at the end of October, he portrayed the latter's charm memorably as follows: 'Both panels of his radiator of geniality were switched on.' However, Carey continued, 'both comforting panels will be switched off the moment the will of the Burmese Trade Union Congress is in any way disregarded by us.' Harper could not help wondering if the authorities in Rangoon were deliberately spinning talks out for their own purposes. 'The longer the Burmese government can keep the ball rolling, the more reconstruction [of oil assets] there would be to take over. And His Majesty's Government's dilatoriness is playing that game for them nicely.'

In November 1949 U Nu set up the *Ad Hoc* Oilfields Enquiry Committee. Before it could get under way, Bowker had to tell U Nu late in December that the British government would be unable to provide a loan for the joint venture. U Nu received that deeply disappointing news without a muscle moving in his impassive face; yet he knew that here was a further blow to his country's grave situation. Indeed, the early months of 1950 were later authoritatively described as the lowest point in Burma's post-war financial fortunes. Even Harry S. Truman's administration in the United States, sympathetic as it was to the new regime, had become convinced that the country was finished as a viable political and economic entity. The Oilfields Enquiry Committee reported in mid-March 1950. Its report sharply criticised Burmah Oil's policies in general and conduct over the Yenangyaung withdrawal in particular. Why, it asked, had oil production in British Borneo and Indonesia recovered so much more dramatically than in Burma, and why had Burmah Oil been so reluctant to pour rehabilitation funds into the country? Burmah Oil's reply was that the post-independence disturbances in the country had greatly exacerbated the problem and that in any case, the oilfields were a good distance from the coast, in contrast with Borneo and Indonesia. To put the case bluntly, the company argued, Burma's problems made it uneconomic to invest money in oil production there when an equivalent sum invested elsewhere would produce more oil at lower cost, not to mention lower risk.

In analysing recent events at Yenangyaung, the report implied that the company had seized the opportunity of a temporary reoccupation of the oilfields by the rebels to escape from an onerous and unprofitable commitment there. Moreover, it continued, Weva and Carey had acted with quite unnecessary haste and had misled the Burmese ministers concerned into thinking that any withdrawal of British staff would be temporary and not lead to a total stoppage of all work there. Weva strongly disagreed with this interpretation of events and made a sworn statement to the effect that he had at the time clearly and fully explained to ministers the consequences for Burmese labour of the withdrawal.

In a private comment on the report, the British embassy staff dryly observed that it was 'too much to expect that a Burmese government committee would admit' that ministers had not had the courage to face the disagreeable implications of the company's decision and to inform their colleagues accordingly. What the embassy did believe to contain a germ of truth was the report's criticisms about the paternalistic attitude of the company, a lack of imagination and of 'human contact' in dealings with non-European staff: criticisms originally made in an official Burmese report on the disturbances of 1938, less valid in post-war conditions but still – according to the embassy – central to the whole problem of the company's relationships with government and employees in Burma.[5] The more perceptive Drysdale, by then a manager in the London office, would have pointed not so much to personal contacts with local staff, which were good, but to the anomalous system whereby a foreign management was striving to cope with economic and political problems which directedly affected the livelihoods of thousands in the country.

On 23 December 1949 the British government informed the company that it would be withdrawing its financial guarantee as from the end of January 1950. The directors had already made it clear that, in the event of such a decision, further large-scale reductions of staff would have to take place: specifically, 2,500 at Chauk and 3,500 at the Syriam refinery. A press report, released in London and Rangoon, expressed the view of Whitehall that the widespread unrest in Burma no longer justified large amounts of expenditure on rehabilitation. At the same time the British government was examining, in consultation with other friendly governments, possible means of providing alternative forms of financial assistance. Carey sent a carefully drafted letter to U Nu. In the fields, he pointed out, the only work that could at the moment be usefully done was the production and refining of the limited quantity of oil which could be marketed locally. Elsewhere in Burma, labour was needed only for receiving and distributing imported oil from the ocean installations at Syriam.

The total expenditure incurred by the oil companies, arising from the extra labour kept on, during the guarantee period from March 1949 to January 1950 amounted to no less than £1.1 million. Just over a half had been spent in the oilfields, a third in the refineries and a small amount on servicing the still non-operative pipelines. British Burmah and Indo-Burma between them were responsible for only 7 per cent of the expenses. Since part of these could not be justified as having been essential, Burmah Oil agreed to accept £700,000 as its share. Bowker, the British ambassador, strove to persuade the government of Burma to assume responsibility for paying the redundant labour for an extra month or two, over and above the month's pay that the company was offering in lieu of notice. The labour forces affected had at once gone on strike, and the matter was referred to the Industrial Court in Burma. The company appealed to the Supreme Court to have the reference quashed, but the Supreme Court ruled that any such application was premature and that it was up to the Industrial Court to decide whether it had the legal powers to adjudicate in this case: this ruling not unexpectedly caused the company much dissatisfaction.

The Burmese authorities brought further pressure in March 1950, when Cecil Maxwell-Lefroy, the oilfields manager, was personally sued in the local court at Chauk for contravening the Trade Disputes Act. On his behalf, the company again pleaded that the dismissals arose from inescapable economic and political factors which prevented the maintenance of normal operations at the fields. It had not been responsible for any victimisation, nor for any illegal actions. There was a slight fear that Maxwell-Lefroy might become the victim of a show trial, but in the event he was released on bail and later quietly sentenced to a nominal fine, which the company paid. The Burmah Oil board later granted him £1,000 for the inconvenience and anxiety which he had undergone.

The directors in London were convinced that all these legal moves were part of an elaborate battle of wits against the company. One of the most acute minds on the Burmese side, the Indian-born M. A. Raschid, who was on the *Ad Hoc* committee and much involved in every aspect of the country's labour affairs, admitted publicly in April that Burma as a virtually bankrupt country had no choice but to seek capital from overseas until such time as it could stand on its own feet. That interim period, he believed, might last as long as 25–30 years, during which his government would have to decide how far existing foreign capital in the country could be constrained and imposed upon without being frightened away altogether.

That a joint venture plan for oil remained very much in Rangoon's mind was demonstrated when U Nu revived the notion in May at an informal meeting with Weva. The prime minister proposed that under the joint venture, topping plant facilities should be increased at Chauk, while a small refinery or topping plant would be erected at Syriam, to be fed by crude oil sent down on barges from the oilfields. Weva declined to discuss any proposals of that kind until the Industrial Court had reported; in any case he viewed such plans as unrealistic since communications by land between the fields and Rangoon were still interrupted by rebel action, and seemed unlikely to be restored for a long time to come. Privately, Weva felt that giving publicity to joint venture proposals at that stage would be counter-productive by raising redundant workers' expectations of more jobs being created, which were quite unrealistic in the existing circumstances.

At the end of May 1950 the Industrial Court announced its findings.[6] The redundancies at Chauk were held to be reasonable, but at the same time illegal on technical grounds, because actual discharge had taken place after the dispute had been referred to the court. Wages should therefore be paid to the end of May, and two months' redundancy payment in addition: that represented an extra expense to the company of about £40,000 a month gross. In London, Foreign Office officials called a meeting a week later to discuss these findings; Harper, Weva, Michie of the Burma Chamber of Commerce and representatives of British Burmah and Indo-Burma were present.

Michie declared that the Industrial Court's finding went against the spirit of the letters exchanged between Attlee and U Nu at the time of the 1947 Anglo-Burmese treaty, which had agreed about safeguarding the interests of British companies in Burma. Harper, too, was so dissatisfied with the court's ruling that, on his board's authority, he arranged for Carey to lodge an appeal with the Supreme Court in Rangoon. Should what he termed a 'reasonable' decision be passed down there, the company would be prepared to increase the output of oil products from Chauk, always provided that communications and transport facilities were suitable. It would also spend some £250,000 on capital expenditure in transferring some recently delivered refinery plant from Syriam to Chauk.

The Supreme Court's decision, announced in October, turned out to be as 'reasonable' as the company could perhaps have hoped for. The Industrial Court was judged to have had no authority to tell Burmah Oil how it should carry on its business. Hence the company's right to discharge surplus labour at Syriam was upheld. At the same time, the discharges at Chauk and the two months' redundancy payments there and at Syriam were declared illegal, but the award of a discharge allowance at Yenangyaung was quashed. The company thereupon paid off the labour, at a total cost of £150,000.

Burmah Oil derived comfort from the fact that it had at least been able to reduce costs to a point at which production and sale of Burmese-raised oil would be showing a profit. Moreover, it was earning a good return on the imported oil products; in the three years since 1946 it had made a direct and indirect profit there of nearly £1.2 million. As the total net trading profit for Burma in 1949 came to £540,000 and in 1950 to £430,000, the company could not have been making much from its indigenous production and marketing there. In an interview with U Nu in November, Carey did not disguise his feeling about the 'colossal tragedy' of so many thousands of men losing their jobs. That tragedy was sadly intensified by the fact, vouched for by the Roman Catholic padre at the fields, that the ex-employees had squandered 60–70 per cent of the redundancy payments within ten days in gambling dens and drinking saloons, energetically assisted by what were described as 'evil exploiters, largely Chinese'.

Now that the various legal tangles were resolved, the government of Burma seemed likely to renew its proposal for a joint venture. That possibility made Harper more than ever determined to play hard to get. As the board minutes put it, he sought 'to remain in the position of the party being pressed to agree to such a joint venture rather than the party asking for it'. This was not merely a tactical move, since the company would then be able to seek, as part of a package deal, a 'constructive programme' of increased output and investment, and it could also insist on the government of Burma contributing its own quota of cash for its one-third share. Soon after the Supreme Court judgement, Carey saw U Nu, and in a conciliatory atmosphere explained the limited programme of fresh investment the company planned to undertake, such as extending the Chauk topping plant for the benefit of the growing domestic market. The renewal of cordiality gave hope that the two parties could move to a swift and mutually advantageous agreement on joint venture.

Towards the end of 1950, a gruelling year by any standards, Carey was clearly feeling the strain. He admitted in a letter to the directors at home – sent by safe hand – that, while he would do his level best to put across to the Burmese authorities the principles laid down by the board during the future joint venture negotiations, he was not looking forward to the task. He went on,

> Frankly, I have great disrespect for some of the people I still have to deal with in this regard, and if it was not my duty to the company to have dealings with them, I should absolutely refuse to have any converse with them.

For the government of Burma, the new year of 1951 brought with it a modest revival of financial and economic prosperity. Underlying that revival was the painfully slow process of attrition against the rebels so that the government's writ still did not run in many parts of the country. Central Burma was largely rebel-held, which inhibited free internal movement of oil products. The outbreak of the Korean war in mid-1950 had led to a sharp commodity boom, in which Burma's rice shared. Hence there was to be in the next few years an unprecedented buoyancy in government revenues and a satisfactory building up of foreign currency reserves. Understandably, the people of Burma pressed for higher social welfare and other public expenditure; yet perhaps negotiations for a joint venture could now at last be opened on a more constructive basis than hitherto. When Weva visited Rangoon early in 1951, he discerned a notable improvement in Burma's political and military conditions, although he was by no means certain that that improvement would continue.[7]

In February 1951 the government of Burma revived the joint venture idea by announcing that it wished to take up a one-third interest, but only if the British government agreed to loan the £5 million that would be required. A formal application for a loan duly went to Whitehall, but a swift reply could not be expected: the Attlee government was yet again facing severe financial problems, this time over defence and increased raw material prices caused by the Korean commodity boom. The ailing Cripps had been succeeded as Chancellor of the Exchequer by Hugh Gaitskell towards the end of 1950.

It happened that Gaitskell knew a good deal about Burma, as his father had been in the civil service there, and his sister Bunty had married Hubert Ashton. Gaitskell was at one with his Treasury officials in believing that Rangoon was 'blackmailing' Britain into making a loan, at a time when Burma had plenty of sterling; in any case – to deploy an all too familiar Treasury argument – surrender in this case would create a bad precedent that other countries would seek to exploit.

However, Gaitskell found himself up against not only Attlee but also certain cabinet ministers such as Philip Noel-Baker and Patrick Gordon-Walker, each of whom had previously served as Commonwealth Secretary and who opposed the cheese-paring Treasury line. Gaitskell, in his diary, described Attlee and Noel-Baker as 'feeling positively passionate about Burma and insisting on giving them anything they wanted. I have voted against this unsuccessfully,' he continued. When the matter was thrashed out at ministerial level, Attlee for once lost his temper, went 'quite red in the face', and angrily exclaimed, 'If you go on like this, you will lose the whole of the Middle East.'[8]

The basis of Attlee's anger was the Abadan crisis, involving the government of Iran and the Anglo-Iranian Oil Company, which had recently erupted when in May 1951 Dr Mossadeq had nationalised that company's assets. Sir William Fraser had given the Burmah Oil board what was minuted as an 'interesting' account of events, and Harper had formally conveyed the board's 'good wishes for a satisfactory solution to difficult problems'. One of the Burmah Oil non-executive directors privately felt that 'one of the causes of our friends' trouble has been insufficient contact with the fields', by which he meant the host country of Iran. At the meeting with Gaitskell, the prime minister clearly feared that Burma too might turn sour and become a centre of discord in South-East Asia as Iran had become in the Middle East.

The Iranian moves against British interests, as U Nu informed Weva in July 1951, had indeed made a deep impression on the Burmese people and also raised their own expectations. U Nu hinted that nothing less than a 50:50 partnership would now do, although Weva after some persuasive argument brought him back to the one-third basis. 'It was also as clear as daylight', Weva reported home, 'that he did not intend to pay a penny of Burmese money for the participation.' U Nu did, perhaps to test out the company, drop hints about getting the 50:50 share by expropriation, but he was not really serious about such a drastic step.

In fact, relations between the government and the largest company in Burma could not have been more different from those in Iran. Remarkably, two very knowledgeable men, the minister of state at the Foreign Office, Kenneth Younger, and the labour adviser of Anglo-Iranian, in memoranda they wrote independently that year, blamed Anglo-Iranian for what had happened. According to the latter, that company was 'confused, hidebound, small-minded and blind'. The former criticised the chairman, Sir William Fraser, for a wanton neglect of the political dimension which Fraser explicitly stated did not concern him at all.[9] Politics of one kind or another were, on the other hand, a constant preoccupation of Burmah Oil's executive and of its general manager in the East.

Nor could Harper or Weva be accused of such insensitiveness towards the country that provided their oil. They understood the Burmese mind from the experience of many years' residence and thereafter the maintenance of regular personal contacts. Relations between the Burmah Oil directors and the authorities in Rangoon may from time to time have become strained, but both sides had a good deal of common ground. At his encounter with Attlee over the loan, Gaitskell retorted, 'It is your policy which will lose us the Middle East. By giving way to blackmail here, you will have it imposed on you everywhere else.' Gaitskell was outvoted, and the British cabinet approved the loan.

With the Iranian crisis rumbling on, and with virtually no prospect of a swift solution, Whitehall very much hoped that Burma at least would deliver an amicable accord. In mid-September Attlee sent a personal message to U Nu. A loan of £5 million would be excessive, he stated, but if the government of Burma and the company could agree on a joint venture scheme, Britain would offer £2.5 million. Since U Nu was persisting in his resolve not to put in any Burmese money, and Weva would not consent to Rangoon's share being less than one-third, an impasse was reached. U Nu merely responded to Attlee by expressing pleasure that Britain had offered a loan, without making public his disappointment that the full £5 million was not forthcoming. Weva privately admitted that he had spent a month or more in fending off a suggestion by Whitehall that the offer of £2.5 million should be linked with a statement that

Burmah Oil would be prepared to make suitable arrangements to underwrite the remainder.

In November 1951 Weva arrived in Rangoon with definite proposals for the government of Burma. A general election had just been held in Britain, and Winston Churchill was once again prime minister. The Burmese were very apprehensive that, as Churchill had been so opposed to what he had called 'scuttle' from empire, Britain's official attitude towards them might sharply deteriorate. In fact, the Foreign Office told Weva before his departure that the new government was anxious to build up cordial relations with Burma, and in particular wished to see a joint oil venture settled. After much discussion, on 30 November an agreement was initialled whereby a new rupee company would be set up in Rangoon, the government of Burma holding a third share. Burmah Oil would appoint three directors, of whom one would act as chairman, and the government of Burma would appoint two directors. That government would in future be allowed to increase its own stake, after giving due notice. Once it had more than 51 per cent of shares, it would be entitled to have three directors and Burmah Oil only two. Marketing would not be affected, since that would remain in the hands of Burmah Oil's trading subsidiary.

The long-term objectives sought by Burmah Oil were written into the agreement, notably that production and refining at Chauk would be increased to about 1.6 million barrels annually and that, when security conditions permitted, the pipeline and Syriam refinery would be reconstructed to permit an eventual output of 3.7 million barrels a year and the restoration of Burma's export trade in oil. The government of Burma had the right to check the valuation of the assets; subject to that, the sale price was set at £15 million and the capital at the equivalent figure of 200 million *kyats*. The *kyat*, of 100 *pyas*, officially replaced the Burmese rupee on 1 July 1952.

Late in December 1951 R. A. Butler, recently appointed Chancellor of the Exchequer, wrote to Anthony Eden, the Foreign Secretary, deploying some 'powerful practical economic arguments' against lending the £2.5 million to the Burmese for the acquisition of what were British-owned assets. Burma, he pointed out, had left the Commonwealth by its own choice, and neighbouring Commonwealth countries could well be jealous if Burma were now singled out for special treatment. Moreover, Britain was short of foreign currency; and so on. The Treasury hostility to this loan had very evidently survived the change in government.

Eden replied with some political and 'politico-economic' counter-agruments. The Burmese government was in a very 'precarious' state; were it to fall, the Marxist element in the country was so strong that Burma might be lost to the West. Moreover, that event could upset the international balance throughout South-East Asia. On the politico-economic side, all peoples in that part of the world were watching carefully the progress of the Abadan crisis in Iran. For Burma, a joint oil venture launched with a loan from Britain could fend off pressure to nationalise outright not merely the oil interests there but also other important British enterprises. An interest-free loan repaid over twelve and a half years would, according to Eden, cost the Exchequer only £2 million in interest foregone: 'as an insurance premium, it does not seem unduly high, particularly if one considers that the Burmah Oil Company last year contributed something like £6$^1/_2$ million to the Exchequer by way of income tax.'

Butler riposted with the further point that the Burmese had not been repaying the money they still owed under the financial agreement of 1947, and that the loan should be withheld until some repayment was made. Eden did not care for the idea of linking the two issues, but as Burma did not appear to be pressing for the loan, the two ministers left the matter in abeyance.[10]

From the political and military viewpoints, conditions in Burma seemed to be somewhat more stable by the end of 1951. A general election had been successfully held there that year. Supervision of the polls may have been lax in places, and bizarre happenings occurred, including local detachments of the armed forces being taken in bodies to vote – naturally for the official candidates. The perhaps over-anxious Burmah Oil board saw the outcome of the election as indicating a 'worsening to the left', with U Nu apparently less securely in control than before. However, world opinion accepted that the renewed mandate for him broadly represented the will of the Burmese people.[11] On the military side, martial law had been brought to an end in mid-1951; although the government still failed to control large areas of the country, the rebels were no longer generally regarded as credible alternatives to the existing regime. As far as the joint venture proposals went, both parties had accepted the principles, and the task was now to settle the financial details.

A valuation commission set up by the Rangoon government duly visited the oilfields and Syriam, and in April 1952 came up with an asset value of £13.5 million. At a time when Whitehall had not yet decided on the precise terms of its loan, the government of Burma sought to place a lien on the sum of £700,000 which Burmah Oil had received from Whitehall for the guarantee period of 1949–50. After a good deal of parleying, the company offered to include the £700,000 in the new company's assets, whereupon Rangoon accepted the valuation in the agreement of £15 million. The government of Burma then tried to have the denial claims – still going through the country's courts at a snail's pace – included as well in the assets. It did not press the matter when the Burmah Oil board refused. 'Somewhat belatedly', as the board minutes described it, Rangoon then sought a ruling from its Supreme Court on whether a joint venture with a minority government stake was permissible under the constitution, which had laid down that the exploration of mineral rights should be entirely or largely in Burmese hands.

Not until February 1953 did the Supreme Court reach its decision on this matter. It held the joint venture to be constitutional, but declined to rule on the validity of Burmah Oil's existing leases after the company's counsel pleaded that it was inappropriate for the court to consider such an 'indefinite question'. However, instead of this decision spurring it into signing the agreement, in April the government of Burma sought to reopen the whole question of joint venture by exploring possible alternative arrangements for operating the country's oil industry.

After the Rangoon government had asked Carey for a detailed breakdown of the company's sources of profit in Burma – which Carey refused to give – U Nu dropped the hint that Weva might care to come out on a visit. Weva, unwilling to appear to be pushing matters, did not oblige, and in the absence of any serious negotiations U Nu blew hot and cold. In June he spoke encouragingly about the proposals, but by September was discussing the possibility of arranging a joint venture instead with certain Japanese and American interests. The latter possibility was not taken very seriously, and a recently arrived World Bank delegation gained the impression that Burmese opinion expected the arrangement with Burmah Oil to go ahead. What did irritate the government of Burma was the chaotic and unsatisfactory situation that had persisted in Yenangyaung, ever since the evacuation of the British staff; that was investigated by the company's board in London, which saw no reason to send its staff back there. Then in October the government of Burma informed British ministers that after all it had no need of the £2.5 million loan, since it would be able to pay the sum required from its own resources: at the end of 1952 the country's foreign exchange reserves had reached the equivalent of £75 million.

Despite all the problems of insurgency, equipment shortages and disrupted communications, oil production in Burma had steadily increased since 1947, as Table 4 shows. There had been a decline in both output and demand during the crisis year of 1949. However, in accordance with the agreement of November 1951, by 1953 the topping plants in Chauk had been replaced by a small integrated refinery, complete with wax processing equipment. This refinery had an initial throughput of 2,500 barrels a day; in January 1954 it was inaugurated by U Nu, who opened a valve, and molten wax flowed out. By the end of that year annual output in Burma, including that of the independent operators there, was just four times that of 1948. The difference between the amount of crude oil production and that of refined products from Burma illustrates the relatively low product yield – compared with pre-1942 – obtained from the topping plants.

Despite the increase in output, and the still high level of oil imports undertaken by the company, the amount of net trading profit contributed by Burma was falling: just over £290,000 in 1951 or almost half that of 1949, although it increased to an

TABLE 4
Oil production and consumption – Burma 1947–54

	Crude oil production (000 barrels)			Refined products (000 barrels)			Percentage of oil product needs from Burma (%)
	'Merger' co's*	Independent operators†	Total Burma	Indigenous	Imported	Total	
1947	72	11	83	n.a.	n.a.	n.a.	n.a.
1948	289	28	317	89	1098	1187	8
1949	219	28	247	86	772	858	10
1950	417	122	539	226	784	1010	22
1951	626	144	770	389	747	1136	34
1952	620	209	829	400	812	1212	33
1953	788	209	997	502	883	1385	36
1954	945	348	1293	707	798	1505	47

* Burmah Oil, British Burmah and Indo-Burma (For 1954, Burma Oil Co (1954) Ltd)
† Estimated

average of £410,000 annually between 1952 and 1954. That represented about 12 per cent of total profit, while investment income was contributing 45 per cent. Unless joint venture were able to increase profits from that source, the country where operations had originally started would soon become a negligible earner for the company.

At the end of 1953 Weva was in Rangoon, and he soon reached a definitive agreement with the government of Burma. Signed on 12 January 1954, it turned out to be substantially the same as the one initialled as long before as 1951. The new corporate body, to take over all functions apart from marketing, was to be called the Burma Oil Company (1954) Ltd. The government of Burma would hold one-third of the £15 million capital, paying £2.5 million in cash and the rest in instalments. The board in London was by then so anxious to resolve the joint venture question one way or another that, before Weva's departure, it had approved in advance a fall-back position of 50:50 shareholding if the earlier terms were rejected. However, this did not prove to be necessary.

Although Weva had done well in the negotiations, the board was not entirely happy with the final outcome. In particular, while the directors had authorised the payment of the £700,000 guarantee money to the new company, Weva had without board permission raised the sum payable to £750,000, just equal to a crore (or 10 million) of *kyats*, as the Burmese rupee was now called.

He had made this extra offer as a *coup de théâtre* on the actual day of signing. A number of cabinet ministers had been unhappy that U Nu had rushed through the accord without insisting on Britain binding itself to provide guarantees over the future capital needed to make Burma self-sufficient in oil. Nor, it appeared, had U Nu tried to gain for the government of Burma even titular control over what they regarded as some of the country's most valuable resources. Therefore ministers might well have vetoed the signing at the very last moment. The directors at home became further irritated when it emerged that the government of Burma was dragging its feet over the initial deposit, agreed at £2.5 million, and offering only £1.5 million in the first instance, with the balance to be paid in

March or April. This infuriated the board in London as
constituting a breach of the agreement and it laid down that the
1954 company could not be registered until the full £2.5 million
had been actually received in London. It seems probable, in
retrospect, that these hiccups led to differences between Weva
and his Burmah Oil colleagues which were never wholly
resolved.

One administrative consequence of a joint venture being
established in Rangoon was that the company's top man there
was no longer designated as general manager in the East.
Perhaps the division of territorial functions, making the general
managers in India and Pakistan responsible directly to London, might have been arranged even as early as August 1947
when both countries received independence. However, it was
only the far more specific new role for the Rangoon general
manager, who was to be made chairman of the 1954 company,
that made the change really necessary. Not until the end of
April was the government of Burma's £2.5 million paid to
London, but the company still had to be formally registered in
Rangoon: as was noted in the Burmah Oil board minutes,
'largely it would appear because of the absence on tour of those
concerned' in Burma.

Subsidiary agreements remained to be signed, but the board
of the new company had been formed and had held its first
meeting. Relations with the Burmese government-appointed
directors were said to be good. On the other hand, the Burmah
Oil board instructed the general manager that, until the
subsidiary agreements had been signed, the new company
would possess no assets and therefore had no right to engage in
trading of any kind. That did not deter ministers in Rangoon
from submitting a list of forty proposed changes to the
agreements, only four of which Burmah Oil after consideration
regarded as substantive. Not until 5 October were all the
agreements signed; shares were then allotted on the 8th. The
Burma Oil Company (1954) Ltd was in business.

The new board lost no time in bringing forward plans for a
new refinery at Syriam, which it hoped to have completed in
two years' time. The former Irrawaddy Flotilla Company,
nationalised in 1948, had been renamed the Inland Water
Transport Board (IWTB): not exactly a name to have set

Kipling's pulses racing. The 1954 company now asked the IWTB to give a firm date when new craft would be available to transport crude oil to Syriam; there seemed no chance of rehabilitating the pipeline within the two years that were contemplated as it ran through dacoit country, so that repairs and maintenance would pose a constant problem. It was irksome that the IWTB charged such high freights; the company pointed out that it cost five times as much to send petrol from Chauk to Rangoon as it did to ship it from the Gulf.

On the Burmese side, an undercurrent of annoyance persisted that Burmah Oil refused to consider making a similar partnership arrangement for its fully-owned Burma trading subsidiary. The latter was earning good profits, still running at £400,000 to £500,000 both on the marketing of indigenous products and on the considerable volume of imports that were being made. This issue flared up in the early 1960s. Meanwhile, however, what mattered was that a new and highly promising era in the oil industry of Burma appeared to have been inaugurated, with goodwill shown by all the parties concerned. Men on both sides of the world must have fervently hoped that the new joint venture would fully live up to its promises.

Notes

1 PRO POWE 33 1565–8, 'Burmah Oil Company's Claim under HMG's Guarantee', 1950–2, and 1569, 'Proposed Participation of Burmese Government in Joint Venture', 1950–1.
2 Tinker, *Union of Burma*, p. 337.
3 I am very grateful to C. A. Maxwell-Lefroy for letting me quote from his unpublished memoirs, especially Chapter 7, 'Burma Oilfields under Siege, 1949–50'.
4 PRO POWE 33/1566, *Report of the Ad Hoc Oilfields Enquiry Committee*, 16 March 1950, pp. 1–65.
5 Ibid. Rangoon Embassy, 'Comments on the Report of the Ad Hoc Oilfields Enquiry Committee', undated (c. March 1950).
6 PRO POWE 33/1565, copy of Industrial Court award, 31 May 1950, and subsequent meetings and correspondence with company. The Supreme Court judgment was reported by a greatly relieved Bevin to Attlee on 26 October 1950. FO 800/441, Bevin Papers.
7 PRO POWE 33/1569, letter of Petroleum Department to Foreign Office, 31 January 1951.

8 P. M. Williams (ed.), *The Diary of Hugh Gaitskell 1945–1956*, 1983, p. 271.

9 Kenneth Younger's memo is in A. Sampson, *The Seven Sisters*, 1975, p. 120. That of AIOC's labour adviser, Sir Frederick Leggett, is in Morgan, *Labour in Power*, pp. 466–7.

10 PRO FO 800/753, Private Papers of Sir A. Eden, Burma 1952 and 1954, correspondence between Eden and Butler 29 Dec 1951–19 Apr 1952.

11 For the 1951 election, see Tinker, *Union of Burma*, pp. 71–2.

CHAPTER VII

The Road to Diversification
1954–9

When India, Pakistan and Burma were granted their independence in 1947–8, the more forward-looking Burmah Oil directors and senior managers, such as William Eadie, saw clearly that the company was on the threshold of a new era. To be sure, the future promised to be considerably less tranquil and straightforward than the past had been. The freshly-acquired authority of the new governments and their high consciousness of national aspirations ensured that there would be bumpy rides ahead. Even so, the company could take comfort from the goodwill it had acquired over the years in all three countries. It had worked reasonably hard at identifying itself with the respective nationals and at pursuing policies in their interests, from oil conservation to the provision of social amenities. Thus there seemed no reason why a good rapport could not be maintained with governments and people alike.

The way in which these expectations were partially fulfilled in Burma, up to 1954, was seen in Chapter VI, and Chapter XI will discuss events in India and Pakistan. As to Burma, the directors in London had hoped to maintain full operational control over oil activities in that country, while the Burmese prime minister, U Nu, and his ministerial colleagues wanted the country's oil to be in the hands of the state. The compromise solution was a joint venture, with the Union government starting off with a minority stake of one-third – two of the five directors being government-appointed – and perhaps gradually building up to full control. As it had taken nearly seven years to reach a point where the new Burma Oil Company (1954) Ltd had come into operation, a considerable period might well elapse before even majority control, let alone full ownership, was achieved.

One national characteristic shared by Burmese and British was a capacity for muddling through. The main agreement to set up the new company had been signed in January of that year; yet one delay after another on the Burmese side had prevented the subsidiary agreements from being concluded. That company was formally established on 31 March, and operations were deemed to have been carried on under its control as from 1 January. A board of directors was appointed, two being Burmese and three British. It met for the first time on 31 May although it had no executive power and no assets until such time as the agreement to transfer these assets had been signed. What the literally-minded Watson would have made of it all can only be wondered at. Rupert Carey was the first chairman, but he was due to retire in July. It disappointed him to hand over so many loose ends to his successor, the 47-year-old Cecil Maxwell-Lefroy; however, there was no one better able to promote the spirit of co-operation with the Burmese than the new general manager and chairman of the Burma Oil Company (1954) Ltd, henceforward referred to as the 1954 company.

Maxwell-Lefroy could perhaps most accurately be described as an idealist without illusions. A Burmaphile by conviction, he understood very well the psychology of his hosts, in whose country he had resided almost continuously in the peacetime years since 1928: in particular, the Burmese propensity to judge the policies of whole enterprises and even governments by the conduct or attitudes of their individual representatives. What he later feelingly termed the 'tortuous mental processes of Burma' caused him sleepless nights as he endlessly pondered on the best way to reconcile conflicting views. Instead of giving way to outbursts of temperament in situations of deep dead-lock, he always sought to relieve tension by bringing smiles to the faces of his humour-loving Burmese interlocutors.

To his own superiors in London he had always been studiously less than obsequious, in the fashion of a very gifted public-school head boy who, without showing overt disrespect, makes it quite apparent that he has little time for the beaks. In his first letter home as chairman of the 1954 company, he straight-facedly observed to Weva that he was 'interested' to learn that the Burmah Oil Company directors had decreed that the level of his company's proposed dividend was a question which need not be referred to them. He continued, 'We had thought that any secretary who gave, to an outside party, his own estimate of dividend without the prior approval of his board [i.e. of the 1954 company] would rapidly be looking for another job.' When a director later wrote to him from home, in quite kindly terms, reminding him that he was only an appointed chairman, there to do whatever his British appointers instructed him to do, he replied in equally kindly vein that the Burmah Oil directors too functioned only by courtesy of the shareholders, who had power to remove them.

One reason why the subsidiary agreements took so long to be concluded was that there was known to be a secret Burmese government committee overseeing the joint oil venture negotiations. Maxwell-Lefroy's best endeavours never succeeded in finding out who the members were. Although the wrangling went on for most of the year, the points at issue were finally resolved without Burmah Oil having to yield any point of principle: it is a tribute to his skill that he was able to convince the Burmese negotiators – one of them at least being openly hostile to the company – that the British were not out to hoodwink them. In September the Rangoon government approved the final terms, and later that month these were debated in the Burmese parliament. There the deputy prime minister, Ba Swe, powerfully countered attacks on the principle of joint venture. If the government had resolved to handle the oil industry on its own, he argued, it would have had to wait fifty to a hundred years before achieving its objective of becoming fully efficient.

The prestigious but moderately outspoken Burmese journal *The Nation*, in commending Ba Swe's speech, underlined the fact that the foreign parties to the joint venture were providing the indispensable capital, technological skills and managerial experience. In addition, they would 'bring to the project the approach of sound commercial practice, as opposed to the bureaucratic attitudes of mind of the government participators'.

The terms of the venture, it continued, were specific and the position of each party was clear. 'This is no donor-recipient relationship, but a down-to-earth, practical arrangement of mutual convenience.'[1]

With these following winds behind it, the final accord (which included an agency agreement) was signed on 5 October. Weva was present in person and the directors in London formally congratulated him, as well they might, on the successful outcome of his protracted negotiations. The Foreign Office's relief that this tiresome matter had at last been settled could be seen in the appreciative letter which he received from the Minister of State there, the Marquess of Reading. 'I have some idea of how difficult the process has been, and the result reflects great credit on your patience and tenacity', the Minister wrote.[2]

The capital of The Burma Oil Company (1954) Ltd was equivalent to the previously agreed figure of £15 million, the government of Burma taking a third and Burmah Oil 55 per cent; the other $11^2/_3$ per cent was shared between British Burmah and Indo-Burma. Rangoon had paid in April the first instalment of £2.5 million, no loan from the British government being in the end called for. However, when in July Weva expected Maxwell-Lefroy to demand a further payment, the latter had to explain that Burmese public finances were in poor shape, since the authorities were reluctant to cut back on government expenditure, and sterling reserves were alarmingly on the decrease; 'Burma has bitten off more than she can chew for the moment', he reported. The directors in London therefore decided to treat the second £2.5 million as an interest-free loan. Burmah Oil's share was nearly £2.1 million, and it received modest repayments each subsequent year until at the end of 1959 there was £1.4 million still outstanding.

Once the October 1954 agreement was concluded, Maxwell-Lefroy discerned a noticeable relaxation of tension among Burmese officialdom: in his words, 'the barometer oscillated less violently'. As could have been anticipated, the authorities in Rangoon treated the 1954 company with far more consideration than was shown towards Burmah Oil's own trading subsidiary, which was the local operator and marketed the final products. The five board members soon settled down and worked together as a corporate team, all being agreed on the objective of carrying oil operations forward in the country, if not always on the means. That harmony at the top was helped by the high calibre of successive Burmese directors, two of whom later became ambassadors and two others cabinet ministers.

The minutes of the bi-monthly board meetings contain a great deal of workaday business such as authorising stores and pondering what to do about reopening the still dormant Yenangyaung operations; there the people in the government-sponsored Oilfield Relief Committee – whom Maxwell-Lefroy nicknamed the oil-thieving gangs – were energetically rehabilitating some abandoned wells which did not belong to them. However, the new board's overriding task was planning to rebuild the Syriam refinery. Weva was anxious to have the proposal brought forward, as under the original agreement of 1951 he had undertaken to work towards making Burma more or less self-sufficient in oil products, by increasing refinery capacity at Chauk.

However, since no less than 63 per cent of oil products were sold in the populous Lower Burma, the restoration of refining at Syriam might seem more logical. The snag was that, according to an internal estimate by experts in the London office, a new refinery there would cost £500,000, despite the survival of the foundations and much of the Dubbs thermal cracking plant which could probably be made serviceable with new pumps and pressure pipes. Undoubtedly, however, the job could be undertaken much more cheaply and, as an earnest of the new company's intention to go ahead, refining experts gave a report to the first board meeting in May, showing how economies might be made.

Plans were rapidly drawn up, and these were agreed with the Union government as early as November 1954, so well had the oil people succeeded in gaining the confidence of officials and ministers. A few weeks later, work was started on clearing the Syriam site, surveying the old plant and salvaging any possibly usable pieces of equipment. The refinery complex was a vast one, and attempts since the war to clear the site had been on a piecemeal basis, to create jobs for local workpeople rather than for any more constructive purpose.

Foster Wheeler Ltd, which had designed some of the pre-war refining plant, were appointed as design and construction engineers. In contrast with the 1920s, the most up-to-date equipment was not required, since newer techniques merely served to economise in space and in the amount of refinery labour needed, and economies of those kinds were not needed in Burma. Work included the repair of the Dubbs plant, the atmospheric and vacuum crude distillation plant, the 40,000 lbs-per-hour steam plant, a candle factory, the facilities for treating and blending refined products, and a range of auxiliary buildings and services. As before, the restored power station would supply electricity to the town of Syriam as well as to the refinery.

The new Inland Water Transport Board – the former Irrawaddy Flotilla Company – was owned by the government of Burma, and the authorities therefore expected the company to continue to use the system of barge trains for conveying crude from the fields to Rangoon, far from ideal as that system was. Apart from the greater expense compared with the pipeline, navigation could be exceedingly difficult at certain seasons when the river fell to an unduly low level. The barge trains, in units of four and propelled by pusher tugs, were capable of transporting 14,000 barrels of crude at a time; enough for four or five days' use once the refinery was working at its full capacity of 3,500 barrels a day. That would represent about one-quarter of pre-war throughput.

The board had hoped that Syriam would be open within eighteen months, say in mid-1956. Unfortunately, during 1955 the Burmese cabinet imposed an across-the-board cut in import licences to conserve foreign currency reserves, and Maxwell-Lefroy protested in vain that half a refinery was quite as useless as no refinery at all. The Foster Wheeler team in Rangoon was with difficulty restrained from pulling out and going home as 'the work creaked jerkily along, never quite coming to a halt and never properly getting under way', in Maxwell-Lefroy's later words. Two encouraging factors kept the project going. First, the clearance operations in the ruins of Syriam refinery, as well as the rival Seikkyi and Thilawa refineries, produced large quantities of serviceable materials, which could be salvaged and adapted for the new installations:

second, the previously low morale of the Burmese refinery workers markedly revived when serious construction work began. Despite continued rebel activity in the surrounding districts and periodic threats to sabotage the refinery, local co-operation was maintained. Under the direction of the headquarters engineering staff in Britain, a 'masterpiece of improvisation' was thus created at a fraction of the cost that an entirely new refinery would have incurred.

One anxiety of the 1954 company board had also exercised R. I. Watson as long before as 1919: the likelihood that the Chauk and Lanywa fields – now the only producers – would run dry in seven or eight years if no new reserves of crude were discovered fairly soon. This was a matter that Weva had earlier discussed with U Nu, and it became a top priority item once the new board began to meet, since a failure to act quickly might mean that the licences to prospect in the Irrawaddy delta would not be transferred, with the other assets, to the new company but would be assigned away to competitors. The necessary prospecting work would be very costly, involving both seismic surveys and test drilling to yield adequate information about the geological strata in the most likely areas. Weva had hoped to keep all exploration in a separate sterling company financed entirely from London. That would have given him a much freer hand than under the joint venture system, but the Rangoon authorities would not agree to this.

Before it had reached a decision about awarding any exploration licences, in June 1955 the Rangoon government announced its overall policy towards capital investment, designed to attract foreign funds. It had in the past year come to suspect that Burmah Oil's board was not treating the issue of prospecting in the Irrawaddy delta with sufficient urgency. To be sure, there was some truth in that suspicion: Burmah Oil was becoming heavily committed elsewhere, with very costly projects under way in India and Pakistan, as explained in Chapter XI below.

Moreover, in April 1955 the company's direction in London had moved on to a new tack. Weva resigned the managing directorship at the early age of 57. He had a variety of reasons for wishing to go. 'I wanted', he said in his memoirs, 'to be freer to play polo at Cirencester, and in low handicap tournaments all over the country.'[3] The other reasons he reported confidentially to the general managers in Rangoon, Delhi and Karachi. 'Partly financial, partly my knowledge that I could not go on for so very much longer without blocking promotion', especially of Eadie, one year his senior. Most intriguingly, there was also 'partly my desire, if it should prove possible, to get more "inside" what is happening, and even to be able to help a little perhaps with defence problems.' No doubt his dream of reliving the magic wartime years of being close to the centre of affairs soon passed away: he did lecture on oil at Camberley and the other staff colleges, including the NATO one at Paris, but otherwise he had to employ his abundant mental energies on the Transport Users Consultative Committee and the Restrictive Practices Court.

In any case, by early 1955 he seems to have found himself out of tune with his fellow directors after the conclusion of the 1954 agreement in Burma, where he had given away an extra £50,000 without authorisation from home. His strength as managing director had been as a masterly negotiator. However, his gifts of administration and of dealing with the minutiae of desk-work were less pronounced, to the detriment of the company at a time when it appeared to be drifting.

Weva had been the maverick in Burmah Oil's mainly conformist herd. As one of the company's top geologists, he had been able to exercise to the full his considerable individualistic talents, and in the army there had been room among the plentiful staff officers for his type of highly original mind. As sole managing director from 1951 onwards, his touch was less certain. To be sure, he had Eadie as a very able assistant managing director, one who tended to stay put when he was off on his many trips abroad, to the Indian subcontinent and the western hemisphere as well as to Burma. Nevertheless, Sir Kenneth Harper's health was not robust and a strong lead was required from the centre. Much attention had to be paid to events in Burma, India and Pakistan, but Burmah Oil also needed to spend time on reappraising its position in the world at large. That need was the more apparent once Anglo-Iranian had in 1954 patched up its quarrel with the government of Iran and was busy expanding elsewhere in the world. That company's new global role, free from the trammels of its origins, was made clear when in December 1954 it changed its name to the British Petroleum Company; BP for short.

Following Weva's departure, William Eadie took over as Burmah Oil's managing director. He was far more dubious than his predecessor about the long-term value of putting money into Burma, where the government was bound to take over the oil industry sooner or later. Like his colleagues on the London board, he was greatly concerned about the security risk to the geologists prospecting in remote areas of Burma which were far from pacified. Even the army commander-in-chief, General Ne Win, disagreed with the British military attaché in Rangoon who had over-confidently declared that conditions in those areas were tranquil enough to permit exploration.

The government of Burma's pronouncement of June 1955 about its future attitude to foreign capital, mentioned above, also stated that there was scope for a number of oil companies to prospect at the same time in Burma, so that newcomers would have to be attracted in. It was therefore prepared to give guarantees that no oil nationalisation would take place for a specified number of years, and that those putting money into the country would be allowed to repatriate their capital and profits. Burma's petroleum legislation was hopelessly out of date, having been enacted as long before as 1924; it would be revised to include these safeguards. Although clearly the 1954 company might well be weakened as a result of this competition from outside, it could hardly object to outsiders bringing in capital and know-how, given its own shortage of capital for the essential and very costly prospecting programme. Gratifyingly, in 1955, profit earned in Burma came to more than £800,000, nearly double the 1952–54 average.

In February 1957, about eight months late, the new Syriam refinery came on stream, and towards the end of the following month was officially opened by the acting prime minister, Ba Swe. The opening ceremony was unashamedly dramatic. It took place at dusk, and when the minister pressed a switch, the whole of the distillation plant was lit up, causing a sensation among the watching crowds. Here was a necessary piece of investment that had demonstrably reached fruition, in contrast with other highly expensive and grandiose official schemes that

Elephant power: loading storage tank on to lorry

Construction of Oil India Ltd pipeline, 1963 (Note mobile crane driver's parasol)

Sir Kenneth B. Harper, chairman
1948–57

Handing over the watch (and clock) end-1964. William E. Eadie, chairman
1957–64 (left) and Robert P. Smith, chairman 1965–71, at Eadie's retirement
ceremony

always seemed to be indefinitely delayed. As the local press took pains to emphasise the next day, people could see for themselves one project that was really going to work. Its productive capacity was indeed only one-quarter of its pre-1942 forerunner but, together with the refinery at Chauk, it was planned to be able by 1959 to supply the whole of Burma's refined oil product requirements, apart from lubricants and aviation fuel which still had to be imported: a quantity of wax was even available for export. Figures of oil production and consumption in Burma between 1955 and 1961 are given in table 5.

The good working relationship, achieved with the Burmese authorities, parallelled the harmony between British and Burmese directors in the 1954 company's board. The government's Industrial Development Corporation had by then introduced a cheap but durable locally-produced kerosene stove; that and official restrictions on the use of firewood as fuel created an unprecedented demand for kerosene. Indeed, the 1954 company had to make representations to Burma Railways for more tank-wagons to meet this demand, and to the water transport board for more barges and tugs at a time when over 2 million barrels of crude oil a year had to be shipped down-river to Syriam. By 1959 the Burmanisation programme among managers and technicians was rapidly going ahead. That year over a hundred Burmese apprentices attended the Chauk Institute of Technology, while 26 employees were being trained in Britain and 3 in India.

Neither the Burmah Oil directors in London nor the British managers in Rangoon could ever forget that political tensions in a young independent country might at any time spark off abrupt policy changes towards their enterprise: in the Burmese cabinet, there had already been rumblings about what some still regarded as the over-generous terms of the joint venture agreement. In June 1956 U Nu gave up the premiership to Ba Swe for a year, so as to reorganise his ruling party, the AFPFL, and to root out corruption.[4] As soon as he resumed office, discontent among ministers erupted, notably about orders he had given to halt the industrialisation and nationalisation programmes so as to correct the endemic budget deficit and

Table 5
Oil production and consumption – Burma 1955–61

	Crude oil production (000 barrels)			Refined products (000 barrels)			Percentage of oil product needs from Burma (%)
	Burma Oil Co. (1954)	Independent operators*	Total Burma	Indigenous	Imported	Total	
1955	996	346	1342	792	953	1745	45
1956	1162	348	1510	866	1147	2013	43
1957	2094	381	2475	1474	751	2225	66
1958	2518	377	2895	2179	245	2424	90
1959	2904	421	3325	2468	282	2750	90
1960†	2979	423	3402			—	
1961†	3088	423	3511	2893	145	3038	95

Notes: * Independent operators' production estimated
† Data for 1960 and onwards incomplete or missing

balance of payments problems. Despite continuing good relations at the top, the oil joint venture periodically came in for its share of criticisms. In June 1958 U Nu took advantage of divisions within his own government to rout the dissidents by sacking fifteen senior and twenty-two junior ministers.

To the company's relief M. A. Raschid, since 1956 Minister of Mines, stayed at his post. In mid-November 1958 he publicised his moderate views about the oil industry which he oversaw as minister. His government could not overlook the fact that substantial amounts of capital were required to develop the industry, and that such capital was not available within the country. Although the 1954 company had been carrying out some exploration, the task was such a vast one that it would have to be shared with other companies which the government was seeking to encourage into Burma. Not only had it brought out new oil legislation, but it would be willing to offset prospecting expenditure against income tax. The government reiterated its promise that nationalisation would not take place for some years and renewed its efforts to maintain law and order. In return, it expected give-and-take, in the form of foreign companies helping to train local personnel, bringing in any capital needed, and agreeing to make local purchases from ancillary industries that showed themselves capable of producing goods of the required quality at reasonable prices.

In retrospect, the period 1956–9 can be seen as one in which, after the immediate post-independence traumas, most elements in Burma – whether political, military or civilian – were broadly striving to make the democratic system work.[5] However, U Nu and his coalition government, while pursuing the path of reconstruction and reconciliation, made two fatal errors. First, they placed social and economic objectives above the restoration of law and order; second, as one expert has put it, they relied on the plausible assurances of certain foreign experts and 'imagined that Burma could at one stride become a modern industrialised community, without undergoing any of the bitter experiences of the older industrial nations'. In October 1958 a rapid deterioration of law and order in many parts of Burma led U Nu to hand over power to his commander-in-chief, General Ne Win, an initially reluctant dictator who agreed to accept office for a limited period only. Although

U Nu returned to office in 1960 and won a landslide victory in a general election that year, the new decade was soon to bring in a change of regime – one of prolonged military rule by Ne Win – and the end of Burmah Oil's operations in the country.

For the company in Britain, 1957 was to prove a decisive year. The 66-year-old chairman, Sir Kenneth Harper, had the previous year been a sick man, and in mid-1957 suffered two coronary attacks; it was clear that his retirement could not be long delayed. Meanwhile, Eadie as sole managing director was effectively in charge of the company, using his authority to draw his colleagues' thinking away from the traditional lines they had become accustomed to follow.

In particular, he composed memoranda to assess realistically the company's current position and future prospects, often with a wealth of figures to back up his line of thought. In May 1956, for instance, he had 'taken stock' of Burmah Oil's situation in the East. In Pakistan, reasonable prospects existed since private enterprise was still allowed a good deal of freedom. However, in Burma the Union government could sooner or later be expected to seek a take-over of the oil industry. In India, as explained in Chapter XI below, the company's high hopes of being able to realise that country's marked oil potential had been considerably hampered by the Industrial Policy Resolution of 1956. Most disappointing of all, the decision to reserve future exploration to the Delhi government alone meant that – with the exception of running the wholly-owned Assam Oil – the company could expect only a steadily diminishing role there.

He therefore found the overall picture in the East none too encouraging, especially when combined with certain financial data which the chief accountant, Jack Strain, had presented to Harper the previous year. The company's operations in Pakistan, recognised as the most stable and promising of the three Eastern countries involved, were making net losses, mainly because of very heavy prospecting expenditure. Regrettably, such losses were likely to persist for some years to come. India and Burma were on the other hand earning profits, Burma at a relatively modest but steady rate now that the 1954 company was in full operation. Those profits were bound to diminish as state control gradually increased. Taking all these factors into account, Strain found it not surprising that the Burmah Oil Group's net trading profit between 1949 and 1955 had fallen from 57 to 32 per cent of total earnings: precise figures are given in Table 6. That fall was of course attributable also to the considerable increase that had taken place in investment income. As long as it maintained existing policies, therefore, the group would sooner or later become little more than an investment company, increasingly dependent on the mounting dividends from British Petroleum and Shell.

A more immediate danger was that of a cash-flow problem. In May 1957 Strain reported that liquid funds were running down so rapidly that the company would have to realise some or all of the £3 million worth of government securities it still held. The following month J. A. Drysdale, currently the senior manager in London responsible for exploration, warned that while geological discoveries in Burma, India and Pakistan had of late been generally as good as in other free areas of the world, Burmah Oil lacked the financial resources to 'hold the British position' in those countries. However, any cut-back in its prospecting would be interpreted as an open invitation to Shell or – worse – American or Iron Curtain oil interests to move in. BP, on the other hand, was under-invested there. 'Everything', Drysdale suggested, 'therefore points to the desirability of Burmah Oil and British Petroleum joining forces in these areas, in order to preserve the joint British oil interests there.' He therefore urged immediate talks on exploration matters with 'the people upstairs' on the BP floors of Britannic House.

As it happened, the parleys that the directors soon opened with their loftier neighbours proved to be on a different topic altogether: concerning the investment rather than the operational side of the business. In about September BP let it be known privately that it was to make a £50 million rights issue of ordinary shares: the first since 1922. That would be the largest industrial issue ever handled by the London capital market, well outstripping the £40 million issue by ICI the previous year. Burmah Oil, with a 26.4 per cent holding, would have to find £13.2 million.

For a number of reasons, that issue would be highly unwelcome to the company. First, at a time when its cash reserves were so depleted, the prospect of finding such a sum, even in instalments, did not appeal. Secondly, it would only become that much more dependent on BP shares both as assets on the balance sheet and as a source of income. There was one alternative: to take up the share rights and then sell them at a profit of £1.50 per £1 share. However, that would reduce the company's holding of the ordinary shares below the minimum level of 25 per cent which the Burmah Oil directors considered vital as maintaining for the company a voting majority in BP. Ever since 1914 the British government had pledged itself never to use its own stake – currently 55.7 per cent – in order to influence operational decisions, so that Burmah Oil attached much value to this important voting power.

The preparations for this mammoth BP rights issue were woefully complicated by a gathering economic crisis, which forced the Conservative government to take countermeasures of a severity not seen for many years. The Capital Issues Committee, an official body controlling stock exchange flotations, scaled down the BP issue from £50 million to £41 million. Then the government decided that it could not afford to retain its own tranche or slice which, even on the reduced figure, would have involved its borrowing from other sources no less than £23 million, a large enough figure to help fuel inflation. It therefore proposed to purchase the rights and dispose of them on the open market. That intention clearly precluded Burmah Oil from following suit, as the simultaneous unloading on the market of these vast quantities of shares could have so depressed their stock exchange prices as to wipe out the expected profit. Hence Burmah Oil would be forced to obtain from the bankers a loan to buy its new stake – just after the monetary authorities had issued strict directions that bank advances must be severely limited to essential purposes.

Richard Fleming, of the company's merchant bankers Robert Fleming & Co., went to see Sir Roger Makins, joint secretary of the Treasury, who expressed sympathy but felt unable to make Burmah Oil a special case. Two days later, in a crisis move, the monetary authorities raised the bank rate from 5 to 7 per cent. Burmah Oil, low on cash, compelled to take up its rights by its self-imposed rule of maintaining a minimum 25 per cent voting share in BP, and facing a bank rate that was higher than at any time since 1921, found itself confronted with some of the tricky problems of being an investment company. Above all, the directors' freedom to manage their own corporate affairs was being gravely hampered by having most of the Burmah Oil investment portfolio in two giant companies, BP and Shell.

There was yet a further complication. Because of its very conservative financial policy of undervaluing balance sheet assets – and, let it be said, none too dynamic leadership at that time – Burmah Oil was highly vulnerable to a take-over, most alarmingly from foreign interests. One method of deterring such a take-over would have been to insert in the company's Articles of Association a clause forbidding it to enter into any arrangement which would transfer its management or control to any foreigner or foreign corporation; a new provision of that kind would need a three-quarters vote of a general meeting to overturn. In 1905, when Burmah Oil had engaged the attention of Whitehall as the only oil producer of any consequence domiciled in the British empire, the Committee of Imperial Defence had, through the India Office, requested the company to introduce similar changes designed to keep it British (see Volume I p. 90). Nothing had come of that request, but early in 1957 the company's lawyers drafted new Articles to make foreign control impossible. That April, Harper saw the governor of the Bank of England, C. F. Cobbold, to seek his blessing for this provision and – perhaps more important as a public relations exercise – to ask whether he would allow an indication of Bank approval to be made public. Mr Governor was unenthusiastic about lending his name to any such pronouncement; once again, therefore, no changes were made.

From time to time throughout 1957 strong rumours were rife that Burmah Oil was considered to be what a former managing director, Kirkman Finlay, had years before lightheartedly termed 'a nice subject for a swallow'. That April the *Investor's Chronicle* confidential news-letter contained reports that a consortium of American oil companies, anxious to secure a larger stake in BP and indirectly in that company's huge Middle East sources of crude, had decided that the most economical method was to increase their holdings in Burmah

Oil. London brokers had therefore been instructed to purchase up to 3 million of the company's 41 million issued ordinary shares. Such reports seemed plausible since the Chase Manhattan Bank had just forecast that between 1955 and 1965 the free world's oil consumption would increase by about three-quarters, requiring Middle Eastern output to be stepped up by 150 per cent.

BP happened to have larger interests in Middle East oil than any other single company: not only did it have a big minority stake in the consortium set up to carry out Iranian production, but it was also involved in Iraq, Kuwait and Abu Dhabi. It held 28 per cent of that region's total reserves and 19 per cent of the world's proved reserves: in volume terms, more than was known to exist in the United States and Canada together. Thus the proposed American consortium could look forward to good growth potential in its investment. The talk faded when no sign of any unusual activity appeared on the London stock exchange. Then a major American integrated oil corporation, the Cities Service Company, was said to be especially interested. Standard Oil of Indiana's president was also rumoured secretly to be working on a plan to take over Burmah Oil, only to be overruled by his executive. Meanwhile, the company's top managers kept a weather eye on its share register, without spying any reefs ahead. Even allowing for the activities of some 'suspect nominees', identifiable American holdings remained on a minute scale: under one per cent of total ordinary shares.

However, even if no foreign predators appeared to be stealthily buying their way into the company, what would the directors do if a head-on bid were to land on their desks? Should they accept, they would incur the wrath of the British government which would be mortified to see over a quarter of the ordinary shares of BP – in which the government itself had a large stake – effectively going to overseas interests. Yet market reaction might force them to yield, on terms unlikely to be much above the current prices of their BP and Shell holdings.

Why might any bid terms be so unfavourable from the company's viewpoint? The answer lay in the lukewarm attitude of the investing public to Burmah Oil's ordinary shares. Ever since the early 1950s, when the BP and Shell holdings together began to figure largely in the company's balance sheet, the value of its stock – already low relatively to other oil shares – had persistently remained below the underlying value of the BP and Shell shares which it held. That allowed purchasers of Burmah Oil stock to acquire a stake in the substantial operations in India, Pakistan and Burma at no extra cost to themselves.

The *Investor's Chronicle* in July 1956 had referred to the widespread criticism, especially among Scottish stockholders, that the increased earnings – mainly from investment income – of recent years had not been adequately passed on to stockholders.[6] The company had instead paid out less in the way of dividends than it had itself received in dividends and interest, and ploughed back the surplus into the business. Given the large financial commitments in the East, that was understandable; however, with hindsight the directors can be criticised for not having publicised more forcefully the case for retentions on such a scale. The article asked bluntly, 'What is the point of sinking more money into countries with increasing nationalistic inclinations and risking the dangers of expropriation on one-sided terms?' The solution it proposed was the familiar one of the company distributing BP and Shell holdings to stockholders and then concentrating on trading activities.

Such were some of the dilemmas which faced Eadie when in November 1957 he was elected chairman on Harper's retirement. He remained as managing director, sharing the post with his former assistant, the 54-year-old Robert Paterson Smith. RP, as he was generally known (Eadie was just Bill), had come into the Burmah Oil hierarchy via Asiatic in Calcutta. Another chartered accountant from Scotland, he had joined the Burmah-Shell organisation on its establishment in 1928. After Indian independence he had worked energetically to safeguard the interests of the British commercial community in Bombay, where life was not always easy for expatriates during the heady transition period. He had been a member of the British Chamber of Commerce there and the committee of the United Kingdom Citizens Association. In 1952 he had been brought back to the London office.[7] Eadie was conscious that the number of executive directors had in recent years been inadequate for the increasing burden of work: four out of nine, if one included the ailing Harper. Jack Strain was therefore appointed to the board as finance director and D. C. Robertson, formerly general manager in India, also became a board member.

Eadie's first few months in office proved to be less onerous than he might have feared. No take-over bid was made, while BP in the end decided to raise its funds in a way that was virtually painless for Burmah Oil. Since over 80 per cent of the shareholding body, namely the Treasury and Burmah Oil, were for their several reasons reluctant to provide new finance, a rights issue was automatically ruled out: eventually in December BP issued £41 million worth of 6 per cent debentures to the general public. The government announced that it would not be subscribing, while Eadie arranged for the Burmah Oil shareholders to benefit in what would clearly be a financially advantageous issue for them, by being given priority in their applications.

The minutiae of that heavily oversubscribed issue, and the pother it caused, are of small interest in themselves after all these years. However, it seems to have been the catalyst for one of the most important memoranda written by the chairman to his board colleagues in the whole post-war period of the company's history. Entitled 'Operational and Investment Policy', this memorandum of 18 September 1957 drove home the message that on the investment side, the company held BP stock with a market value of £17.3 million: a 'vast sum', on which Burmah Oil was getting only 2.3 per cent return tax free, well below the 15 per cent return at par value. Was the company therefore employing those resources to the best advantage? What he called the company's 'time-honoured' policy, pursued ever since the government had bought its way into BP as long before as 1914, had been to retain at least a 25 per cent voting position; yet to attempt to use the veto at BP general meetings, in the face of the government and all outside shareholders, would be quite unthinkable. Hence, he argued, a holding of not less than 20 per cent was perfectly adequate, and would give the company scope to sell up to 5 per cent of the stock, for reinvestment in any alternative project it chose.

Eadie had previously argued forcefully that the company must not allow itself to become simply an investment trust. What he now sought was the acquisition of operational outlets for the money that would be freed by such sales of stock, in the form of direct investments which the company would control. 'Where should we look for new opportunities?' he asked. Having reminded his readers of the company's limited operational prospects in India, Pakistan and Burma and its indirect interest through BP in the Middle East, he went on, 'The obvious answer must be west of Suez and perhaps west again – Canada.'

That country presented great opportunities, but also problems. One problem was that Canadian industry, then mainly in the east of the country, needed to stretch across the continent and establish itself closer to the oil areas, which were in the west, before a reasonable return could be expected on what could well be a considerable investment outlay. The company might therefore in the first instance seek some appropriately-sited Canadian gas or oil transportation or production enterprise, which had already reached a remunerative stage, and use it as a 'watching base' for possible development or expansion of direct investment in oil.

From that time on, for good or ill, the Burmah Oil Company was embarking on a new and totally uncharted course. For that shift in direction Eadie, and Eadie alone, was responsible. In one of the most over-cited passages in Shakespeare's *Julius Caesar*, Brutus states:

> There is a tide in the affairs of men
> Which, taken at the flood, leads on to fortune;
> Omitted, all the voyage of their life
> Is bound in shallows and in miseries.
> On such a full sea are we now afloat,
> And we must take the current when it serves,
> Or lose our ventures.

The nineteenth-century author James Russell Lowell usefully glossed this quotation by pointing out, 'Truly there is a tide in the affairs of men; but there is no gulf-stream setting forever in one direction.' Lowell's remark seems so apposite to the history of Burmah Oil in this period that it is used as an epigraph to the present volume.

Yet Eadie's signal achievement was not so much to launch his company on a tidal current that was already flooding, as to work long and patiently to give momentum to that current. He eventually induced the directors to realise that the company's operations no longer needed to be confined to the East, but that new ventures could be started up anywhere on the globe. Even so, it took the best part of two years before the board agreed even to a modest joint exploration venture in the western hemisphere, and it was the end of 1959 before Eadie won – after a tough battle with some of his colleagues – the general principle of diversifying operations geographically. In those years 1957–9 he produced a stream of memoranda, gradually nudging directors towards accepting the logic of his argument.

Like many company chairmen, Eadie needed some confidant with whom he could privately discuss problems as they cropped up. The man he relied on was Lord Bilsland, a non-executive director since 1947.[8] Bilsland was a bakery millionaire and a knight of the Thistle, with interests in many other fields of Scottish commerce, including the Bank of Scotland. Many of his qualities appealed to Eadie. Above all, he was a man of commonsense, which he demonstrated by the sage advice on many questions of company policy he proffered over the years. While not seeking to be an innovator himself, he was good at thinking through and then assessing the proposals of others that were designed to cope with change.

Bilsland took his position on the board very seriously, several times complaining that the non-executive directors were being hampered in their job by not being given enough information. He fully backed Eadie in his diversification programme, while at times counselling caution. For more technical advice Eadie turned to Richard Fleming, who was to become a Burmah Oil director in 1959. Despite being much occupied with his work in the bank and with some very influential outside directorships, he always found time to help Eadie and his colleagues over financial problems that beset the company. The Scottish directors were said to appreciate obtaining, for a non-executive director's fee, advice that they would otherwise have had to pay for at full consultancy rates.[9]

The first of the company's serious enquiries outside the traditional areas seems to have been made in February 1958. A proposal had come to its notice for acquiring production interests in Venezuela, then the second largest oil-producing country in the world: one which Burmah Oil had in the early 1920s considered entering but decided against. An American oil corporation, the Atlantic Refining Company, had recently uncovered substantial new Venezuelan fields, but its own outlets were restricted mainly to the United States, where there was a glut of oil, so that it could not hope to profit adequately from that discovery.

Atlantic was also short of money. It therefore sought a partner to take over the disposal of the oil, to provide all the capital for developing the fields and to pay all operating costs for eight years in return for 75 per cent of the sales proceeds. That partner would need to spend the equivalent of £7 million over three years and then £4 million over the following five years. The Treasury, not yet out of the economic crisis that had erupted the previous autumn, could make no promise about releasing from Britain's still inadequate reserves the substantial sum of dollars that would almost certainly be needed. Even so, Eadie thought the proposition well worth following up.

Although he had just come back from a gruelling trip to India, and confessed that he had been through a period of indifferent health, Eadie at once made preparations for a visit to the United States and Canada, taking Drysdale with him. His principal task was to go to Washington in order to seek finance from the World Bank for the newly-formed Oil India Ltd (see Chapter XI below). However, they also made a point of visiting Atlantic's Philadelphia headquarters; within a few days Eadie had hammered out an 'understanding' with the company's president, one that each expected would quickly be ratified by his own board.

If Eadie had hoped for a swift conclusion to the deal, he was to be disappointed. Burmah Oil's cash problems, while still evident, had eased somewhat, but he knew it was essential to find a partner to share the £11 million cost of the deal with Atlantic. He had already sounded out the BP directors, who would consider taking a share if the terms were right. It was an attractive offer, as the government shareholding in BP would otherwise have debarred it from obtaining concessions in that country. In May 1959 he formally offered to Harold Snow, deputy chairman of BP, a half share in the Venezuelan venture. Eadie did not hesitate to apply moral pressure by pointing out that as Burmah Oil gave BP assistance over refining and marketing in the East – for instance, by selling Iranian oil in India and Pakistan, it was reasonable to expect reciprocal help in the West.

Disappointingly, Snow expressed reservations about the terms of the deal, but offered to help with disposing of any crude oil from Venezuela. That left Burmah Oil in the lurch, and still faced with two weighty problems. First, however attractive the opportunity of securing profuse quantities of crude in what was politically a more or less safe area, the company would not be investing in a properly integrated enterprise. Second, how to pay for the venture? When in mid-May Eadie was called in to see Cobbold, the governor of the Bank of England, Cobbold admitted that the Bank by then could afford to be more liberal over releasing funds for overseas investment. However, he was not happy at the prospect of a deal between Burmah Oil and Atlantic being financed by an exchange of shares, as a sizeable block of Burmah Oil shares – with their underlying stake in BP – would then be going overseas.

Cobbold had also wished to discuss with Eadie the possibility of enlarging the Burmah Oil board, now that the company was geographically spreading its wings. Moreover, he was anxious to know if there was any evidence of block purchases by outsiders of its ordinary shares; Eadie was able to assure him that there was not, but the governor wanted to make sure that the board had contingency plans to forestall any take-over bid from the United States. No one specifically mentioned Harper's idea of changing the Articles of Association, but Eadie did at once raise the matter with the company's auditors and solicitors. However, no changes of note occurred.

If it seems strange that the governor should spend time in discussing the internal affairs of a privately-owned oil company, the reason was clearly that the Bank, as the government's financial adviser, would be concerned about any move that would even indirectly affect the shareholding structure or profitability of BP, the nation's most important overseas trading investment. Cobbold more or less conceded this when he advised Eadie to examine the take-over possibility in conjunction with Neville Gass, chairman of BP from 1957 to 1960: this was in one of the exceptional periods when the chairmen of the two companies got on very well together. Whether discussions actually took place is not recorded in the Burmah Oil files.

Eadie still needed to secure from his board a statement of principle on diversification, which he suggested should be affected by reducing the company's shareholding in BP. Towards the end of July 1959, therefore, he arranged a special meeting of directors to discuss the matter. Not surprisingly, the Burmah Oil director who was most forthright in expressing his opinions was the formidable Lord Strathalmond, until 1955 Sir William Fraser, retired chairman of BP. He came down strongly in favour of the company undertaking portfolio rather than direct investment: that would of course have made it more, not less, of an investment company and thus would have defeated Eadie's plans. If Burmah Oil did acquire the shares of enterprises in the western hemisphere, Strathalmond would prefer this to be done by a straight exchange of BP shares for the stock of such enterprises, as causing less disruption to share prices than would a sale followed by a reinvestment of the proceeds. He therefore seemed less worried than Cobbold about BP shares going abroad, directly or indirectly. Although some of the directors, such as Bilsland, seemed to be influenced by Strathalmond's powerfully expressed view, Eadie summed up positively, stating that 'diversification by disposal of the company's holding of BP stock and acquisition of investments in integrated concerns in the western [hemisphere] oil industry seemed to be the wish of the meeting'. His management would therefore examine and put forward recommendations for the board to consider.

The Venezuelan project thereafter faded, in favour of one from the eastern hemisphere, first considered in August 1959. A French government oil exploration agency had discovered a gas field in the Sahara, 300 miles south of Algiers, and reported to be by far the greatest natural gas reservoir in the world. Britain's publicly-owned Gas Council had been concerned for some time that coal gas was seriously uncompetitive, whereas basing production on either heavy oil or naphtha could make the local gas boards over-dependent on the oil industry. A promising alternative was to use natural gas. In the later 1950s, the Gas Council decided to join with a firm of American experts in refrigerated transportation – Union Stockyards of Chicago – and two oil companies – Continental Oil and Shell – to convert a small tanker, the *Methane Pioneer*, for the transport of experimental cargoes of liquefied methane gas from Texas to the Thames.

A pioneer in the use of natural gas in Britain was the chairman of the North Thames Gas Board, who assured the Burmah Oil directors that he would be more than happy to contract for supplies of Saharan gas should the company acquire the concession. However, there were considerable political difficulties in the way. The northern departments of Algeria were at this time an integral part of France, while the southern territories which included the Saharan oil and gas fields were administered as a French colony. Successive French governments had rigidly controlled the activities of foreign oil companies under the petroleum law of 1928. Perhaps most worryingly, Algeria persisted in a high state of political unrest and even violent insurrection between 1954 and General de Gaulle's declaration of Algerian independence in 1962. These problems of instability and government control were all too reminiscent of those which Burmah Oil was facing in Burma and India. Not surprisingly, therefore, the company had second thoughts.

It is one of the 'might-have-beens' of history that Burmah Oil, which had earlier been the progenitor of the Middle East oil industry and which later was to make the first oil strike in the North Sea, could well have become the supplier to Britain of Algerian gas from the early 1960s onwards. In the event, others were to introduce what became known as 'high-speed gas' from the Sahara, which – before Britain's own reserves of gas were discovered off her coasts – revolutionised an important source of energy for her industrial, commercial and domestic consumers alike.

To Eadie, the decision not to go ahead with the project in the Sahara was in no sense a major rebuff. He had what he felt to be a sound strategy for Burmah Oil, and if not yet a full mandate from the board, at least adequate authority to investigate potentially worthwhile projects. What he now needed to do was to remain on the look-out for an initiative that was within his company's means and technical expertise, and preferably in the New World.

The beginning came about in an unexpected way. In November 1958 an American oilman, described by the bankers Morgan Grenfell as 'an able businessman and a good friend of ours', sought an interview with 'someone in the highest level' in Burmah Oil. He was Charles H. Murphy, president of the Murphy Oil Corporation of El Dorado, Arkansas.[10] Murphy Oil, incorporated in Louisiana in 1950, was of high reputation as a progressive independent company. In addition to its interests in the United States and Canada, it owned 52 per cent of the Ocean Drilling and Exploration Company, of New Orleans. The latter, known as Odeco, had under Charles Murphy's chairmanship pioneered offshore operations in the Gulf of Mexico, and was in the forefront of design, development and use of deep-water drilling vessels and marine production and storage facilities. Murphy was put in touch with Eadie, his prime objective being to discuss the possibility that their two companies might join in an offshore exploration programme off the coast of Burma. They soon reached agreement in principle, provided that they could obtain the consent of the Burmese authorities. The company expressed a willingness in turn to assist Murphy Oil and Odeco with exploration in Papua and Canada, as well as in the Gulf of Mexico. (Papua and later developments in Australia will be considered in Chapter XI below.)

A team came over from the United States to Burmah Oil's headquarters to be briefed in detail about conditions in Burma and the Irrawaddy delta, which seemed the most suitable locality for offshore operations. In April 1959 Murphy himself went to Rangoon, where he held discussions with M. A. Raschid, the Burmese Minister of Mines. He later submitted a formal application for a joint venture, to involve Burmah Oil, Murphy Oil and the government of Burma. However, General Ne Win was then prime minister; while civilian officials kept an open mind on the proposal, their military masters were sceptical and hostile, and the venture got nowhere.

By then relations between Charles Murphy and Eadie had become close, especially after H. R. Tainsh, Burmah Oil's chief geologist, had visited the headquarters of both Murphy Oil and Odeco and expressed complete professional confidence in the companies' operations. In August 1959 the Burmah Oil board approved an agreement between all three companies which provided for joint exploration of leases in the Gulf of Mexico offshore from Louisiana. The crude oil already being raised there was piped into offshore storage tanks, from which tugs or barges collected it at regular intervals and took it to Murphy Oil's refinery close to New Orleans. That same year, the company set up The Burmah Oil Western Company to handle its affairs there. The second joint test led to gas and oil being found in May 1960. Another subsidiary, BOC of Canada Ltd, was registered in November 1959 to undertake joint operations in north-western areas of Canada together with the Murphy-Canada Oil Company.

The two ventures were described in Burmah Oil's report for 1959 as marking 'a significant milestone in the history of the group', since it was only the second occasion on which the group's activities had spread successfully beyond the borders of its traditional areas of operation, namely Burma, India and Pakistan. The first had been in Persia, the inglorious joint venture with Shell in Trinidad (see Vol. I, Chapter XVIII) having been properly forgotten.

While the board in London was not yet convinced of the need for major diversification, it had accepted the involvement with Murphy Oil since it was on a relatively modest scale and confined to exploration. As Eadie well knew, whether his fellow-directors wholeheartedly backed diversification or not would become clear only when they had to decide on a larger proposition.

He was offered such a proposition in the autumn of 1959 while in New York for a meeting with the World Bank over finance for India. The British-controlled Ultramar Company Ltd, which owned oil and gas interests in North and South America – notably crude oil production in Venezuela, offered him participation in a Panama refinery, coupled with a marketing organisation in California. What impressed Eadie was the thorough investigation that had been carried out by

Ultramar, concerned as it was to build up an integrated organisation with downstream acquisitions as outlets for the plentiful Venezuelan crude. To help with financing, Ultramar needed a partner, and a 50 per cent participation by Burmah Oil would cost the equivalent of £6.2 million for the Panama and California ventures combined. That investment might yield £500,000 a year after tax.

Eadie held a board meeting in December 1959 to consider this proposition, in the context of his general diversification principle. He sent to directors a note on 'Future Policy', which stressed the inadequacy of the current and expected future returns from Burma, India and Pakistan, and recommended the Ultramar proposals as 'something worthy of serious consideration', since they could be of complementary value in the event of the joint venture with Murphy in Louisiana being successful.

Regrettably, details of the board meeting have not survived but McCreath wrote to him afterwards, expressing 'admiration of the courage with which you have recently put forward your views in the face of strong opposition'. Although McCreath had not backed him in supporting the principle, he admitted that Eadie might turn out to have been right. The Ultramar proposals as such fell by the wayside, but Eadie had won the day over the principle that the company should diversify through direct investment, which was never challenged again by the Burmah Oil board. Meanwhile, through his initiative, the oldest British oil company already had several look-out posts in the new world, and it remained to be seen which would be the integrated North American enterprise that would eventually join the Burmah group.

Notes

1 Tinker, *Union of Burma*, pp. 117–8.
2 PRO FO 371/111999, 'Burma – Joint Venture', Marquess of Reading to Weva, 14 January 1954.
3 Abraham, *Time Off*, p. 66.
4 Tinker, *Union of Burma*, pp. 90ff.
5 Ibid, p. 386, cf. p. 128.
6 *Investor's Chronicle*, 7 July 1956, pp. 12–13.

7 For R. P. Smith, see obituaries, *The Times* and *Financial Times*, 1 June 1971.
8 Bilsland's obituaries are in *Scotsman*, 11 December, and *Glasgow Herald*, 11 and 14 December 1970.
9 *Sunday Telegraph*, 7 July 1963, 'London Week by Week,' p. 3.
10 For Murphy Oil's activities, see *Burmah Group Magazine (BGM)* No. 13, Spring 1968, pp. 2–6.

CHAPTER VIII

The Denial Case 1948–65[1]

The departure of R. I. Watson from the scene at the end of 1947 did not diminish the anxiety of the Burmah Oil directors to pursue with the utmost vigour the denial claims against the British government. Chapter V showed how the company, on the advice of Sir Stafford Cripps, began lawsuits in the Burmese local courts, later transferred to the High Court in Rangoon, to claim £54.4 million compensation for the assets denied to the Japanese in 1942. As a number of companies were bringing their own actions – there were 36 separate claimants in all – the plaintiffs agreed among themselves that Indo-Burma, the sole locally-registered company involved, should proceed with the test case in Rangoon.

The Burmese authorities at once countered with the argument that they had neither any legal obligation to pay nor any intention of doing so. The wartime destruction, they maintained, had been carried out in the interests not of Burma itself but of Britain and her allies, and it was the British who had given the necessary orders. Cripps himself had hinted at the possibility that their claims might be rejected, but he had made clear that the *ex gratia* payment, of which £4.67 million was Burmah Oil's share under the Carter committee award, would be his final word. To be sure, the affected companies were in an unique predicament in having to resort to lobbying tactics or to the courts in pursuit of their rights. Much to Watson's regret in 1942, the hastily put-together war damage compensation arrangements in Burma had specifically excluded the oil

229

industry; that was why he had then given orders that all written orders by the authorities regarding any destruction must be secured and carefully preserved.

The vessels of the Irrawaddy Flotilla Company had been requisitioned on the orders of the governor, who had later given instructions for their scuttling. That company was thus legally entitled to the compensation, amounting to £1 million, it duly received after the war. The oil installations in Sarawak and Brunei too had been demolished under the terms of agreements made with the authorities soon after Pearl Harbor and the outbreak of war with Japan. No one had at that stage dreamt that Burma would be overrun.

A further legal twist was that, after the terrible losses of the First World War and the barrage of claims arising from those losses, Lloyd George's government in 1920 had passed an Indemnity Act to bar further claims being raised in the courts of law. Since widespread war damage schemes had been introduced in the Second World War, no similar legislation was felt to be necessary after 1945. Owing to its haste over the granting of independence to Burma a year or two later, the British government failed to protect the compensation rights of British firms which had sustained war damage in that country. By contrast, similar firms were protected in other countries such as North Borneo, Brunei and Sarawak. Again, had Cripps in 1948 introduced a short bill translating into parliamentary draftsmen's terms his notorious phrase about the claimants having to whistle for further compensation, then that would have been the end of the matter.

The advent of a Conservative government in October 1951 appeared to offer the claimants a prospect of finding more sympathetic ears than previously in the corridors of power. Of the new senior ministers, R. A. Butler (made Chancellor of the Exchequer) had in 1947 been briefed by Harper, who was concerned about the parliamentary bill passed into law that October to grant independence to Burma, and what he regarded as the lack of safeguards for British companies that continued to operate in that country. Again, Sir David Maxwell-Fyfe (the new Home Secretary) had provided counsel's opinion on the relevant clauses in that bill, and also on the denial case in 1948 and 1950. However, it was not long before incoming ministers, in pursuit of broad continuity in government policy, were learning to be as beastly to Burmah Oil as their predecessors had been.

When in June 1952 J. K. Michie, on behalf of the Burma Chamber of Commerce's home committee, sent to Butler at the Treasury a memorandum outlining the history of the denial claim, the discouraging reply was that the British government had already made *ex gratia* payments. Ministers, it argued, could not rightly propose to parliament that the United Kingdom taxpayer should incur any further burdens over this affair. Butler dismissed out of hand Michie's (and ultimately Watson's) suggestion of independent arbitration as 'not practicable', now that Burma was a sovereign nation.

The next appeal by Michie, complete with memorandum, was made in May 1956 to Butler's successor as Chancellor, Harold Macmillan. In reply, Macmillan declined to modify the government's previous attitude, which was that any legal liability rested with the government of Burma and not with itself. That was disappointing to the Burmah Oil directors, all too aware as they were of the delays occurring over the test case in Rangoon. Two months later, in July, they sent a memorandum to both the Treasury and the Foreign Office, pointing out the political and economic consequences likely to flow from pursuing their claim in Burma any further. Particularly galling was the fact that, although down for hearing on various occasions, the Burmese test case was constantly being postponed on one pretext or another, notwithstanding the efforts and protests of counsel. R. P. Smith, managing director from 1957 onwards, had a by no means complete list of twenty-two occasions on which postponements had been granted. That year the company consulted the Scottish advocate Christopher (later Lord) Guest, to see whether it appeared to have a sound claim in Scots law; his opinion was that it did.

The directors therefore decided in April 1957 that enough was enough, and proposed to start legal proceedings of their own against the British government. By then the six-year time limit applicable to the recovery of debt under the statutes of limitation barred any recourse to the English courts. However, in Scotland the equivalent period was twenty years, which in practice would give them until the early months of 1962: not all that far ahead when allowing for the law's delays. As it happened, in July 1960 the Burmese High Court at last delivered its verdict, totally rejecting the claim of Indo-Burma. On counsel's advice, no appeals were lodged.

In October 1960 Michie made a final appeal, this time to the recently appointed Chancellor of the Exchequer, Selwyn Lloyd. Instead of the six-week delays of his predecessors – just long enough to unearth and blow the dust off the files, Lloyd took nearly five months to reply. This suggests a fairly thorough review of the whole case by government lawyers. Not that his eventual response was any different. The government, he declared, had no *legal* responsibility for denial compensation, while the Carter award had fully discharged any *moral* liability that could possibly have existed.

The Burmah Oil directors at once took advice of leading counsel. The opinion received was unequivocal. They had a legal duty to pursue their claims energetically against the authorities by every practicable means, and to default on this obligation would render them personally liable to their stockholders. Having read Lloyd's reply, the board resolved in April 1961 that the company should start up a test case in Britain; to that Michie and his fellow committee members readily agreed. Burmah Oil was not only the most considerable of the plaintiffs, with the largest claim, but was a Scottish-registered company and therefore able to take advantage of the statutes of limitation there. On 30 October 1961, only four months before the twenty-year period expired, the company brought its action against the Lord Advocate, William Grant, the senior government law officer and legal representative of the crown in Scotland. Under the normal procedure, the case went first to the outer house of the Court of Session.

Until that date, there is no evidence that Whitehall had taken the company's claim at all seriously; perhaps an over-reliance on the case dragging on interminably through the Burmese courts and on being protected by the statutes of limitation had engendered official complacency. Now the Attorney-General, the tough Sir Reginald Manningham-Buller, was sufficiently alarmed to have the whole matter referred to the Home Affairs Committee of the cabinet. There he argued that, while in his opinion the claims of the company and the other plaintiffs had no merit in law, it would be 'intolerable' if the Exchequer were to find itself having to meet the full cost, which in his estimation could well exceed £100 million when simple interest was included, or nearer £160 million at compound interest. Should the courts by any chance decide in the plaintiffs' favour, he continued, then it would be right to introduce legislation to set aside such verdicts. Hence there would be advantage in warning the plaintiffs of the government's intentions before they started to incur further heavy expenditure on litigation.

To its credit, this powerful cabinet committee, chaired by Lord Hailsham, the Lord President of the Council and himself a highly experienced barrister, did not lightly accept these audacious proposals. Such an attempt to warn off plaintiffs by threats of retrospective legislation, it argued, could well expose the government, already in choppy waters over its economic and other policies, to unnecessary criticism. After all, the courts might well reject the claims, but in any case the gravest charge would be that the government had deliberately sought to interfere in a lawsuit actually pending before the courts. As against this, some members of the Home Affairs Committee argued that if the plaintiffs were to persist with their claims despite any warnings issued, the government would be that much better placed to introduce legislation. The views of the hawks prevailed, and the committee agreed to recommend the Attorney-General's proposals to the cabinet.

The matter came before the cabinet on 31 May 1962. It was probably the first time since 1924, when the plans for a merger with Shell had been finally overturned by the refusal of Ramsay MacDonald's administration to sell the government holdings of Anglo-Persian shares, that Burmah Oil's name had been mentioned in full cabinet. The Lord Chancellor, Lord Kilmuir, presented a memorandum on this issue, along the lines of the committee's deliberations; Kilmuir was the Maxwell-Fyfe who had formerly been retained by the company. After discussion, the cabinet accepted the committee's recommendations, approving the general terms of a warning letter already drafted, with the riders that the letter should be sent out as soon as possible, as any victory in the courts by the plaintiffs would create a vested right to damages, and that the Lord Advocate should not be the signatory, since he was a party to the case. The final version of the letter was to be prepared by the Chief Secretary to the Treasury, Henry Brooke, in consultation with the Attorney-General and the Lord Advocate.

On 13 June the warning letter was sent out to the plaintiffs. No doubt after a great deal of internal discussion, it was signed by the deputy Treasury Solicitor. On cabinet recommendation, a final paragraph was added offering the *douceur* that if the plaintiffs were at that stage to abandon their claims, the government would be prepared to consider defraying some of the legal expenses they had so far incurred.[2]

This blatant attempt to warn them off, barely a month before their case was due to open in Edinburgh, clearly strengthened the Burmah Oil directors' resolve. The two distinguished Scottish counsel, to whom they at once referred the letter, declared that its receipt did not by any means warrant abandoning the case. 'We do not consider', they maintained in carefully chosen words, 'that the legal position or (though this is scarcely our province) the political situation is so adverse to the claimants that further steps would be useless.' Counsel therefore drafted a letter for the solicitors to send to the Lord Advocate, complaining that the letter had gone directly to the claimants 'without courtesy of intimation to us. They are couched in terms which we consider offensive to the companies and those who advise them in law'. They therefore reserved the right to bring the matter to the court's attention.

A further grievance was over the signature on the letter, which was claimed to be illegible. Had the solicitors troubled to consult the list of government functionaries at the less garrulous front end of *Whitaker's Almanack*, they would readily have identified him as (Sir) Harvey Druitt, later to become Treasury Solicitor and no doubt chosen because for many years he had wrestled with legal aspects of the denial case. The Lord Advocate's reply was somewhat more temperate, confirming that the terms of the letter accurately represented the government's views and intentions, and conveying the assurance that there had been no intentional discourtesy in sending it to the plaintiffs rather than to their legal advisers.

By the time they had received this reply, the directors were beginning to glean some important political intelligence. The former junior minister Sir Toby Low, by then Lord Aldington and the deputy chairman of the Conservative party, had been horrified to learn from Michie about the letter of 13 June. He had at once reported it to Conservative Central Office and taken it up directly with the Attorney-General, having what he later called a fairly confused and unsatisfactory exchange of letters with him. He subsequently revealed that a number of ministers felt on reflection that the Attorney-General had 'bulldozed' the plan through cabinet by citing clearly exaggerated figures of the sums involved.

Aldington shared with the directors a total disbelief that, in the somewhat more settled – although far from tranquil – economic climate of 1962, ministers would adhere slavishly to the stern Crippsian 'not a penny more' line of 1948. Nicholas Williams, the company's in-house legal adviser since 1961,* interpreted the wording of Druitt's letter, notably the paragraph on possibly contributing to the company's expenses were it to withdraw, as 'indicative of a desire on government's part to avoid litigation'. Indeed, he felt it to be 'the first, albeit clumsy, move towards settlement': a reading which the more cautious R. P. Smith characterised, in a pencilled comment, as 'optimistic'.

Important outside evidence spoke out strongly against Williams's sanguine view. Sir Hubert Ashton, now an influential back-bench MP and a church estates commissioner, at Smith's request took up the case directly with the Lord

---

* As this is the first reference to Williams, his background will be outlined here. Of Cornish descent, he was born in Calcutta during 1925; he later played rugby and cricket for Cornwall. Early in his career he became involved in the activities of Burmah Oil in the East as a partner in Pakistan's largest firm of solicitors, Surridge & Beecheno. There had, however, been a hereditary link: his great-grandfather, a lawyer in Rangoon, had acted for the company there at the end of the nineteenth century. Williams was adviser to Jack Strain during the negotiations of 1960 to revise the joint venture agreement in Burma (see Chapter IX). The company was so impressed with Williams' ability that the following year he was offered and accepted the post of head office lawyer.

Advocate. After a full discussion with him, Ashton wrote with the utmost circumspection to Smith, 'I have never been very optimistic that you would be successful, and I believe it would be a mistake to place your hopes too high.' Undeterred, and with the backing of counsel, Williams refused to accept that the government would be determined to use its powerful double-barrelled gun to pick off the company with the second, legislative, shot if the first judicial one misfired. He accepted that 'there must be an element of face-saving' to allow the government to back down with dignity, and favoured an unofficial approach, using the Carter committee's full award to the company of £17 million – of which Burmah Oil had later received the scaled-down sum of £4.67 million – as a basis of settlement. The government's preliminary pleadings in the case had made reference to that award, which suggested to Williams that here might be the 'hint' for the plaintiffs to pick up.

Williams discussed the possibility of a negotiated settlement with the two counsel early in July. A problem was that starting up negotiations with government would render valueless an important new card in the company's hand, namely the warning letter. Counsel insisted that great advantage would accrue from keeping it for presentation in court; Williams went further and felt that the threat of publicising it – for as yet it was a private document – might be more effective in inducing the government to parley than the publicity itself. The Burmah Oil directors may already have heard from Aldington that some ministers were apparently having second thoughts. Quoting a far lower figure than hitherto and expressing willingness to bargain over that figure might therefore do the trick. Counsel agreed to sound out the Lord Advocate and to mention the possibility of publicising the warning letter.

Something then went seriously amiss, and with hindsight the last real chance of reaching a compromise settlement with government appears to have been lost. Perhaps the Lord Advocate regarded as provocative the threat to reveal the contents of the letter, or perhaps Harold Macmillan's dramatic cabinet reshuffle of 13 July (in which Kilmuir was one of seven cabinet ministers to be sacked and Manningham-Buller, freshly ennobled as Lord Dilhorne, took his place as Lord

Chancellor) at a time of renewed economic crisis, stiffened ministerial backbones. As arranged, therefore, the hearing was opened in Edinburgh on 17 July; for the company R. P. Smith and Williams attended as observers. Williams later wrote an account, and it is through his eyes that we can view the proceedings.

In defence the crown sought to prove that Burmah Oil's denial operations had not been under the royal prerogative but represented acts of necessity, comparable with the blowing up of a house to halt a fire raging in a town, for which no public compensation would be payable. Alternatively, if under the royal prerogative, the denial would fall into the category of battle damage, which again historically did not give rise to compensation. Neither of these arguments, in Williams' view, went down well with the judge, and the company seemed to be some way towards establishing its case.

Smith informed Roper afterwards that 'win, lose or draw, the Burmah had had better value for their money in the court from their counsel than the crown had from the Lord Advocate'. Williams in his account believed that Grant and his second had been 'out of their weight' and deployed a far less effective case than did the company's counsel, who had liberally and effectively quoted from authorities between the year 1400 and very recent times. To some extent, he admitted, it was a disadvantage to field better advocates than the opposing side's: 'there is always an inevitable tendency in the circumstances such as these when the judge has, so to speak, to write one side's argument for him to convince himself of its correctness.' All in all, however, 'the case went very much better than anyone on our side had hoped.'

Until the very early days of the hearing, the crown had probably not appreciated the strength of the case deployed against it. Williams put this down to the crown's original thinking, which went back to Cripps's days, being based entirely on English law under which a number of insurmountable technical defences could have been ranged against the company. Williams therefore believed that the time had come to propose an out-of-court settlement. If it could be suggested 'at a sufficiently high level' that an *ex gratia* payment of, say, £10 million would be acceptable to the directors, then it would be

reasonable to expect this to be tax-free, as Cripps's payment
had been. Claims for a higher sum could only lead to tax
complications. In default of a settlement, the help of MPs might
be enlisted to oppose the principle of retrospective legislation
foreshadowed in the warning letter.

On 14 August the judge, Lord Kilbrandon, handed down his
judgement: that proved to be in the company's favour. It was
later to be commended as 'scholarly' and as establishing the
line of the subsequent debates.[3] Above all, he sought to draw a
distinction – while admitting its narrowness – between denial
damage, where assets were destroyed under the royal prerogative so as to prevent them from falling into enemy hands, and
battle damage, which occurred accidentally during military
operations. The former was properly subject to compensation
and the latter not. Referring to the warning letter, Kilbrandon
criticised the phrase that the claim was not one which ought to
be met by the British taxpayer, as if there were some moral
principle involved 'which must override the common law of
Scotland and the notion of justice of our forebears'.

Eadie, a non-executive chairman since the beginning of
1962, had played no direct part in the denial case. When
Bilsland congratulated him on 1 August over the 'double' he
had achieved of the Lobitos acquisition (see Chapter IX) and
the judicial success in Edinburgh, Eadie confessed that the
latter had been 'to some extent a surprise to me but a very
welcome surprise'. However, he cautiously regarded it as 'just
at the beginning' although he felt gratified 'to be standing at
"fifteen-love" in the match'.

If the company did offer to negotiate on the morrow of the
victory in the outer house – and no evidence has survived that it
did, that offer must have been immediately rejected. The Lord
Advocate at once lodged an appeal with the Scottish higher
court, the inner house of the Court of Session. In the long term,
that meant a fight to the finish: whichever side were to win on
appeal, the loser was bound to take the case to the House of
Lords. Even before the appeal hearing was opened in February
1963, Williams had begun seeking written evidence from
surviving witnesses who could throw direct light on the events
of 1942. As he wrote to a key witness, Sir Harold Roper, the

basic facts of denial were generally admitted; what still needed to be established were the exact circumstances under which denial took place. Since there seemed to be very little first-hand testimony, he was anxious to build up, for eventual submission, 'a whole picture of what actually happened'.

About sixty statements were taken altogether, from the top military commanders such as Field-Marshal Lord Slim and General Sir Thomas Hutton to pensioners who had held quite junior posts in the refineries or the fields. Two men, approached by Williams, had difficulties over acceding to his request. Leslie Forster, the top witness outside the company who had (in his own engaging words) made a 'substantial negative contribution' to the company's finances took a typically independent line, insisting on giving testimony on his own behalf rather than in support of either party in the case. When Williams tried to induce him to challenge the crown's argument that battle and denial damage could not be separated as the oil installations would in any case have been demolished by subsequent acts of war, he took the crown's side; yet he was later incensed by the government's ultimate refusal to pay anything more.

Sir Eric Berthoud, by then a distinguished retired diplomat, judged that he could properly appear only for the crown, and saw problems in showing Burmah Oil the two memoranda he had composed for the Treasury Solicitor, the first being a statement similar to all the others and the second a more wide-ranging narrative of the British government's oil strategy towards the enemy in the Second World War, the latter in particular being covered by the official secrets act. That memorandum the Treasury Solicitor considered to be 'a very helpful background to the crown's legal argument'.

While both sides were assembling their respective depositions, in March 1963 the four judges of the inner house unanimously overturned that of the outer house and found in the crown's favour. Three out of the four reaffirmed the general principle being sought by the company, that denial damage was entitled to compensation, but they unanimously declared that, in the circumstances, the demolitions in Burma had been battle damage. Each justified that view according to his own criteria, such as proximity to the actual fighting or the fact that the denial was an integral part of Britain's overall military strategy. Not unexpectedly, the presiding judge made reference to the warning letter and echoed Kilbrandon's severe strictures on it. While explaining that his remarks did not affect the merits of the case as he and his colleagues saw it, he rubbed home the breach of professional standards created by the solicitor to one side directly communicating with the client on the other: a piece of conduct for which – he correctly pointed out – no explanation whatever had been given to his court.

In April 1963 the board of Burmah Oil considered this disappointing judgment, as well as counsel's opinion on its terms. As the principle had been clearly established about compensation being payable for denial, the board decided that the case should be taken to the House of Lords. There, the directors considered, a reasonable chance existed of being able to prove the crucial point of fact: that the demolitions were for denial purposes and nothing to do with the battle as such. The case was opened in the House of Lords on 27 January 1964.

After one or two preliminary matters had been got out of the way, such as under which nation's law the case should be heard – English law, since Burma had then been a possession of the crown – the five Law Lords went on to the two questions at the heart of the case. Was the crown expected to pay compensation for assets which had been commandeered and/or destroyed under the royal prerogative, and if so, did the company's installations fall within or outside that category? To be sure, there were few reliable precedents in law to go on. As an authoritative account in the *Harvard Law Review* later put it, 'both sides sought to back up their views by digging into the ancient authorities', even though the kinds of war waged in earlier centuries, however savage, had been relatively limited in their impact: 'the scorched-earth concept was unknown' to lawyers of those days.[4]

In this largely uncharted territory, with few landmarks to help them, the majority of the Law Lords concluded that while the demolitions had been deliberate and properly planned, they could not be held to fall into the catetgory of battle damage, since they had not occurred in the midst of the fighting and had not formed an integral part of army tactics against the

A meeting at Shillong, Assam, India
1954. Front row, left to right, David C.
Robertson, director 1957–63, John A.
Drysdale, director 1960–69, and John
C. Finlay, chief representative, India,
1962–76

John F. Strain, director 1957–73, deputy
chairman 1967–71

Nicholas J. D. Williams, director
1965–74, managing director 1969–74

(Sir) Alastair F. Down, managing director BP 1962–69, later deputy chairman of BP 1969–75 and chairman of Burmah Oil 1975–83

Leslie W. Farrow, CBE, chairman of C. C. Wakefield Ltd, later Castrol Ltd, 1943–66, director Burmah Oil 1966–70

An example of sponsorship by Castrol: motor racing, early 1960s

Castrol House, Marylebone Road, London, 1966 ('a cool and astringent flash in a brick and concrete waste')

Anglo filling station, Guyaquil, Ecuador, 1964
(Anglo-Ecuadorian Oilfields, a subsidiary of Lobitos)

Drilling rig *Ocean Prince* 1966 (First rig to strike oil in North Sea, October 1966)

Japanese. Curiously enough, that conclusion seems to have been influenced by the old small-scale conflicts rather than by more recent precedents. The Lords disregarded an American case, where Caltex had been ordered by the military to hand over for destruction its Philippines oil installations at the end of 1941, on the grounds that the Supreme Court definition of 'use', for which the installations had been commandeered, was too restrictive in the circumstances. On 21 April the Law Lords found for the company, three being for and two against.

Burmah Oil had therefore won, by the slenderest of majorities, in the House of Lords. Even now, however, the battle was far from over: the company had achieved no more than a confirmation at the highest judicial level that it possessed a legitimate claim for compensation. A further laborious task had next to be undertaken, namely a return to the courts in Scotland, which would have to investigate the facts and circumstances in which the denial had taken place, and assess the precise damage caused. To use Eadie's earlier terminology, the company was still far from the game point, but only at thirty-fifteen.

When replying to Roper's warm congratulations, Eadie expressed no personal gratification at the outcome but merely thanked him for the help he had given. Williams and his colleagues in Burmah Oil were meanwhile very much occupied in amassing the evidence on the denial, and hiring experts to help draw up the denial assessments. Everyone in the company appreciated that they still had a very long way to go. Similarly, investors in general saw no reason to celebrate a decisive victory: the price of the company's ordinary shares on the London stock exchange did not rise when the House of Lords verdict was announced. Uncertainty, ever a depressing factor on stock market prices, would remain as long as the threat of government legislation hung over everything.

At that stage the company is believed to have made approaches to the Treasury but, as it declined to reduce the size of its claim, it could have got nowhere. On the question of when the case would be heard, serious congestion was known to exist in the Scottish courts, so that the hearing could not possibly be held before the New year. Both parties strove hard to engage the star witnesses who could well be decisive influences as to which way the next stage went. Roper was solidly on the Burmah Oil side, as Berthoud was on the side of the crown. Field-Marshal Slim had publicly expressed harsh views about the government's conduct over compensation; even so, the Treasury Solicitor hoped to bring him in as a crown witness.

Forster was highly embarrassed by the Treasury Solicitor's blandishments, as he reiterated to Williams – who was also energetically wooing him – that he wished to be an independent witness: a stance that appealed to neither side. The Conservative government drew up a bill, which – according to a later report – was then considered at a lugubrious meeting of the cabinet's Economic Policy Committee: Selwyn Lloyd, by then Lord Privy Seal and therefore outside the committee, did not see the bill as drafted. No cabinet decision was made to introduce it. The next parliamentary session was not due to begin until November 1964, but a complication was that a general election had to be held before the statutory five-year period of office ran out in October. From May onwards, the lead that Labour had enjoyed in the opinion polls began to shrink, so that by September the margin was down to nearly one per cent: that suggested a very close finish at the polls.

The general election, that October, returned a Labour government under Harold Wilson with a wafer-thin overall majority of four. A rather over-dramatic revelation of the critical state of Britain's finances on the morrow of the election, showing a rapid deterioration in both the home and the overseas accounts, combined with fears that the steel industry would be re-nationalised, caused a sharp fall in sterling's international value. By December the country's reserves of gold and convertible currencies had fallen to £826 million, the lowest for many years, and the prospect of having to pay out £100 million or even more to a bunch of rapacious capitalist claimants made it all the more attractive to introduce a short bill that would cut them out. The Labour government must have taken a particular delight in being able, for this purpose, to use the identical bill that the Conservatives had drafted before the general election.

Once the result of the election was known, the company's

solicitors wrote at the end of October to the new Lord
Advocate, Gordon Stott, about the new government's intentions. Stott replied on 17 December that legislation to inde-
mnify the crown from Burmah Oil's claims would be brought in
without delay, and that the company would be well advised for
the moment not to incur the expense of preparing its proof.
That same day the bill to enact the War Damage (No. 2) Act
was published. It sought to abolish the common-law right to
compensation for property damaged or destroyed by acts
lawfully done by the crown, or on its authority, during a war.
Any proceedings to obtain compensation would be automatically set aside. Since there were no other cases outstanding, the
immediate targets of the bill were perfectly plain, as Stott had
indicated. It had been called No. 2 since there was already an
act for 1964 which was concerned purely with air-raid damage
in Britain, but cynical observers inevitably regarded the second
bill as a convenient Labour resuscitation of a frustrated
Conservative design.

Williams at once had Scottish counsel briefed for an opinion
on any constitutional questions the bill appeared to throw up.
In their reply, counsel pondered on whether the judiciary
might have power to review any oppressive act of the legislature
that purported to destroy constitutional rights enjoyed by the
individual citizen; however, they felt this path was too speculative, as well as unprecedented in Scots law. A less unrealistic
approach would be to examine how the bill might impinge on
the safeguards to the citizen written into the Act of Union
between Scotland and England in 1707. Early in 1965 Williams
asked counsel to explore the latter approach and the timing
factors involved; for instance, whether it would be inoperative if
and when the bill were passed into law.

Meanwhile, for the company a very pressing task was to put
its case over to MPs, peers and the general public. H. H.
(Oliver) Twist, the public relations officer, energetically
embarked on a programme of lobbying city editors of the main
newspapers and business journals; just as important, now that
the new media were increasingly influential in moulding public
opinion, he briefed the editors of the various BBC and ITV
news programmes. However, all too conscious that 'some fast
work on the PR side' was vital – especially as the Treasury

Information Division was already publicising the government's point of view – Twist obtained R. P. Smith's permission
to engage a public relations firm, CS Services Ltd. That firm at
once prepared an action plan, the overall objective being 'to
delay the introduction of the bill for some time in order to build
up a head of steam against it'.

According to the CS Services plan, campaign leaders were
needed on the Labour as well as the Conservative side;
moreover, briefing letters should be sent to categories of MPs
likely to be interested, such as those with Scottish constituen-
cies, lawyers, ex-army men, and also to Scottish peers and peers
with oil and chemical interests. Back-bench committees also
needed to be approached, such as Labour's economic affairs
and finance committee and its legal and judicial committee,
and the Conservatives' Scotland, Scottish law, law and finance
committees. The Chancellor of the Exchequer and the Scottish
secretary should be asked to meet deputations. CS Services
believed that officers in the forces could also exert pressure on
public opinion: the consultants were already in touch with both
the War Office and the army's London district. These and
other measures would seek to demonstrate that 'the bill
embodies a major issue of principle; that it is a hot potato; that
it will be contested; is directed mainly at one company, and is
morally wrong and legally bad'. The firm dismissed the notion
that Conservatives would be embarrassed because their party
had considered introducing a bill. 'That is past history', the
consultants declared, and besides, the Tories had not after all
brought it in.

What Nicholas Williams called the 'first shots' in the
campaign were discharged in a letter to *The Times* by Sir John
Foster, QC, MP and a short piece in the *Sunday Telegraph* both in
the company's favour, on 17 and 18 January. The Burmah Oil
directors soon became aware, however, that it was going to be a
hard struggle to build up a sufficient pressure of public opinion
for the bill to be rejected; instead, a number of specific
criticisms of the company were being made. Newly appointed
chairman as well as managing director after Eadie's retirement
(see Chapter XII), R. P. Smith acepted that these would have
to be vigorously countered. With a battle in parliament clearly
ahead, the company decided additionally to appoint Watney &

Powell, highly regarded as specialist consultants on the Westminster scene, to reinforce its representations there. Smith gave a press briefing on 21 January. He rebutted the damaging charge that excessively high sums were being claimed. Cripps had years before been unhappy about any compensation money from the government going to shareholders or helping to weaken Britain's overseas currency reserves; at the beginning of 1965 similar fears were being voiced afresh. Smith therefore agreed to differentiate between aspects of the company's claim that were incontrovertibly attributable to denial, and those aspects that were more arguable.

This downward revision of the claim was a genuine one, based upon the need, mentioned above, to prove before the Court of Session the details of the amounts claimed. The denial losses included not only wells and surface installations such as derricks destroyed but also the forgone quantity of recoverable oil stocks. More reliable estimates of these items were by then available because of the knowledge gained from working the fields since the war. On the recommendation of the head geologist, Percy Evans, an independent expert had been commissioned to produce new estimates of oil losses. At the press briefing Smith quoted a figure of £20 million as one which he would seek to prove in the courts. *The Economist* a few days later picked up this modified figure and urged both sides to 'climb down' so as to avoid the necessity of passing a 'bad bill' and to seek to agree an additional *ex gratia* payment, over and above the Carter award.[5] The company seems to have disregarded this well-meant advice.

On 3 February 1965, the War Damage Bill had its second reading in the House of Commons. According to *The Times* some ten days before, opposition would be less than whole-hearted, as a recent meeting of the Conservative shadow cabinet had revealed fundamental differences of opinion on how to tackle the bill.[6] Opening for the government Niall MacDermot, Financial Secretary to the Treasury, stated that the bill sought to restore the common law of England and of Scotland to what those laws had been generally considered to be before the House of Lords decision. He dealt first with the part of the bill intended to establish the law for the future; in fact, no one believed that this part was of much practical significance. As to the second part, which dealt retrospectively with claims arising out of the past, he asserted that the denial claim for Burma by all the parties, totalling £39 million, would at compound interest accruing since the late 1940s put the figure at nearly £160 million.

Selwyn Lloyd, replying for the opposition, stressed the difficulties involved in the bill; the legal principle, he said, was both complex and far-reaching. Moreover, (in his words) 'rightly or wrongly', successive governments of different parties had taken identical attitudes towards Burmah Oil's claim. He refused to be drawn on the merits or otherwise of the case but, while agreeing with MacDermot that the common law was being restored to what it had earlier been thought to be on the matter, he hoped that the government would think further about the bill, especially as the sums likely to be at stake now appeared to be very much smaller than previously understood.

After Lloyd had spoken, several members of parliament attacked the principle of retrospective legislation, especially because it appeared to be widely altering the common law and would provide a poor example to Commonwealth and other overseas countries. For the Conservatives, Patrick Jenkin brought in the entirely novel point that there had been a precedent, in Sarawak and Brunei, where the British government had paid compensation to the oil companies concerned after arranging in 1940, well before the war in the Far East, for the destruction of their assets in the event of a Japanese invasion. The agreement had provided for full compensation to be paid. Jenkin therefore reasoned that, as Chapter II above showed, similar contingency arrangements had not been made with the companies there because no one before 1941 had seriously contemplated the possibility that Burma would be attacked.

In his winding-up speech for the second reading the Attorney-General, Sir Elwyn Jones, had no answer to the Sarawak case. On 5 February Jenkin therefore wrote to him about it. On the 19th Jones replied that first, the Sarawak demolitions had been ordered immediately after the attack on Pearl Harbor, and were therefore – in terms of the earlier legal distinctions – denial damage. In Burma, on the other hand, destruction was carried out 'at the last possible moment in the face of an advancing enemy' and was therefore more akin to battle damage. (This conveniently overlooked the point that the Japanese had at the time wished to capture the oilfields intact, rather than wanting them to be destroyed.) Second, the signing of a formal agreement over Sarawak proved that the common law right to compensation was not considered to apply in that case.

Also on 5 February Williams wrote to MacDermot about the very large sums which the Financial Secretary had quoted in the debate. Williams claimed that the 'grossly exaggerated' figures had come into play because the Treasury had not allowed the directors to meet a minister in order to discuss them. To avoid misunderstandings in the future, he asked that Smith should be allowed to call and deliver 'more exact figures than it would appear are available to you at the present time'. He also enclosed a copy of a letter by Smith to *The Times*, actually published on the 9th. That dealt not only with the magnitude of the claim, but also with a point made by the Attorney-General, that the company would if successful be gaining preferential treatment over the millions who had suffered war damage. On the contrary, Smith argued, it was the company that had been placed at a disadvantage by the government, which was now seeking to overturn Burmah Oil's rights in law as established by the judiciary.

By the time the Treasury replied to Williams in mid-February, ministers were confident that they had gained an upper hand in the propaganda contest. Public opinion remained singularly unmoved by the whole issue, despite some attacks on the bill by the weekly press, for instance in *The Economist* and one by Alan Watkins in *The Spectator*, who stressed that the retrospective principle, formerly restricted to a very narrow range of cases such as taxation and acts of indemnity, was being widened almost to an 'act of attainder'.[7] (Watkins was suggesting, in his own inimitable way, that the government would be able to enforce retrospectively the forfeiture of property far more extensively than had been possible in the recent past.) The second reading had produced a majority for the government of nearly a hundred, with no senior Conservative ex-ministers or law officers voting against it. Not surprisingly, the Treasury's response to Williams was that the compensation figures quoted had been taken from the company's own submissions, and had never been amended, but that the record could be altered in the usual way. 'As, however, there could be no question of negotiations with H.M. Government, the Financial Secretary sees no advantage in the meeting', the reply concluded.

With ministers so intransigent, Burmah Oil redoubled its public relations efforts, providing briefs both for MPs before the Commons committee stage and for peers against the time when the bill would be sent to the House of Lords. However, the company's main target for persuasion was undoubtedly Selwyn Lloyd, whose refusal to vote against the bill had seriously blunted the vigorous attack on it by the Liberals and by one or two Labour members such as Harold Lever. On 1 March Smith had a 25-minute meeting with Lloyd and also with the former prime minister, Sir Alec Douglas-Home. Smith argued that the bill was totally unjustifiable and set a precedent of withholding compensation which other countries where Burmah Oil had large interests – such as India and Pakistan – might be tempted to follow. He then showed the ex-ministers the minute of the meeting in October 1947 with Sir Stafford Cripps, mentioned in Chapter VI, where Cripps had stated that there had been two views about legal liability for denial damage; only in 1948 had Cripps offered an *ex gratia* payment and told the company that it should fight in the Burmese courts but could whistle for anything more from the home government. Lloyd said that he had not seen the minute before, and felt that if legislation to veto any claims had been intended, it should have been brought in at the end of the war. In his view, the company had thus been right to take legal action against the government; however, once the judges had made a final decision, then it was up to the government to legislate or not as the circumstances seemed to justify.

Lloyd asked about a matter raised in the debate, that the Japanese were expected to (and did) overrun the oil installations within hours, so that those assets could be regarded as having effectively been worthless. Smith was able to explain that the company had been in touch with the Japanese war historians, who had replied that the high command's orders to the invading forces had been to destroy nothing and to keep intact as much production and refining capacity as possible. Once satisfied by Smith on this point, Lloyd said that he planned at the report stage – after the bill had come back from the standing committee – not to launch an all-out attack on the government but to work towards uniting the whole of the opposition, so that the narrowness of the final vote would be a signal to the Lords about feelings generally over the bill.

Lloyd warned that the House of Lords was unlikely to make a constitutional issue of the bill as there were more clear-cut battles, such as steel re-nationalisation, in the offing. He therefore expected the bill to be amended by the Lords but not thrown out. Smith stated that the company 'certainly did not want to be mixed up in this sort of thing', namely direct political embroilment. When Lloyd added that the size of the company's claim was a key consideration, Smith replied that he had already declared his willingness to see the claim reduced and to accept, say, a credit for the amount, but only if a negotiated settlement were reached in advance of any judicial decision on the size of the claim. As the meeting was simply to clarify the matters discussed, Lloyd asked that it should not be publicised in any way.

The following day, on 2 March, the report stage of the War Damage bill was held in the Commons. Selwyn Lloyd moved an amendment, stating that the act should not come into force until a draft order had been approved by a resolution of each house. After three hours of vigorous debate, enhanced by a typically robust intervention from Quintin Hogg (later Lord Hailsham), the amendment was rejected by twelve votes, and the bill was then read for the third time. John Harvey, an MP who was a director of the Lobitos group, a recently-acquired Burmah Oil subsidiary, did not intervene in the debate; however, in an account of the debate he sent to Williams, he expressed his disappointment that so few members on either side really seemed to know what they were talking about. Rather than become entangled in the far more debatable legal and constitutional aspects, he felt, the government had 'decided to concentrate on building up an ogre-picture of a big oil company seeking to amass further wealth at the public expense'. Too often, therefore, the bill's opponents found themselves having to counter specific government arguments rather than pressing home matters of principle.

With the bill on the point of being referred to the House of Lords, Harvey suggested that, when briefing peers, the company should concentrate on the factual side of the case and leave the constitutional and legal arguments – of special concern to the upper house after the Law Lords' verdict – to the legal experts among peers. He also recommended striving to 'spike the government's guns' by formally complaining to the prime minister about the way in which MacDermot had sought to mislead the house by deploying certain arguments to his side's advantage rather than giving a full and fair portrayal of the whole case. The company duly sent a letter, and on 22 March the prime minister's private secretary rejected this complaint.

Three days later the House of Lords gave the bill its second reading. Much to the company's disappointment, Lord Dilhorne – who as Attorney-General had initiated the warning letter of June 1962 to the company – urged his Conservative friends not to vote against the bill. On 13 April the bill was considered by a committee of the whole house, where Lord McNair proposed an amendment to remove altogether its retrospective character, thereby making it totally ineffective. According to information reaching the Burmah Oil directors, the Lord Chancellor, Lord Gardiner, disliked the bill on principle; however, in winding up he spoke forcefully against the amendment.

On 13 April, after its report stage, the House of Lords decided to amend the bill, as proposed by Lord McNair. Among those voting for the amendment were Earl Alexander of Tunis and Viscount Slim, who had been ultimately responsible for the denial decisions in 1942. The bill was then sent, in its amended form, back to the Commons. Contemplating substantial delays in its progress should the Lords refuse to give way on their amendment, Williams met the Scottish lawyers to discuss the legal implications of Burmah Oil's compensation award being granted in Scotland before the bill became law. He was strongly advised to proceed with the legal case of proving compensation, and to request the Lord Advocate for permission to cite secret documents in open court. Smith realistically minuted on the note of the meeting, 'There is a great deal to be done in a very short time.'

In the shorter run, Williams felt that the time had arrived to propose a compromise solution to government. It would, he believed, be pushing the company's public-spiritedness too far to offer an unconditional withdrawal of the lawsuit in return for the government's withdrawal of the bill. Instead, he hoped the government might let the bill 'drift into limbo' by accepting the Lords' amendment and at the same time undertake to advance the company £25 million line of credit, usable only in Britain, for prospecting and other oil and chemical operations in Commonwealth countries. On 10 May Smith wrote to MacDermot along these lines; two days later he received an outright rejection.

By then the Burmah Oil Company had effectively suffered defeat over the denial issue, and the government had only to maintain its obdurate stance to pick up the spoils of victory. In the House of Commons the opposition had been in disarray, with only Selwyn Lloyd – a late convert – and Quintin Hogg supporting their back-benchers, and that house's future was in any case unaffected by whether or not the bill was passed and in what form. The House of Lords, on the other hand, would become embroiled in a constitutional crisis if the Commons rejected its amendment and the Lords refused to accept that rejection, thereby inflicting a year's delay on the bill before it could be ultimately passed by the provisions of the 1949 Parliament Act. The prime minister, Harold Wilson, had already threatened in public speeches to seek a general election on the issue of the Lords versus the people: in April, public opinion polls showed Labour some seven points ahead of the Conservatives.

One of Wilson's back-bench colleagues, the leftward-inclined Willie Hamilton, playfully sought to intensify the opposition's discomfiture by introducing a private member's bill to abolish the House of Lords' delaying powers. His main object was to reveal, from the share registers in Companies House, that 38 of the 144 peers who had voted for the amendment were Burmah Oil shareholders. This pin-prick had the desired result of placing the Lords heavily on the defensive when on 25 May they debated the Commons' rejection of the amendment. However, swayed by the advice of the elder statesman Lord Salisbury and the Conservative leader of the House of Lords, Lord Carrington, peers were finally dissuaded from continuing to oppose the bill. It was thus, in the end, passed as originally drafted.[8] Smith at once reported to the Burmah Oil board his grave disappointment at this outcome, since the company had clearly lost the case not on its merits but entirely because of party political considerations. Yet he was resolved not to make any public statement until the annual general meeting on 3 June, at which he intended to 'take the opportunity of saying something, leaving the subject stone dead, and refuse to be drawn into any further discussion'.

If Smith felt that the company had reached the end of the road over this matter, Nicholas Williams was far less convinced. On 2 June he wrote to Smith, then in Glasgow for the AGM, about a draft submission just received from Scottish counsel, arising out of the previous month's consultations in Scotland. This challenged the War Damage Act (as it had become that day, with the royal assent), on the ground that it was in conflict with the Act of Union between Scotland and England. That Act of 1707 had provided that no Scottish laws concerning private rights could be altered to harm those rights, and the common law of Scotland allowed the crown to pay compensation when property was damaged or destroyed in a legitimate war. The War Damage Act was 'accordingly *ultra vires* and is null, void and of no effect'. As Williams put it to Smith,

If such an argument were to succeed, nothing short of repealing the Act of Union, which is after all the constitution of the United Kingdom *[sic]*, could enable government to put matters right. You will appreciate, therefore, that the constitutional issues involved are both far more fundamental and quite different from those previously before the Commons.

Williams therefore asked of Smith the question, 'Does the balance of commercial advantage lie in the courts or in accepting the present position as final?' If the former, then the action could be kept alive for up to two years, perhaps until a Conservative government had been returned. 'On the other side, there is the powerful argument that a company in our position cannot afford to go on indefinitely fighting the Treasury.' He professed himself 'terribly undecided' on this question, although he later admitted to one of the counsel, 'I am only sorry that we did not have a go on the Scottish point, and the Act of Union.'

Smith had no time whatever for these heady and stratospheric principles of constitutional law. On 3 June 1964 he persuaded the board, at its meeting in Glasgow, to agree that the denial issue should be considered closed, 'as it was not deemed prudent to continue the litigation.' At the annual general meeting a few hours later he read out a statement explaining this decision and the board's refusal to consider invoking the Act of Union. He did not believe that the latter step would enjoy any chance of success; however, in any case, 'the Burmah Oil Company has never in its history been involved in political issues.' He hoped that good relations with the British government, of whichever political persuasion, would not be impaired, 'and that the whole issue will in every way be regarded as exceptional.' He did not live to know that his hopes on the latter count would be in vain, and that the company would one day again find itself seeking redress in the courts over a question of what it regarded as grossly unjust treatment by the British authorities.

Notes

1 The anonymous but very well informed article on 'The Burmah Oil Affair' (see Chapter III, footnote 7) is the best outside account of the denial case. As the references there are so full, they need not be repeated here.

2 The warning letter of 13 June 1962 was only partly read out in the House of Commons ('Burmah Oil Affair', p. 616, footnote 13). A full version, with minimal drafting changes, is in Hansard, HL 254, col. 739, 25 March 1965.

3 'Burmah Oil Affair', p. 617.

4 Ibid., p. 621.

5 *The Economist*, 23 January 1965, p. 372.

6 *The Times*, 25 January 1965.

7 A. Watkins, 'The Burmah Oil Affair', *Spectator*, 12 February 1965. This was commended by R. P. Smith, in the issue of 19 February, as the 'best objective analysis' of the 'current situation' he had yet seen.

8 Janet Morgan, *The House of Lords and the Labour Government 1964–70*, 1975, p. 138 regrettably gives only a sketchy outline of this episode's constitutional implications.

CHAPTER IX

An End and A Beginning
1960–3

Early in February 1960 a general election was held in Burma, the third since independence. Commonly agreed to have been conducted with remarkable smoothness and regularity, its outcome was a decisive victory for U Nu and his coalition; between them they gained two-thirds of the 250 seats in the chamber of deputies.[1] With parliamentary democracy apparently assured, Ne Win prepared to transfer power back by April to the civilians. Few of the latter regretted the passing of military government. Its stern discipline fitted in ill with the easy-going Burmese character; yet it had brought certain distinct advantages. Public administration had been noticeably more efficient and freer from corruption than at any time since 1948. That efficiency had resulted in a budget surplus for 1959/60 equivalent to £1 million, the first since 1950/1, and in foreign exchange reserves rising to an unprecedentedly high level.

Civilians might be taking over political power again, but the period of Ne Win's rule from 1958 to 1960 had nevertheless left one large area of public life in which army control had been irreversibly established. As long before as 1950, the Ministry of Defence in Rangoon had set up the Defence Services Institute (DSI), a non-profit-making body on the lines of Britain's NAAFI or the American PX, for the sale of consumer goods to servicemen and their families.[2] From modest beginnings it had moved on to selling books and then tendering for government contracts. Under Ne Win the DSI had prospered wonderfully, setting up a bank and firms engaged in insurance, housing construction, mechanical and electrical engineering, and transport – including a shipping line – among others; many such firms were expropriated foreign-owned companies. The DSI had behaved commendably in eradicating the black marketeers and middle-men who had preyed on the consuming public. At the same time, these DSI-controlled firms were generating, from levies on their profits, quite considerable extra-budgetary funds for the army and creating jobs for the boys.

The Burmah Oil Company could only view with concern this tangible evidence of the Burmese road to socialism. In February 1960 Ne Win paid over the £1.4 million outstanding on the loan for his government's one-third stake in the 1954 company. Shortly afterwards, on the 23rd of that month, the clearly well-briefed paper *The Nation* announced in Rangoon that the government of Burma was likely to increase its stake in that company to 51 per cent before the new parliament met, and that Stephen Glover, Maxwell-Lefroy's successor as general manager, was returning to Britain for consultations.[3] In the stir caused by the announcement, informed opinion in Rangoon had no doubt whatever that Ne Win was behind such a move, even though he was on the point of retiring as premier and the moderate M. A. Raschid was heading the Ministry of Mines. Now that the military had had a taste of power and had built up such an impressive presence in the significant foothills of the economy, it would be looking to the commanding heights and especially to establish control over oil.

To be sure, the board in London had in its hands a binding contract in the joint venture agreement of 1954; however, political, military and economic realities meant that the contract would be valueless in the event of a showdown. It was not merely that 51 per cent would mean conceding control to the Burmese, but other unwelcome consequences might follow. At worst, the group's stake in the 1954 company and the Burma trading subsidiary could be expropriated without compensation or bought out in inconvertible Burmese currency; at best, these stakes were worth considerably less than a few years before, as prospecting since then had yielded no new sources of crude oil in the country.

When he met the London directors, Glover advised that everything possible should be done to stave off any precipitate move in Rangoon, and that a loan on easy terms might be offered as an inducement to postpone further demands for another five years or so. At its meeting on 3 March, the board conceded that the oil companies – which included British Burmah and Indo-Burma – could effectively raise no objection. However, the repercussions of the move to a 51 per cent Burmese stake would be grave for the oil industry in Burma. The directors therefore resolved to be willing to discuss any proposals that might come from Rangoon, but certainly not to take any initiatives.

It happened that a Canadian civil servant, the deputy minister for mineral resources for the state of Saskatchewan had been visiting Burma as a United Nations adviser. He had recommended that the government should acquire the 51 per cent stake as a way of strengthening its influence in what was by any criteria a good investment, and that it should terminate the marketing agreement with the still British-owned Burma trading company as being unfair and harmful to host-country interests. Such advice was music to the ears of many Burmese, especially as the 1954 company was under constant and almost obsessive attack in the local press for an alleged unwillingness to discover more oil deposits. The British embassy in Rangoon summed up to the Foreign Office the Burmese mood over the joint venture affair as one of 'fretful impatience'. It recognised that the most cogent argument against the 51 per cent Burmese stake was that the people there were incapable on their own of running their oil industry; but that was hardly an argument that could be usefully deployed.

No developments occurred before U Nu returned to power on 4th April 1960. In his address to parliament, he stated that his main economic intentions were to see trade and industry Burmanised as far as possible, but not to nationalise any more private firms during his coming four years of office. A few days later Glover attended a meeting with Raschid and other government representatives. When asked to prepare counter-proposals, he submitted a plan on the 18th for a 50-50 agreement, which could if necessary be underwritten by a loan from the Burmah Oil Company. Given the touchy feelings generated by earlier exploration failures, he added that the company in London would be prepared to see far greater resources being spent on searches for oil. The affair then went quiet again.

Eadie, in his usual detached way, professed himself to the Foreign Office as not being too worried by these pressures in Rangoon, although some of his board colleagues took them more seriously. Reliable information reaching him from the East suggested that the Burmese were not genuinely seeking a controlling interest, but had merely made noises in order to get some kind of dialogue going. Raschid himself was reportedly not in a great hurry to move in the matter, but had been compelled to give support in principle because questions had been asked in the chamber. While Eadie was prepared at any time to fly out to Burma for discussions, he had been advised by Glover to wait: his well-publicised arrival in Rangoon would simply stir things up by drawing attention to a matter that the government of Burma would rather let ride for the moment.

At a press conference in mid-May, U Nu revealed that his government was still considering the 50-50 proposals. However, although Raschid was in London briefly in July, he made no attempt to follow them up there. Not until 17 August was Glover informed that his proposals of 18 April had been rejected, and that the government intended, on 30 September, to pay the required sum in sterling to bring its stake up to 51 per cent.[4] It would also acquire a 51 per cent interest in the Burma trading company.

Despite this abrupt announcement, both Glover and his principals at home felt encouraged by all the indications of friendliness that accompanied it. Burmah Oil directors were asked to submit ideas on how, as minority shareholders, they would be prepared to carry on the agency and also pay their share of additional capital for new projects. R. P. Smith as managing director, in a note to his board, stressed that, while the political climate in South-East Asia was not all that favourable to long-term foreign investment, 'we are there, and Burma is a growing market for oil products.' Thus, if it could negotiate the right terms, Burmah Oil would be well advised to continue in the country – provided that it could remain actively in the oil business and not be relegated to being merely the provider of expert staff, materials and technical advice. Unless its representatives had an effective voice in the running of the 1954 company, any investment of further capital would be hazardous.

Towards the end of August, after a lunch with Ne Win, Eadie felt so uncertain about the future as to confess in a private letter, 'Quite frankly, personally I would prefer to have £2 million with the Bank of Scotland [then the company's British bankers] than an IOU in Burma!' He must have been relieved when, a month later, the government of Burma remitted the sum due for its 51 per cent stake. Burmah Oil received £2.2 million, and its precise status as a 49 per cent shareholder urgently needed to be agreed on the spot. On 9 October, Jack Strain, the company's finance director, travelled out to Rangoon with draft terms which his board and legal advisers had approved. Just over a fortnight later, on the 25th, he and the secretary of the Ministry of Mines signed a formal agreement which appeared to safeguard for Burmah Oil a suitably effective role in the industry's affairs.

Above all, the government agreed not to acquire any further shares in the 1954 company for 15 years. It was also willing to see that company's operations conducted in such a way as to yield a reasonable return on the shareholders' capital. Burmah Oil would continue to act as agents for at least ten years. In return, the 1954 company would take over the Burma trading company from the beginning of 1961. Together with British Burmah and Indo-Burma, Burmah Oil was willing to subscribe 49 per cent of the new capital needed for the projected expansion of the Syriam refinery and a pipeline from Syriam to Dunneedaw on the opposite side of the river. It also agreed that the search for oil in Burma should be stepped up, at a cost equivalent to £1.6–£2 million a year in 1961–3. Moreover, the 1954 company would continue a policy of accelerated Burmanisation.[5] The press communiqué issued in Rangoon emphasised that both parties considered the accord to represent 'a reasonable and equitable arrangement for the continued prosperity and efficient working of the joint oil venture'. When the Foreign Office in London passed on the details to the Ministry of Power, an official in the latter department had no doubt as to which party had done the better out of it. 'To my mind, it concedes quite a lot to the Burmah Oil Company, and little to the [Rangoon] government', he declared.

In the aftermath of the agreement, it was unfortunate that Burma almost at once lost its self-sufficiency in oil products because of increased demand. Despite the Syriam and Chauk refineries working flat out, an acute shortage occurred in kerosene, petrol and diesel oil, so that over 200,000 barrels had to be imported during 1961. Tenders were invited for these imports, and although both BP and Shell put in bids, the Russians undercut their prices by 20 per cent and moreover agreed to accept payment in Burmese currency. Late in March 1961 *The Nation* voiced renewed suspicions that the 'British oil companies' were not pressing a search for oil energetically enough. Other local papers also criticised apparent shortcomings in the oil scene: for instance, that the number of petrol stations in Burma remained totally inadequate, especially by international standards, and that Burmanisation was proceeding far too slowly. They alleged that no Burmese employees of Burmah Oil had a degree in petroleum engineering, while Burmese boys of 12 or 13 were being sent to independent schools in England to receive a general rather than a technical education; moreover, most of the sub-agents were still Chinese.

Almost a year into the new civilian regime's period of office, there were a number of straws blowing about in the chilly winds fanning Burmese hostility. In general terms, standards of public administration had noticeably fallen since military rule ended. U Nu and Raschid had clearly hoped to go in for some dawdling over future policy towards Burmah Oil. They made no attempt to implement the agreed plan to take over the trading subsidiary. Then in March 1961 Raschid invited the new general manager, D. H. Cozens, to tea and told him in the strictest confidence that Ne Win – still commander-in-chief but quite unconnected with the government machine – had asked to see the papers about the proposed take-over. That request had clearly embarrassed ministers, but they could hardly tell the general to mind his own business. All the non-routine Burmah Oil correspondence to and from Rangoon went by safe hand, sometimes in the embassy's diplomatic bag, so that Cozens was able to comment frankly to directors at home. 'It seems extraordinary,' he remarked, 'that the views of the army commander should apparently be considered of such importance in what is purely a civil matter.' As Ne Win was about to leave for Russia in a visit lasting until May, and Raschid would be at an international conference in Geneva during June, no further moves were likely to be made until well into the summer.

In June it was reported that a Burmese committee of enquiry had toured the Burma trading company's branches round the country and in a report had valued its assets at the equivalent of £1.6 million, whereas Burmah Oil was demanding £2 million. Moreover, as negotiations about a take-over had been started in Ne Win's time, his deputy Brigadier Aung Gyi was to discuss the enquiry committee's report with U Nu. These demonstrations of the army's steadily growing interest in oil matters made depressing news for Burmah Oil's directors. That year a Burmese Economic Development Corporation (BEDC) had been set up under an act passed by the chamber. The corporation was, like the DSI, to be run by military personnel and had the task of co-ordinating, supervising and financing the DSI subsidiary firms. BEDC would therefore be a very powerful arm of economic planning in the country. It was no secret that the BEDC and DSI were looking forward to absorbing the whole of the oil industry.

Ne Win's reading of the files dealing with the October 1960 agreement appears to have borne no fruit until late in November 1961, when U Nu informed his cabinet that a number of criticisms of that agreement had been brought to his notice. The cabinet therefore ordered that enquiries should be made to find out exactly what the bases of these criticisms were, since no one in government really knew. Moreover, Burmah Oil should be informed through the British embassy that the government would in consequence almost certainly wish to renegotiate the agreement. Desmond Dewhurst, by then the general manager in Rangoon, privately expressed surprise that this matter had come up, but told London that it could probably be turned to the company's advantage. R. P. Smith found it most disturbing, but warned Dewhurst in the meantime to make no comment apart from expressing dismay.

Dewhurst soon reported, in a hand-written letter despatched by an extra-secure route, why the army did not like the agreement. They felt that fifteen years was too long a period to promise no further increase in the government's stake, and that the terms offered for the Burma trading subsidiary were too generous. Yet the real underlying grievance was that the army had not been properly consulted at the time, despite its wish to have what he called 'some say in or some cut from' the profits of the 1954 company and the Burma trading subsidiary. He made clear how unhappy and embarrassed ministers were over the whole business. They saw no possibility of future agreement unless the army became involved. 'Our only hope of security of tenure (if we want it) is to bring the army – the real power – in with us,' Dewhurst concluded.

As nothing much had happened in December, R. P. Smith – who had just become sole managing director – instructed Dewhurst on 3 January 1962 to see Raschid and find out what the latter's attitude was to the 1960 agreement and whether the government really did intend to renegotiate it. Raschid and his ministry turned out to be quite content with that agreement, as they had been all the time; if renegotiation did become essential, it should be later rather than sooner. Meanwhile the British ambassador in Rangoon, fully aware of Burmese objections after the November cabinet discussion, was worried that Burmah Oil might possibly over-react to what he regarded as an 'irritatingly vague threat' hanging over its head. He asked the Foreign Office to brief the directors in London on what the embassy had found out – which seemed to be precious little of any substance – and to ask what they intended to do. When the Foreign Office consulted other departments on the ambassador's suggestion, the Treasury, ultra-cautious as ever, deemed it inadvisable to vouchsafe any opinions whatever to the company, while the Ministry of Power insisted that the ambassador's fears that Burmah Oil might over-react were scarcely matters that could be passed on to the directors. 'The company is not in business at the stockholders' expense to prosecute the cold war or maintain British political influence or prestige', a senior civil servant minuted sententiously.

Then out of a seemingly cloudless sky, came Ne Win's *coup d'état* of 2 March, and the re-establishment – this time indefinitely – of a military regime.[6] One reason given for this coup was that some civilian ministers resented the army's increasing hold on the economy, and that Ne Win had acted to forestall any attempt to wrest the subsidiaries of BEDC and DSI from army control. Ne Win's deputy, Aung Gyi, took over the key portfolio of Industry and Trade Development; he was known to belong to the more pragmatic wing of the revolutionary council. When it was rumoured that that council had decided to nationalise the oil industry, he was questioned at a press conference and replied, 'I do not intend to be another Mossadeq': a reference to the man who had sought to vanquish another powerful oil company, Anglo-Iranian, in the early 1950s. Instead, he insisted that his aim was to improve the oil industry's operations. For that statement – Dewhurst subsequently learnt – Aung Gyi was privately reprimanded.

As Dewhurst saw it, the problem for Burmah Oil was the irreconcilable split within the revolutionary council between the pragmatic and the doctrinaire members. Aung Gyi and those who shared his views were not prepared to see the public sector in Burma augmented at the expense of private enterprise, and sought to emulate neighbouring countries such as India, Pakistan, Malaya and Thailand where sound industrial progress had been achieved within mixed economic systems. Between these opposing groups stood Ne Win, reported to be bogged down in petty detail, sometimes harassed and irritable, sometimes tending to seek policy guidance from the 200 or so anonymous letters he received and personally read each day. The company in London feared that he might act precipitately, but rather unkindly took comfort from his seeming involvement in trivial matters, which gave hope that he would 'literally not have the time to make a mistake on important ones'.

Meanwhile, Eadie in his role as Burmah Oil chairman was determined to maintain good personal relations with Ne Win. On 22 March he wrote and conveyed his good wishes on (as he tactfully put it) the task which the general had undertaken; he stressed how vital it was for the Burmese and British sides to work successfully together, and offered to come out for discussions on 'mutual arrangements'. Ne Win did not reply directly, but instead complained to the British ambassador about the 1960 agreement, which he found in some ways even worse that the 1954 one. 'As usual,' he claimed, 'clever British business had taken advantage of the inexperienced Burmese.' The ambassador pointed out that the 1960 accord had been concluded with the legal government of Burma, to which Ne Win retorted, 'that was why members of that government were behind bars!' While expressing personal confidence in Eadie, Ne Win did not seem to be in a hurry to discuss with him the process of furthering the revolutionary council's nationalisation policy.

Dewhurst, well aware that 'we are not going to be able to dodge the problem', was meanwhile looking round for a suitable Burmese minister with whom Eadie could in due course seek to do business. Ne Win seemed too far removed from the realities of life; Dewhurst therefore sought an appointment with Aung Gyi, to no effect, and had to subsist on rumours. The Burmese chairman of the 1954 company had sent a private report to Ne Win on that company's working, and when some colonels had spoken privately to its Burmese employees, an impressive number of those employees had stressed that the government would be incapable of taking it over completely for a considerable time. No one in authority seemed to be answering letters any more, ministers were reportedly overworked and Ne Win in a testy mood, so that nothing was to be gained by trying to force the pace. As so often in Burma, everyone had to wait and see.

Early in May 1962, Malcolm MacDonald, former commissioner-general in South-East Asia and current British roving proconsul *par excellence*, touched down in Rangoon and had a talk with Ne Win. On oil matters, the general maintained that Burmah Oil had in the past to some extent done the Burmese down. He was not prepared to see the company cheating him any longer, but would negotiate changes in a calm and constructive way. MacDonald remarked that the company was working quite happily with the government of India, and then suggested that he should accept Eadie's offer to come out. Ne Win took the view that no good would result from such a meeting, as the rest of Burmah Oil's board did not share Eadie's clearly progressive views.

How the ruler of Burma came to believe that there was

disunity in the company's board has never been explained. Dewhurst, when told by the ambassador, at once declared that, on the contrary, Eadie was firmly in command and the board solidly behind him. No internal evidence has survived of that alleged disunity; perhaps Strathalmond may have been regarded as a hawk, capable of insisting that the company should uphold its rights to the letter. The three directors who mattered, Eadie, Smith and Strain, had between them about a century of direct and indirect experience of the East. They knew they must allow the issue to come to a head in its own good time, for the revolutionary council was still busy grappling with complex political and constitutional questions. Then, once the moment for action had come, they must avoid truculence or an over-legalistic stance which could well cost them the whole of their investment in Burma.

An apparent provocation occurred in August when two newly-appointed Burmese directors turned up unannounced at the premises of the 1954 company. Pointedly ignoring the British managers and employees, they summoned their own nationals to a private meeting. There they boasted that rapid Burmanisation was about to be introduced and warned that the Burmese staff would have to put up with salary cuts. The (British) acting general manager, H. Shepherd, told London that this episode showed how far the 1954 company had become a pawn in the political game; to him the only solution lay in complete disinvestment. Then the matter blew over. A few days later Shepherd and his fellow-director, the geologist Stanley Churchfield, were called in to meet the two Burmese directors, who proceeded to apologise for their high-handed behaviour, thereby disposing of any notion that the revolutionary council had instigated this piece of psychological warfare.

As autumn approached, opinion in Rangoon hardened to the view that the authorities there were resolved to buy out the Burma trading subsidiary, with its lucrative marketing, importing and exporting functions, but would continue to allow Burmah Oil to hold its 49 per cent share in the 1954 company. Since the two British directors there could always be outvoted by their three Burmese colleagues, British interests would receive scant consideration. Instead, Burmah Oil would be expected to do little apart from paying its share of the refinery and other capital projects and the heavy prospecting costs. A foretaste of things to come was the board meeting of the 1954 company early in October, with thirty items to consider: the days of leisurely consideration of a thin agenda comprising charitable donations and stores indents had gone beyond recall and Dewhurst, now back from home leave, had to argue each item at length as the meeting spilled over to no fewer than three days. Then on 6 October a government decree laid down that oil imports into Burma were to be transferred from the Burma trading subsidiary to the BEDC, and the officially-inspired Rangoon newspapers carried rumours that the subsidiary would be nationalised as from the beginning of 1963.[7]

Dewhurst, in writing home to Smith, reckoned that these surprise moves represented a distinct watering down of Ne Win's original plans for the oil industry. Oddly enough, since BEDC apparently had no interest in the day-to-day work, so that the Russians or Romanians had seemed likely to take this over, the Israelis were now being encouraged to become the new agents. The Israeli ambassador, when discussing the matter with the British embassy, appeared very well briefed about Burmah Oil's affairs and had clearly held detailed discussions with Burmese ministers. The fact that Israel, through the Arab boycott, was cut off from all Middle East supplies did not escape the Burmah Oil directors; then Ne Win, who had been away in Europe, returned and no more was heard of this scheme.

Dewhurst, reviewing all the words and deeds of the Burmese authorities, could only assume that those were co-ordinated examples of what he called 'Hitlerian' tactics, whereby Burmah Oil's influence was being whittled down by stages, 'in such a way that it is unlikely that we will kick up a very great fuss over each one.' Comfortably withdrawn from the deafening hurly-burly on the spot, the directors in London thought that Dewhurst was taking the Burmese to be 'much more Machiavellian than they are', as John Drysdale put it. Yet they had to note very seriously Dewhurst's considered view, echoing the celebrated bulletin on George V's last illness, that 'the operations of the Burmah Oil Company in Burma appear to be drawing peacefully towards their close'.

It undoubtedly helped the embattled Dewhurst to have a

personal talk at Rangoon airport with R. P. Smith, on his way home from Australia, on 17 October. The seven points which they agreed made bleak reading. Briefly, they accepted that the Rangoon government intended to nationalise the oil industry piece by piece, that neither the 1954 company nor the Burma trading subsidiary could any longer be run on truly commercial lines, and that both local organisations had effectively slipped from Burmah Oil's control. 'This being so, our aim must be to obtain the maximum possible payment for our business holdings by sales of shares or assets', the two men concluded.

However logical these assessments – and they still had to be put to the Burmah Oil board – the political ferment in Burma towards the end of 1962 suggested that a clean break with the past, on terms of anything like reasonable compensation, might not be all that easy to achieve. The one hopeful factor was the personal goodwill between Eadie and Ne Win, both as it happened dedicated golfing enthusiasts. In September the general had at long last replied to the former's letter of March, and had approved a meeting between Eadie and his own negotiators in Burma. Eadie decided that he could not go himself at that time but suggested that Strain should travel in his place and arrive early in November. Oddly enough, although Strain had negotiated the 1960 agreement that was in such bad odour among certain Burmese, no one on the spot seems publicly to have objected to his coming out.

Strain arrived in Rangoon on 5 November. He was armed with instructions from his board, but in the last resort had virtually plenipotentiary powers. The responsibility on his shoulders was considerable, for one incautious step might have precipi- tated a seizure of all assets without compensation, as had happened to a number of other British enterprises in that country since 1948. He started up two parallel series of negotiations: one on the take-over of the Burma trading subsidiary with the BEDC chairman, who was also on the revolutionary council, and a separate negotiation on the future of the 1954 company with the secretary of the Defence department. Although Strain wrote a courtesy letter to Ne Win, there was no reply. When he called on Aung Gyi, the latter confirmed the main reason why the revolutionary government refused to accept the 1960 agreement: ministers had failed to consult Ne Win at the time. Strain tactfully suggested that Ne Win had not then been a member of the government, only to be told sharply that the general was the most important person in Burma and should as a matter of course have been consulted.

That the 1960 accord was detested primarily because of personal resentment on the general's part was some comfort to Strain, who soon learnt that while the Burmese would on principle refuse to discuss that accord, they fully accepted the previous one of 1954. The fact that the moves against the Burma trading subsidiary and the take-over terms were in breach of the 1954 agreement was to work in London's favour. It soon became evident that, in return for this breach of agreement being kept quiet, the regime might be prepared to give Burmah Oil more generous terms than otherwise. Strain's negotiating position was thus clear, and he pursued it very astutely.

His first objective was to agree a figure for the sale of the Burma trading subsidiary's assets. At a meeting with BEDC on 12 November, he suggested a price equivalent to £2.3 million; however, the Burmese were prepared to offer only £1.3 million or even less, since the sale value depended on political considerations rather than on any commercial valuation. Though brisk, the discussion was cordial. At a subsequent meeting with the defence secretary concerning the future of the 1954 company, Strain at once got down to business. In a letter handed in soon after his arrival, he had offered an outright sale of the 49 per cent stake in the 1954 company. Now he argued his case in some detail. Proceeding from the agreement of 1954, still valid in Burmese eyes, he declared that when the government of Burma acquired 51 per cent of the 1954 company's shares, it had intended to do likewise with those of the Burma trading company. Since the BEDC now wanted the whole of the latter's shares, it 'could perhaps be deduced' that government would wish also to buy the balance of the 1954 company's holding.

As a gesture of goodwill and to preserve good relations, Strain continued, Burmah Oil would allow the payment of the £6.5 million for the remaining stake to be spread over a number of years. He argued that total buy-out seemed logical now that Burmah Oil appeared to have no future in the country. On the other hand, if the current arrangements were to continue, he required an assurance on two matters in the interests of his own shareholders: a reasonable level of dividend (which followed from the declaration in the 1954 accord that the company would be run on commercial lines) and some British say in the management. Whatever the outcome, he concluded, Burmah Oil would be glad to furnish all the technical assistance required for as long as the government needed it.

This option by Burmah Oil of a virtually complete withdrawal had clearly taken the Burmese by surprise, and Strain requested a reply by the following day on the purchase of the 1954 company's 49 per cent. He was leaving for Karachi on the night of the 13th, and could return to Burma on the 19th or alternatively after the Burmah Oil board meeting on 7 December. In fact, it was not until 27 November that the government in Rangoon announced its refusal to give assurances on dividend levels and management, but agreed in principle to buy the 49 per cent stake, with payment to be made by instalments.

Meanwhile, events in Burma did nothing to encourage the company to stay on. The news of the Burma trading subsidiary's take-over was reported in the press, which led to much labour unrest, springing from well justified fears that government control would lead to inefficiencies and reduced pay. The Burmese chairman of the 1954 company and the secretary of the Ministry of Mines therefore visited the Chauk oilfields in a bid to calm feelings. Dewhurst was asked and agreed to accompany them: an experience he found 'interesting if humiliating'. The others spoke in Burmese throughout and the chairman gave orders to all and sundry even though those orders often went against board policy. Dewhurst's sole function was to speak to the expatriate staff, which he did reluctantly since he felt such a move to be divisive. The only solace was that in the Burma Corporation, the mining firm that had operated a joint venture with the Burmese government since 1951, the British directors on similar visits were made to 'trail round like puppy dogs' and were openly snubbed by that firm's Burmese chairman.

The chairman was also reported to have given instructions that, among other things, wells should be spudded in only on auspicious days, after suitable propitiation of the '*nats*', or spirits. When the casing became stuck in a well and could not be shifted, Keith Wilson, then chief engineer in Burma, was informed that this was because the *nats* had not been sufficiently appeased. The necessary ceremonial was at once upgraded, whereupon the casing was removed without difficulty.

Back in Rangoon, Dewhurst found no other tidings to cheer him. A British embassy official had spoken to the secretary of the Ministry of Finance, who asserted that BEDC was so 'broke' that it would need a thirty-year interest-free loan before it could buy the Burma trading subsidiary. This bad news was corroborated by the chairman of the central bank, who added that the balance of power in the revolutionary council was shifting from Aung Gyi's pragmatism towards the dogmatic wing. The embassy dared not pass this on to the Foreign Office people in London 'lest they get too depressed', according to Dewhurst. Problems were also looming for the Burmah Oil staff in the country: whatever was to happen, they had little assured future there, and Dewhurst pleaded for some announcement from London about staffing policy.

Strain returned to Rangoon on 9 December. At the board meeting in London two days earlier, directors had agreed that Burmah Oil's stake in the 1954 company would, because of political realities and the failure to discover new sources of crude, have to be sold at well below the price laid down in the agreements of 1954. He found that the Burmese had no proposals of their own to make, but were awaiting the terms of his offer. He at once drew their attention to the relevant clauses in the 1954 agreement: if the Burmese would pay the agreed value, equivalent to £7.4 million, he would throw in the Burma trading subsidiary (now valued at £1.4 million) 'as part of a package deal, at no value'. The counter-offer was £3.8 million for the whole package, raised at a subsequent discussion to £4.1 million. Strain rejected these, but was willing to accept £1.4 million for the Burma trading company and £4.7 million for the 1954 company; the latter sum was roughly the oil companies' share of net capital assets plus the depreciated value of all fixed assets. At this point, both sides refused to budge.

On 17 December Strain sought to break the deadlock by splitting the difference of £2 million, making a total sum payable of £5.1 million, which he would accept in three annual instalments. The Burmese side would not accept and said that their cabinet would have to make a decision the following week. As both Ne Win and Aung Gyi were out of the country, Strain said he was prepared to wait until he could see one or other of them, or at least until the 22nd. Then on 21 December the leader of the Burmese delegation called and started off by accusing Burmah Oil of having in 1954 overcharged the government by £3 million for its share by over-capitalising that company; he then added that the newly-returned Aung Gyi would see him the next day. On the 22nd Aung Gyi announced that £4.5 million was his final offer and that if it were unacceptable Strain had better return home and consult his board. After one and a half hours' argument Strain said he would accept £4.7 million if it were paid in two instalments with interest at 3½ per cent free of Burmese tax. Aung Gyi accepted, and the sale was arranged as from 1 January 1963.[8]

The instalments were not due to be paid until March 1963 and March 1964 respectively, but were in fact remitted in January and December 1963. The speed of settlement and relatively liberal terms to the company encouraged other firms in the queue, with local assets of some £8 million, including Burma Corporation, the Bombay Burmah Trading Corporation and subsidiaries of Unilever, British Oxygen and the British Match Corporation, to expect similar treatment: in this they were to be sadly disappointed. The smooth and mutually acceptable hand-over of the Burmah Oil Company's interests in the country to the People's Oil Industry remained a unique phenomenon in Burma's progress towards socialism, and must have been rare enough among all the post-1945 transfers to host countries of oil assets throughout the world.

So ended the British oil presence in Burma, just over a century after the first expatriate businessmen had established a distilling plant not far from Rangoon. Burmah Oil's own involvement spanned more than three-quarters of a century, broken only by the Japanese occupation of 1942–5. It was not simply the material capital that passed out of its hands at the beginning of 1963, but a further dimension, of human capital, as well.

Although the top level negotiations had been brought to a conclusion untinged by any bitterness among the participants, British employees were afterwards unnecessarily delayed, whether by bureaucratic muddle or worse, when leaving Burma at the end of their service; often, too, their bank balances, pension contributions and baggage were held up for unconscionably long periods. Even worse was that a file in London quickly grew fat with heart-rending stories – often smuggled out – of Burmese ex-employees who were dismissed from 1963 onwards and were subsequently reduced to poverty and isolation. Strain and others were tireless in their efforts to try to help such people, but many suffered grievously for their former loyalty to a company they had come to respect and even love. Keith Wilson, one of the last of Burmah Oil's British employees to leave the country, had a poignant experience of this affection. On the eve of his departure, members of his workshop team came quietly to his bungalow under cover of darkness to present him with the traditional parting gift of a retirement bowl. They apologised for the fact that they dared not show such friendship openly in daylight. The documents show clearly that, at this watershed in its existence, the Burmah Oil Company tried not to turn its back on the human tragedies that followed a severance that was not of its own making.

The end of its long association with Burma intensified the company's need to seek new developments elsewhere in the world. However, there was one irksome barrier to expansion that would have to be overcome, dating from the 1928 Burmah-Shell agreements. This will now be explained.

In one clause of those agreements, Watson had in 1928 undertaken that should Burmah Oil for any reason possess oil that was not indigenous to India, the company would offer it to Shell and Anglo-Persian for disposal elsewhere in the world. That would serve to maintain the orderly market in the subcontinent which had underlain his strategy there. Even in the sombre days after 1942 when he had doubted if his company could return to Burma, at the most Watson contemplated extending his purchases of shares in other oil companies; namely portfolio investment. It never entered his mind that Burmah Oil would one day deliberately set out to invest directly in (say) the New World; yet that is precisely what Eadie had done by joining with Murphy Oil in both the US and Canada. By 1961 some crude oil had started to appear. Burmah Oil duly informed Shell and BP, which had replied that they were not interested in purchasing the small amount then on offer, but would wish to know if and when the quantities involved became substantial.

Eadie and Smith believed that the most satisfactory way of overcoming this problem would be to revise the Burmah-Shell agreements and omit that particular clause. Intensive discussions with Shell and BP then followed, which taxed the negotiating skills even of Smith and Drysdale. 'I have been having a pretty tough time over this', the latter admitted after a particularly long bout of talks on some issue or other, but in the end a new agreement was hammered out which satisfactorily addressed Burmah's concerns. That came into force as from the end of 1961.

Also in 1961 another Canadian venture was launched as the result of an initiative in the East. The Great Plains Development Company of Canada was named after the extensive prairie provinces of Western Canada which also happened to house the dominion's principal oil deposits. Great Plains was founded in 1950 at Calgary, Alberta. The president was Lewis MacNaughton, the geologist who ran an oil consulting firm of world renown, DeGolyer & MacNaughton Inc. of Dallas, Texas.[9]

MacNaughton's first contact with Burmah Oil was for the purpose of providing annual surveys of the oil and gas reserves of the Nahorkatiya and Moran fields in Assam. Burmah Oil had of course had outside consultants from the days of Sir Boverton Redwood onwards (see Vol. I pp. 39ff.), but the employment of the Texas firm showed how the frontiers of oil technology had now moved to North America, so that the technical problems of the eastern hemisphere were being overcome with know-how from the West.

By the early 1960s Great Plains had become a considerable independent company, with production of one million barrels a year and annual profits of C$400,000 after C$500,000 depreciation. The capital was C$1 million with a market value of some fifteen times that figure. It confined itself entirely to the upstream activities of prospecting and production, mainly in the Pembina field in Alberta, covering half a million acres and the largest producing field in Canada yielding both oil and natural gas. Its policy was, during the current years of oil surplus, to plough back its income into exploration, drilling and the acquisition of oil properties; it thereby hoped to be advantageously placed when oil demand began to outstrip supply, as it was expected to do in the middle of the decade.

Early in 1961 MacNaughton approached Eadie and asked if he would purchase a stake in Great Plains, since large amounts of finance were needed to carry out the bold strategy which yielded no immediate income; the first dividends were not paid until 1964. To Eadie the attraction of this offer was that the oil deposits were already proved. He admitted that he was really after an integrated company, but he went on to discuss with Charles Murphy whether between the three of them they could not organise an 'arrangement from the well to the consumer.'

A possible link up was very much in Eadie's mind in July 1961 when he wrote a memorandum, the product of 'Sunday afternoon musing in the garden' of his house in Kent, declaring that,

> To maintain our position as a live and active oil organisation, we should seek and consider any suitable and acceptable remunerative avenues of progressive interest elsewhere in the world within our ample means.

He was thinking specifically of Great Plains, 'assuming our detailed examination confirms'. The following September, Burmah Oil acquired a 20 per cent holding in Great Plains shares, with options on further purchases; by the end of 1962 it held 31 per cent of the capital. The main negotiator for the company was Drysdale, working very closely with Eadie.

Meanwhile, the directors at home had been planning the largest and most far-reaching acquisition of the company's life so far. Valued at £22 million, it was to take Burmah Oil's operations into new areas – including Britain itself – and into refining new types of products, including speciality oils, although these downstream developments were the consequences rather than the initial prime objectives of the deal.

Lobitos Oilfields Ltd, known on the stock exchange floor as 'Lobbies', was a London-based company registered in 1908, a few years after British enterprise had discovered oil near Punto Lobos (or Wolves' Point) on Lobitos Bay in the northern part of Peru, and went on to build up a major presence in the country's oil refining and marketing.[10] The first producing well was said to have been found after the managing agent on the spot, Alexander Milne, despairing of finding oil by more conventional methods, had asked an old fisherman named Pablo to throw Milne's hat into the strong wind that was blowing. Drilling proved successful where the hat fell to earth. Equally improbable stories of this wildest form of wild-catting have been related in several regions of the globe, Burma included.

By the early 1960s Lobitos had begun oil operations in Ecuador as well, through its interest in a major refining and marketing subsidiary, Anglo-Ecuadorian Oilfields Ltd. It also owned a British refinery, built in 1934, at Ellesmere Port on the River Mersey; this processed nearly two-thirds of the crude exported from Peru. In 1960 Lobitos had acquired the Manchester Oil Refinery Ltd, dating from 1936 and situated at Barton on the Manchester Ship Canal.[11] Both refineries had been built to produce specialised products and were therefore small compared with such giants as BP's refinery at Llandarcy. Their combined throughput was only 2.5 million barrels. However, their activities illustrated the importance of speciality oil products to so many facets of industrial activity in Britain.

The three founding fathers of the Manchester Oil Refinery were Dr Franz Kind, Dr Georg Tugendhat and Dr Paul Frankel, who came to Britain as the tide of Nazi persecution began to rise in Europe. Horrified at the amount of so-called waste currently being burnt in the boilers of conventional British refineries, they bullied their technicians into finding uses for these fractions. As one of them put it, 'We must valorise our products'; that is, seek to discover new marketable products of potential high value in the process of reducing avoidable waste. Some additional by-products were being developed in the Ellesmere Port refinery.

Seventy years before, the Burmese refineries, like others

round the world, had sought to produce mainly kerosene, with some wax and lubricants, burning off the lightest fractions as of no use – for petrol came later, while the residue was suitable for the boilers of tankers or to be recycled as fuel in the refineries themselves. Since then, the steady advance of technology had evolved a number of by-products; indeed, many were inno- vated by the skills of Lobitos or Manchester Oil technicians. In addition to motor vehicle lubricating oils and hydraulic oil, marine, industrial and aircraft engines all required specialised lubricants. The electrical industry needed transformer and cable oils. On the pharmaceutical side, various kinds of petroleum-based products were being turned out, from medi- cinal paraffin to white oils and waxes for the cosmetics industry. Moreover, white oils, sulphonates and other specially formulated products were increasingly required by the rapidly growing plastics and synthetic rubber industries.

There were other related areas in which Burmah Oil was about to find itself involved for the first time. Two subsidiaries of Lobitos were Dussek Brothers Ltd and Campbell Technical Waxes Ltd.[12] Dussek contributed not only saturants and industrial waxes for cables but also bitumastic paints, putties and mastics for the building industry. Campbell was the largest wax-blender in Britain, and probably in Europe. It supplied waxes not only for the packaging industry but also for an impressive range of uses from printing inks to cosmetics and chewing gum. Another subsidiary was Flexibox Ltd, which manufactured mechanical seals and associated lapping machines. The prototype had been designed by Manchester Oil Refinery's chief engineer to prevent the leakage of fluids or gases along rotating shafts, for instance those in pumps or mixers, or of obnoxious substances in the chemical phase of lubricating oil refining. He later developed flexible mechanical couplings for use with these same types of machinery and also with the main drives of naval vessels.

Lobitos's chairman was Frederick C. Bowring, who also headed the insurance, shipping and trading firm C. T. Bowring & Company Ltd. A relative of his, Sir Thomas Bowring, one-time director of Assam Oil, had until 1915 been on Burmah Oil's local London board, defunct since 1928 (See Vol. I, p. 115). Correspondence about a chance event late in 1960, concerning the Bowring directors' wish to buy from Burmah Oil some shares in the latter's portfolio, referred to what Frederick Bowring called 'the very happy relationship which has existed between our companies for many years'.

Then in March 1962 two apparently unrelated events brought the two companies closer to each other. The first was that Eadie, in a further memorandum on geographical and operational diversification, mentioned that Lobitos had been suggested – almost certainly by Drysdale – as 'fitting the bill'. At that time Lobitos' price (on its 25p ordinary shares) was 85p, giving a total market value of £12.6 million. As Burmah Oil's ordinary share price was then £1.75, he recommended that a share exchange of one of its ordinary shares for two of Lobitos would be appropriate, although 'incentive odds' might stretch the ratio to three of Burmah Oil's for five Lobitos shares.

Ten days later Bowring wrote to Eadie, seemingly out of the blue, to say that Lobitos was seeking partners to help develop two leases in Cornwallis and Ellesmere islands, in the arctic wastes of Canada. These islands were icebound for eleven months in the year, and he therefore floated the intriguing idea that if substantial quantities of oil were to be found, the most efficient method of shipping the oil out would be by submarine tankers. He assured Eadie that cargo-carrying submarines were entirely practicable from a technical point of view. It would have been instructive to have the response of the hard-headed Eadie to what must have seemed Jules Verne-type fantasies, but he did ask Drysdale and a company geologist, K. V. Stringer, to investigate the proposal; he told Bowring that he appreciated 'the opportunity of having a look at this interesting proposal'.

Eadie then spoke to Richard Fleming about using this approach by Bowring as an opportunity to suggest a merger. Fleming's reply was that if no hidden snags emerged, he would back such a merger project as the most attractive for Burmah Oil that he had come across for a long time. He had recently met Lobitos' managing director, George Mardall, and found him 'a very nice and most capable administrator' who would be a congenial man to work with. Mardall had previously been managing director of Trinidad Leaseholds Ltd until that firm had been taken over by Texaco and, since joining Lobitos, he had undoubtedly done much to promote that company's growth and profitability. However, its share price was low in relation to its assets, and there were lively fears of an American takeover bid.

Burmah Oil eventually decided not to become involved in the polar regions, but in August it felt ready to launch merger proposals. Then the Lobitos board announced that its standing in the market for specially blended oil had been greatly strengthened by its recent acquisitions in Britain, notably Manchester Oil and Dussek Brothers, which provided enhanced scope for future diversification. It was therefore making a one-for-one bonus issue of shares, and undertook to pay a dividend on the increased capital of not less than 20 per cent, a considerable improvement on the previous year's 14 per cent.

Much to the Burmah Oil directors' dismay, they saw Lobitos' share price shoot up from 85p to £1.10 by mid-August. They therefore had to contemplate raising their proposed offer from three to four of their ordinary shares for every five of Lobitos, but decided that those terms would still be worthwhile. When the bid was made, on 10 August, *The Economist* was not the only financial paper to regard the terms as 'distinctly generous'. The *Sunday Telegraph* complained that the offer price was too high, but it was known – as Richard Fleming told Eadie – that the financial editor had a 'bee in his bonnet' about having Burmah Oil's holdings in BP and Shell distributed to its shareholders, and 'this article was merely a peg on which to hang this particular hat'.[13] The Lobitos board accepted the offer with alacrity.

One of the promises Burmah Oil made was stated as follows in the press release after the bid: that Lobitos would 'maintain its identity and generally carry on business as usual'. Bowring and Mardall joined the Burmah Oil board, while Smith, Strain and Williams were appointed to the Lobitos board. The offer was of course subject to the approval of the latter company's shareholders, but in the end 90 per cent of them accepted. A discordant note of a different type was struck by the *Investor's Chronicle*, which maintained that Burmah Oil would 'add the difficulties of South American politics to those of Burma, India and Pakistan'.[14]

It was true that the governments of Peru and Ecuador shared

the instability common to many Latin American states and that since 1959 Peru had restricted exports of oil to no more than 20 per cent of output. Although in both countries large areas seemed well worth exploring for their oil potential, these were on the whole remote and inaccessible. Hence Lobitos had of late preferred to look elsewhere in order to reduce its dependence on that part of the world. Its operations in Canada seemed promising but had as yet produced no oil. Even so, that company's overall prospects and advantages were attractive enough to Burmah Oil.

Not until 6 September was the offer formally reported to the Burmah Oil board, two days after publication of the offer document, although Eadie had consulted all the directors individually about the bid. Three weeks later an extraordinary general meeting was held, to increase the company's authorised capital to £110 million by creating new ordinary shares to permit the share exchange. Other provisions were that Burmah Oil's ordinary shares would then become ordinary stock and that the number of directors would be increased from twelve to fifteen.

In his address to that meeting, Eadie stressed four points. The expected profit would provide an enhanced earnings cover for Burmah Oil's dividend. Lobitos' Canadian operations would greatly strengthen the company's own presence there. Since Lobitos concentrated on speciality lubricants and waxes, there would be no clash with BP and Shell outside South America, where there was little conflict in any case. Lastly, the merger would provide substantial tax advantages. He tactfully omitted to add that the planned return on the additional capital looked as if it would be appreciably higher than operations in the East were currently yielding.

The extraordinary general meeting did not go entirely smoothly. Two Scottish shareholders complained that the terms represented a bad bargain for the company, with the exchange ratio being too favourable to Lobitos. Echoing the *Sunday Telegraph* man, they proposed that the BP and Shell holdings should be distributed to stockholders, and that a bargain should be struck with Lobitos on the basis of the resulting relative trading value.

Eadie's reply was that the paramount criterion had been to

safeguard the Burmah Oil stockholders' dividend prospects. The offer had been pitched so as to ensure, as far as possible, that the income from Lobitos would more than cover the part of the Burmah Oil dividend on stock issued to acquire Lobitos. 'So long as you are satisfied that the income or prospective income from the Lobitos investment would match up to that yardstick, we feel this is something we should go for', he concluded. The mini-revolt collapsed, and the resolutions were all passed. In a vote of thanks to Eadie, another stockholder commented both on the fact that Burmah Oil had 'passed the hundred million-pound mark in capital, a very astonishing feat for a Scottish company', and on the highly amicable nature of the takeover. Eadie replied that 'the decision we have taken today is unique and momentous in the company's history'. Whether one personally liked it or not, he went on, 'the pattern today of industrial development and economic advance – I might almost say economic survival – seems to lie in the way of larger and international institutions and organisations. This merger today is therefore conforming to this pattern.'

He was in fact pursuing the same policies, albeit on a smaller scale, in Canada. The company's subsequent consolidation of its Canadian venture well illustrates the effectiveness of the strong head-office team master-minding the venture, namely, Eadie, Smith and Drysdale. The Lobitos acquisition usefully brought in two 80 per cent-held subsidiaries, Lobitos Oilfields Canada Ltd, with an issued share capital of C$2.3 million and net assets of C$8.8 million, and the Round Valley Oil Company, carrying on exploration in the arctic islands mentioned earlier by Bowring. In July 1963 BOC of Canada acquired the Canadian operations of the Colorado Oil & Gas Ltd, with reserves – estimated at fifteen years' production – in all the 'great plains' provinces, for C$9.3 million. That had an annual production of 600,000 barrels and net profit of C$700,000.

The purchase of Colorado gave the executive in London an opportunity to merge all these properties into an integrated wholly-owned Canadian subsidiary, with strong local management – which was an essential pre-requisite in that country – and the capacity to be as far as possible self-financing. That July the interests of BOC of Canada and Lobitos Oilfields

Canada, plus C$3.5 million contributed in cash by Burmah
Oil, were exchanged with Great Plains for an equivalent
number of its own shares. As a result of this transaction,
Burmah Oil owned about 67 per cent of Great Plains' issued
capital and was able to nominate the majority of directors. In
addition to declaring dividends from 1964 onwards, Great
Plains was able to continue its acquisition programme by
buying two smallish Canadian oil concerns. The whole operation was thus a text-book example of what could be achieved by
careful assembling of different oil properties into a properly
co-ordinated entity. The government of Canada's national oil
policy, emphasising the need for growth in the country's oil
resources, greatly helped this process along.

All these far-reaching moves, as part of a radical new
direction for Burmah Oil, needed not merely financial strength
but also top managerial expertise. Ever since becoming
chairman in 1957, Eadie had relied on four outside directors for
advice: Lord Bilsland on the major issues that passed over his
desk, Richard Fleming – an adviser and then director in 1959 –
on financial matters, J. A. Lumsden of the solicitors Maclay
Murray & Spens – a director since 1957 – on legal questions,
and Lord Strathalmond as a seasoned international oil man.
Relations with the last-named were more at arms length than
with the others, since he necessarily had the interest of BP, his
own company, at heart.

However, within the company, Eadie could have done with
more executive directors, as shown in Chapter VII. He had the
dedicated support of R. P. Smith, who was appointed sole
managing director when Eadie became part-time chairman at
the beginning of 1962, backed up by the probing mind of J. F.
Strain who was both a skilled overseas negotiator and financial
director. Drysdale was regularly on the move on exploration
and kindred matters in the New World, as Strain was in the
East. The only other full-time board member, working on staff
matters, was David C. Robertson, known as Bertie. In 1957 he
had been promoted to the London office from his post as
general manager in India. He turned out to be a good staff man,
if rather silent during board discussions. He retired in 1963.

Now that Lobitos was part of the Burmah group, and other
major acquisitions were being contemplated, senior managers

would be needed to help integrate these newcomers and gain the benefits of consolidation. With hindsight, this managerial aspect of the group's overall strategy was never properly thought through, a weakness that in the longer term was to be of the utmost consequence for its future. The far-sighted Eadie had rightly stressed the unique and momentous nature of the merger that had just taken place, itself a promising first step in his programme of diversification pursued so single-mindedly from 1957 onwards. However, it was building up many administrative problems that were to prove as difficult for the group as any that had arisen in the whole of its history.

Notes

1 Tinker, *Union of Burma*, p. 92. Kingsley Martin, on the other hand, emphasised the bitterness engendered by the election, *New Statesman*, 12 March 1960, p. 355–6.

2 For Defence Services Institute, see Tinker, *Union of Burma*, p.227.

3 *Financial Times*, 1 March 1960.

4 *The Times*, 20 August 1960.

5 *Petroleum Press Service*, July 1961, pp. 253–5.

6 Tinker, *Union of Burma*, pp. 60–1, 386–8.

7 Forecast in the *Guardian* (Rangoon), 3 October; *The Times*, 8 October, *Financial Times*, 9 October 1962.

8 *Sunday Guardian* (Rangoon), 23 December, the *Guardian* (Rangoon) 25, 29 December 1962, cf. leader in the *Nation*, 2 January 1962 [*sic*]. The fullest report given in British newspapers was in the *Glasgow Herald*, 28 December 1962.

9 'Great Plains Profile', *BGM* No. 4, Winter 1965, pp. 18–23. For Lewis MacNaughton, see ibid., No. 13, Spring 1968, pp. 7–8 and No. 18, Summer 1969, p. 17.

10 For the early history of Lobitos, see *Oil*, Spring 1962, pp. 16–21, Vol. 5 No. 6, 1963, pp. 12–15.

11 'The M.O.R. Story,' *BGM* No. 4, Winter 1965, pp. 3–7. For Franz Kind, see *Journal of Institute of Petroleum* XLI, 1955, p. 215, and for Georg Tugendhat see ibid., LIX, 1973, pp. 144–5.

12 Dussek is described in *BGM* No. 6, Summer 1966, pp. 23–6, No. 16, Winter 1968, pp. 20–1; Campbell Technical Waxes in ibid., No. 11, Autumn 1967, pp. 2–7, and No. 16, Winter 1968, pp. 20–1; and Flexibox in ibid., No. 7, Autumn 1966, pp. 3–7, and No. 19, Autumn 1969, pp. 8–9.

13 *Economist*, 18 August 1962, pp. 635–6; *Sunday Telegraph*, 16 September 1962.

14 *Investor's Chronicle*, 21 September 1962.

CHAPTER X

Relations with British Petroleum and Shell 1950–64

By 1950 all the trends suggested that Burmah Oil, so far from remaining an integrated oil producing and marketing company, was steadily turning itself into an investment trust. In 1941, shortly before the denial of its Burmese installations, just under three-quarters of its income represented trading profits, almost all earned in Burma or the Indian subcontinent, and only a quarter from investment. The proportions had changed to 50-50 by 1951 and were to tilt even further in the new decade, to a 32 per cent trading contribution as against a 68 per cent investment contribution to overall profit in 1955 (see Table 6 below). On the whole disappointing results from the newly independent successor states to the Indian empire – Burma, India and Pakistan – helped to explain the relative decline on the trading side. At the same time, the dramatic extension of both Anglo-Iranian's and Shell's activities world-wide had sharply increased the dividends accruing to Burmah Oil, from nearly £134,000 and £60,000 respectively in 1941 to £882,000 and £121,000 in 1950. The corresponding dividends for 1955 were to rise as high as £3.49 million and £364,000 respectively.

Such a heavy reliance for its income on the performance of two major oil companies, however gratifying at first sight, was bound to be less than comfortable if viewed as a long-term and seemingly permanent trend. One of those especially worried was Hugh Spens, one of Burmah Oil's non-executive directors since 1937 and partner in the Glasgow law firm of Maclay Murray & Spens. In 1950 he suggested to Harper that this

problem of over-reliance could be largely overcome by distributing the company's total holding in Anglo-Iranian ordinary
shares to the Burmah Oil stockholders. Some of the latter, as
well as popular journals such as the *Daily Express*, had long been
campaigning for a distribution of that kind. Spens's proposal
was that Anglo-Iranian should acquire all Burmah Oil's
ordinary stock by offering £1 of its own shares for every £2 of
Burmah's. Since the latter totalled just over £13.7 million, some
£6.85 million worth of Anglo-Iranian stock would be required.
The nominal value of Burmah Oil's own holdings came to
£5.35 million, so that Anglo-Iranian would need to provide
roughly an additional £1.5 million of its stock. It could do that
by increasing its ordinary share capital by £6.85 million, all of
which would then be allotted as bonus shares to Burmah Oil
ordinary stockholders, enabling the £5.35 million worth of the
Anglo-Iranian stock held by Burmah Oil to be cancelled.

Spens's ingenious brainchild had one defect: it would result
in throwing the baby out with the bathwater since Burmah Oil
would in the process end up as a fully-owned subsidiary of
Anglo-Iranian. Theoretically Burmah Oil's 46,000 ordinary
stockholders, who between them stood directly to acquire 26
per cent of Anglo-Iranian shares, could collectively exercise a
voting power over the latter company; in practice, however,
there was no reason to expect them to act in unison, any more
than would any other widely dispersed shareholding body.
Even so, neither Harper as chairman nor Weva as managing
director raised serious objections to the possibility of being
taken over in this way. Weva admitted that in the long run
Anglo-Iranian was 'almost certain to get bigger and bigger,
whereas Burmah [Oil] must get smaller and smaller', relatively
speaking. Hence if terms for any take-over could be agreed that
would give Burmah Oil's shareholders 'something
approaching what they would probably get if we carried on
alone', he would be content.

During the next few years, the principle of Spens's capital
reorganisation was not challenged. Although discussed interminably among the executive directors and with outside
advisers such as Sir John Craik Henderson of the company's
Glasgow solicitors Miller Thompson & Henderson and the
auditors Brown Fleming & Murray, it was not brought

formally to the board, presumably because Anglo-Iranian's chairman, Sir William Fraser (later Lord Strathalmond) was a member. During 1951 the chief object of debate was the distinctly derivative one of how best to deal with Burmah Oil's preference stock, which carried what were then excessively high interest rates of 6–8 per cent. Redeeming it seemed one possible answer. Then in August the Chancellor of the Exchequer, Hugh Gaitskell, announced that he was introducing legislation to limit dividends. That made any plans for repaying preference stock unattractive, and that part of the scheme was therefore abandoned.

The return in October 1951 of Winston Churchill's Conservative government, pledged to release the British economy from its by then onerous post-war controls, does not seem to have encouraged the Burmah Oil directors to pursue more vigorously any effort to implement Spens's plan. Instead, in June 1953 Harper contacted Hubert Ashton, an MP since 1950 and parliamentary private secretary to the Chancellor, R. A. Butler, over rumours then current that the government would be glad to dispose of its 56 per cent holding of Anglo-Iranian ordinary stock, and that one of the largest British insurance companies was anxious to purchase it. Harper said that according to R. I. Watson, the government had undertaken to give Burmah Oil directors the first refusal should it ever wish to sell the holdings; 'possibly a verbal agreement', Harper added cautiously, as nothing had ever been put into writing. He tactfully suggested that if the rumours were true, Burmah Oil would be very interested in acquiring the whole or a large part of the holdings.

Ashton, having discussed the matter with Treasury officials and then with the Chancellor, replied in mid-July, 'I have spoken to the people concerned and can let you know that the question which you raise is not a live issue to H.M.G.' However, he promised to see that the correspondence remained in the files in case the matter ever did become active. His reply prompted Harper to remind Ashton of the merger scheme of 1915–24 (see Introduction above). That scheme had proposed to transform the 60 per cent Dutch-owned Royal Dutch-Shell into a British company by amalgamating it with Burmah Oil and with Anglo-Persian. Figures produced in 1921, setting out relative market valuations to show how the three companies (including the British part of Shell) jointly gave a narrow British majority over Royal Dutch, could – he pointed out – be parallelled by the current proportions, as follows:

	1921	1953	(%)
Burmah Oil	10.7	6.7	
Shell (a)	33.2	33.2	
Anglo-Persian/Iranian	6.3	10.3	
Total British	50.2	50.2	
Royal Dutch (b)	49.8	49.8	
Total	100.0	100.0	

Notes: (a) 40 per cent of Royal Dutch-Shell
(b) 60 per cent of Royal Dutch-Shell

In fact, the post-1945 world was quite unconducive to reviving a merger scheme of that kind, especially now that Anglo-Iranian's percentage share had grown while Burmah Oil's had declined. Only the previous year the United States Federal Trade Commission had issued a staff report on *The International Petroleum Cartel*, detailing the way in which the world's oil industry had become monopolised during the twentieth century: Royal Dutch-Shell and Anglo-Iranian together already accounted for nearly a fifth of world oil production and held almost a quarter of known crude oil reserves.[1] The Government and international regulating bodies alike would frown on any attempt to reassemble a merger package of that kind.

It was equally out of the question that Burmah Oil, with net operating assets of £46 million, would have been capable of buying all or even a large part of the government's Anglo-Iranian holding, which had a market value not far short of that figure. Even if feasible, such a purchase could in any event have compounded the investment trust problem that was already exercising the company. By 1954 the Burmah Oil directors had

more realistically reverted to the main problems which surrounded their current shareholding in Anglo-Iranian. How
could it be disposed of for the maximum benefit of Burmah
Oil's stockholders; how could their voting rights be safeguarded, and how could they make efficient alternative use of
the proceeds from any disposal?

These questions were in practice self-contradictory. To
transfer the holdings of Anglo-Iranian shares to Burmah Oil's
stockholders would deprive Burmah Oil of voting control over
this rapidly growing company. In any case, its assets would
then be run down by the amount of that stake forgone; the
company's income would also be reduced and hence its ability
to expand along alternative lines should it wish to do so. During
1954 Spens proposed certain internal accounting adjustments
to expedite his plans; the precise methods he put forward need
not detain us here. That he was allowed to go on so long,
generating reams of correspondence between those concerned,
shows up the absence of overall corporate strategy at that time.
The company just did not have any clear idea where it was
going.

Those mainly responsible for the drift were the chairman and
managing director. Harper, an administrator who for years
had concentrated on personnel matters, and Weva, a geologist
with particular skills in face-to-face negotiations, seemed lost
and even lacking in interest when detailed questions of
corporate finance were raised. Perhaps also they would not face
the need, perceived and later pointed out by their senior
accounting staff, for the company to plan for the future and to
adopt a more assertive strategy. Indeed, the days when the
company could manage without its own financial experts had
now vanished. Even the legally-trained Watson, who for years
had no experts of this kind in-house, had in 1941 brought back
the accountant William Eadie from Burmah-Shell to build up
an accounts department in London. So central was the
accountant's role to become in Burmah Oil's overall direction,
as to that of most large British companies, that in the years after
1955 the chairman or the managing director (and often both)
were almost invariably trained accountants.

Eadie, although designated chief accountant in 1948, did not
join the board until mid-1950. Even after becoming assistant

managing director in 1951, he scarcely felt it his place to argue about the principles of the Spens plans. Yet he was far from happy with them. Above all, it could not help the company if a large slice of its own stock were to be held by a category of shareholder concerned only with Anglo-Iranian's affairs and dividends, and with no personal interest in Burmah Oil's need to prosper in its own right. When later that year Anglo-Iranian (later to be renamed British Petroleum) announced a bonus issue of four ordinary shares for every one share held, and Spens quickly concocted a scheme to pass on these bonus shares to Burmah Oil's stockholders, Eadie saw his opportunity to stress the quite intractable problems that would arise from such a scheme. Under this cold douche of realism, the Spens proposals at last died a natural death.

In the second half of the 1950s, Burmah Oil's troubles over the BP shareholdings became only one facet of a more general problem. Now that the company had adopted the practice of distributing the BP and Shell dividends in full so as to avoid having to pay tax on them, Burmah Oil's dividend had in addition to be boosted by at least half the trading profits; that left retained earnings that were all too inadequate to finance the very costly investments needed in the East (see Chapter VI). Moreover, to join such post-war horrors as rock and roll, spivs and steam-baked bread, the era of the take-over bid had arrived. Burmah Oil, because of its highly conservative asset valuations and large holding in two of the giants of the oil industry, was especially vulnerable to corporate predators, particularly from overseas. In April 1957 Harper and Eadie, now chairman and managing director respectively, met Sir John Craik Henderson to consider drafting new Articles of Association so as to prevent foreigners from serving either as directors or holding shares in the company. According to the current *Stock Exchange Year Book*, only a handful of British quoted companies had such restrictions. Apart from shipping companies, such as Cunard and P. & O., these included some industrial and trading companies, notably Attock Oil.

Before putting such amendments to stockholders, the Burmah Oil directors were advised to seek from the Treasury and Bank of England a declaration that it was in the public interest for the company's stock to be held only by British subjects. Harper did not for one moment believe that such official blessing would be forthcoming, and was proved right. When he formally approached the governor of the Bank of England, C. F. Cobbold, he came away empty-handed. Cobbold was no more helpful when Eadie went to see him in May 1959 (see Chapter VII above); he did not discuss possible changes in the Articles of Association but suggested that Burmah Oil should tighten up its existing corporate rules in order to make it harder for possible take-over bids to succeed, and should keep in touch with BP over the matter. Clearly the traditional practice of ear-stroking rather than arm-twisting applied in the Bank's dealings with industrial enterprises as in the world of banking and finance.

It has to be said that relations between Burmah Oil and Anglo-Iranian (later BP) were not of the most cordial during the 1950s. Watson had enjoyed an excellent rapport with BP and also with Shell. Harper remained on good terms with Shell, of which he was a director until 1960. No one from Burmah Oil thereafter replaced him on that board. His relations with Anglo-Iranian, or at least with Lord Strathalmond – chairman until 1956 – were strained (see Chapter V). Another area of difficulty was the oil supply contract for Burma, India and Pakistan, which the company had needed ever since its own crude oil production in Burma had been so greatly cut back.

Negotiations over a new supply contract had dragged on through the late 1940s. No definitive arrangement had then emerged, although Anglo-Iranian had agreed to supply Shell with its oil on a profit-sharing basis; that is to say, at actual production and refining cost, then splitting the difference between that cost and the market price. Strathalmond was prepared to offer comparable terms to Burmah Oil, but this would have cut across the Burmah-Shell agreement under which Anglo-Iranian had the right of supplying, at the same price as Shell, half Burmah Oil's requirements for India and Pakistan. The Burmah-Shell terms were very much more favourable for Burmah Oil than those currently applying to oil earmarked for Burma, and the company pressed hard for similar terms in all three countries. Then in July 1951, after the

Abadan crisis had severely cut its crude resources, Anglo-Iranian announced that it could not make even provisional arrangements without first consulting Shell.

All this uncertainty over supplies, at a time of such crisis, made Burmah Oil's top people distinctly jittery. They recalled Watson's words in 1940, 'A distributor who is not a producer of petroleum products exists only on the sufferance of those who have the production.' By the time Eadie joined the BP board on Weva's resignation in 1955, inter-company relations were at an all-time low, and he set out to do what he could to heal the breach. A further source of friction had arisen over the contract for crude oil supplied to the Burmah-Shell refinery near Bombay which had been opened in 1955; the fee was based on 'cost-plus' but, when it proved to be a undue burden on the refinery's earnings, it had to be renegotiated in 1957 in favour of one based on the refiner's margin. To forestall any hostile reaction by the government of India, the charge had to be made retrospective, but Burmah Oil compensated BP for its reduced income earned in the two years 1955 and 1956. BP expected the compensation to continue; instead, Burmah Oil and Shell – themselves beneficiaries of the refinery's augmented earnings – offered BP half of Burmah Oil's investment in the Burmah-Shell refinery and in its marketing company. BP brushed aside that offer, as providing no benefit to itself.

In 1961 – as part of the renegotiated Burmah-Shell agreement mentioned in Chapter IX – BP at last agreed to supply all the imported crude which Burmah Oil required in India, but on a profit-sharing basis. The director concerned, Sir Harold Snow, raised the question of retrospective compensation from 1957 onwards, then still in deadlock. This matter came to a head not long after the genial Sir Neville Gass had been succeeded as BP's chairman in 1960 by the more hawkish (Sir) Maurice Bridgeman,[2] which suggests that it was Bridgeman's idea to get tougher with Burmah Oil. R. P. Smith, the latter's managing director and a BP director since Harper's retirement in 1957, did not help matters by proposing to Snow at the end of 1961 that BP should simply write off the claim for compensation.

No further noises came out of BP until six months later, in June 1962, when Smith received a visit from two of its managing directors, (Sir) Eric Drake and Robert B. Dummett. They brought what Smith later called 'a most unpleasant surprise': news that they had submitted all the papers on the compensation quarrel to counsel, who had advised that there was a strong case against Burmah Oil. If the BP directors did not pursue it, they could under company law be held personally liable for any consequences. They therefore proposed to take out a writ against the company, but hoped – in so many words – that commonsense would prevail and that Burmah Oil would cave in without further ado.

Eadie told Lord Bilsland, his closest confidant among the non-executive directors, that litigation between the two companies was 'unthinkable. I personally am most distressed that they should have taken this action', he continued, 'no matter how necessary it may have been from their side, without at least intimating to me that they were taking this "protective" measure'. His endeavours, 'for quite a number of years' to rebuild the good relations 'which should always exist between BP and ourselves', had been largely successful 'and therefore it is all a bitter disappointment to me that steps of this nature should have been taken "behind my back"'. Three weeks later he saw Bridgeman; as he reported to Bilsland, he 'cleared the relationship aspect of our inter-company contacts quite satisfactorily' and apparently convinced Bridgeman that it would be highly damaging to both parties for any difference of this kind to go before the courts. Bridgeman, while refusing to give way directly, did agree to having the question resolved by arbitration.

If there was one lesson to be learnt from this unhappy episode, it was that Burmah Oil's directors had been put on notice that they could not expect any favours from their BP counterparts. Even so, in his anxiety to improve relations between the two companies, Eadie proposed in April 1963 that Bridgeman and one of the BP managing directors should join the Burmah Oil board. The BP nominees would at least learn something of the company's point of view. Bridgeman rejected the idea. Soon afterwards, Burmah Oil was to receive another unexpected and even nastier shock from the same direction.

The London stock exchange was and is no stranger to erratic surges in demand for particular shares from time to time. Yet the buying spree for Burmah Oil's stock and the accompanying rumours about its future during much of 1963 were noteworthy by the standards of that time. Beginning the year at less than 45s (£2.25), by early April its £1 ordinary stock had risen above 50s (£2.50). That month the directors announced an issue of debentures and unsecured loan stock, totalling £10.2 million, to help finance the pipeline being built by Oil India Ltd. Although that issue was an entirely routine operation, stories at once began to circulate about an imminent capital reorganisation, involving a plan to sell off all or part of the BP and Shell shareholdings.

With the results for 1962 now eagerly awaited, the rumour-mongers' expectations were fanned early in May by the fortuitous publication of a highly sanguine study of Burmah Oil, made by an American oil share analyst for a leading London firm of stockbrokers. Whereas the market had tended hitherto to look on Burmah Oil as primarily an investment company, so that its shares were priced at little more than the value of those investments, the study emphasised the contribution being made by its trading activities, including the considerable oil and natural gas operations in both India and Pakistan, and the rich possibilities of the recently acquired Lobitos. It therefore strongly recommended purchase of Burmah Oil ordinary stock. Since the analyst concerned, Robert A. Gilbert, was known to have been briefed in some detail by the company and to have met outside experts during a fact-finding trip to London, his study – widely distributed in the United States by a Wall Street firm – made a great stir on both sides of the Atlantic.

By mid-May Burmah Oil stock was up to 52s (£2.60), fuelled not only by the analyst's report, but also by 'whispers' of a take-over bid in the offing; the latter R. P. Smith was at pains to discount. Royal Dutch, widely tipped as a possible bidder, also issued vigorous denials. Nothing daunted, the city pundits trotted out the age-old cliché that there was no smoke without fire. The company's 1962 results, published on 14 May, revealed the encouraging news that profits after taxation were up from £11 million to just under £14 million. Of this, £1 million was due to improved dividend payments from BP and Shell, but the analyst Gilbert's optimism seemed to be confirmed by a gratifying 50 per cent increase in trading income, largely attributable to Lobitos's activities.

Since he had no knowledge whatever of any impending bid, Eadie in the annual report said nothing on this score. As he would have been expected to be aware of any possible take-over moves in Britain, market opinion inferred that the persistent buying pressure on Burmah Oil stock must be coming mainly from American interests, attracted by Gilbert's recommendations and by the highly favourable yield on the stock, currently more than 7 per cent.

The annual meeting in Glasgow, on 7 June, gave Eadie a suitable platform to quash the rumours which refused to go away. Virtually no one, he pointed out, even a consortium, would be able to make a bid attractive enough to induce the board to recommend acceptance; in his words, 'it is just not on.' Yet rumours persisted, being accompanied by what were termed 'widespread and speculative' dealings in the stock; Gulf Oil of America was said to be buying heavily. However much the company issued disclaimers, some of the 'best brains' in the city of London were reportedly sticking to their conviction that a bid could be expected at any moment.

City editors suggested it was about time that the Burmah Oil board made an official statement to the Stock Exchange Council, only to be met by the entirely sensible response that the directors knew of no reason for doing so. The editors failed to ask why the two watchdogs in the City, the Bank of England and the Stock Exchange Council, had raised not a woof between them. By hindsight, it can be inferred that they may conceivably have been fed with some titbits of information withheld from the Burmah Oil directors, and felt no great concern about the unsettling effects that an unusually protracted palaver was having on the stock market generally. As to the Stock Exchange Council, a spokesman dismissed the speculation as set off by no more than 'intelligent anticipation'.

From 19 June onwards, activity in Burmah Oil stock continued. The price shot up for the first time above 55s (£2.75), while in the following seven days to 27 June no fewer than 1.6 million of the 94 million issued ordinary stock units changed hands. Even so, the unsuspecting Eadie saw no reason for postponing his planned golfing holiday in Nairn near Inverness where, on Wednesday 26 June, he was surprised to receive a visit from Alastair Down, one of BP's managing directors. Then in his late forties Down had, after spectacular wartime service in which he had gained four decorations and lost an eye, become a high-flyer in the BP hierarchy. He had recently returned to London after eight fruitful years spent in establishing a BP presence in Canada. As a Scottish-born accountant, he had personal affinities with both Eadie and Smith, who were in any case colleagues of his on the BP board. The object of his visit was to break to Eadie the startling news that BP and Shell were jointly making a bid for Burmah Oil.[3]

The take-over terms basically involved reconstructing Burmah Oil's capital, which would then be acquired by the two companies. The ordinary stock would be cancelled in return for the distribution to existing stockholders of the company's ordinary shareholding in BP and Shell. The proposal, which had piquant echoes of Spens's schemes of the early 1950s, envisaged that each holder of £100 Burmah Oil ordinary stock would by that exchange receive £85 and £4.25 of BP and Shell ordinary stock respectively, and almost £46 in cash.

As £94 million of Burmah Oil ordinary stock was in shareholders' hands, nearly £80 million of BP shares would be needed for the exchange. The company's BP holding had a value of nearly £64.2 million; BP therefore undertook to provide about £15.8 million of its own shares to make up the required total. The existing Shell stock held by Burmah Oil would be sufficient for that part of the offer. BP and Shell would also provide £47.8 million in cash to meet both the money payment to ordinary shareholders and the cost of buying the preference share capital. The debentures and loan stock would remain and be guaranteed by BP and Shell.

Since its assets would remain intact, apart from the BP and Shell holdings after distribution, Burmah Oil would be expected to issue further ordinary stock to BP and Shell once they had become owners of its assets. As Burmah Oil was a Scottish registered company, it would almost certainly have to lodge a petition with the courts in Scotland to sanction a scheme of arrangement under the Companies Act of 1948. That required meetings of stockholders and debenture holders to be held where major capital reorganisations were proposed.

The news of this audacious bid came as a total shock to Eadie; he returned at once to London together with Down. To avoid any possibility of further rumours being set off, Down's travel reservation had been made in the name of Smith. During their deliberations, Eadie no doubt raised some very searching questions; with his usual benign courtesy, he gave nothing away to Down. Although Eadie could not properly deliver a considered response until he had consulted his board, Down seems to have imagined that he was favourably disposed towards the bid. In fact, Eadie shared with R. P. Smith a deep sense of betrayal: despite both being members of the chief predator's board they had been kept in complete ignorance of that board's intentions. Furthermore, contrary to stock exchange conventions, the bid itself had been made entirely without prior consultation.

The next afternoon, 27 June, when both Eadie and R. P. Smith were present at the regular monthly BP board meeting, they were asked to leave before the bid was discussed. Then, after Bridgeman had gained his board's approval of the letter setting out the terms of the bid, which he signed at 4.45 p.m, Down took it from the fourth to the first floor of Britannic House to give to Eadie. Judging by the thumb-prints that to this day adorn the original, no document in the whole of Burmah Oil's history has ever been as closely scrutinised as that letter.

Eadie's written acknowledgement was formal and brief. The proposals, he stated, would be discussed at the next meeting of his board on Thursday 4 July, and the board's views communicated to the chairmen of BP and Shell. He at once sent a copy to all outside directors, saying that his executive colleagues were working on the proposals. 'I hope to be in a position to make a recommendation to our [board] meeting,' he concluded. When the company released a press announcement that evening, his only public comment was to advise stockholders not to sell.

The Burmah Oil people thus gave themselves a week in which to make up their minds. Eadie himself had no desire to preside over the extinction as an independent entity of the company he had worked for since 1921, and had so recently directed into new paths; his closest colleagues were equally resolute. In their hour of extreme vulnerability, it occurred to this bunch of canny Scots that the large government holding in BP might prove the Achilles heel of the principal predator. Drysdale recalled that the export marketing director of Lobitos, which Burmah Oil had acquired the previous year, was a Conservative MP – John E. Harvey (see Chapter VIII). He arranged to see Harvey on the morning of the 28th and asked him to inform the Chancellor of the Exchequer at once that the Burmah Oil board intended resolutely to oppose the BP-Shell bid. Harvey telephoned the Chancellor – Reginald Maudling – who agreed to meet him at the Treasury at noon. By 1 p.m. Harvey reported back to Drysdale: Maudling had seemed greatly put out by the possibility of serious opposition from Burmah Oil, saying he had been assured by BP that there would be no trouble. Thanking him for having so quickly made Burmah Oil's attitude clear to the Chancellor, Drysdale mused, 'So they've been told there will be no trouble. Well, trouble there is going to be.'

Back-of-envelope calculations within Burmah Oil showed the market value of the bid to be over £300 million.* It was therefore by far the largest take-over scheme Britain had seen, easily topping the £190 million bid by ICI which Courtaulds had successfully fought off in 1961–2.[4] That earlier bid had severely discomfited Whitehall, unleashing fierce parliamentary criticisms – by no means confined to the opposition benches – of serious government complacency over growing corporate take-over trends. The ministers involved had promised to bring forward practical measures to curb such take-overs, but had signally failed to deliver. The battle of the state-owned Richard Thomas & Baldwins Ltd for Whitehead Iron & Steel Ltd the previous winter had further embarrassed the government. This latest and largest bid, which the victims were resolved to contest, seemed capable of stirring things up to an alarming degree.

---

* At the market prices of 27 June, Burmah Oil's holding of BP stock was worth about £173 million and of Shell stock about £33 million. In addition, the bid provided for £90 million to be paid for Burmah Oil's trading assets, £42 million being the value of the new BP shares to be provided, and £47.8 million in cash.

There were political reasons, too, why the cabinet at that point had no stomach for a row over a politically tender issue. Since the beginning of 1962 the administration of Harold Macmillan, within eighteen months at most of a general election, had been consistently behind Labour in the opinion polls, and at that moment found itself the most unpopular government since 1945. Macmillan's sacking of nearly a quarter of his cabinet in mid-1962 had been widely interpreted as a sign of panic; early in 1963 his abortive attempt to gain entry into the European Economic Community had added to the feeling that Supermac had lost his touch.

To cap it all, a rash of scandals had indicated further serious government shortcomings: notably the Vassall affair of 1962 and that of John Profumo, who had resigned as a minister in disgrace only a few weeks before the bid. Small wonder, then, that the Chancellor of the Exchequer was visibly shaken and annoyed when he discovered that Burmah Oil's directors were squaring up for a fight, despite the assurances he felt he had been given to the contrary.

On the Burmah Oil floor of Britannic House, Friday 28 June was a day of robust activity. The company's financial adviser and perhaps the most weighty outside director was Richard Fleming. It so happened that he was in New York for a wedding, but when R. P. Smith telephoned him early that morning (New York time) he unhesitatingly declared that the bid must be contested. Unfortunately his firm, Robert Fleming & Co, would be unable to act for Burmah Oil since it advised BP as well; he therefore recommended Baring Bros whose managing director, A. H. Carnwath, had an impressive record of having beaten off a string of bids.

Carnwath's most celebrated scalps had been those of Sir Charles Clore, who had bid for the brewery group Watney Mann in 1959, and of Sir Paul Chambers, chairman of ICI who had master-minded the recent bid for Courtaulds. As Fleming had been adviser to the defeated ICI, he well recognised Carnwath's abilities and resourcefulness. Similarly, because Burmah Oil's auditors Brown Fleming & Murray were also auditors to BP, Thomas Lister of the prestigious accounting firm Thomson McLintock & Co was engaged. The equally well respected London law firm of Allen & Overy was brought in to work with the company's Glasgow solicitors Miller Thompson Henderson & Co, in place of Linklaters & Paines which also acted for BP.

Writing from New York that same day, Fleming sympathised with Eadie for being 'so rudely precipitated into such a difficult, unpleasant and I can't help thinking unnecessary affair. . . . Keep the temperature low,' he sagely advised, 'state the facts and let the shareholders – if HMG don't intervene – decide what they want. It will be a sad day if Burmah loses its identity, and I feel if BP had spoken to us, we could have worked out something to suit all of us.' As it was, he suggested instructing the accountants to draw up, within one month, a projection of the company's trading and investment income over the next two years. To back up this forecast, a detailed valuation of the company's major reserves of oil and natural gas would be needed: he recommended calling in the world expert, Lewis MacNaughton of the Dallas oil consultants DeGolyer & MacNaughton and chairman of Great Plains (see Chapter IX). Fleming also enclosed in his letter a lengthy draft statement that might be issued to shareholders: not a bad morning's work, virtually at a moment's notice, with none of his files handy for reference.

Eadie, as well as briefing these advisers, began to contact some of the company's largest shareholders, urging them to stay loyal. R. P. Smith for his part saw the London press, adopting the low-key approach enjoined by Fleming. He emphasised that the directors felt no bitterness or ill-will towards BP or Shell. Bridgeman, too, was energetically briefing the press. To the *Evening Standard* he declared with breathtaking confidence, 'There is no ill-feeling between myself and the Burmah directors who sit on the BP board. I believe they are quite grateful that the bid was made in the way it was.'[5] From the information he imparted to the quality Sunday papers, on 30 June the allegedly grateful Burmah Oil directors for the first time found out how long-standing BP's and Shell's plans had been.

Nearly nine months before, in October or November 1962, BP and Shell had apparently begun talks about a joint take-over. Bridgeman seems to have contrived the scheme, having felt – it is said – that he was not too highly regarded by his fellow oil company chairmen, so that this was an opportunity to show his mettle. His allies had been J. H. Loudon, chief executive of Royal Dutch – which had therefore been disingenuous in denying the earlier rumours – and Sir Harold Wilkinson, a Shell director. BP, too, bypassed Robert Fleming & Co and sought as financial adviser Viscount Hampden, a managing director of Lazard Brothers & Co. According to the press, the matter was kept so secret that Hampden did not even divulge this assignment to his fellow directors.

By January 1963, with heads of agreement amicably settled between the parties, Bridgeman felt ready to see the Treasury, as BP's controlling shareholder, and secure its approval; clearly the Bank of England must also have been made privy to what was going on. Just as the aggressor in a war is said to defer launching his offensive until after the harvest is gathered in, so here the predators refrained from moving while the respective companies' accounts and reports for the previous year were being drawn up. According to the newspapers Shell took three board meetings to approve the terms of the bid, whereas BP agreed them in one: presumably that of 27 June after Eadie and Smith had been asked to leave. Later press comments pointed out the exceptional knowledge the two bidders seemed to have of their potential victim's affairs. Circumstantial evidence was also quoted to indicate that, despite the efforts at total secrecy, a leak did occur about 19 June, causing Burmah Oil's stock-market price to soar to a level (56s, or £2.80) uncomfortably near the value of the bid itself, estimated by the financial press at the not over-generous level of 61s 6d (£3.07).[6] When the *Sunday Times* correspondent put it that the terms of the bid were too low, Bridgeman roundly replied, 'Absolute poppycock!'

While the bid could be all too correctly described (by the *Guardian*) as 'one of the stock-market's worst-kept secrets for some time',[7] it was not disclosed that, as the planned date approached, Alastair Down had argued powerfully among his BP colleagues that it would scarcely be right to spring the bid on the totally unprepared Burmah Oil directors with no prior indications whatever. He was therefore allowed to travel to Nairn to forewarn Eadie.

Down had a further distasteful task to perform on Monday, 1

July. The week-end's papers had widely assumed that the proposals represented merely an opening gambit, allowing Burmah Oil a chance to bargain for an improved offer. Down was therefore instructed to deliver a message through Robert Fleming & Co that there was 'no intention whatever of raising the value of the proposals above the present figures'. If anything was calculated to harden the Burmah Oil directors' resolve to stand and fight, it was to be told that they must take it or leave it.

What were the motives for the bid? The reason revealed by Bridgeman to the *Sunday Telegraph* was the need to forestall any take-over by an American company, which could have automatically transferred nearly a quarter of BP's ordinary shares into foreign ownership.[8] For his pains Bridgeman received a wretched press from the quality Sundays. One paper, the *Sunday Times*, further pointed out that the United States would not in fact have been able to finance an acquisition by dollar payments. The Interest Equalization Tax of that year effectively prevented new issues being made on the American stock-market for use overseas, so that the $840 million or so required would have had to come partly from swap sterling; namely, currency accruing from the sales of other shares. That would have entailed the British authorities in providing an interest-free loan for an American purchase of a key British company: a wholly unacceptable proposition.

The city editor of the *Sunday Telegraph* dismissed as 'telling fairy stories to the press' the explanation that BP needed to break up Burmah Oil's 24.6 per cent stake. He listed the six or seven blatant implausibilities in the story, and quoted R. P. Smith's declaration that at no time had the BP people ever informed Burmah Oil that they wished to see the holding split up. Instead, the truth seemed to be that the two companies were really after Burmah Oil's own trading interests, mainly those in India. Not only was the Indian subcontinent expected to be one of the fastest-growing markets in the world for oil products, but also 'BP and Shell may well feel that they are better equipped than Burmah is to engage in the *realpolitik* of oil in Asia.'

If deeds were more eloquent testimony than words, then

those interests in India and Pakistan were indeed regarded as vital pawns in the game. As soon as the bid was made, Shell had secretly despatched two senior executives to Delhi and Karachi respectively, to inform the governments concerned that Shell would strive to maintain and even strengthen the friendly relations built up by Burmah Oil. In the event, both governments reacted strongly against the proposed take-over.[9] British business in the Indian subcontinent had on the whole a reputation for gentlemanly behaviour and mutual trust, to which these events had dealt a blow. Ministers there regarded Shell as 'too big and powerful and uncompromising', and certainly as showing none of the flexibility and sensitivity which had largely been the hallmark of Burmah Oil's conduct: so much for the *realpolitik* which the oil majors imagined they could exert in that part of the world.

Ministers in Delhi disliked above all 'the idea of bargains being struck in London whereby the ownership of large parts of their natural resources and industry changes hands without their wishes being considered at all'. They actively considered acquiring Burmah Oil's 50 per cent stake in Oil India Ltd if the bid went through, and comparable steps to purchase Burmah Oil's interests in Pakistan were being mooted in Karachi. So John Drysdale discovered when he was sent hot-foot to Delhi a few days later – R. P. Smith had wanted to go in person, but could not be spared, while Jack Strain visited Karachi, to reassure both governments of the company's continued friendship and loyalty. Other examples later came to light of some smart groundwork by the two predators: for instance, BP representatives in the United States had been busy compiling detailed data on Burmah Oil's interests in New Orleans.

In the exceptionally crowded week beginning 1 July, no outside event was more critical for Burmah Oil than the parliamentary questions to the Chancellor of the Exchequer on Tuesday the 2nd. Maudling admitted to MPs that the government had been consulted in advance, quite properly from his viewpoint as a change in BP's structure would be involved, and he had seen no reason to object to the proposed bid. A Scottish member complained that the breaking up of Burmah Oil, one of the most important of Scottish companies, would be 'a further step in the concentration of economic power in London'. As Burmah Oil's operations were predominantly outside Britain, Maudling replied a little disingenuously, the problem of market power at home did not arise.

James Callaghan, Labour's shadow Chancellor, condemned the government for having failed to put forward a general review, as promised, over giant mergers. Maudling dodged the issue and instead dealt with the allegation of earlier leaks by stating that the matter should be referred to the Stock Exchange Council.[10] It really began to look as if the government was seeking to distance itself from the bid. A magisterial leader in the following day's *Times* commended the Chancellor for deciding not to become involved. It set out the reasons for the bid: fears of Burmah Oil being taken over by foreigners; the attractions for BP and Shell of its interests in the Indian subcontinent; and Burmah Oil's recent appearance on the British oil scene by acquiring Lobitos. 'BP would probably be the first to admit', declared the clearly BP-briefed leading article, 'that Burmah, with her new acquisitions, has been showing all signs of competing not only overseas but in the home market also.'

The more independent *Guardian* pointed out that Maudling's remarks did nothing to resolve the enigma of the motive. 'We still have to learn what it is in Burmah's assets that BP and Shell so badly want,' the paper stated.[11] By hindsight the answer can be given with some confidence. Shell would have been happy to inherit the assets which Burmah Oil had built up in the East, although – as shown above – the reactions of the Indian and Pakistan governments might have sensibly diminished that inheritance. BP, on the other hand, aimed to remove Burmah Oil's perceived threat to its own aspirations in the western hemisphere and particularly in the US and Canada.

What also mattered for the Burmah Oil directors that week was the strength of the case their advisers could build up against the bid. The press concluded that in Carnwath, Lister and MacNaughton the company had a 'formidable trio', with the last-named due to arrive from Dallas in about a week. Armed with the data so far assembled, the directors held an informal meeting on Wednesday 3 July. They were unanimous that the bid was too low. By then the Burmah share price was up to 65s (£3.25) and therefore well above the original terms;

and the bidders had cut off any escape route by refusing to countenance negotiations. The directors without further ado resolved to recommend rejection of the bid.

Eadie drew comfort from receiving a hand-written letter from Alastair Down. 'I just want to wish you well and the best of luck at tomorrow's meeting, *whatever* the outcome.' At Burmah Oil's full board meeting on the 4th, five advisers – including representatives of the Glasgow and London solicitors – were also present. The board formally agreed to minute the unanimous view of the directors that the value of the proposals did not adequately represent the worth of the company's assets nor the future earning capacity of its operations. They were therefore unable to recommend the acceptance of the proposals. As soon as possible a circular would be issued to stockholders, setting out the reasons for the board decision and giving forecasts of its future prospects. Draft letters had already been prepared for despatch to BP and Shell, and these were approved and then signed by Eadie. Within a few hours of the letters reaching their destinations, the two companies had withdrawn their bid unconditionally.

The scenes on the stock exchange which followed the bid's rejection and speedy withdrawal were variously described by the press as ones of 'confusion', 'uproar', 'turmoil' and more staidly by *The Times* as 'hectic if not chaotic'. Burmah Oil stock plunged to 56s (£2.80), then soared to over 66s (£3.30) before closing at 61s (£3.05). The market then had to await Burmah Oil's circular, duly published on 20 July. That set out the company's overall stretegy: to remain independent as a significant British oil company; to operate in such ways and areas as not to conflict materially with its interests in BP; and to retain its holding in BP as an integral and essential part of its activities, since that holding was far more valuable to the company than indicated by the current share price. It therefore ruled out the defensive move, widely predicted in the press, of a distribution of its BP shares to its own stockholders. The Shell shares, on the other hand, would be treated as a 'marketable investment for use as required from time to time'. The company did however, pledge itself to continue to pass on in full dividends from BP and Shell and BP cash distributions.

Burmah Oil's future trading income was forecast to rise from £5.9 million after tax in 1962 to 'some £8 million' by 1966.

Perhaps inevitably, after all the excitements of recent weeks, the circular proved somewhat of an anti-climax. For one thing, as *The Economist* pointed out, it lacked the dash of the Courtaulds document produced to combat the ICI bid, with 'brilliantly conceived profit projections, stock distributions and hive-off of investments' plus graphic diagrams to drive home the message.[12] To be sure, Courtaulds' had been a campaign document, issued while the bid was very much on; for Burmah Oil the battle was already over, as BP and Shell had retired hurt. Besides, it had to keep some shots in the locker just in case a further bid came along. The content of the circular, too, was felt to be something of a let-down. Many commentators criticised it as being a bit thin and not exactly forthcoming; for instance, it failed to give estimates of asset values, difficult as these would have been in the case of oil and gas reserves. In the event, however, what mattered was that the market in general clearly approved of the company's stand, and Burmah Oil's stock retained its strength on the London stock exchange.

The post-mortem on the bid produced brickbats from the financial press on all the parties concerned. To some, Burmah Oil was to blame for being secretive, financially over-cautious and generally rather stodgy. For many, the behaviour of BP – widely recognised as the prime mover – attracted pungent and largely displeasing comment. William Rees-Mogg of the *Sunday Times* listed six obvious mistakes, 'of a particularly amateurish character', which BP had made 'with some help from Shell'. In his view a cardinal error had been to employ Lazards, characterised as a first-class bank for handling new issues, acceptances and other credit work, but with a record of recurrent failure in contested take-overs: 'one should choose a fighting bank as one chooses a fighting solicitor', he suggested.[13] 'Lex' of the *Financial Times* went so far as to regard BP's conduct over the whole affair as 'a form of juvenile delinquency'. Even so, the paper declared, the current strained relations between Burmah Oil and BP were not really tenable for long, and would at some stage have to be resolved.[14]

Bridge-building would indeed come later, but first Eadie felt that he must have his say on the BP board. That determination was not weakened when word came back to him that the Shell top management were furious with BP for having misled them over the expected reaction of the Burmah Oil directors to the bid. Eadie let it be known that he would be making a personal statement at the next BP board meeting.

His original plan was to put BP directors on the spot and ask some penetrating questions. Why were the Burmah Oil representatives on the board kept in the dark? Had the government appreciated that BP was seeking to dispose of its majority non-government stockholder? Had BP conducted itself with due propriety in the circumstances? 'One could use much stronger terms, but to say the least, such action cannot but leave an embarrassing taste.' If any possible clash of interest were to arise in any part of the world, Burmah Oil as an independent company would always be ready to discuss it freely with BP. As he had said to Bridgeman even in recent months, 'surely we are big enough as men' to be able to agree mutually acceptable arrangements. However, after what had happened, Burmah Oil was considering ways of ensuring that such a situation could never recur.

Such was the gist of the draft statement which Eadie had prepared. Perhaps wisely in the circumstances, he contented himself at the BP board meeting on 25 July with a few brief comments. He felt he must communicate the Burmah Oil board's 'grave concern' at the manner in which this major initiative had been handled, 'in view of the close relationship of our two companies and especially in the light of the Burmah's majority public holding.' He went on,

> As the longer serving members of this board will know, I came here when the relations between Burmah and BP were under some strain, which to me at any rate seemed a deplorable state of affairs.
>
> I have endeavoured to narrow this apparent gap – at least at a personal level – but I can only judge that from the way in which this recent matter has been handled, it would seem any success I may have had has been somewhat limited.
>
> Although there are many aspects of this matter on which one could seek clarification, I feel the first concern of both our boards is to ensure that relationships between our companies are re-established on a proper basis of mutual understanding and confidence.

Alastair Down for one lost little time in striving to improve relations. On 30 July he called on Richard Fleming and admitted that the two companies could not restore full mutual confidence on matters where they might be in competition as long as the existing atmosphere of conflict persisted. Down then went on to have a talk with John Drysdale, since 1960 the Burmah Oil executive director most concerned with operations in North America. Both agreed that there was no immediate area of friction to hold up a process of *rapprochement*.

Eadie's relations with Bridgeman took longer to improve. Not until the end of November did the two men meet for an informal talk; as Eadie later reported to Bilsland. 'I feel we have at last got off to a good start in the right atmosphere.' To Strathalmond, Eadie put it more vividly: 'I found that generally we were seeing the long-term future through the same pair of spectacles.' He added that a small working party of two top men on each side would be set up to discuss matters of common concern. One of them on the BP side would be Alastair Down, who would also be keeping a watching brief on BP's behalf over Burmah Oil's activities.

As the months wore on it became clear that, for Burmah Oil, life could never be quite the same again. The bid was proving a catalyst, revealing the perils of being basically a relic of colonial enterprise located in a remote part of the former British empire. Unless the company were to start transforming itself into an enterprise of truly international status, it could not expect to survive long in a world where the globally operating 'majors' – as the oil giants were now known – increasingly made the running.

No one grasped the significance of this development more than Eadie. At 67 he was ready to think about standing down; yet he knew that his successor, whoever he was, must be one who would be recognised in oil circles as a businessmen of international standing. In August 1963 he therefore floated the idea that one of Burmah Oil's non-executive directors, with a presence in various branches of British commerce and industry, should at once become vice-chairman and in due course be elected chairman. As that director was still in his forties, he could be expected to serve the company as chairman for a long period. R. P. Smith, sole managing director since 1962 and the heir presumptive, who had already passed his sixtieth year, had to be told that he was being passed over, on the grounds that the new chairman would need at least ten years to see through his new strategy. However, Smith would be given enhanced status as deputy chairman and chief executive.

It was the formidable ex-BP chairman, Lord Strathalmond who, when told by Eadie of this plan, put the boot in. He declared that the chairman must be an oilman, as happened in every oil company of any standing, as otherwise he would be 'out of his depth' in negotiations with rivals at home and abroad. Why not look for an outside oilman in either BP or Shell, he asked, to be brought in with a view to taking over? Eadie, still bruised by those two companies' recent pranks, felt that such a move would be extremely tricky, and dropped the idea.

At this stage the appointment of Nicholas Williams to the board was also considered. The non-executive directors believed that while he had proved his value as a legal adviser, he had not yet had the opportunity of proving himself in a specific executive job. They suggested that he should be given the task of organising the incorporation of Lobitos in the Burmah group; in fact he was appointed co-ordinator of operations in the East. In June 1964 R. P. Smith duly became deputy chairman. Whereas Eadie had soon recovered his equilibrium, R. P. Smith never quite overcame the feeling of outrage over the BP-Shell bid.

Even so, Eadie wanted to see the Burmah Oil board strengthened with expertise in the international oil arena. Now that Strathalmond was about to retire, in May 1964 he again asked Bridgeman to join the board, or, failing him, one of his managing directors. No doubt he had in mind the experienced and adroit Alastair Down, and it is interesting to speculate how different the history of Burmah Oil over the following decade might have been had Down been so appointed. Bridgeman in fact refused the request: however, soon after Eadie retired from the chairmanship at the end of 1964 and R. P. Smith succeeded him, Lord Inchcape, who had been a non-executive director since 1959, was nominated to the board of BP as a representative of Burmah Oil in Eadie's place.

Not only in the Burmah Oil boardroom was the shortage of managerial expertise recognised. The sequence of untoward events in the East during and after the war had disrupted the usual flow of talented men back to the London office, to be groomed for the top jobs. Perhaps the lack of suitable men had been responsible for the company's failure fully to integrate Lobitos into its own organisation. Even as late as January 1966, when reviewing the company's financial progress since the BP-Shell bid, Jack Strain declared, 'If we are to buy income, we must also buy management. Managing the old Burmah Oil Company with its eastern trading was one matter; managing businesses in the competitive markets of this country is another.' The issues were clear. Would the Burmah Oil directors have the resolve and imagination to make the leap forward towards becoming a truly international enterprise, or would their past orientation and almost wholly Eastern experience prove a limiting factor as they sought to conquer the West?

Notes

1 See Chapter I, footnote 10 above.
2 For Bridgeman, see *Dictionary of Business Biography* I, pp. 440–3. Of other senior men in BP, mentioned in the present chapter, entries for Alastair Down and Eric Drake are in ibid. II, pp. 158–60 and 169–72 respectively.
3 The press coverage of the BP and Shell takeover bid was immense; the bid itself was all over the papers of 28 June 1963. Only a few of the more important press sources are noted here.
4 See D. C. Coleman, *Courtaulds: An Economic and Social History III 1940–65,* 1980, Chapter X for the ICI bid for that company.
5 *Evening Standard*, 28 June 1963.
6 *Sunday Times*, 30 June 1963, also for Bridgeman's 'poppycock' remark and for the motives discussed later in the chapter.
7 *Guardian*, 28 June 1963.
8 *Sunday Telegraph*, 30 June 1963.
9 Ibid., 14 July 1963.
10 Hansard, HC 680, cols 204–7, 2 July 1963.
11 *The Times* and *Guardian*, 3 July 1963.
12 *The Economist*, 27 July 1963.
13 *Sunday Times*, 7 July 1963.
14 *Financial Times*, 22 July 1963.

CHAPTER XI

India, Pakistan, Australia
1945–66

India[1]

Even more so than in Burma, the company's activities in India during the two decades to 1966 were bound up with the vagaries of official attitudes to oil there. The Burmah Oil Company found itself having to react to government policies or intitiatives rather than being able to promote a strategy that would in its view benefit the people of India and at the same time yield reasonable returns for itself. Its presence in the country was initially a considerable one. It controlled the only large producer, Assam Oil, while Burmah-Shell, in which it had a half interest, effectively dominated the distribution of oil products there. The only 'reserved' market area was that of Assam, for which its India trading subsidiary was responsible.

The vast Burmah-Shell organisation had its headquarters in Bombay and four branch offices in Bombay, Madras, Calcutta and Karachi (transferred to Burmah-Shell of Pakistan in 1947). From each branch office radiated a network of divisional offices and depots. There were seven port installations, 48 airfield outlets and over 3,500 petrol filling stations. As early as 1930 it directly employed 3,000 clerks, and also 200 travelling inspectors who enforced product price and quality controls on its retailers. The total Indian workforce numbered 10,000, with an annual wage bill equivalent to £375,000; the 1930 average level of wages was above the going rate for that period, and in addition security of employment was offered. To facilitate the transportation of products into the remoter parts of the country, its managers encouraged each local administration to construct good roads, and as a means of generating higher purchasing power – as well as greater revenue for itself – it fostered the mechanisation of agriculture.

After 1945 Burmah-Shell continued to supply most of India's substantial oil needs. By 1946/47 Assam Oil, its crude reserves badly depleted by over-production during the war, was able to provide no more than 9 per cent of national requirements of kerosene, 11 per cent of petrol and 5 per cent of fuel oil. Attock Oil's contribution was even smaller, less than 1 per cent of products generally. Imports made up this shortfall, between 80 and 90 per cent coming from Iran, while Caltex imported limited quantities from Bahrain, say 9 per cent of kerosene and 2 per cent of fuel oil. Now that Burma itself no longer had a surplus to ship overseas, and only a meagre amount was of Indian origin, the Middle East seemed to have established itself as the natural source of the country's oil supply.

When independence was granted in August 1947 and the subcontinent was divided, Assam Oil remained in India while Attock Oil, being in the western part of the Punjab, found itself in Pakistan. India was initially very short of foreign exchange, necessitating every possible economy in oil imports. The authorities strove to develop substitutes, such as charcoal gas and power alcohol, but these did not prove cost-efficient. They also maintained wartime rationing of products until well into 1950, helped by the full co-operation of Burmah-Shell's country-wide organisation. Even so, a high level of economic activity, involving transport as well as industry, kept Indian demand for oil extremely buoyant.

From 1947 onwards, the high profile of Burmah-Shell in India, combined with official pressures to economise in the supply and finance of oil, inevitably caused a good deal of friction with the government in Delhi. Although the other overseas oil companies had their own tangles with authority, these were on a minor scale. The American-owned companies accepted Burmah-Shell's market share through understandings that were, for anti-trust reasons, informal. To Indians, foreign control over all oil activities, from prospecting to retail sales, provided an all too visible reminder of a phenomenon still common to much of the developing world: that a country might have attained to political independence, but the road to true economic independence was longer and more difficult than had ever been imagined.

That the shoe of economic imperialism pinched more painfully among the Indian authorities than with the more easy-going Burmese is clear. The structure of Burmah-Shell's management, and to a lesser extent that of Assam Oil, which parallelled the pre-independence Indian Civil Service (ICS), was partly to blame. At the top came the executive assistants, available to work anywhere in the country. Being usually graduates of British universities, they were very similar in background and in attitude to their British ICS counterparts before 1947. Perhaps the main difference was that character and sporting prowess were considered to be no less important than intellectual qualities as such.

Just as before 1924 (see Vol. I p.158), sport was a general interest of many who came to work in the East, and Burmah Oil did much to encourage competitive and other activities of all kinds. An impressive number of Oxbridge sporting blues and, after 1945, no fewer than three Scottish internationals, in different sports, served with the company. Many others enjoyed more or less energetic games as forms of agreeable recreation out of working hours. After a probationary period, a Burmah-Shell assistant would be put in charge of a small up-country divisional office and be set a sales target, with instructions to make his own decisions without troubling higher authority unnecessarily. Mistakes, if not too grave, were condoned as part of the training process.

The headquarters staffing department in Bombay shifted these assistants around from job to job every few years, and followed a management development programme designed to bring on the more promising among them. The more senior posts in India, as elsewhere in the freshly independent countries, required considerable negotiating ability and diplomatic skills. The general manager in particular had to deal with top civil servants in Delhi or the Indian states and with the ministers concerned. Not only would they be in constant touch with the Burmah-Shell head office in London, but also accompany directors (including those of Burmah Oil and Shell) who had come out from London when discussions were held on the spot.

A later Burmah-Shell chief executive, an Indian national who had served with the organisation since the early 1950s, approved of the decidedly unstarchy way in which it was run. As he put it,

> Free expression of opinion and indeed dissent were encouraged down to junior levels. Even a junior employee with a real or imaginary grievance had access to the top. In other words, the atmosphere was fair and friendly without being lax in discipline.[2]

Although Shell was the main recruiting agency, the organisation maintained much of the Burmah Oil tradition of carefully listening to the man in the field.

The second level of management was of local and branch assistants and people at the supervisory level, such as district sales representatives and depot superintendents, largely Indians; at first they were given little opportunity of promotion to the top jobs. This changed in the late 1950s when the first and second tiers were amalgamated to create a unified management structure. Internal promotion became common and privileges such as separate washrooms and lunch facilities were abolished. Specialist staff such as accountants and technicians tended to be located at the headquarters and branch offices, and had their separate entry and promotion systems; one or two were Indians from the outset. Work in Assam Oil and the India trading subsidiary was necessarily confined largely to the Digboi area, although the former had a representative and a small office in Delhi to maintain liaison with government.

How much did the Burmah group earn from its activities in India? During the early post-independence years, that country was by far the largest contributor to the group's net trading profit, as Table 6 shows. Assam Oil was both highly lucrative and a very variable earner over these years, its average annual profit between 1949 and 1955 being just under £750,000. On the other hand, profits from Burmah-Shell rose dramatically as general demand for its products increased.

TABLE 6

Sources of Burmah Oil net profit 1949 and 1955

	1949		1955	
	£000s	%	£000s	%
Net trading profit				
India*	1,670	62	2,078	36
Pakistan	−904	−34	−649	−11
Burma	540	20	804	13
Other (e.g. wax)	232	9	−331	−6
Total net trading profit	1,538	57	1,902	32
Investment income				
BP	882	33	3,486	60
Shell	121	5	364	6
Government, etc	141	5	100	2
Total investment income	1,144	43	3,950	68
Total net profit	2,682	100	5,852	100
* of which:				
Production (Assam Oil)	1,146		647	
Product sales	150		1,017	
(Burmah-Shell area)				
Assam 'reserved area'	241		349	
Tinplate Co. of India	133		65	
	1,670		2,078	

Delhi knew well the magnitude of the profits that Burmah Oil was making directly or indirectly in India. From the outset, therefore, it sought to strike at two key elements in these profits: the retail price charged, and the inadequate refinery capacity in the country itself. Indian opinion remembered certain grievances expressed in the minority report of the Tariff Board enquiry of 1928 (see Chapter I), regarding these two issues. During the war, the then authorities had allowed

Burmah-Shell a very favourable price formula, which their successors were anxious to squeeze. As India retained price controls after the war, throughout the following two decades the foreign companies had to battle hard with Delhi for any price increases.

From 1947 onwards, the government of India also forced the question of indigenous refineries. Throughout the world, the former practice of refining at or near the point of production was breaking down, for financial as well as political reasons. The larger sizes of tankers allowed considerable quantities of crude oil to be transported relatively cheaply; buoyant demand in developed or developing nations permitted local or regional refineries of an economic size to be built, able to take full advantage of rapid advances in refining technology. The dollar shortage made it worthwhile to import crude and save on the value added at the refining stage, and newly independent countries looked on their own refineries as symbolic of their national prestige, in the same category as their own airlines.

India's need for refineries was the greater because of its grave balance of payments difficulties, while the problem of national security was intensified by worsening relations with Pakistan. The dispute with its neighbour over Kashmir brought the two countries to the brink of war, and the outright hostilities of 1965 were merely a culmination of years of tension. In 1949 the government in Delhi therefore requested Burmah-Shell and the other oil companies to send out a delegation of technical men, to assess the economic case for constructing refineries in India.

The question of possible sites presented no difficulty. Bombay was an obvious choice as being the nearest Indian port to the Persian gulf, and enjoying good harbour and bulk installation facilities and well developed rail and road communications with the rest of India. Indeed, its geographical advantages had been amply demonstrated during the war. Vizagapatam on the east coast was also recommended, as being almost equidistant between Calcutta and Madras.

At the same time, the delegation unanimously concluded that there was no economic case for India having its own refineries unless products there could be sold at 10 per cent above the Gulf-plus parity price. Delhi at once rejected that condition, and the refinery issue then became deadlocked.

Calculations were radically altered by the oil crisis in Iran, set off by Dr Mossadeq's move in March 1951 to nationalise Anglo-Iranian's operations there. As shown in Chapter VI above, this startling event raised expectations in Rangoon that the Burmese would be the next people to win greater oil participation. The government of India, too, had been given the opportunity it sought, and in October 1951 Sir Kenneth Harper had to tell the Burmah Oil board:

> Events at Abadan have knocked the bottom out of our case for refusing to consider the building of a refinery for imported oil in India, and it is clear that we must be prepared to share in the cost of such a refinery in order to defend our trade.

Harper quoted a figure of nearly £10 million for constructing a one million ton (6.25 million barrel) refinery and £18 million for one twice that size. The board accepted his proposal, subject to satisfactory arrangements being concluded with Delhi.

Two months later, in mid-December 1951, Burmah-Shell signed an agreement to build a 1.5 million ton (9.4 million barrel) refinery at Trombay island, near Bombay; in 1952 the capacity was raised to 2 million tons (12.5 million barrels). It came on stream at the beginning of 1955 and soon afterwards was turning out 45 per cent of India's total requirements of oil products. Stanvac built a refinery, also at Trombay, which came on stream in 1954, and Caltex built one at Vizagapatam, operative in 1957. Burmah-Shell's was the largest refinery in India, being larger than the other two combined. By comparison, Digboi's throughput was about 2 million barrels.

To finance the new refinery, in November 1952 Burmah-Shell Refineries Ltd was registered in Bombay as a rupee company, with an authorised capital of Rs 250 million (£19 million), of which each London parent provided half. To some Indian critics, the terms agreed by the government of India represented a sell-out to the foreign interests concerned. One critic even suggested that the agreements read like treaties between sovereign states rather than the usual commercial accords under which private concerns were permitted to operate in foreign countries.[3] Indeed, Delhi does seem to have conceded most of the oil companies' demands; having asked for equity participation, ministers did not press for it when that request was turned down.

For Delhi a major embarrassment was that the terms conflicted with the official Industrial Policy Resolution of 1948, which had envisaged a strong state control over oil, and also with the Industrial Development and Regulation Act, which in 1951 had laid down guidelines for controlling private-sector enterprises. The wide-ranging scope of the latter had made the local Burmah-Shell general manager 'nervous', but in the event his company was readily granted exemption from its provisions. Clearly, therefore, Delhi was anxious to see refineries constructed as speedily as possible, and acknowledged its own lack of sufficient know-how to do the job itself. Official calculations showed that India would save 24 per cent on average: the purchase price of a ton of imported oil products was estimated as costing the equivalent of £10.60, while the aggregate cost of importing crude and refining that ton at home would be just over £8.

The companies were allowed to retain full ownership of the refineries and to choose the sources from which to import crude. The refinery actually cost Burmah Oil and Shell a total of £24.4 million for the full capacity of 2 million tons.

The question of oil exploration in India was no less contentious than that of refining. The old prospecting rules were replaced by new rules in 1949. Under the former system, Assam Oil had already been granted a geophysical permit over nearly 6,300 square miles of the alluvial belt of upper Assam. Before the seismic surveys were suspended at the outbreak of war in 1939, the geophysical findings were positive enough to suggest drilling at Nahorkatiya, about 25 miles south-west of Digboi.

In 1951 Delhi granted Assam Oil a prospecting licence over a small area of Nahorkatiya. The first well was spudded in there during May 1952. Nine months later oilsands at about 10,000 feet were tested, and gave clear indication that a large oilfield had been discovered. This find encouraged the drilling of appraisal wells in that field, and also extensive geophysical surveys, some covering the entire Upper Assam valley. Geologists then selected a further area for test drilling near the village of Moran, about 50 miles from Nahorkatiya. Once again they were successful; the first test well indicated an oilfield there, which was proved in 1956.

Nahorkatiya and Moran were jointly estimated to have recoverable reserves of close on 300 million barrels: the largest oil discovery the Burmah group had ever made. That also opened up the prospect of uncovering further fields within the vast alluvial area. Since the crude oil would need to be transported to a refinery, the company made plans, as a temporary expedient, to construct a pipeline to Digboi and to raise the throughput of the refinery there. In 1954 a new gasoline plant and lubricating oil distillation plant were added, at a cost of £440,000. Between 1952 and 1956 throughput therefore rose by 52 per cent, from 1.7 million barrels a year – the same as in 1945 – to 2.6 million barrels; by 1958 it was up to 2.9 million barrels.

Clearly other refining capacity would be needed as well, and that would depend on the agreement of the authorities in Delhi. However, the Indian minister of natural resources, K. D. Malaviya, was determined to reduce the dominant role which the company had hitherto played in India. He therefore arranged not merely to take over control of all future exploration, but also to separate production from downstream activities. Until the recent oil finds in Assam his government had had neither the money nor the expertise to take any interest in prospecting. Then in 1955 he set up an Oil and Natural Gas Division of his ministry, which four years later became a statutory body, the Oil and Natural Gas Commission (ONGC). That body took over all oil exploration and production outside the areas in Assam already explored. He then invited in experts from western Europe, Canada, Romania and Russia. With their help the ONGC discovered other oilfields in Assam such as Sibsagar and also in western India, at Gujarat and offshore at Bombay.

Also in 1955, Malaviya made an extensive world tour to seek technical and financial assistance for building refineries. Only Russia and Romania gave a positive response. They offered credit on terms that were very advantageous for India, the rates of interest being low and the loans repayable in rupees, and they were also willing to provide the necessary expert help.

In 1956 Malaviya set up an international committee of

experts to suggest possible sites for the proposed new refineries. The experts' choice was Budge Budge, near Calcutta, which Burmah Oil also favoured since it already owned storage installations there (see Vol. I p.50). However, the state government of Assam at once protested that its oil would be 'stolen' if taken outside its borders to be refined. Together with the state of Bihar, north-west of Calcutta, Assam therefore offered to provide the necessary land without charge and also power and water supplies at reasonable rates. Delhi accepted that offer, and in July 1957 asked Burmah Oil to participate in the Assam refinery. The exact terms of the request are not on record, but doubtless a joint venture was suggested with the Indian share being paid for by a low-interest loan from London.

Unfortunately, this request came just when the company was being faced with one financial difficulty after another (see Chapter VII). The board, having carefully considered India's request, therefore had to turn it down. Eadie knew well the possible consequences of this refusal. 'Any real security of tenure [in India]', he concluded pessimistically in September 1957, 'becomes in fact non-existent in these circumstances.' That December he travelled to Delhi, but what he found there did not encourage him. The Romanians were to be asked to build a refinery at Nunmati in Assam, 260 miles from Nahorkatiya, and the Russians one at Barauni, 460 miles to the west in Bihar. Both would be owned and operated by the government of India.

Eadie did, however, secure an agreement in principle for setting up a rupee company to finance and administer upstream activities, to be called Oil India Ltd (OIL). That would have a capital equivalent to £20 milion and be one-third owned by the government and two-thirds by Burmah Oil. It would sell the required amount of crude – up to 1.3 million barrels a year – to Assam Oil to keep the newly expanded Digboi refinery at full capacity, and the remaining production would go to the new refineries; Burmah Oil would be guaranteed a 10 per cent net dividend.

This agreement became bogged down in Delhi over the fine print. The general manager of Assam Oil and Burmah Oil's representative in India, W. P. G. (Bill) Maclachlan, was responsible for the day-to-day negotiations. Then in October

1958 Eadie was invited to Delhi, in order to attend the financial summit meeting of the World Bank there. Although not expected to do more than 'listen quietly to the deliberations of the financial pundits and enjoy calmly the sunshine of Delhi', he was determined to seize the opportunity to break the deadlock with the government of India. Malaviya was absent from the capital, but Eadie did have useful discussions with his senior civil servants and also attended an *ad hoc* meeting of the OIL shadow board. His efforts paid off. As he wrote to Bilsland on his return,

> For some time, I have had an uneasy feeling that our relationships with Delhi were slipping badly through the long drawn-out talks to clear a number of points preparatory to the incorporation of the new company. We have been bewildered by the lack of understanding – or so it would seem – of matters relating to company administration and organisation on the other side [in India]. Be that as it may, I made up my mind to endeavour to clear all decks while I was in Delhi so that the new company [OIL] could take shape almost at once.

> I am glad to say that I have come back in much greater ease of mind that I had been [in]. I believe I have re-established our relationships with government on a firm basis of understanding and mutual goodwill and confidence. If, as I hope, the few remaining hurdles of detail are cleared this week, then the new company can be formed right away. That would put us back relationship-wise where we should and must be if this joint venture is to prosper.

Eadie had made a point of briefing the UK High Commissioner, Malcolm MacDonald, about progress of the talks. Clearly he felt that Britain's representatives aboard, notably those of MacDonald's calibre, were more understanding and co-operative than officials and ministers at home. In a letter of thanks to MacDonald for all the High Commission's help, he saw his recent visit as 'the second milestone along the road to progress of this joint venture; it had been pretty rough in spots since we passed the first [milestone] last January.' A month later R. P. Smith, during a general tour of the East, spent three days in Delhi; thanks to the groundwork provided by him and by Eadie, Maclachlan was able to clear up the still unresolved details. OIL was then incorporated in February 1959.

Maclachlan was the first chairman of OIL; two of the other board members were British and three Indian. K. B. Kanuga, the Indian operations manager at Digboi who was also on the OIL board, became the managing director of OIL and helped to move that company's headquarters to Zaloni, a new township near Nahorkatiya. In contrast with Burma, a considerable number of very able indigenous Indian office and technical staff had been recruited by Assam Oil, most being graduates of Indian universities; the first Indian works manager at Digboi took over in 1960. That company was therefore able to take on the considerable additional administrative and technical work involved in developing the new Assam fields. Many of these employees later achieved senior positions in the oil industry or in government service. A further responsibility for Assam Oil entailed having to provide facilities for OIL until such time as the latter was able to set up its own organisation. Thus the Burmah group was encouraging Indianisation by every means.

What did inhibit progress on the OIL board was the power of veto exercised by the government-nominated directors when questions of national interest were held to be involved. That was based on the veto available to government nominees on the BP board. Whereas the latter has apparently never been used, in OIL it was exercised so frequently that the taking of important decisions was substantially slowed down, as the points at issue had to be referred back to Delhi. As a result, efficient functioning of the company became increasingly difficult.

In the hope of encouraging a more constructive relationship generally with the government of India, Burmah Oil in 1960 decided to strengthen its representation in Delhi, by moving its headquarters in India from Digboi to the capital. Michael J. Condon was transferred from Pakistan to become the first general manager in Delhi, while Bill Maclachlan, who had been general manager in Digboi, moved to Karachi to take over from Condon. However, in his two years in Delhi Condon did not find it easy to achieve the same kind of rapport with the host government as in his previous post, and the inadequate understanding of corporate matters among official circles in Delhi, deplored by Eadie, persisted.

Malaviya continued to intervene personally in all questions to do with oil. As a protégé of the defence minister Krishna Menon, he was known to be close to Jawaharlal Nehru, the prime minister. Nehru's overall attitude was therefore of key importance. His second five-year plan, from 1956 to 1961, was concentrating on industry but had run into severe balance of payments difficulties, culminating in an international rescue plan organised by the World Bank in 1958.[4]

This economic setback, combined with widespread criticisms of public-sector inefficiencies, so unnerved Nehru that he publicly attacked private enterprise in India as anti-democratic and ripe for being swept away. That kind of talk well suited Malaviya and his officials, whose resentment towards foreign oil companies was exacerbated by a feeling that the latter were all too ready to run to their home governments for support against Delhi. For its part, the Burmah Oil executive remained highly sceptical as to whether it could count on any real support from Whitehall, which refused to stand up on any issue of substance against Nehru on the ground that only he stood between India and Communism: so deeply was the cold-war mentality engrained in British government thinking of the late 1950s.

Where Burmah Oil was given scope for its expertise was over constructing a pipeline between Nahorkatiya and the sites of the new refineries. The government of India gave the company's pipeline subsidiary the task of designing it, supervising its construction, and operating it for twelve months after it was completed. During that time the company would have to rectify any faults at its own cost. Much of the credit for the successful laying of the pipeline was due to B. R. (Dick) Kemp, who had previously been concerned with the rehabiliation of the Burma oilfields and had then been general manager in Pakistan (see below). As general manager of the pipelines subsidiary, he had to set up the project organisation for constructing the pipeline.

The cost of laying the whole 720 miles was estimated at nearly £35 million, of which £21 million represented rupee expenditure; that would be borrowed in India by OIL on debentures. The other £14 million would necessarily be in foreign currency for overseas outlays. Burmah Oil was willing to make a considerable loan, but hoped that Whitehall would share in the lending. However, as the Burmah-Shell general manager in London reported to R. P. Smith, British ministers were concerned mainly with the question of how to sell plant and materials to India on deferred credit terms, in order to relieve unemployment in Britain's less prosperous regions, and not at all with the wider issue of how to safeguard British interests in India by making an imaginative loan offer.

Soon after his return from Delhi, in November 1958 Eadie and his financial adviser Richard Fleming visited Sir Denis Rickett, second secretary at the Treasury in Whitehall, to see if the World Bank might be induced to give help. The Treasury agreed that its representative in Washington, Sir Guy Thorold, should ask the World Bank to participate in a loan. Thorold was rebuffed. India, he was told, had already absorbed quite a substantial amount of the bank's capacity during the first five-year plan of 1951–56. Moreover, the bank believed that the Indians should leave oil matters entirely to foreign private-sector finance. As its chairman, Eugene Black, put it a year or two later,

> They can't afford to waste scarce resources by putting prestige ahead of real need, by ignoring economic calculations [or] by refusing to accept [private foreign] productive capital.[5]

Yet national prestige had to be taken into account, and Eadie was sufficiently alarmed by this refusal that he arranged to go to Washington in December; he combined this trip with a visit to Atlantic Refining in Philadelphia to discuss possible joint operations in Venezuela (see Chapter VII). At the same time he instructed Smith, then in Delhi during his tour of the East, to urge the government of India to put in a formal application for finance on behalf of OIL. Delhi, still smarting under the earlier rebuff to Thorold, would not agree. So Eadie, despite a very sympathetic reception from the bank, came home from the USA without a loan.

In 1959 Whitehall agreed to lend £3 million to the government of India, provided that the money was spent in Britain. Burmah Oil was then prepared to lend the remaining £10–£11 million, which it financed partly with unsecured bank loans and partly with a $6\frac{1}{4}$ per cent debenture stock offered to the

British public. For some unexplained reason, the company did not have to pay the money over until 1963. Delhi was regular in its repayments to the company, and the principal sum outstanding was down to £7.5 million by the end of 1966.

Because both the Nahorkatiya and Moran crudes had a high wax content, they tended to solidify at the low winter temperatures experienced in the Assam valley, which penetrated to the depth of soil in which the pipeline was buried. Since heating the entire 720 miles of pipeline would have been prohibitively expensive, the company started up an extensive research programme in its laboratories to find a solution. That was to heat and then cool the crude under controlled conditions before pumping it into the pipeline. The process was tested in a British pilot plant with the help of BP's research scientists, after which two special crude conditioning plants were constructed, one in each field. Without this discovery, the cost of operating the pipeline would have been substantially greater.

The first stage of the pipeline, the 260 miles to Nunmati, was started towards the end of the 1960, and reached completion in March 1962. The second stage, covering 460 miles from Nunmati to Barauni, was laid in 1962 and ready in mid-1963. One of the longest in the eastern hemisphere, the pipeline was noteworthy also in terms of technical sophistication. It was operated from a central control building by automated remote control systems, at that time reckoned to be more advanced than those anywhere else in the world. Even so, it was completed within the budget estimate of £35 million.

This efficient laying of the pipeline did undoubtedly help to improve the group's standing with government in India. During 1961 Delhi sought to increase its stake in OIL from one-third to a half. As a *quid pro quo* it gave OIL rights over a further 1,800 square miles of prospecting land near Nahorkatiya. As part of the deal Burmah Oil persuaded the authorities to abolish the right of veto enjoyed by the government directors, thereby speeding up decision-making. The group agreed to accept deferred instalments for £1.5 million of the equity which it was surrendering. Those were fully repaid by 1965.

Despite the underlying hostility that still existed in Delhi, Eadie felt that a great deal had been achieved. In the 1961 annual report he wrote that the widening of the state's involvement in the Indian company, and also that in Burma during 1960 (see Chapter IX), represented 'major steps in the reshaping and consolidation of the group's operational interests in the east', which had put these interests on a much more stable footing than before. 'I hope', he concluded, 'that this [stability] will be maintained for many years to come.'

Sadly for the Indian economy, the refineries did not by any means make comparable progress. The two state governments in Assam and Bihar had later withdrawn the offers of land they had made, and also held out for a 15 per cent stake in their respective refineries. Delhi therefore reduced its own share in each to 85 per cent. The sites turned out to be far from ideal, being too remote from the main centres of demand. Moreover, the layout of the refineries left much to be desired, with less advanced specifications than could have been provided by Western oil companies, and took insufficient account of the climatic and other conditions specific to India. At Barauni, for instance, the floating roof storage tanks were provided with extra fixed roofs, of the kinds used to keep snow out during Russian winters, but quite unnecessary in snowless parts of the world. In the vicinity of both refineries, large new townships had to be built and social welfare facilities laid on. Hence costs were appreciably higher than if Western oil companies had been free to choose more suitable sites and had undertaken the design and construction. Whereas Burmah-Shell's refinery at Trombay had cost the equivalent of £24.5 million, the one at Barauni, also of 2 million ton capacity, cost £33.3 million, not including expenditure on the local township. Nunmati, of only 750,000 ton capacity at the outset, cost £13.5 million.

Furthermore, serious delays ensued. The Barauni refinery was not commissioned until 1964 and did not reach full capacity until 1967. Nunmati's was not on stream until 1962 and four years later was extended to 1 million tons capacity. Thus a decade passed before the new oil discoveries in Assam resulted in finished products flowing into the Indian economy.

On top of all the other points of conflict, those over the distribution of oil in India remained very lively. Official discontent over prices, which had been rumbling on ever since the Tariff Board enquiry of 1928, became even sharper when the Indian authorities learnt that the majors were offering secret discounts off the posted prices of crude, in which India did not share. Then in the later 1950s Russia and Romania offered to supply oil, not only at prices well below those being charged under the Gulf-plus system but also in exchange for inconvertible rupees, which those countries would use for imports from India.

Here indeed were many overtones of the Russian incursion into the Indian market of the late 1920s (see Chapter I above), although this time there was no question of regarding Russian oil as having been filched from the West. Burmah Oil reacted badly to news of this offer, and to Delhi's request for its help in distributing the Iron Curtain oil. Much as their predecessors had been in the 1920s, the directors were convinced that long-term security of supply, even at higher prices and involving a foreign exchange burden, was preferable to the disruption caused by interlopers into an orderly market. In 1966 the Russians arbitrarily suspended the supply of cheap oil. Having gained a share of the Indian market, they raised the price of their oil so that its earlier advantage disappeared; the only remaining benefit to India was its payment in inconvertible rupees.

Burmah-Shell therefore declined to undertake the distribution of this oil. Instead, it offered to meet the foreign currency problem by extending its credit terms for imports from three to six months. Delhi rejected this compromise, which simply spread out these payments and did not ease the underlying drain on resources.

To break the impasse, in 1959 Delhi set up the state-owned Indian Oil Company Ltd (IOC), to undertake the marketing of Russian and Romanian imported oil. Once it had established itself, it was given the additional task of marketing the output from the state and jointly-owned refineries. In 1964 it absorbed Indian Refineries Ltd, set up in 1958 to administer the refineries at Nunmati and Barauni, and changed its name to the Indian Oil Corporation. Thus by 1966 the IOC was well on the way to distributing all finished products except those from the foreign companies' own refineries.

Burmah-Shell had in 1964 submitted a bid for a refinery in

Madras which the government had put out to tender. The proposed capacity was 2.25 million tons, capable of being expanded to 4 million tons. The company offered a 51 per cent equity to the government, plus an elaborate system of dividend limitation. In fact, the contract went to a consortium of the National Iranian Oil Company and Amoco, which offered more favourable terms over credits and the like. Burmah Oil, already heavily committed in the subcontinent and elsewhere, must have been relieved not to have become involved.

By the early 1960s, therefore, Burmah Oil was still prepared to maintain its interests in India – with no expectation that they would remain in British hands for longer than another decade or two – but was faced with growing state intervention in every phase from exploration to marketing. Then in the autumn of 1962 it encountered an outside threat to its Assam property, as unexpected as had been the threat from Japan in 1942. A frontier dispute between India and China had been simmering for some years; after a series of provocations, late in October the Chinese invaded north-west Assam.[6] On 20 November, when the Chinese forces were half-way to the River Brahmaputra, there was what J. K. Galbraith, the American ambassador, called 'the day of ultimate panic in Delhi, the first time I have ever witnessed the disintegration of public morale'. That was after a catastrophic broadcast by Nehru, which indicated that he had little power to protect Assam.

The impact of the invasion on the Assam town of Tezpur, 200 miles west of Digboi, carries some bizarre echoes of happenings in Burma two decades earlier, thereby seeming to bear out Marx's assertion – taken from Hegel – that notable events appear the first time as tragedy and the second time as farce. Once the Chinese were rumoured to be only hours away from the town, the authorities announced by loudspeaker that they could no longer guarantee civil safety. Politicians then harangued the townspeople and urged them to stay put, but themselves decamped, whereupon the people followed them. The crowds besieging the ferry point across the Brahmaputra to safety included newly released convicts and mental hospital patients. On orders from Delhi, the local branch of the State Bank strove to incinerate £300,000 worth of notes and coin;

attempts to jettison bags of coin by dropping them in a nearby lake had a predictable outcome when local divers went down and fished them out again.

Cash was not the only asset in the state earmarked for destruction. The Director of Civil Defence in Delhi had been despatched by the government of India to carry out a scorched earth policy, and army engineers were standing by at power stations and waterworks, explosives at the ready. On 25 November the governor of Assam sent written instructions to Tony Gowan, the general manager at Digboi, to K. B. Kanuga, managing director of OIL and to the other top managers concerned, about Operation Sledge-Hammer. That would involve denying, by making unusable for a period of two years, the Digboi installations, the oilfields at Nahorkatiya and Moran, the uncompleted Nunmati refinery, and the pipeline.

The denial programme would be in three phases: training, preparation, and demolition. For the first, an explosives expert would soon be arriving to provide the necessary instructions. Any employees who were liable to panic should be evacuated by rail; armed protection would be supplied to prevent looting of property and intimidation of the denial teams. A note personally signed by the governor would authorise the actual demolition. These written instructions were sent out five days after the Chinese had declared their intention to cease fire and withdraw behind the *de facto* frontier. Having completed their punitive expedition and given no comfort to the Indian army, they were content to depart.

The only serious Indian resistance to the Chinese was led by Brigadier Naveen Rawlley, whose brigade effectively defied the enemy by trench warfare some 60 miles north of Digboi. Interestingly enough Rawlley, who later became general manager and Burmah Oil's chief representative in Delhi, had been involved in the British stand against the Japanese at Kohima in April 1944, when the same tactic of digging in had been used. On the morrow of the Chinese announcement about withdrawal, Eadie's comment to Bilsland neatly summarised the relief felt in London. 'I am breathing a little more freely this morning, in view of the dramatic and unexpected twist of the dragon's tail last evening.'

In the four critical weeks of hostilities, everyone in Digboi remained under very considerable stress. For the second time in a generation (see Chapter IV) the Assam Oil Company's properties had been under serious risk of destruction, in the face of an oncoming enemy. Although there was a teleprinter link with the general manager's office in Delhi, that was not much help in steadying nerves at a time when so little hard news appeared to be available in the capital. Hence exaggerated rumours of imminent air attacks were rife. As in Burma twenty years earlier, the managers had to face the sometimes self-contradictory pressures of maintaining output, of ensuring the safety of personnel and dependants, and of denial.

Production of petrol for service aircraft and vehicles was especially vital, at a time when Digboi's total throughput was about 3 million barrels a year. In mid-November, government orders at last arrived to evacuate the wives and families of senior personnel. These were taken off from a nearby airport in planes of the Indian Air Force and, following the earlier pattern in Burma, the managers then shared accommodation in bachelor messes. After the Chinese withdrawal, the dependants arrived back just in time for the Christmas and New Year celebrations.

The episode of the Sino-Indian border war was politically significant in weakening further the already tarnished reputation of the 73-year-old Nehru as a Third-World statesman of high principle and a seeker after peace. It also went some way towards projecting him out of the enclosed environment in which he had existed for too many years. As he said at that time,

> We were getting out of touch with reality in the modern world and living in an artificial atmosphere of our own creating, and we have been shocked out of it, all of us.[7]

For Burmah Oil, this greater realism at the top in Delhi was to be helpful in the next few years, as it led to some relaxation of official antipathy towards foreign oil operations. Krishna Menon resigned the defence portfolio after the débâcle of the war with China, and Malaviya was in turn forced to resign a year later from the Ministry of Natural Resources. R. P. Smith, when he announced the resignation to the board, said that he intended to go to Delhi shortly in order to establish relations with his successor.

The official policy of steadily expanding the public sector for a time gave way to one of encouraging private enterprise. Burmah-Shell was allowed to extend its refinery capacity at Trombay from 2 million to 3 million tons, a step that Malaviya had strenuously resisted. The high calibre of the company's representation in Delhi was a further boost to the improvement in relations that followed. At the beginning of 1962 John Finlay, grandson of Kirkman Finlay (see Introduction) became chief representative of the group in India and also managing director of OIL. He reacted imaginatively to the more conciliatory atmosphere then prevailing in the capital.

In particular, Finlay speeded up the programme of Indianisation in OIL, which by then had an Indian chairman. By a systematic programme of staff training, he reduced the number of expatriates in that company from 69 in 1962 to one only seven years later. He was strongly supported from home by Maclachlan, who in 1962 had been posted to the London office and appointed group regional co-ordinator for India and Pakistan. In 1964 Burmah Oil was willing to collaborate with Shell in developing the petrochemical and fertiliser industries in India, using naphtha as a feedstock. Yet future events, at that moment quite impossible to foresee, might all too easily reawaken the latent official predilection for state controls and bureaucratic hostility to private business, undoing much of the hard work of the past two decades.

How could Burmah Oil's record in India since 1947 be summed up? If the company had prevented that country's lamps from being extinguished during the First World War (Vol I, p.228) and had significantly helped to keep road transport rolling and aircraft flying in the Second World War, its more recent experiences had been mixed. One supreme achievement had been to discover the large Nahorkatiya field, and to open up the prospect of other major finds in Assam. However, not through its own fault, there had been much delay before the products that would result from that discovery were to become fully available to consumers. It had reluctantly joined in building one refinery, but had then found subsequent refineries being entrusted to other parties. Its marketing power, jointly with Shell, was being whittled away by the state setting up an alternative marketing organisation and by other official restrictions. Another achievement, completed to general satisfaction, had been to construct the oil pipeline.

The paramount question remained. What future, if any, did the company have in the country? Drysdale, as exploration manager of Burmah Oil, had declared in 1957 that its concession areas in India, as in Burma and Pakistan, were geologically speaking exceptionally good compared with other known areas in the free world. However, two years later Eadie, when putting forward the case for diversification away from the East, pointed out that Burmah Oil had since 1945 invested £37 million in India and received only £24 million profits after tax. By 1962 he expected the total investment outlay there to have risen to £44 million and profits only to £32 million.

In the ten years between 1947 and 1956, the average annual profit of Assam Oil and the India trading subsidiary were just under £1.5 million, but in the following ten years 1957 to 1966, the average was down to £410,000. Assam Oil's losses from 1963 onwards were due partly to the high prices it had to pay for the crude it bought from OIL, and partly to official controls which kept down retail prices. Then in 1966 those companies had jointly been faced with a huge loss of £2.2 million after the devaluation of the rupee. Although Burmah Oil would certainly not wish to turn its back on India, the balance of its newly developing activities was moving inexorably towards the West.

Pakistan

Burmah Oil's activities in Pakistan, during the period from 1947 to 1966, were fully as eventful as those elsewhere in the subcontinent. Yet on the whole relations with the government there caused the board in London far less anxiety than relations with India, or indeed with Burma. Eadie explained this to his fellow directors in 1959 as follows. The outlook of the governing classes in Pakistan seemed to be more akin to the British outlook than to that of the regimes in Burma or in India. Dealings between government and company were thus on the whole smoother owning to the co-operative attitude that was engendered in Karachi. What he called the 'more or less autocratic forms of government which have persisted there in different forms since independence' also led to far more continuity in Pakistan's policies towards oil.

However, the first decade of independence was not one of great progress for Pakistan as a whole. After the death in 1948 of Mohammed Ali Jinnah, the first governor-general, administrations seemed to lack a consistent unity of purpose as well as the resources to intensify the pace of economic development in what was by any standards a very poor country, extremely deficient in energy resources.

As national income in that decade increased at the same rate as population size, it was a time of zero growth per head. Hence the demand for oil remained sluggish. Of that, only a small amount of motor spirit was required, an average quantity of kerosene by Eastern standards, but a substantial quantity of fuel oil, especially for the railway system.

Although an officially-sponsored planning commission was set up in 1953, it was hampered by political instability; over the following five years there were no fewer than five governments. Then in 1958 General Ayub Khan gained power in a bloodless coup; he remained president until 1969. Hence, as Eadie put it, 'to a large extent British-trained civil servants and army officers have been in main charge, and politics have not had quite the free rein as elsewhere'.

More tranquil relations with government therefore followed, especially in the oil sector. The division of the subcontinent had required the company to set up separate operating units for concessions and for trading. In 1948 the 33-year-old Michael J. Condon, then manager of the Pakistan concessions subsidiary at Karachi, was appointed to head the Burmah Oil's operations in Pakistan. A large man in more than one sense, he used a combination of intelligence, drive and panache to establish a unique degree of confidence among his hosts. He remained in his post for twelve years, a record for post-war general managers.

The confidence shown by the Pakistan authorities in Burmah Oil and its general manager was the more welcome, given the continuing hostility between Pakistan and India. The fact that the company had interests in both countries does not appear to have provoked charges of partisanship either way; more specific accusations about wells on one side of the border draining off oil on the other side could normally be disproved quite conclusively.

As in Delhi, the post-independence government in Karachi was anxious to revise the rules about oil concessions. It gave the company, together with Pakistan's other producer, Attock Oil, an opportunity to discuss the draft proposals. The Pakistan petroleum production rules were issued in 1949. Although both companies were allowed to retain full control of already discovered fields, new rupee companies had to be set up for future operations. Condon therefore helped to set up Pakistan Petroleum Ltd (PPL) which was incorporated a year later to take over new concessions work. Burmah Oil at first had 99 per cent of the equity, reduced a few years later to 70 per cent. To comply with the official policy of encouraging private share ownership, the public in Pakistan then acquired an 0.3 per cent holding and the state took the remaining 29.7 per cent. In 1952 Attock Oil established a rupee company named Pakistan Oilfields Ltd, with a 70 per cent stake, the other 30 per cent being taken by the state and indigenous shareholders.

Condon was the first chairman and managing director of PPL, with G. F. (Scout) Wilson as exploration manager; Wilson remained there until 1953, when he beame fields manager at Digboi. Burmah Oil had already resumed prospecting work in both West and East Pakistan and put down test wells. The most important early test was at Lakhra, in Sind province, drilled down to over 12,600 feet in 1948–50 without success. At that time it was one of the first deep tests in South-East Asia, and the depth was only exceeded a handful of times in Pakistan before 1966, all wells proving to be dry.

Another area of early exploration was further north at Balkassar, about 50 miles south of Rawalpindi. There PPL and Attock Oil had adjoining concessions over a large geological structure, and both companies drilled a number of successful although small-yielding wells by 1955. In accordance with the official production rules, they were required to share production on the basis of the respective proportions of proved recoverable reserves estimated as lying below the two concessions. However, implementing the rules posed certain difficulties, some technical, and on several occasions the two parties had to go to arbitration. All crude oil raised by PPL would be processed in Attock Oil's Morgah refinery near Rawalpindi, which was to be expanded accordingly. By the late 1950s PPL was supplying about 22 per cent of the refinery's annual throughput.

On downstream activities, the government was anxious to see a refinery built in Pakistan, both on grounds of national pride and to economise in foreign exchange: much as in India. Attock Oil's refinery had a throughput in 1949-50 of only 700,000 barrels. The Burmah Oil directors, aware that a large proportion of the ensuing expense would fall on their company, decided to stall on the refinery issue until such time as the current exploration programme produced commercial strikes of oil. By 1951 prospecting expense in Pakistan was more than £1 million a year, which so alarmed the board that it insisted on every effort being made to reduce this burden.

In the risky business of oil prospecting, it is often the unexpected that occurs. One licence issued to the company was at a desolate place some 350 miles north of Karachi. Geologists had known about seepages of oil and gas 80 miles from that locality ever since the 1880s, when a small quantity of oil had been raised. In 1914 a Burmah Oil geologist had mapped the region, and others had carried out more intensive surveys. However, as the prospective area was on Baluchi tribal land, the British authorities before 1947 had refused to issue any concessions there. PPL was now permitted to explore in the area and decided to carry out deep test drilling.

That area resembled many other promising sites around the world in being in the middle of an inhospitable desert, with ultra-high temperatures in the torrid season. It was then uninhabited, its characteristics graphically described as showing

> no sign of life except for a passing camel train, no water to sustain even a temporary settlement, only a boundless rugged plain baked hard by the excessive heat of countless summers.[8]

Literally in the middle of nowhere, a mere blank patch of desert, it possessed no name. Eight miles to the east were to be found the remains of the old Sui fort; the PPL geologists therefore named the location Sui.

The nearest railhead was 35 miles; away, and a connecting road had therefore to be built, along which 6,000 tons of drilling machinery, stores and technical equipment for the test was transported. No fewer than 150 workers had to be engaged, and a camp sprang up from scratch, being provided with electric light and power, workshops, a garage, store yard, canteen, hospital and airstrip. A water supply was piped in from the railhead. In the months that followed, Sui gas was used to bake the bricks for the buildings of the township that was soon to emerge, with its dwellings, shops, offices, mosque, clubs, cinema and other amenities. In order to create gardens, soil was brought in from miles away. Desmond Dewhurst and Vincent Stewart, the chief engineer, were responsible for the local organisation of this mammoth undertaking. Such provisions of the wide-ranging needs of civilisation were a far cry from the very inadequate preparation of the 1880s, when the heat and shortage of drinking water had caused the death of one prospector and almost killed another.

In October 1951 the first exploratory well was spudded in and, as it progressed, indications became positively encouraging. Thirteen months later it was down to 10,700 feet. To the initial disappointment of all concerned, however, only gas was found, in thick limestone. Then the evidence began to mount up that here was a very substantial gas discovery. A second well five miles away served to confirm its magnitude. Eventually the experts calculated that the entire field contained no less than eight million million cubic feet of gas, equivalent to about 950 million barrels of oil. That placed it globally among the ten largest natural gas reservoirs known at that time.

The government of Pakistan at once asked for some gas to be pumped to a fertiliser plant not too far away. Burmah Oil, which was then almost entirely PPL's paymaster, refused to become directly involved in the marketing of the gas, although it stood ready to provide what technical advice it could. The reason for this refusal was clear. In 1953 it had to pay out £3.5 million as its share of capital requirements for Burmah-Shell's operations in both India and Pakistan and for the Trombay refinery. During the five years 1949-53, according to Eadie's calculations quoted in Table 6, the Burmah group lost a little over £2.6 million in Pakistan, and that cumulative loss rose to nearly £2.9 million by the end of 1955. PPL itself lost over £1 million in 1953 and smaller losses in the two subsequent years.

When in 1956 it went into the black, it had to sign a profit-sharing agreement with the state. To finance these capital projects, the group did have a large holding of British government securities, built up during the war, which it was able to draw down. However, that source of funds would soon be exhausted.

Even in the early 1950s, when it was still a relative rarity, natural gas found on such an enormous scale represented a noteworthy discovery; yet many people in and outside the Burmah group seriously doubted if any commercial potential existed in a country as underdeveloped as Pakistan. PPL therefore commissioned a market survey from Snodgrass Associates of Washington, DC. The agreeably named Cornelius Stribling Snodgrass, Strib for short, was a distinguished oil consultant, well known in western Europe for having inspected the major refineries there on behalf of the US administration for the Marshall aid programme.[9] His report highlighted the revolution in Pakistan's fuel prospects which the gas would bring about, since it would be able to supply heating power equivalent to 1.6 million tons of coal annually for the next 60 years. However, to launch the revolution, a pipeline would have to be built to Karachi, the country's largest port and commercial centre, initially to supply large customers such as power stations. Intensive marketing should then encourage other suitable concerns to switch to gas.

The estimated cost of the 350-mile-long pipeline to Karachi was £9–10 million, and the government of Pakistan at once applied to the World Bank for a loan. Although the bank's president, Eugene Black, agreed to give this application top priority, he was doubtful if it could be granted. That was because the government had not explored the possibilities of private finance; in any case the bank did not care for certain aspects of the proposal, especially the extent of government control envisaged.

In November 1953, therefore, the government of Pakistan requested Weva, then Burmah Oil's managing director, to fly out from London to Washington in order to impress on Black and his fellow directors the vital importance of the project for the country's economic future. Weva found this exercise in very high-level financial diplomacy to be one of the most interesting experiences in the whole of his post-war career with the company. Early in 1954 Black therefore sent two American natural gas experts, Ralph E. Davis and E. O. Bennett, to review the company's calculations about the gas reserves and commercial prospects. These the experts approved, and in June the Bank overcame its scruples and lent £5 million to cover the foreign exchange expenses. The chairman of the state-owned Pakistan Industrial Development Corporation (PIDC), Ghulam Faruque, was so enthusiastic about the pipeline project that he agreed to put up £2 million together with a local partner. Burmah Oil stood ready to lend the remaining £1–2 million.

To take responsibility for the purification of the gas and for its conveyance from Sui by pipeline to the major outlets in the south, in February 1954 the Sui Gas Transmission Company (SGTC) was established. Burmah Oil's Pakistan trading company was appointed as managing agency, Condon being the first managing director of SGTC and Dick Kemp the operations manager. The capital was the rupee equivalent of £4 million, 51 per cent being held by the PIDC and private investors locally – the latter issue being five times oversubscribed – while Burmah Oil and the recently established Commonwealth Development Finance Company each held $24^1/_2$ per cent, or just under £1 million. Since the Burmah group also had a majority interest in the production of the gas, through PPL, it was heavily involved as far as the Karachi end of the pipeline.

Work on the 16-inch pipeline was preceded by an aerial and land survey of the proposed route, carried out by engineers of the company. Begun in autumn 1954, it was completed in the summer of 1955, the first gas supplies being delivered to customers that August. The close co-operation of the office and technical staff was neatly captured in a parody of 'Widdicombe Fair' written in 1954. The second verse read,

Appointments with MD[Condon] are hard to arrange,
All along, out along, down along, lee,
For he's floating a company [SGTC] on the exchange,
Wi' Dick Kemp, Harry Hall, Mervyn Jones, Alizai, Hugh
  Brown, Stan Walker, Phil Swales, Arthur Cockle,
And C. Stribling Snodgrass and all,
And C. Stribling Snodgrass and all!

Those mentioned in the fourth line were the operations manager, the US consultant engineer, chief resident engineer, general assistant, office manager, two more engineers and the company secretary.[10] In all no fewer than 4,000 men were employed, of whom 125 were British and American technicians, and 40,000 tons of steel pipe, made by Stewarts and Lloyds Ltd of Glasgow, were used. The Karachi terminal building, near the southern end of the pipeline, was conspicuous by its tall radio mast; the communications network included mobile units, teleprinters and radio telephone services. At a ceremony there to inaugurate the pipeline in November 1955, after a reading from the Koran a gas flare was lit, and the crowds of onlookers were able to enjoy the visible evidence of the way in which their country's lucrative asset was being utilised commercially – only four years after the start of the first test well. Earlier, the engineers had had to purge the line of foreign substances and test the flare at close to its full capacity. The result had been spectacular: the roar of air and then gas escaping from the line sounded like an approaching hurricane, and the sky was obscured with the smoke that belched from the flare. The inaugural ceremony was by comparison no more than a discreet shadow of the initial test.

The distribution and marketing of the gas were undertaken by the Karachi Gas Company, the chairman being Ghulam Faruque; Arthur Cockle became the general manager. That company made its first sale of gas at the end of 1955; eight months later it had twenty industrial customers and by March 1957 was serving fifty-eight industrial outlets and six factory canteens. The gas was eventually piped to any number of small consumers, replacing a variety of scarce fuels: not merely petroleum products but also firewood and imported coal.

A further pipeline was then planned, to run north-east of Sui to Multan, about 220 miles away. That was completed in October 1958. To extend the pipeline northwards from Multan, a new company was established in mid-1963: Sui Northern Gas Pipelines Ltd (SNGP). Burmah Oil, which seconded Cockle as the first general manager, held a one-third interest. The majority shareholder was the West Pakistan Industrial Development Corporation, which had owned the Sui-Multan line and now sold it to SNGP. Attock Oil had its pipeline network from Dhulian to Rawalpindi and the new capital city of Islamabad; that network was also sold to SNGP, which planned to construct the intervening section from Multan to the junction with Dhulian.

This 350-mile section was costed at £21.3 million, of which £8.6 million would be needed for acquiring the sections already built and £12.7 million for the new construction. The foreign exchange component was £7.4 million, the World Bank being requested to lend £5.4 million. Once again, intensive negotiations had to take place in Washington, Burmah Oil's chief representative, Hugh Brown, acting for the Pakistan side. As delays were to be expected, Jack Strain offered, during a visit to Pakistan at the end of 1963, to provide interim finance of £1 million. Then in June 1964 the World Bank authorised the loan. Two years later, the pipeline had reached within 50 miles of the Dhulian system. While the daily offtake of the gas had been 23 million cubic feet in 1956, it had risen to 167 million cubic feet by 1965. Over the same period the saving to Pakistan in foreign exchange, in terms of the imported coal and fuel oil replaced by natural gas, rose from £1.6 million to £5 million.

Despite all the attention that had to be paid to the gas discovery and its development, the government of Pakistan was resolved to keep alive its earlier calls for a new indigenous refinery. In January 1957 the finance minister argued that two were now needed, one at Karachi and one at Chittagong. Six months later he invited Burmah Oil to head a consortium for a Karachi refinery of 1.5 million ton capacity, later increased to 2.1 million tons. Shell, Stanvac and Caltex were the other members. Some time elapsed before the project passed the planning stage. The government insisted that its private investors should be allowed a 40 per cent participation, and on that basis signed an agreement with the consortium in October 1959.

The Pakistan Refinery Ltd was registered in May 1960, Burmah Oil's 15 per cent contribution amounting to £1 million. The refinery was planned to cost £11.5 million, half by loans from banks and half from equity. It was opened in 1962 by President Ayub Khan. The Burmah group knew that the arrangement could only work to its disadvantage. The government had the right to buy its own requirements of finished products, up to 40 per cent of throughput, and that was bound to reduce Burmah-Shell's and the group trading subsidiary's marketing volume. The state-owned Pakistan National Oil Ltd was set up in March 1962, to import and market petroleum products, and was clearly intended to be a serious competitor to the British firms.

When in 1959 Eadie put to his colleagues some cogent reasons for diversification, he stated that the excess outlay in Pakistan since the war – that is, the amount paid over by the company less receipts – had been far greater than in India, being £11 million as against £2 million. Investment had cost £14 million and profits after tax had brought in only £3 million. By 1962, he estimated, the investment total was likely to be up to £20.5 million and profits after tax only to £5 million, raising the shortfall to £15.5 million. Thus some years at least were likely to pass before the company received an adequate return on all its money invested in the country.

Eadie was particularly concerned that Burmah Oil, like rival companies, had suffered 'severe and costly disappointment' over exploration for oil, especially in West Pakistan. Even had a worthwhile oil strike occurred, the size of the find would have undoubtedly been far smaller than in such areas as offshore Louisiana or Texas. 'Moreover,' he concluded, 'due to the smallness of the Pakistan market and the proximity to the large cheap surplus Middle East supplies, the prospects of profitable disposal are also less than in, say, the gulf of Mexico.' He thus took the opposite view to Drysdale about the extent and economic value of future discoveries in the East.

The Burmah Oil board accepted Eadie's advice and in 1960 arranged for its investment strategy in Pakistan to concentrate on producing and developing the natural gas, rather than continuing with the largely unsuccessful oil exploration. In any case, the government of Pakistan was now intent on undertaking exploration in its own account, using staff and equipment loaned by the Russians on a long-term basis.

Turning to East Pakistan, before 1939 Burmah Oil had undertaken a considerable amount of exploratory drilling at Badarpur in Assam, near the East Bengal border (see Chapter

II and Vol. I p.226). The wells were abandoned in 1933. After its establishment PPL continued the exploration work. In 1952-53 it put a well down to below 10,000 feet at Patiya, near Chittagong, which proved to be dry. It had more success in 1955 with a test well near Sylhet, a railway terminal in the north-east corner of East Pakistan. That well contained a considerable volume of methane gas, but it unfortunately blew out and caught fire. The rig was lost and the well had to be abandoned. Later the gas field was reopened. Together with a subsequent discovery nearby at Chhatak, PPL established a small production of gas, which was used by a fertiliser factory at Sylhet and also by a cement plant at Chhatak and another across the Indian border. As to oil, for the same reasons as in West Pakistan, PPL did not feel that exploration was likely to be worthwhile. PPL did not pursue further exploration in the region, as the many geological structures which remained to be tested were considered mainly as gas, rather than oil, prospects. Also the terrain, with its many rivers and monsoon problem, presented formidable technical problems over trans-portation to markets which could only be limited ones. Other interested companies later confirmed that view.

Marketing operations were on a much smaller scale than in the Western part, given the economic backwardness of the region. Burmah-Shell of Pakistan operated in all but the 'reserved' area in and around Chittagong, which was run by Burmah Oil's Pakistan trading subsidiary. The latter had a large and modern ocean installation and packing factory at the port. By 1961 the government of Pakistan was making it clear that it expected these marketing organisations to become rupee companies, with majority national participation, although without imposing an actual deadline. When the two parent companies appeared to be dragging their feet, it set up the rival Pakistan National Oil Ltd, mentioned above. In fact, while Burmah Oil was anxious to follow government wishes, Shell held contrary views. Early in 1964 Burmah-Shell, on Shell's prompting, offered a 30 per cent local participation; according to word reaching the company, ministers privately 'ridiculed' the smallness of the offer. R. P. Smith thereupon decided to take a strong line with the Shell directors in London.

'I think that it may not be too much to say that the issue

could be one of survival for Burmah-Shell,' Smith explained. French interests had already been granted the new refinery at Chittagong, and if Burmah-Shell remained 'foreign', it might not be allocated products from that refinery for marketing, and its trade would suffer further. (In fact, the Chittagong refinery was taken over by Burmah Oil before it came on stream.) After considerable pressure from Smith, in February 1965 Shell agreed to participation in East Pakistan, but only to the extent of selling to Burmah Oil, in sterling, the Shell half-stake in the Burmah-Shell assets there. Burmah Eastern Ltd, 49 per cent owned by Burmah Oil, became a public company in 1966, when the remaining 51 per cent of its shares were offered to and taken up by Pakistanis.

Not until the late 1960s did Burmah-Shell in West Pakistan become a rupee company, with 50 per cent being taken up by local investors; this time Shell maintained its interest. When Maclachlan returned on a visit to Pakistan early in 1965 after three years' absence, he declared himself 'struck by the distance which government had travelled to give effect to their declared intention to develop Pakistan interests in commerce and industry'. That process, of steadily restricting the role of foreign concerns in the country, was carried out with great effectiveness and largely without arousing rancour on the part of the foreign concerns themselves.

To sum up, Burmah Oil's outstanding achievement in Pakistan over this period had been the discovery of natural gas, which by the mid-1960s was contributing about 28 per cent of the country's fossil fuel needs, coal providing 19 per cent and oil 53 per cent. Of its demand for oil, less than one-sixth came from domestic sources. The none too robust economy of Pakistan could have done without this foreign exchange burden arising from imported oil, but the efforts made by Burmah Oil to stimulate the use of gas were recognised by the government with whom the group's relations remained good.

As to the financial outcome, Eadie's forecast of 1959 turned out to be a not too inaccurate one: of a £15.5 million deficit, compared with £12 million in India, by the end of 1962. The actual results for Pakistan showed that investment outlay had been slightly lower than anticipated, at £18 million, while profit was £5.2 million as against an expected £5 million. That revealed a deficit of £12.8 million. The largest investment item was exploration, at £8.4 million: money which, to Eadie's way of thinking, had been largely wasted.

As a means of appraising the Burmah group's operations in the Indian subcontinent towards the end of the period, it would have been helpful to provide comparable figures to those given in Table 6 for earlier years. Unfortunately, ready-made data do not seem to have survived. Instead, Table 7 gives a rough

TABLE 7
Burmah group: net trading income (after tax) 1963

Geographical breakdown

	£000s	%
India	3,350	54
Pakistan	1,450	23
Burma	—	—
Peru and Ecuador	1,190	19
US and Canada	110	2
UK etc*	120	2
	6,220	100

of which

	India		Pakistan	
	£000s	%	£000s	%
Oil and gas production (Assam Oil, OIL, PPL etc)	770	13	450	7
Refining (Burmah-Shell refinery, Pakistan Refinery Ltd etc)	1,020	16	20	—
Product sales (Burmah-Shell, India and Pakistan trading)	1,450	23	980	16
Tinplate Co. of India	110	2	—	—
	3,350	54	1,450	23

* This is net of £400,000 loss on parent company's expenses and £80,000 loss by tankers, both of which may have been shared *pro rata* worldwide rather than being borne solely by UK.

breakdown of net trading income after tax in 1963, which includes income from trade investments (ones in which the group had no direct control over operations) but not dividends from BP or Shell shares or government securities. The calculations involved have necessitated the making of some assumptions on the basis of inadequate information. However, the orders of magnitude are believed to be about right.

In the early 1960s India was the major trading earner, but Pakistan was then making a profit, partly it seems because of the reduction in exploration expenditure. For the £5 million or so being earned there, the group in London and in Pakistan had to devote much entrepreneurial effort. Each of the various activities, from concessions to refining to marketing, had its own subsidiary operating companies, and the subsequent initiatives of the indigenous governments led to the setting up of further rupee companies over which the London office had at least some control. The burden of work on the Burmah Oil directors, who had not only to monitor this corporate network by correspondence at long range and by periodical visits, but also to negotiate with ministers on often very complex and sometimes quite contentious issues, must have been quite substantial.

From the early 1950s onwards, the director who was undoubtedly the most actively involved in the subcontinent was Jack Strain. Eadie and Smith were from time to time on the move to the East, but the main negotiating tasks were frequently left to Strain. Among his most noteworthy achievements was his restructuring of the group's interests in Pakistan to take full advantage of the Sui gas finds. The rapport he established with ministers and civil servants alike ensured a reasonable share of the benefits to both sides.

Below the Burmah Oil board level were the interlocking affiliated companies, from the sterling ones such as Assam Oil and Burmah-Shell to the various subsidiaries which embraced India and Pakistan trading, concessions, pipelines and the like; senior executives in London not on the main board became directors of these affiliates and contributed their expertise to their running. For the rupee companies, the boards in each country were manned by senior managers there, increasingly joined by indigenous colleagues. Burmah Oil's chief representatives – as the general managers came to be called – were given increased powers by London as their functions took on a higher profile; from the 1950s onwards, they all flew home at the same time once a year to discuss jointly with the group directors, common problems and policies.

It would have been difficult to draw up organisation charts which precisely reflected the complex inter-relationships. That the system worked to the broad satisfaction of host governments was brought home in several remarkable ways during 1963. The disengagement process from Burma was as harmonious as could have been expected. Similarly, that year the governments of India and Pakistan (see Chapter X above) were so ill-disposed to the attempts in 1963 by BP and Shell to take over Burmah Oil, which they feared could have subjected those governments to far less sensitive treatment than they had received from Burmah Oil, that they seemed prepared to sever connections entirely by purchasing outright all the Burmah group's interests in their countries.

Herein lay the central problem that faced Burmah Oil's top executives after 1945. Was it likely that the considerable managerial exertions in these Eastern countries, coupled with the constant demand for risk capital, could be at all adequately repaid in material terms? Given the enticing prospects for oil endeavour elsewhere in the world, notably in the western hemisphere, did Eadie have any real alternative to diversifying away from the East? Having faced up to political reality in negotiating its way out of Burma, could the company be reasonably expected to maintain its commitments to India and Pakistan, with no certainty as to whether or when – or on what terms – either country might choose to end the relationship? With oil increasingly becoming the mainstay of the industrialised world, Burmah Oil was to find the pull towards new interests more and more irresistible.

Australia[11]

Burmah Oil's interest in the antipodes began in November 1958 when the president of Murphy Oil Corporation, Charles H. Murphy Jr, was introduced to Eadie (see Chapter VII).

Murphy Oil had a 50 per cent concession right from the Australian firm Camelot Nominees Ltd to a 9,500 square mile area offshore in the Gulf of Papua, a territory then administered by Australia. Only two years before, BP had discovered an onshore gas field at Barikewa in Papua, and in 1959 Burmah Oil began discussions with the BP Exploration Company and a local BP subsidiary, the Australasian Petroleum Company Pty Ltd, about the possible development of the Barikewa field. The government in Canberra was known to be willing to subsidise approved exploration projects likely to benefit the Australian economy.

The combination of all these benign factors – congenial and highly experienced potential partners; hopeful indications, at least of gas; and the prospect of financial assistance – persuaded the company to despatch G. F. (Scout) Wilson, one-time exploration manager in Pakistan and currently its drilling and engineering adviser in London, Thomas F. A. Armstrong, an engineering manager there, and Keith Wilson, seconded from Pakistan, to investigate on the spot the geological possibilities at Barikewa. Murphy Oil suggested that Burmah Oil should become the operator and offered it half its own stake in the Camelot Nominees concession.

In November 1959 the Burmah Oil directors considered the possibility of joint operations with Australasian Petroleum, to bore test wells on the land side of the boundary between the two concessions. The company's hope was that these tests, and a concurrent marine seismic survey of the offshore area that was started at the end of 1960, would determine whether or not further exploration was justified. A local operating company, BOC of Australia Ltd, was registered in January 1961, the directors being R. P. Smith, John Drysdale, Jack Strain, Bob Tainsh and Scout Wilson. Meanwhile, Burmah Oil was discussing with the British registered company Conch Methane Services Ltd the commercial possibilities of liquefying and transporting liquid natural gas (LNG) from Papua to Sydney in Australia.

Despite the very primitive conditions in which they had to work, Scout Wilson and his team at Barikewa were initially quite impressed with the prospects for the natural gas fields. However, as Smith reported to his board colleagues in June

1961, the offshore tests in Papua – which had been studied on the spot the previous March by Percy Evans, the geological adviser from the London Office – revealed no outstanding indications that seemed worth following up by test drilling. The evidence was sent to London and thoroughly investigated by the geological staff there during 1962, which only confirmed the earlier verdict. It was clear that the gas reserves could not be developed commercially without financial help from the Australian government to meet the substantial costs of setting up a liquefaction plant in Papua and of building LNG carriers for the transportation to Sydney. As Canberra declined to offer any such assistance, Burmah Oil agreed with Murphy Oil to call off its involvement in Papua.

In June 1961, at the board meeting where the disappointing outcome in Papua was discussed, Smith reported that he and Charles Murphy were favourably impressed by the long-term prospects in Australia. In fact, it had been Burmah Oil's promptings which had directed Murphy's attention to these prospects. Since exploration and production possibilities in the dominion were likely to be identified in the coming year or two, and since Burmah Oil's operational efforts in its traditional areas of the East were being steadily reduced, Smith felt that the company's representative in Australia should keep himself closely informed about potential opportunities on behalf of both companies. This was, of course, a similar arrangement to maintaining a 'watching base' for oil possibilities which Eadie had proposed for Canada in 1957: one which had proved highly beneficial to the company (see Chapter VII).

Early in June 1961, in preparation for his retirement from executive duties at the end of the year, Eadie carried out some wide-ranging discussions with his fellow directors about the company's future strategy. Australia, he believed, resembled North America in being a politically and economically secure country where Burmah Oil could use its technical expertise to good effect. At the beginning of 1962 BOC of Australia opened up a small office in Sydney, headed by Scout Wilson, to start up its 'watching base' function. It also undertook some geophysical surveys and drilling in New South Wales and Queensland that year, both as operator and 40 per cent shareholder in a consortium comprising Murphy-Australia and the locally registered Southern Oil Company Pty Ltd. The results of these operations were discouraging, and the possibility of Australia turning out to be, geologically speaking, another Papua could not be ruled out. The general manager of BOC of Australia from 1963 to 1965 was Desmond Dewhurst, himself a geologist, former general manager in Pakistan and more lately in Burma.

However, a new area of Australasia was being investigated by K. V. Stringer, who became chief geologist when Tainsh joined the Burmah Oil board in 1963. Stringer and his colleagues had been studying the geology of the island of Timor, north-west of Australia, where the indications were complex but hopeful. Some 300 miles offshore to the south lay the Australian North-West Shelf, which Stringer considered could well be an area much more likely to contain oil than Timor.

The well-known law about oil, that deposits tend to be situated in the more inaccessible and difficult parts of the globe, was not invalidated here. The shelf stretched over a total of 1,250 miles from north-east to south-west, and was as remote from the large centres of population as was possible even in Australia. The coastal areas to the south were both sparsely populated and lacking in properly developed natural harbours, while a road system in the state of Western Australia and in the adjacent Northern Territory was virtually non-existent.

Quite independently, the chief geologist of the Woodside (Lakes Entrance) Oil Company, Dr Nicholas Boutakoff, had also become interested in the North-West Shelf, after studying a submarine contour map. Woodside had been formed as recently as 1954 to take over the interests of the Gippsland Oil Company, but was near to closure as the monies raised for a variety of minor ventures had produced no discoveries of note. Its shrewd chairman, the Melbourne stockbroker Geoff (Tiny) Donaldson, insisted that Woodside could not survive indefinitely by playing a series of small-time gambler's hunches. It must seek concessions over larger exploration areas and then negotiate partnerships with interested companies which understood the cost factors involved in oil exploration and which were prepared to commit sizeable budgets accordingly. Against this background, Woodside sought to obtain from the government of Western Australia exploration rights over 270,000 kilometres of the North-West shelf.

It is possible that Woodside's managing director, Rees Withers, already knew of Burmah Oil's own researches in that area. At any rate, soon after being awarded that concession, Withers flew to London and secured Burmah Oil's agreement to take a one-third interest therein. Drysdale, negotiating on behalf of the company, successfully insisted that Burmah Oil should be the operator. Withers then went on to the Royal Dutch-Shell headquarters in The Hague, where he had a less straightforward reception. Shell demanded a 51 per cent participation: he would not concede more than a third. He gave Shell only a few days to reach a decision, but within that deadline received acceptance of his terms.

Initially, therefore, Burmah Oil, Shell and Woodside held equal shares. However, as future prospecting costs were likely to be considerable, all the partners farmed out part of their holdings to others. Drysdale persuaded BP to acquire half of the Burmah Oil stake. It is said that company geologists were angry that he had failed to extract a premium from BP for giving it an entry into such a promising operation. Drysdale apparently replied that he hoped to be offered in return a share in BP's current exploration in the North Slope of Alaska, which it was as yet fruitlessly prospecting (see Chapter XII). BP did not oblige with a *quid pro quo* of that kind, so that a transactional bridge was never built between the North Slope and the North-West Shelf.

With this strong consortium in place, prospecting on the shelf went ahead with great vigour. Since the required know-how was not adequately available in Australia, Burmah Oil as the operator sent out highly trained and experienced men for the purpose. As was usual in joint ventures these were represented on a committee of technical and financial experts from all the companies involved, which worked out the exploration budgets and programmes. It was encouraging that in 1963 an aeromagnetic survey of the entire shelf established that the sedimentary rocks were thick enough to make exploration worthwhile. However, the experts soon encountered a number of initial difficulties, so that they had to pioneer improved methods of acquiring and interpreting the necessary data. For instance, new techniques refined the seismic sections in such a way as to make them far more straightforward to read, although problems of distinguishing between accurate and false readings of seismic waves took a considerable time to overcome. Then digital recording of the seismic information permitted high-speed computers to be used. As Dewhurst later wrote of those arduous but exciting days,

> Within the geophysical files of the [Burmah] group there exists . . . a classic documentation of the rapid evolution of offshore seismic methods since 1964.

The obvious success of these painstaking efforts to extend the frontiers of technical knowledge encouraged Drysdale as exploration director to seek further involvement in Australia. During the spring of 1965 he visited that country, and after his return he put proposals to the board for increasing its exploration activities there. With the aid of an able presentation by Stringer, who emphasised the progress made in the past few years, the good prospects for rapid economic development generally, and the favourable prospecting opportunities in Australia, Drysdale in June obtained board approval for the Burmah group to buy a 14 per cent interest in Santos Ltd. That company, round which the agreeable aroma of coffee might have been expected to hover, was in fact an Australian concern with the full name of South Australia and Northern Territory Oil Search Ltd.

Despite this agreement in principle, the Burmah Oil board was clearly worried about the financing of the Santos acquisition. Strain, as his memorandum of July 1966 (see Chapter XII) made clear, felt that the £5½ million already spent in Australia was doing precisely nothing to overcome the company's immediate problems of generating more income as soon as possible. For some time to come, that expenditure would not yield any return which then would suffer a UK tax disadvantage as it would be overseas income. Whatever representations he may have made at the June 1965 board meeting, it could not have been helpful that the company's then bankers, the Bank of Scotland, refused to lend the necessary funds. The money was in the end obtained on debenture from a local firm, through

Burmah Australia Ltd, a marketing subsidiary which had been set up in 1964. Then in 1966 the group increased its stake in Santos to 22 per cent.

Santos' concession was in the Cooper Basin, in the north-east corner of South Australia which appears to cut a chunk out of the state of Queensland. In 1964, in conjunction with another partner, it had made a major gas discovery at Gidgealpa, about 450 miles north of Adelaide, and another equally significant gas find at nearby Moomba. Although these discoveries set off intensified prospecting, only small quantities of oil were discovered. For once, the distance from the main cities was not too far, and before the end of 1966 the company's representatives had opened talks with the government of South Australia and other parties about piping the gas to Adelaide. In that year also, the Burmah Oil board judged the prospecting rights on the North-West Shelf to be so encouraging that it acquired a 30 per cent interest in Woodside.

Thus by 1966 the company's exploration in Australia was still at a preparatory stage, with considerable expenditure sunk in the country but only modest returns. That year only one per cent of the group's trading income was earned in Australia, compared with 64 per cent from Asia, which meant India and Pakistan. It was clear that Burmah Oil, while it shared in some significant interests in Australia, had not as yet established much of a presence. It was in fact others, notably the Esso-Broken Hill Proprietary Ltd consortium, who were making really substantial oil discoveries offshore in the Gippsland Shelf off the coast of Victoria.

Here, perhaps, more than anywhere else in the world, the basic dilemmas in Burmah Oil's strategy as a medium-sized oil concern were shown up. As the company admitted a few years later, in the mid-1960s it enjoyed considerable operational strength, employing a technical workforce of high ability who were willing to experiment with and often helped to evolve advanced methods to deal with conditions without precedent. The company also had a financial strength sufficient to enable it to deploy these skills in new areas, since it was largely free of corporate debt and had behind it the substantial uncommitted backing of its holdings in BP and Shell.

In two ways, however, Burmah Oil laboured under a grave disadvantage compared with the majors. On the financial side, it was currently finding it very hard to generate enough income, from its trading activities, to meet investment needs and at the same time to pay the level of dividend which stockholders had come to expect. As to the geographical spread of its operations, the group was diversifying with some success into new areas of the world. In the US and Canada, for instance, it had built up a still fairly modest but potentially lucrative presence. Even if only 9 per cent of its trading profits in 1966 was derived from these countries, that contribution could be expected to rise markedly in the coming years.

For a late-comer such as Burmah Oil, the entry price into what were regarded as the more economically and politically stable parts of the world was bound to be high. The relatively untried geological structure of Australia, and the vast distances involved, must have caused concern among executives as to how the company could sustain a major role there if success in exploration were to lead to heavy demands for finance of high-cost offshore development and production. With all Burmah Oil's other current commitments in its quest to diversify away from its traditional area of operation, the minds of the directors must have been greatly exercised about its ability to sustain world-wide its growing upstream activities as the 1960s drew to a close.

Notes

1 An important scholarly study of oil in India from 1947 until the early 1970s is R. Vedavalli, *Private Foreign Investment and Economic Development*, 1976. B. Dasgupta, *The Oil Industry in India: Some Economic Aspects*, 1971, despite its errors of fact and interpretation, can also be usefully consulted. The house magazine of Assam Oil, *Digboi Batori* (Vol. I 1953 onwards), is a primary source of information.
2 Patwardhan, *Oil and Other Multinationals*, (see Chapter I, footnote 8), p. 89. The whole of Chapter 13, 'The Human Side of the Enterprise' is highly recommended.
3 Vedavalli, *Private Foreign Investment*, p. 33.
4 For second five-year plan, see B. N. Pandey, *Nehru*, 1976, pp. 358–60 and M. Edwardes, *Nehru, A Political Biography*, 1971, pp. 261–4.

5 For relations between the World Bank and India (and Pakistan), see the authoritative work E. S. Mason and R. E. Asher (eds) *The World Bank Since Bretton Woods* Washington, DC, 1971, esp. pp. 372–3, 665–6, 675–83.

6 N. Maxwell, *India's China War*, 1970. Galbraith's remark is on p. 410 and the Tezpur episode on p. 412. For Pakistan, see ibid., pp. 665–75.

7 Pandey, *Nehru*, p. 427; Edwardes, *Nehru*, p. 305.

8 'The March of Sui Gas', *BGM* No. 5, Spring 1966, pp. 11–17.

9 For Snodgrass see *BGM* No. 15, Autumn 1958, p. 19.

10 *Forward* (Journal of Pakistan Petroleum, Karachi), Vol. 2 No. 3, March 1954, p. 8. This magazine, started at the beginning of 1953 and renamed *Progress* in August 1956, has been extensively used here.

11 A. Tengove, *Discovery: Stories of Modern Mineral Exploration*, North Blackburn, NSW, Australia, 1979, pp. 165–96. J. D. Dewhurst, 'Exploration on the Continental Shelf of North-West Australia', *Petroleum Review*, January 1973, pp. 14–22. Background information is given in J. Turner, 'The Oil Industry in Australia', *Petroleum Review*, January 1969, pp. 1–8. See also *BGM* No. 7, Autumn 1966, pp. 18–19 and No. 11, Autumn 1967, pp. 2–7.

CHAPTER XII

The Sleeper Awakes
1964–66

The take-over bid by BP and Shell in June 1963 had been a brief
but traumatic episode: the more so because the main instigator
had been not some American raider but Burmah Oil's own
offspring, on whose board the company had two representatives, and with which it actually shared Britannic House.
Although the Burmah Oil directors had seen off the would-be
predators, the problem remained of how to live with BP. Shell
was thought to have been no more than BP's reluctant
accomplice, so that relations with Burmah-Shell in India and
Pakistan were scarcely affected.

Towards the end of July Nicholas Williams, Burmah Oil's
legal adviser who had lately been promoted to one of the
company's principal line management posts, that of regional
co-ordinator of the Indian subcontinent, produced several
memoranda for Jack Strain, the finance director. Referring to
the recent letter to stockholders, which had included a firm
statement of policy and forecast future profit and dividend
levels, he was anxious to explore 'certain matters which are in
the public eye and on which the [stock] market will expect to
see something concrete done in the next few months'.

Externally, the overriding question was that of corporate
relations with BP. Since these had in the past depended so
heavily on the personalities of those involved, possible alternative ways of tackling this question had been obscured. Meanwhile, two internal topics needed urgent consideration: the
reorganisation of the Burmah group along more efficient lines,

and 'the building up of a Burmah image in the US as an operating oil company'. On the former, he observed how little had been done to absorb Lobitos into the group; indeed, the top managers in that company had ever since the acquisition not seen much of their colleagues in Britannic House, and Williams now highlighted the consequent wasteful duplication of managerial and financial control. In Lobitos and its subsidiaries, considerable opportunities existed for reducing the number of independently operating companies and placing them within divisions of one or more UK trading companies.

As to the company's public image, that was virtually non-existent. 'It has been a matter of comment that what Burmah does is not known to the public in the UK.' Such ignorance was partly due to its occupying the same building as BP. To be sure, that would shortly have to change as BP was planning to move to new premises, perhaps as soon as 1965.

> The acquisition of a Burmah House [he added] would go some way in building up a Burmah image, but a certain limited amount of prestige advertising and a carefully conducted PR campaign might well pay dividends: it seems a pity not to capitalise on present favourable press inclinations.

This 38-year-old man, recently appointed a director of Assam Oil and clearly one of the rising stars in the Burmah Oil hierarchy, was not afraid to touch on one or two of the company's tender spots. The forecasts in the letter to stockholders had indeed made a take-over attempt that much more difficult, but by the same token it implied more specific commitments than before. These commitments at the same time presented opportunities. 'It is doubtful whether any major company in any industry has built [its] position up without any direct operating position in its home market.' Traditionally, the only contribution of Burmah Oil to Britain's oil needs had been that of wax, and of late that had become no more than a minority interest in Candles Ltd (Volume I, pp. 287–8). Yet the acquisition of Lobitos and of its refining capacity had given it a 'foothold' in Britain: namely the chance of 'setting up the nucleus of an integrated industry based on an enlarged refinery at Ellesmere Port'. The crude oil supply was regarded as a secure one, available from BP. The Lobitos management had the expertise to suggest ways of building up operations in Britain, and should be set to work – together with a nominee from head office – to plan for increasing the group's UK profit by, say, £500,000 a year. As vital as the financial aspect was the question of management development. 'With no recruitment for the East or for South America, where are we to get the new generation of managers if we have no UK operations?'

The problem of how to live with BP could be dealt with in tandem with these internal reforms. He started from the premise that 'a greater pulling together of BP and Burmah is desirable in the interests of the stockholders of both companies'. Now that the route of a take-over by BP had been tried and failed, the only practicable alternative was for Burmah Oil to use its levers of control, namely the two directors' votes on the BP board and the shareholding, now 23 per cent. It could, for instance, acquire shares in BP held by the outside public, in exchange for its own stock. That had the immediate attractions that the relative prices of both sets of shares were currently 'about right' (the price of Burmah Oil's £1 ordinary stock at the end of July being the equivalent of £3.15p and BP's of £2.93p) and that the BP shareholder would thereby acquire an interest in countries where BP could not participate by reason of its government holding.

Burmah Oil should therefore establish effective voting control over BP, so as to force it into accepting an agreement that could determine once and for all the two companies' respective spheres of influence. Such a demarcation of geographical areas would doubtless allow Burmah Oil to concentrate its efforts on India and Pakistan, South America, the United States and Canada, while leaving the rest of the world to BP. Burmah Oil already had an effective presence in the first two countries and in Peru and Ecuador, and had made a promising start in Canada, where integration of its various interests was under way. However, 'in the USA there is still a long way to go.'

To achieve a real breakthrough in the United States, Williams claimed, the company must recognise two overriding needs: to seek out as a take-over target an integrated oil corporation, fully involved in downstream activities as well as in prospecting and production, and to be prepared to expend considerable sums. How far would any initiative be affected by the American anti-trust laws? Good legal advice in the US was essential there; if it turned out that the company were limited to 'a single bite of the cherry', then the acquisition of a larger shareholding in BP seemed a logical first step to build up the company's standing. Should more than one bite be permitted, then perhaps a smaller US concern could be bought initially for, say, $40–50 million (£14–18 million), in which case the BP share purchase and a major American acquisition could be left until later.

Yet sooner or later, he continued, the company's possession of 50 per cent of those BP shares not held by the government was desirable. Once that was achieved, relations with BP would change radically. Burmah Oil could then set up a holding company, 'possibly renamed the British Oil Company or some such', which would hold the BP shares and the whole of 'a new operating Burmah Oil Company, for which we could use the overseas company and/or Lobitos, renamed'. Clearly, agreement with the British Treasury, owning 51.3 per cent of the ordinary BP shareholding, would be required; although he did not discuss this, he appears to have assumed that there would be no difficulty on this score. By November 1963, when Williams redrafted his note, he admitted that 'with present personalities involved' – undoubtedly the implacable Bridgeman as chairman and Eric Drake, an accountant powerfully committed to his company's interests, as deputy chairman – the BP people would accept a holding company only on terms that would effectively ensure that they themselves controlled it. Some alternative means of exerting pressure on them must therefore be found.

Williams' alternative suggestion was a move that would provide the means of exerting pressure through a worthwhile US acquisition: he recommended the Atlantic Refining Company. That was a suitably integrated corporation, with good oil and gas reserves, of which 60 per cent was in North America and 30 per cent in Venezuela. It also had extensive refining and marketing facilities. As Chapter VII showed, Burmah Oil had in 1958–9 negotiated with Atlantic over possible production interests in Venezuela, but the talks had foundered. Now his proposal was to seek a controlling, say 60 per cent, interest in Atlantic.

That company's post-tax earnings, as a percentage of market valuation, were 9.4 per cent, compared with BP's 9.8 per cent and Shell's 8.2 per cent. Since its ordinary stock valuation was $487 million (£171 million), Burmah Oil would have to expend about £103 million to obtain 60 per cent. The combine would then have a net market value of some £400 million; its large interests in the US would make it both far more difficult to take over and 'immeasurably stronger in dealing with BP', the net market value of which was about £765 million.

According to Williams, a further advantage of buying into Atlantic would be to acquire badly needed and up-to-date technical and marketing expertise from the western hemisphere, including knowledge of the new growth area of petroleum-based chemicals and plastics. It could then offer such knowledge back to BP, which was also becoming interested in that area. As he put it,

> Indeed, if [Atlantic] were acquired, the lapse of time [since the 1963 take-over bid] plus the greatly increased size of the Burmah operation might go a long way towards making the solution of the BP problem possible without any direct action by Burmah.

On the other hand, should Burmah Oil feel it advisable to provide a nudge by positive action, it could acquire enough shares to give it an absolute majority of non-government held BP shares: the extra one per cent required would give Burmah Oil 25.4 per cent of voting shares as against outsiders' 23.3 per cent and would cost about £8.5 million.

These proposals, in the aftermath of the BP-Shell bid of 1963, have been summarised at length for two reasons. Williams himself was in a few years' time to be given even greater responsibility within the company, and his thoughts at this time therefore have an importance of their own. Second, he neatly pinpointed Burmah Oil's opportunities and dilemmas at that time. The comments of Eadie as chairman or Smith as managing director would have been instructive, especially as Eadie regarded it as totally unthinkable for the company ever to use its voting power for coercive purposes at BP board meetings. However, Drysdale, whose brain was no less probing that that of Williams, did write a memorandum in February

1964 on 'Group Policy and Burmah Oil/BP Relations', which partly drew on these earlier notes but is very much stamped with his own original thought.

This memorandum revealed that the company – probably in the person of Williams – had made a preliminary study of a number of major integrated US corporations. Two turned out to be the most 'promising and well suited', namely Atlantic and, by a curious coincidence in the light of later events, the Richfield Oil Corporation. The company had officially sounded out Atlantic, which was prepared to consider a possible amalgamation of interests, although it would have preferred a complete merger in a joint holding company rather than the acquisition by Burmah Oil of a controlling interest. Illustrating his arguments with some figures, Drysdale felt that once a Burmah Oil-Atlantic merger had been achieved, 'the BP board would find integration in a joint company impossible to resist, and . . . in that integration the influence of Burmah would be greatly enhanced by the prior merger with [Atlantic].' Great Plains' chairman, Lewis MacNaughton, the Dallas consultant who had helped to assemble data for the letter to stockholders, fully shared that view.

By August 1964, when Drysdale composed his next memorandum, a British general election was that much closer, having been announced well in advance for the coming October, and Labour was a good eight points ahead of the ruling Conservative party in the public opinion polls. The almost inevitable return to power of Labour, pledged to resolute action against mergers of all kinds, would put paid to the kind of link-up that had seemed so enticing to Burmah Oil's senior management only a few months earlier. BP's executive remained unwilling to pursue discussions aimed at restoring good relations. A further difficulty, which had become more pressing in recent months, arose from Burmah Oil's undertaking to pass on to shareholders the BP and Shell dividends in full, and the need to top up those dividends with a large part of its own trading profits.

The results for 1963, announced in April, had shown that trading income after tax was up slightly from £5.9 million in 1962 to £6.3 million; not a large enough improvement to ensure meeting the £8 million target by 1966 indicated in the letter to stockholders. True, there had been a loss by Assam Oil caused by the high price of crude demanded by Oil India Ltd. At the same time, total net profit had declined from £13.1 million to £12.6 million. The company was therefore effectively prevented from being able to finance from retained earnings the scale of exploration needed to break out of undue dependence on India, Pakistan and Peru. That August Drysdale again urged an amalgamation with Atlantic, which could be carried out by an exchange of shares. There could be a Shell-type arrangement which Williams had favoured, whereby Burmah Oil would have a 60 per cent holding to Atlantic's 40 per cent, or else Burmah Oil could agree to acquire the whole equity.

Despite the initial enthusiasm and continuing goodwill of Atlantic's executive, negotiations for a closer relationship proceeded at a depressingly slow pace. Periodic meetings were held in London or New York, but never seemed to get any further. This unpalatable delay meant that relations with BP hung fire, and one wonders what, if any, objective grounds existed for believing that Burmah Oil had any chance of winning BP over into the kind of closer association envisaged by Williams and Drysdale.

In truth, at that period BP was in the doldrums, virtually for the first time since the early 1920s. At the date of the 1963 take-over bid, over 99 per cent of its crude oil deposits were situated in Middle Eastern countries, where host governments were becoming increasingly assertive. Hence this geographical concentration of resources in an unstable part of the world gave rise to a risk factor which tended to make its shares that much less attractive, in relation to its asset values and earnings, than those of rival companies with more diversified reserves. Indeed, since June 1963 Burmah Oil ordinary share values had remained consistently above those of BP, often by as much as four or five shillings (20–25p) per share; towards the end of that year, the differential rose to 30–40p. Only in April 1964 did the gap narrow and BP once again overtake the Burmah Oil share value.

Both companies were finding it difficult to achieve an overall profit improvement large enough to provide for higher dividends, for prospecting, and other development expenditure. From 1958 to 1961, BP's net profit had been static at an average of £62 million, rising to £70 million in 1962 and averaging £82 million in the three years 1963–5. Hence its desire to spread risks – only partly assuaged by some exploration successes in Nigeria and Libya during 1964 – and to investigate new sources of profit. The western hemisphere was an obvious target area. Only just over 10 per cent of its products were sold there, and it had no production or refining facilities. The latter would provide the downstream profitability and the stability it was seeking.

One of BP's senior policy advisers later revealed that his company's determination to establish a presence in the Americas had been sparked off by the Suez crisis of 1956.[1] Until then its directors had regarded the cost of entry in North America as too high, while – as Williams had also pointed out – in Latin American countries the British government's shareholding in BP effectively barred that company from applying for concessions. In Canada Alastair Down was its chief representative; in 1957 he became president of the BP group in Canada, which indicated its intentions to move upstream from marketing to production.

That year BP signed an agreement with the Sinclair Oil Company of New York, short of crude but well endowed with downstream facilities. Sinclair would import BP oil from the Middle East to the US, and joint exploration would take place in the western hemisphere. The former objective received a fatal setback in 1958 when the US administration introduced quotas which drastically reduced imports of crude oil, while the latter languished when the two companies failed to agree about one extremely remote exploration area selected, Sinclair's concession on the North Slope of Alaska. Unlike his opposite number in Sinclair, the chief geologist in BP was convinced that Alaska was one of the few areas in the free world where a good chance existed of finding an oilfield of vast dimensions, such as that in Kuwait.

The proving of the Alaska field had still not been achieved by 1966, and in the meantime turned out to be as arduous and relatively costly an operation as the original efforts in the Persian oilfields had been before 1908. Apart from technology, the main difference was that temperatures were intolerably low rather than ultra-high. In a decade of persistent balance of payments difficulties, the UK exchange control regulations debarred BP from financing American expenditure with funds remitted from Britain; it was fortunate that some small acquisitions, especially in California, provided BP with enough dollar revenue to maintain prospecting on the North Slope. From the viewpoint of the early 1960s, therefore, Burmah Oil's top management had some justification for doubting whether BP would ever achieve a major presence in the western hemisphere. At that moment a really large oil strike in Alaska must have seemed very speculative. Moreover, once Burmah Oil had made a deal with, say, Atlantic, any acquisition by BP in the US – unlikely as it appeared, given that company's financial difficulties – could well encounter anti-trust problems because of Burmah Oil's shareholding stake. Thus there must have seemed a reasonable chance of the two companies concluding an agreement that would cut out BP from any continuing operations in the US.

These debates about the future direction that Burmah Oil might pursue were strictly confined to the top executives and not formally put to the board, and were overtaken by an event necessitating radical reconsideration of the company's future development path. As had been forecast, in October 1964 Harold Wilson's Labour government came into power. The new Chancellor of the Exchequer, James Callaghan, at once announced a new system of taxing companies in Britain, based on the American practice. That was designed not to increase the total volume of corporate taxation but to redistribute the burden; taxes on profits distributed to shareholders would be increased but those on retained earnings would fall. One provision of the new Corporation Tax would have the effect of penalising companies with income from overseas but with little or no offsetting earnings in Britain, since they would lose double taxation relief. Burmah Oil, which fell into that category, claimed to be the British company most adversely affected by the proposals.

Early in December, R. P. Smith as managing director wrote to the Earl of Cromer, Cobbold's successor as governor of the Bank of England, as the Bank was collecting the views of industry about the proposed tax. Since Callaghan did not reveal even the main structure of the tax until a few days later,

Smith could only deal in generalities. However, he did point out the unfairness of singling out companies with substantial overseas interests, which were in any case large earners of foreign exchange. Burmah Oil's share price would fall and the company would find it that much more difficult to raise capital in Britain, so that it would become a more attractive subject for a take-over by a US or other foreign country. It was, moreover, effectively an investment company, passing on to shareholders the dividends received from its principal investments, and should not therefore be penalised by an Act designed to curb dividends.

In January 1965 Smith, now chairman, took up with the Board of Inland Revenue a remark which the Chancellor had made, that where problems arose because overseas taxes could only be credited against Corporation Tax paid in Britain, he would consider introducing transitional arrangements. Smith maintained that a more permanent system of relief was the only remedy. In a letter to Callaghan on the same day, Smith outlined the serious consequences he anticipated for his company, which would no longer be able to hold its own with overseas competitors. Stockholders would suffer because their dividend incomes would fall; an important consideration, as 70 per cent of them currently held £500 or less of the company's stock. The British economy would also suffer, since incentives to invest in the oil industry overseas would be reduced, thus diminishing exports of capital and other equipment for operations abroad. Burmah Oil itself had over the past five years placed orders for no less than £20 million worth of such equipment from British manufacturers. Despite these pleas, however, Smith was given the stock reply that his views would be considered when the legislation was being drawn up. In fact, the measure went through, but companies such as Burmah Oil were granted 'overspill relief', on a declining scale, for a period of five years. That was to total £1 million for 1966/7, but its limited duration caused the directors much dissatisfaction.

So far from being able to implement major schemes for an American link-up, calculated at the same time to overcome the BP share problem, the Burmah Oil executive found itself saddled with the urgent task of finding income in Britain, on a big enough scale to offset the new tax burden. Williams had already suggested one route: to restructure operations at the two refineries at Ellesmere Port and at Barton, involving a major expansion of the former. Although, as suggested in Chapter IX, their highly specialised range of products was of considerable value for industrial purposes, both refineries lacked sufficient marketing facilities to dispose of their entire production directly; hence they had to sell substantial quantities of products to competitors, so that potential profits were being foregone. To the extent that UK profits might be increased by taking over one or more of the company's smaller rivals, the Burmah Oil board did consider later in 1964 making one possible acquisition; yet the business concerned was really too insignificant and the proposal was dropped. Of other medium-sized companies of the type being sought, Williams was known to be on the trail of one in particular. In fact, more than a year was to pass before the quarry was tracked down.

The new year of 1965 brought a change at the top of the company. Eadie retired from the chairmanship and was succeeded by the 61-year-old R. P. Smith. As explained in Chapter VII, Smith was a Burmah Oil man by adoption rather than birth, having originally been recruited to Burmah-Shell through the Shell side. Although coming from the same background, that of a Scottish-born accountant, he was subtly different from his predecessor. Eadie, who married late, had an ailing wife but no children, and felt most at home in the impersonal ambiance of company bungalows and golfing hotels. Largely free of family commitments, he had ample time to think in depth about company matters and to know his own mind. R.P., on the other hand, was very much a family man, with two daughters, and perhaps in consequence more amenable to argument and persuasion.

The *Financial Times* once well encapsulated the two sides of Smith's life: it portrayed him as talking of pipelines and prospects in much the same reflective way as he spoke of how his roses were getting along. He was an enthusiastic fisherman as well as a keen gardener. Although by nature a conservative man, he was concerned to keep up the momentum of growth.

Negotiations with Altantic were still proceeding in their lethargic way. In mid-1965 that company's president, H. Supplee, and its finance director met Drysdale and his senior financial manager, Robert Elliott, in London. The four men agreed to continue discussions in New York that autumn: when the meeting did take place, in November, Supplee had to tell Drysdale that he had been approached by the Richfield Oil Corporation. A merger duly took place in January 1966. The Atlantic Richfield combine had a stock market valuation not much short of Burmah Oil's, so that any prospect of merging on the basis of a straight exchange of shares was out of the question. The fundamental dilemma over Burmah Oil was that although its holdings in BP and Shell contributed massively to its asset values, its income, net of dividends from these holdings, was only the equivalent of $40 million compared with Atlantic Richfield's $68 million.

Both sides' representatives therefore considered inviting BP into the combine, but then decided against such a move. The Labour government in Britain had brought in its promised Monopolies and Mergers Act of 1965 to curb merger activity, and in any case the Treasury, much as in the early 1920s, would be very reluctant to see BP's freedom of manoeuvre hampered inside a partly foreign-owned corporation. Without BP as a partner to boost relative income proportions, progress on amalgamation was ruled out, although both parties undertook to keep in touch with each other. These major talks were in addition to proposals, discussed several times that year by the Burmah Oil board, to enlarge existing operations in the US, especially those offshore Louisiana, and to make them financially self-supporting.

In 1965–6 the board decided to reduce its portfolio investments by selling for $4.3 million the stock it held in Standard Oil of New Jersey. The nucleus of that stockholding had been acquired by R. I. Watson in the early 1930s, as part of his policy of establishing links with other oil companies by agreements and shareholdings. The company had steadily built up that stock over the years, but given its current expansionist policy in the US, the sale would release dollar funds for operational use. In November 1965 Drysdale made an offer to purchase a 60 per cent stake in Southdown Inc of Louisiana, which had significant royalty interests in oil and gas onshore, but no direct exploration or production of its own. Drysdale's intention, achieved early in 1967, was to merge all the company's interests in the offshore areas of the Gulf of Mexico – hitherto held by the Burmah Oil Western Company and its exploration affiliate – into the Southdown Burmah Oil Company. That combine was expected to be able to generate enough dollar income to pay for both prospecting and the expansion of output. Although in 1966 only 9 per cent of the group's trading income was earned in North America, compared with 64 per cent in Asia and 13 per cent in Britain and Europe, here was plainly a significant growth area. Drysdale's further objective was to merge Burmah Oil's Canadian interests with those in the United States to form a single North American company, thereby securing the maximum advantages of efficiency and of easing the tax burden. It would also provide a corporate framework within which any future acquisitions, large or small, could be conveniently fitted. Burmah Oil Incorporated was established early in 1968.

These successive steps to build up and rationalise the group's activities in the western hemisphere clearly needed to be parallelled by measures aimed at overhauling its structure at home. As shown earlier in the present chapter, Williams in 1963 had pointed to the gains in efficiency and economy that would spring from such an overhaul. The Lobitos board had already proposed its own reorganisation, through rationalising the structure of its marketing subsidiaries within the Lobitos and Manchester Oil Refinery companies. However, it deferred any action on learning that Burmah Oil had set up a small committee to consider the feasibility and possible mechanics of merging all its British trading activities into one company. All manner of technical problems had to be looked at, such as how to merge or liquidate the preference shares and debentures as well as the pension funds of acquired companies and ensure the continuity of agreements and contracts. However, the committee found that all these problems were perfectly capable of being resolved.

In September 1965 the committee submitted to the board a memorandum on 'Corporate Reorganisation in the UK'. That proposed establishing a single company to take responsibility for all Burmah Oil's trading in Britain and also carry out all the head office functions, which ranged from accounting and technical services to staff matters. The main advantage was to create a far simpler corporate structure for tax purposes, so that head office expenses could as far as possible be offset against trading income. Moreover, the considerable amount of overlapping and consequent unnecessary paperwork could be eliminated. The unit chosen to become the new trading company was Lobitos Oilfields Ltd, which would be appropriately renamed.

The board agreed to a new operating company being set up, within which functional divisions would be created; it rejected as artificial the notion of conducting business through dormant agency companies. A committee of directors, headed by R. P. Smith and including Strain, Drysdale and Williams was set up to oversee all the multifarious routine measures, including 'deeds, agreements, transfers, letters, consents, declarations, indemnities, guarantees and the like'. On 1 January 1966 all the trading companies involved were merged into Lobitos Oilfields which on 1 March changed its name to Burmah Oil Trading Ltd, familiarly known from its initials as 'Bottle'. The committee agreed that there should be four divisions: the Group Management and Services Division; Lobitos Division, for refining and marketing the lubricants and other oil products; Dussek Division, for blending and marketing a variety of products such as cable saturants and waxes; and Flexibox Manufacturing Division to produce the mechanical seals and associated lapping machines mentioned in Chapter IX. Not until 1969 was the group fully organised along functional lines, with three divisions to deal with oil, industrial products and engineering respectively.

Other candidates for reorganisation were the often well-scattered premises occupied by the group's various units. Looking first at the head office, its accommodation on the first floor of Britannic House had been strained to the limit as early as 1950 and additional office space was rented in Salisbury House, across the way in Finsbury Circus. In November 1963, after Lobitos and its subsidiaries joined the group, the directors searched for larger premises. A number of buildings were considered; early in 1965, when BP was constructing its new head office in nearby Moor Place, Burmah Oil sought to obtain the tenancy of the whole of Britannic House. Instead,

BP decided to sell the building and Burmah Oil, advised by Knight Frank & Rutley, bid some £2 million which was regarded as a fair price at that time. However, much higher bids were received and the company had to look elsewhere.

A new air-conditioned office block in Victoria Street was turned down as the directors felt it essential to stay in the City. Instead, in early 1966, the company purchased Academy House, a seven-floor office building erected on the site of a former warehouse in Chiswell Street, close to Whitbread's brewery.[2] This building was converted internally for company use under the supervision of Burmah Oil staff. The administrative director mainly responsible was the former chief geologist, H. R. Tainsh, who had joined the board in 1963. Part of the block was to be occupied by Whinney Murray & Co, the company's accountants who in 1965 had taken over its original auditors – and those of BP – Brown Fleming & Murray. In July 1967 the first board meeting was held in what had been renamed Burmah House. Thus one tangible aspect of Williams' desire to see the group present a more positive and definite image of itself had been fulfilled. The other aspect, of expanding the company's public relations on a scale commensurate with the activities of rival companies and of establishing appropriate relationships with government, was not implemented at this time. That omission was in various ways to work to the company's disadvantage during the final years of the decade.

For Burmah Oil, one of the drawbacks of being a substantial ordinary shareholder in BP was the risk that it might at any time be called upon to find the money for a rights issue. To be sure, the need had not actually arisen since the early 1920s. BP had succeeded in financing its considerable growth either from internal funds or by alternative means such as debentures. Yet in the mid-1960s, especially after the return of a Labour government, Britain found itself in a period of economic stringency and Burmah Oil might at any time be asked to stump up money it could ill afford, or accept a decline in its share of BP's ordinary stock. In 1957–8 (see Chapter VII) the company had been caused much anxiety by BP's plan to make a rights issue which would have involved Burmah Oil in a £13 million cash outlay. Mercifully, BP had changed its mind and gone for a debenture issue instead; all the same, it had been a nasty scare.

Towards the end of 1965 BP proposed a rights issue, and Burmah Oil's share of its cost would amount to £14.8 million. Late in December Smith went to see Sir William Armstrong, Permanent Secretary of the Treasury, to explain the dilemma the company faced. If it decided to pass on its right to stockholders, it could well incur capital gains tax, which had not existed in 1958. However, taking up the rights would not merely compound its problem of having an already high dividend income but also involve recourse to the market for funds, which might prove difficult as well as expensive at that stage. Armstrong could only offer to put him in touch with the Inland Revenue experts, but he did point out that the government was on a knife-edge with a very slim parliamentary majority, which could force Harold Wilson to go to the country at any time. In those conditions, Armstrong made no secret of the fact that BP hoped to push through the rights issue before an election was called. Whereas a re-elected Labour government would undoubtedly take up its share rights so as to retain its majority holding in BP, a Conservative government might well refuse to subscribe, in which case BP would probably have to settle for a more modest debenture issue, as had happened in 1958.

Smith, convinced that Burmah Oil's interests would be best served by passing on the BP rights to its own shareholders, sought counsel's opinion as to whether that step would raise any legal problems. One QC spoke for the majority of the experts consulted when he declared that it was 'not on'. The ever resourceful Williams, while not criticising the QC's view, pressed Smith to make the rights issue proposals an 'excuse to get talks started with BP'. Smith, still very bitter after the 1963 take-over bid, had nothing he wished to say to BP at that juncture. Instead, he put the various options to the board, which decided that the company should itself take up the rights if they could be satisfactorily financed. In the end Burmah Oil chose to make a £15 million rights issue of its own of $7\frac{1}{4}$ per cent preference shares, which was duly floated in March 1966 and turned out to be handsomely over-subscribed. Smith was encouraged by the fact that of the 17,500 applicants, no fewer than 16,000 were from stockholders applying for 1,000 shares or less.

While some of Burmah Oil's jitters over the BP rights issue were due to its unwillingness to become even more of an investment company than it already was, it was also unhappy about the problem of how to increase profits. That problem was faced squarely by Jack Strain, in some 'thoughts' he composed in January 1966 on 'The Present Burmah Group Financial Position'. He reminded his executive colleagues of what they appeared to have overlooked of late: the forecasts and pledges contained in the letter to stockholders of July 1963. In particular, net trading profit for 1965 would be well down on the 1963 forecast: between £5 million and £5.5 million, and certainly nowhere near the £7.3 million target if £8 million were to be achieved in 1966.

To be sure, the reasons for these disappointing results were clear enough. Assam Oil, caught in a situation in which it could not adequately recoup, from its product marketing, the high price it was forced to pay for Indian crude oil, had yet again incurred substantial losses: in 1965, as large as £500,000. The outlay on exploration was currently reducing net trading profit by about £1 million a year. Whereas the 1963 letter had assumed that prospecting would be confined to Louisiana, it had since been started up in Australia and in Britain's North Sea; the last-named operations will be described later in this chapter. Moreover, just at a time when the Corporation Tax provisions made the earning of UK income essential, income from the Lobitos trading subsidiaries at home was falling, due mainly to an economic squeeze imposed by the new government.

Strain was also concerned about the dividends being paid out to stockholders. Before the 1963 bid, these had comprised the BP and Shell dividends in full but only a relatively small sum from trading income. In 1963 and 1964, on the other hand, no less than £4.5 million was paid out each year as dividend, leaving no surplus for reserves. All the company's investment income and 75 per cent of its trading income was thus being distributed. Even so, stockholders could claim with some justice that they would have received considerably more income if the company had accepted the 1963 bid. To put matters right, therefore, the group needed to be reorganised, by amalgamation or otherwise, and then retain more profits.

Only three alternatives were open to the company. The first was an approach to BP; however, Burmah Oil was currently in a much weaker bargaining position than in 1963. The BP top management was 'not sympathetic' and was, like Burmah Oil, anxious to increase its own UK income. The new Labour government, shortly to be re-elected in March 1966 with a large majority, had declared that it intended to maintain its majority interest in BP. Strain thus concluded that 'we have little to offer at this moment'. The second alternative was to hope for 'an early bonanza from our prospecting fields'. Strain had always been sceptical about putting money into overseas prospecting, because such money seldom yielded a quick return. His scepticism was reinforced by the Corporation Tax provisions because most returns on exploration represented overseas income and there-fore a tax disadvantage. The North Sea was probably the best short-term bet, especially if gas were discovered. His third alternative was 'buying income', and that should be done quickly.

Strain had three warnings there. First, the company could not expect in future to earn in any country the handsome margins obtained in India and Burma before the war. Second, as quoted at the end of Chapter X, the company must also buy management, which in the harsher world of 1966 was an entirely different matter from managing the old style Burmah Oil with its Eastern trading. His final warning was that in the meantime, long-term investment and prospecting expenditure must be restricted as much as possible. 'Although we have built up a very sizeable trading organisation since the war, we are now for the first time short of funds and we are very vulnerable.'

In August 1966 he reiterated his earlier point that the company's financial constraints made it absolutely essential to be 'more conservative' in future over long-term investment. Expansion must be by acquisitions and mergers, involving share exchanges, in order to build up trading operations and hence the vitally needed cash flow and retained profits.

As it happened, by the summer of 1966 a British candidate for acquisition was emerging that would at once gladden the hearts of the expansionists and soothe the fears of the more cautious board members. As a bonus, it was in the preferred field of blending and marketing high-quality lubricants. 'A certain project', as it was cryptically termed in the June board minutes, was to be investigated by a panel of directors. On 7 July their favourable conclusions were put to the full board, which authorised Smith to approach the company concerned. Five days later he and Richard Fleming met Leslie Farrow at the offices of Fleming's bank. Farrow was a highly esteemed chartered accountant; in his late seventies, he had recently decided to ease up, paring down his multifarious business commitments to no more than 63 directorships and 28 chairmanships. Of the companies that he chaired, the one being targeted by Burmah Oil was Castrol Ltd.[3]

There was no other oil company quite like Castrol. Relying heavily on its own expertise in the fields of lubricants and speciality oils, it chose to purchase its feedstocks from others and blend them in accordance with its established formulae. The largest independent lubricating oil company in the world, it had its own distribution facilities in practically all non-communist countries. It sold its products even behind the Iron Curtain through a variety of agency arrangements. Castrol was the great survivor among the scores of specialist concerns, most of which had been gobbled up by the oil giants in the preceeding fifty years or so. It could no longer boast, as it had been able to do in 1939, that more than half the cars and motor cycles in Britain used Castrol, with overseas sales the largest in the British empire. Yet despite very severe competition, largely by the oil giants, it still held more than 30 per cent of the British market for motor oil; in 1966 over 50 per cent of its total sales were made overseas.

Established in 1899, the firm owed its success very largely to the founder Charles Cheers (later Lord) Wakefield, who had begun by supplying lubricants to the railway companies. Early in the new century he had foreseen the dramatic commercial possibilities of the internal combustion engine. Having evolved his Wakefield motor lubricating oil, he named it Castrol, from the castor oil base then used in blends for racing cars. So much did the castor oil smell become part of racing drivers' consciousness that, as formulations later changed, an odoriferous additive was specially introduced in some racing grades largely for the sake of nostalgia. He was a textbook type of entrepreneur, not willing to stray outside his speciality and promoting high growth by lavishly ploughing back profits into the firm.

Following Wakefield's death in 1941, the equally astute chairmanship of Farrow had fostered Castrol's interests in the two functions which really mattered to it. One was research and technical development. In 1935 it had been the first oil firm anywhere in the world to blend specially formulated chemical additives into motor oils; these were oleates of tin and chromium, designed to ward off oxidation and corrosion. It had striven ever since to keep ahead of rivals in research into the temperamental habits of the often ill-used motor-vehicle engines, and in the many types of marine and aircraft engines. Among the many 'firsts' it had claimed since the war was the introduction in 1953 of the first normally priced multi-grade oil, Castrolite, to be joined seven years later by a new synthetic jet aircraft lubricant, Castrol 98, which incidentally broke into a world monopoly until then held by an American-owned company. Many of its lubricants were formulated for agricultural or for industrial use, including shipping of all kinds, electricity generation and nuclear reactors. It was also the leading supplier of insulating oils and cutting and metal-working oils in Britain.

Marketing, of both the consumer and the industrial varieties, was the second main function. Extensive advertising was backed up by the dedicated efforts of a highly efficient sales force at home and overseas. A top manager once facetiously described Castrol as a company of 'barrow boys': like those itinerant traders, it had no production or refining overheads, apart from research facilities. It took its base oils from others and seemingly dressed them up for sale on its 'barrow'. This was, however, a considerable over-simplification, since the process of 'dressing up' took Castrol increasingly into the realms of high technology that consolidated the forward-looking reputation the company had so long enjoyed. There was, therefore, much from Castrol that the Burmah Oil people would need to learn if they were to be successful in pursuing their new diversified role. In the East Burmah Oil's refined products had more or less sold themselves, and besides, it had left the actual marketing chores to local – in Burma usually Chinese – agents, so that the British office staff were somewhat removed from the hurly-burly of the bazaar. Jack Strain had, as noted above, reminded his colleagues of the more up-to-date – especially market-orientated – styles of management needed in the new competitive world of the West.

Castrol would also bring into the Burmah group some diversified subsidiaries. Edwin Cooper & Co formulated chemical additives and marketed, sometimes to competitors, such of its output as was surplus to Castrol's own needs. Expandite Ltd produced and marketed materials for the building industry, such as joint fillers and sealants, mastics and sealing compounds; many fitted in well with Dussek's range of products. Melwood Thermoplastics (later Castrol Plastics Ltd), which concentrated on PVC materials, had expertise that seemed of potential value. The Atlas Preservative Company specialised in protective processes and coatings for rust prevention and removing corrosion from metals. Founded by Thomas Thatcher, it had been sold by his son Denis to Castrol as recently as 1965.[4] Denis Thatcher was in 1967 appointed a director of Castrol and later planning and control director of Burmah Oil Trading Limited; his wife Margaret was an MP and a former Conservative junior minister. Currently the second opposition spokesman on Treasury affairs, in 1967 she joined Edward Heath's shadow cabinet with responsibility for Energy.

Castrol, then, provided the opportunity for a new injection of commercially-minded talent into the rather establishment hierarchy of Burmah Oil. The joint managing directors of Castrol, Angus Barr and Arnold Watson, had both come up through its publicity department. Overall, the direction of the firm was imaginative, with the maximum possible delegation of authority. Managers overseas were given considerable freedom within broad guidelines, remarkably reminiscent of Burmah Oil's former managing agencies.

The head office, Castrol House, was an elegant edifice of green glass and steel, incorporating a fifteen-storey tower block. It was happily described as a 'cool and astringent flash in the brick and concrete waste of Marylebone Road' in London's

West End. It contrasted piquantly with the somewhat oppressive grandeur of Lutyens' Britannic House. When the BBC was planning a television drama series, 'The Troubleshooters', about the goings-on in a fictitious oil company named Mogul, Castrol House provided an appropriately modern backdrop.[5]

Some still vividly recall an early illustration of the wide gulf in thinking between the two companies. Castrol, organised along modern sales-orientated lines, provided company cars for its senior staff and maintained its own garage for servicing these vehicles. In Burmah Oil, Watsonian traditions of parsimony were so deeply embedded that, when four of its directors visited Castrol House together for the first time, they all travelled in one London cab, much to the astonishment of the Castrol people waiting to meet them. It was thereafter decided that R. P. Smith should have a company car and chauffeur. Idiosyncratically, out of all possible vehicles he selected a taxi: a sensible decision given the parking difficulties in the city of London, but one with drawbacks. When of an evening R.P. was dropped at London Bridge station to catch his train for Sussex, the driver had to move quickly to prevent would-be fares from hopping in as R.P. alighted.

Despite this, the characteristics of Burmah Oil and Castrol were in many ways so complementary that the matrimonial metaphors rolled effortlessly off the keyboards of the commentators' typewriters. Burmah Oil enjoyed a presence in all phases of oil activity from exploration to refining, but had virtually no retail marketing interests in Britain. Castrol, on the other hand, possessed no upstream facilities. Overseas, Castrol was 'big in Europe', where Burmah Oil was very small, and in Australia it outpaced its prospective parent. Burmah Oil, on the other hand, had by far the larger interests in the East.

Echoing sentiments already expressed to him by Williams, R. P. Smith euphorically declared to Farrow, on their initial meeting, that a merger with Castrol could be one of the corner-stones in the creation of a third major company, after Shell and BP, in the British oil and petrochemicals fields. He made it clear that, if a merger did take place, Burmah Oil would be unable to provide any management resources for Castrol, so that Castrol must be encouraged to carry on as an independent unit and act as a nucleus of marketing interests for

Burmah Oil in Britain. Farrow in turn disclosed that Castrol's relations with certain major oil companies had for some time been far from easy.

Sales of lubricating oil in Britain, he explained, were really at the mercy of Shell and Esso – which also happened to be substantial suppliers of lubricating oil base stocks – and those giants could put Castrol out of business at any time by an all-out price war. Why, then, did they not do so? 'Because Shell and Esso did not like each other', but that mutual antipathy could always change. The oil majors had also sought to harm Castrol by banning its brands from their tied filling stations. Castrol had complained to the Board of Trade, and a subsequent report on petrol distribution by the Monopolies Commission had upheld these complaints.

BP was another important rival, and Farrow was apprehensive that in any quarrel between BP and Castrol, Burmah Oil would automatically side with BP. Smith unequivocally replied that Burmah Oil was a totally independent company. In the event of a merger, 'we shall actively look after the interests of Castrol, even if it meant that our relations with BP suffered.' (These relations were already at a low ebb, but there was no point in dwelling on them at that juncture.) Once Smith and Farrow had broken the ice, further meetings of the top managements produced agreement that the scheme would yield considerable mutual advantages through vertical integration and marketing economies.

The relative sizes of the two companies were agreeably appropriate, Burmah Oil's issued capital and reserves totalling £157 million as against Castrol's £26 million. The amalgamation scheme was made public late in October: oddly enough, it was not formally put to the Burmah Oil board until early November. The deal involved an exchange of shares, three Burmah Oil ordinary £1 shares plus £10 of $7\frac{1}{2}$ per cent loan stock being given for every six ordinary 10s (50p) shares in Castrol. Although the merger would further reduce the number of sizeable independent lubricating oil firms in Britain to a handful, the Board of Trade decided not to refer it to the Monopolies Commission. From the Burmah Oil side, Smith declared publicly that Castrol would continue to run its own business, which it was doing well, with 1965 trading profits before tax of £5 million compared with Burmah Oil's £5.9 million – slightly higher than Strain's earlier forecast.

Press comment on the merger was on the whole guardedly approving. Some city editors spotted that the holdings in Shell, which Burmah Oil had in 1963 indicated would be sold to finance acquisitions, had not been used in this instance and were therefore being kept in reserve for a future bid. Yet the correspondents still found it hard to know what to make of Burmah Oil. It seemed too much a prisoner of its past, with continuing heavy commitments in India and Pakistan and the legacy of the BP shares, which were in various ways a burden, neither generating funds for growth nor being readily marketable.

On the morrow of the Castrol announcement, the *Sunday Times* referred to Burmah Oil as a 'sleeping enigma'.[6] Well, at last the sleeper appeared to be stirring, and observers were anxious to see whether it would remain sufficiently wide-awake to break free from the past and seize the opportunities at home and abroad that were still available in the later 1960s. A warning note was struck by the following week's *Investors' Guardian*.[7] In retrospect, the journal declared, 'it can be said that Castrol represented the only avenue effectively open for Burmah Oil to spread its wings within the UK while still retaining its image as an oil group.'

For the remainder of the decade these two themes, of an old-established company rousing itself like a strong man after sleep, and of its dilemma over the next move it should make because there were no more Castrol-type British enterprises on offer, overhung Burmah Oil's strategy. The purchase of Castrol had indeed helped the company's growth. Net operating assets were up from £177 million in 1965 to just under £220 million in 1966, a rise of nearly 24 per cent, while total net profit increased by 44 per cent, from £16.8 million to £24.2 million. Yet this was still not a large enough or potentially profitable enough acquisition to overcome the problem into which Burmah Oil seemed to have become locked. Above all, UK income needed to be on a scale sufficient to offset its Corporation Tax bill. Behind this more immediate need was a longer-term one. If it were to aspire to the third place in Britain's oil industry, behind

BP and Shell, and become a genuine competitor with the majors, it would need to acquire both a really substantial company at home and an integrated oil corporation in North America.

For a company that was of no more than medium size in operational terms, these twin goals of extra income at home and a large-scale purchase in the US could be achieved only after the most careful planning, if the company were not to find itself overstretched in the process. As part of these aspirations, a great opportunity was provided by Britain's North Sea, although this was also a potentially huge drain on funds. For some years Burmah Oil's geologists had been following with close attention the growing indications that there might be really substantial oil finds off the coast of northern Europe, similar to those off, say, the US and Australia. The discovery in 1959 by a Shell-Esso consortium of large natural gas deposits at Groningen, in north-east Holland, engendered a not unreasonable hope that, if such deposits could be proved to extend into the North Sea shelf between Britain and Europe, the UK and its oil companies stood to be substantial beneficiaries.

It is instructive to recall that few in the oil industry had believed, at the outset of the 1960s, that the discovery of oil or gas off Britain's east coast was even remotely likely, according to existing survey evidence; nor would it have seemed credible that any deposits found could be successfully brought ashore, as neither geological nor production techniques were sufficiently well developed. Even if the prospecting problem could be solved, the perils of operating in the often gale-swept and dangerous waters of the North Sea would have to be faced. A further difficulty was that no legislation existed to regulate any offshore operations of that kind. However, the United Nations conference on the law of the sea had in 1958 drawn up a convention which gave each country having a coastline exploration rights over its contintental shelf out to a depth of 200 metres, or 656 feet. The oil industry at once set up committees to give specialist advice to interested governments about possible legislation, and Burmah Oil played a major role in these committees. The convention was ratified by Britain in 1964.

Meanwhile, certain oil companies – but not Burmah Oil –

had joined together to undertake detailed surveys in the North Sea using the latest techniques. Preliminary findings increased the likelihood that oil and gas deposits would be located there. In February 1963 Murphy Oil, always on the look-out for promising exploration opportunities, suggested to Drysdale that their two companies should together undertake a large programme of geophysical mapping. The Burmah Oil board, while prepared to allocate £116,000 for this purpose, made it clear that all further financial commitments in the North Sea must be specifically authorised in advance. That year the Burmah Oil Exploration Company (BOEC) helped in a mapping programme over an area of 60,000 square miles. The company was kept busy sounding out various possible partners, including the American companies Atlantic, Sun Oil, Superior Oil, and the British chemicals giant ICI.

The consortium which it finally assembled, known as the Burmah North Sea Group (BNSG) was one in which Burmah Oil and ICI each held 40 per cent, with Murphy Oil (including Odeco) holding the other 20 per cent. BOEC was designated as the operator. The British parliament passed the Continental Shelf Act in 1964 and specified that the Ministry of Power (as it was then known) would allocate licences for individual blocks in the North Sea, each of 100 square miles in area. This block system, familiar to the company from its experience in other countries, was considered preferable to sole concessions over far more extensive areas, in speeding up exploration and in preventing any one group from gaining monopolistic advantages. Rather than auctioning off blocks to the highest bidder, they were allotted according to the applicant's experience and record, and the work programmes that each application had to submit.

The BNSG was successful in two applications, being granted five licences covering a total of 34 blocks, 26 in 1964 and a further 8 in 1965. Seismic work was soon started on these blocks. As the company's chief geologist Kenneth V. Stringer wrote, 'To enter upon a limited programme [of exploration] is to indulge in gambling with the odds heavily against success.'[8] For him and his team, therefore, an essential task was the most meticulous assembling of data, assisted by exchanges of information with rival consortia.

For the drilling, a semi-submersible oil barge, of the same pattern as those employed in the US, was built by Smith's Dock Company Ltd of Middlesbrough, not far from the BOEC headquarters: the first ever to be constructed in Britain. Named the *Ocean Prince*, it was owned by Odeco (UK) Ltd, half the capital coming from the US firm Odeco and a quarter each from Burmah Oil and ICI. Most of the crew were British. It had eight 10-ton anchors to secure it on the sea bed before its rig began drilling.[9] A supply ship, the 700-ton *Lady Alison*, described as a 'surface lifeline between the shore and the rig', was built at the same time.[10] Late in January 1966 the company's first North Sea well, in block 42/23, was spudded in 28 miles off Flamborough Head (now in Humberside). Some of the worst storms experienced off north-east England for 40 years held up drilling progress. Then in October an oil strike was made in a second well, in block 48/22 off Cromer; this was the very first crude oil to be discovered in the North Sea.[11]

For a fleeting moment, the company entertained high hopes that history was repeating itself and that it would pioneer North Sea oil no less decisively than it had pioneered Middle East oil in Persia nearly 60 years before. That was not to be, as tests soon showed the yield to be only 400 barrels a day, compared with 10,000–15,000 barrels in the Middle East. Reaction to the news was therefore muted until stronger evidence had emerged about the extent of the find. Then a fall in pressure confirmed that the strike was not commercially viable.

The North Sea represented only one possible route to prosperity, and if it offered the hope of glittering prizes in the long term, it was meanwhile turning out to be painfully expensive, with costs ever on the increase. In 1966, for instance, the company's share of operating cost was put at £888,000, an increase of about £250,000 on the original estimate. Thus in the middle years of the 1960s, Burmah Oil's top executive was badly in need of a properly co-ordinated and costed overall strategy. Indeed, a considerable amount of financial and other information was already channelled into the London office, but it was largely going to waste because it was not fed into a consistent programme. However, two of the company's senior accountants, William R. Gage (who became finance director in 1968) and

Robert Elliott, devised a system of monthly reporting of performance by each unit and five-year forecasts to impose control over budget expenditures. Nicholas Williams had lately shown his capabilities as co-ordinator of Eastern operations, and in July 1965 was appointed executive director in charge of group planning. He soon set up a Corporate Planning and Development function in the London office.

Williams began from the premise that planning – and in particular acquisition policy – had until then been on an *ad hoc* basis, each new opportunity being judged on its individual merits rather than as an intrinsic part of a master plan. That system could well lead to financial problems because the required volume of cash would not necessarily be self-generating, and to management problems because the extra demands on top executive time might not become fully apparent until it was too late to reverse any decision.

As it happened, Shell had developed a sophisticated UPM (Unified Planning Mechanism) and agreed to sell the rights to its Burmah-Shell partner, Burmah Oil. UPM embraced both planning and control of revenue and capital expenditure within a planning cycle. The advantage to Burmah Oil was that its corporate structure was relatively simple so that the system could be rapidly introduced by being slotted into the current round of operations and into any newly-acquired units as they joined the group. Furthermore, in many ways it was formalising what was already being done less formally, for example in the budgeting and monthly reporting introduced by Gage and Elliott. However, while R. P. Smith personally welcomed its introduction, some senior managers feared lest it might cut across their individual authority. It was in fact soon adapted to the group's own requirements and renamed Planning and Control Mechanism, PCM for short.

Certain fundamental group planning objectives were laid down: first, to increase to 10 per cent the average return (net of taxes) on capital employed in trading operations; second, to improve the company's cash flow and increase the amounts available for retention and reinvestment out of company reserves; and third, to spread risks by starting up trading in areas of lower political and financial risk than existed with many current projects.

Within these basic objectives, each level of management would submit its own plan covering the next five years. In a way, this acknowledged a principle deeply embedded in the Burmah Oil philosophy, which went back to the management agency era, that the man on the spot could best judge local conditions. Each individual plan would be incorporated in the plan at the next higher level, but would be formally submitted to Burmah House each September. That was then considered at autumn meetings in Britain between the chief executives of the relevant units and headquarters staff, and helped to determine the company's overall strategy.

On the basis of that strategy, the planning department wrote individual objectives letters to each operating company, to chief representatives abroad and to managers of the respective areas. The monitoring aspect put responsibility on individual managements to check the performance of their units against the targets set. Since they had to submit regular returns to head office, as well as attend the regular autumn meetings, there would be both supervision from the centre and a feedback of ideas there. Thus if PCM worked as well as it was expected to do, the Burmah Oil group would at long last have the organisation to ensure that all its component parts were interacting to move in the desired direction.

The core of PCM was the objectives memorandum. Williams drafted the first one, discussed below, in the shadow of a sterling crisis in July 1966. James Callaghan, the Chancellor of the Exchequer, then had to impose all the apparatus of the 'stop' phase in the 'stop-go' system of demand management which had passed for government economic strategy ever since 1945. His measures included a 7 per cent bank rate, tax increases, credit restraint and a standstill in prices and incomes. Burmah Oil was forced to cut back on its priority capital projects and restrict them within the estimated figure of depreciation allowances to be generated in the coming twelve months. However, Smith as chairman proposed that, while the company must perforce accept the government-imposed restrictions, it should continue to work on planning the group's development in order to be ready to move forward as soon as these restrictions were eased.

The board accepted Smith's proposal, given the overriding

need to tackle Burmah Oil's fundamental weakness, namely the current marked disparity between its trading and investment income. In 1965, for instance, net operating profit had been only £5.9 million, higher than Strain's forecast £5–5.5 million but only 20 per cent of total earnings: income from associated companies and trade investment had been £8.2 million or 28 per cent and the BP and Shell dividends no less than £15.6 million or 52 per cent. 'An increase in the trading income to £20 million would be envisaged', the board minutes stated, with top priority being given to obtaining a substantial part of the figure from operations in Britain.

Having taken account of all these aspirations and constraints, in December 1966 Williams submitted his draft Objectives Memorandum for 1967/72 to the board. He began by accepting that Britain's economic difficulties for the moment overshadowed the group's investment and expansion policy. He assumed that the period of financial stringency would persist for at least two years, before giving way to improved economic performance and liquidity in Britain and the rest of the world. What was the planning base he had in mind? The three overriding group objectives, mentioned above, could be converted into the goal of a group trading income, net of tax, of £25 million by 1972. That figure would make trading and investment income about equal. As priority would have to be given to an increase in UK trading income, for Corporation Tax purposes, substantial acquisitions would be required at home.

A striking diagram graphically illustrated the boldness of this target. If a trading profit level of £8 million were reached in 1967 – a year late on the 1963 forecast – the equivalent profit on existing products and markets would in 1972 be no higher than £10 million. A gap of £15 million was therefore left to be filled. Should that gap be covered by acquisitions, fresh discoveries of crude, new markets, new products, internal reforms, diversification, or a combination of some or all of these? The group's financial and management resources would not be strong enough to undertake direct investment in new projects that needed to be built up from scratch. On the other hand, acquisitions through share exchanges of profitable established companies, with good management in place, would pose none of these problems. Certainly, as he admitted, 'every effort to achieve integrated operations both nationally and internationally will be made', while any existing unit with no prospect of a 10 per cent return on capital by 1972 must be a candidate for disposal. A major step should therefore be new capital investment in acquisitions and projects to the tune of about £120 million during the period. That figure was later raised to £200 million, of which no less than £90 million would be in the UK and £60 million in North and South America; most of the remainder would be spent in the East and the increasingly prosperous EEC countries.

How, then, to raise this vast amount of money? The Shell shares might fetch £30 million, while acquisitions would be paid for with the company's own stock, by borrowing, and by new share issues for cash on the London market. For overseas ventures, funds would have to be sought on the spot in local currency, perhaps on the security of the BP shares or other assets. Exploration and other longer term projects could be financed out of the group's cash flow. On the question of raising money in the market, since governments always tried to engineer booms just before elections, and one was due in late 1970 or early 1971, by (say) 1969 economic conditions might have eased enough to permit a major funding operation of up to £40m. Dividends would need to be kept down to existing levels in order to allow for the necessary increase in profit retentions.

In any case, a vigorous policy of diversification was required. That should concentrate on the need to refine, manufacture and market lubricating oils and speciality products. However, in this quest the company must not provoke a direct clash with the oil majors. It would therefore enter into the main product field, such as petrol, only as far as necessary to 'sell the whole barrel' of oil, so that some extension to the Ellesmere Port refinery and perhaps even the acquisition of some petrol service stations might follow, a course which he had been anxious to pursue ever since 1964, as mentioned earlier in the present chapter. Fertilisers, too, represented an important growth area, especially as the current American administration of Lyndon Johnson was promoting policies which would certainly set off a major revival of agriculture there.

Williams' programme had significant implications for the

group's staffing policy. Clearly the acquisitions that were contemplated should provide a satisfactory number of competent and suitably qualified staff both for line and for general management; some, after wider experience, might be promoted and transferred elsewhere in the group. However, major exploration successes and other integrated operations would require staff of suitable calibre, who in the short term would have to be trained people brought in, where possible, from Burmah Oil's subsidiaries; in the longer term, qualified juniors could be recruited locally and then trained up as quickly as possible. Overall, much greater attention must be paid to the systematic training of technical and managerial staff.

Williams' Objectives Memorandum was thus extremely wide-ranging both in the issues it raised and in the objectives it set for the company. The structure of Burmah Oil was very different from what it had been four decades earlier. The reforms of R. I. Watson had pulled together the poorly co-ordinated operations in the East into a unified enterprise tightly controlled by the London head office. In Watson's day all the trading income had been derived from those Eastern operations. By 1966, thanks largely to Eadie's vision of diversifying by direct investment, and to the talents of his successors, less than two-thirds of trading income was earned in the East, while Britain, Europe and South America accounted for a quarter and North America and Australia for one-tenth. The changes now being planned were calculated to bring about markedly different geographical breakdowns of contributions to earnings.[12]

Of the spheres of activity that an observer might have pinpointed as fundamental to Burmah Oil's future at the end of 1966, two stood out above all: the growth of technology, and changes in consumer preferences. Past technological change could be seen in the wide range of industrial and consumer products brought under the group's wing by the Lobitos and Castrol acquisitions, including the speciality items turned out by the Ellesmere Port and Barton refineries, Castrol's own resolve to keep ahead of its rivals in the lubricating oil business, and the increasing interest within the group in petrochemicals, plastics and further by-products of the oil-refining process.

A major reorganisation of research and development facilities, essential if it were to remain generally a progressive company, was carried out by integrating the Lobitos and Castrol research laboratories into a group R. & D. division. The second fundamental sphere of activity related to the changing pattern of consumer demand. Burmah Oil, being a medium-sized operating company and therefore more flexible in its response to change, could be better placed to gratify changes in peoples' tastes than its larger rivals, provided that the products demanded were compatible with its own overall strategy. Britain was becoming a nation of car-owners; perhaps the most noteworthy statistic was that in 1964 private road transport accounted for nearly two-thirds of all passenger mileage in the UK, estimated to cover no fewer than 125,000 million passenger miles. Through Castrol, Burmah Oil already supplied the largest single share of lubricants sold at home.

In October 1966 the board therefore agreed that Williams should obtain estimates for the expansion of the Ellesmere Port refinery. That would provide most of the lubricating oil base stocks required by Castrol, and at the same time a wider range of speciality products to meet projected market growth. Increased quantities of light fractions would inevitably be produced, and those would be turned into petrol. From early 1967 onwards, the company began to acquire suitable independent networks of petrol stations in order to maximise sales through its own outlets of this growing production. It was in the light of this board decision and its consequences that Williams – managing director from 1969 – became increasingly interested in wider aspects of the developing motorists' market.

As one successful entrepreneur at that time put it, the car should be thought of not just as an outlet for petrol and oil, but as a source of pride and joy to motorists in an increasingly affluent era. Their needs included brake fluid and anti-freeze compounds, tyres and batteries, detergents to keep car bodies clean and waxes to make them shine, rust-proofing materials, touch-up paints, and an infinite variety of articles that provided real or cosmetic improvements. Literally and metaphorically, behind the car came the caravan; that implied a further step in potential sales from the motorists' market to all the growth prospects of the leisure market. These and similar concepts played their part in influencing the acquisition policies of Burmah Oil in the immediate post-Castrol phase from 1966 onwards.

Meanwhile, the directors never lost sight of the need, so often expressed in recent years, for truly integrated oil operations in the United States through the purchase of a large American corporation. They were willing to accept that this purchase might threaten to put the company's aspirations in conflict with those of BP. Yet all the effort appeared to be well worthwhile, as the world's need for oil and its products was clearly insatiable. The days in which Burmah Oil had exerted such great influence over the British oil scene under R. I. Watson's leadership seemed about to return. The 1970s promised to be the most dynamic and exciting decade yet in the company's long history.

Notes

1 R. Belgrave (Policy Planning Adviser to BP), 'How BP Made It in the US', *Petroleum Review* LVII, 1971, pp. 83–8.
2 Academy House (renamed Burmah House), Chiswell Street, is illustrated in *BGM* No. 10, Summer 1967, p. 27.
3 See Castrol Ltd, *Wheels, Wings and Water*, privately printed for 75th anniversary, 1974, pp. 67–71. For Farrow and his directorships, see *Guardian*, 19 November 1966.
4 For Expandite and Atlas, see *BGM* No. 16, Winter 1968. For Denis Thatcher, see *Sunday Times*, 2 December 1979.
5 'Castrol House', *BGM* No. 9, Spring 1967, p. 13.
6 *Sunday Times*, 30 October 1966.
7 *Investors' Guardian*, 4 November 1966.
8 K. V. Stringer, 'Offshore Exploration', *BGM* No. 7, Autumn 1966, pp. 25–9, gives a useful background to the completion of the first well. The quotation is on p. 27.
9 For *Ocean Prince*, see *BGM* No. 1, Spring 1965, pp. 4–5; No. 3, Autumn 1965, pp. 18–19; and No. 5, Spring 1966, pp. 2–9.
10 For *Lady Alison*, see *BGM* No. 4, Winter 1965, p. 10.
11 This oil strike was the lead in the *Evening Standard*, 20 October, and in many of the London papers on 21 October 1966.
12 Many of the concepts discussed here, including that of the Ellesmere Port refinery project, are dealt with in the company's *Special Report to Stockholders*, issued in February 1973.

Postscript

History has to relate a very different and far more sombre scenario for the 1970s than Williams and his fellow-directors could ever have contemplated. The story of all that was attempted in the quest for achievement is too long to be related here. Briefly, however, Burmah Oil did indeed after 1966 make a number of major acquisitions, the most important being that of Signal Oil & Gas Inc in the United States, and entered into further exploration commitments in the North Sea, Australia and elsewhere. It also became involved in tankers. All these additions to its activities, while falling within the overall strategy for oil and gas already laid down, had three grave drawbacks: they burdened the company with very heavy financial commitments; the pace of acquisitions proved too great for them to be properly digested and consolidated; and time would be needed before satisfactory management practices, especially supervision from the centre of rapidly spreading world-wide operations in many different fields, could be adequately enforced.

All might still have been well had external disaster not struck, when OPEC quadrupled oil prices in 1973–74 and the stock-market in Britain subsequently collapsed, thereby substantially depressing the worth of the BP shareholdings. Since the holdings had been used as collateral for the loans to acquire Signal, these loans were now put in jeopardy. Moreover, the company's tanker commitments became a crippling liability at a time when tanker demand was drastically falling. At the end of 1974 it had to be rescued by the Bank of England, at the eventual cost of selling – at the current ultra-low market price – its 23 per cent stake in BP. Williams then resigned as managing director.

A new hand-picked managerial team, headed by Alastair Down – who retired from the deputy chairmanship of BP to become the Burmah Oil chairman, had to put the stricken company back on its feet by massive sales of oil assets as scattered as those in the US, Australia, Canada, Ecuador and the North Sea. The total value of the disposals was no less than £865 million. Those executives who formed part of the team remembered the years from 1975 onwards as ones of almost intolerable stress, but also of heroic endeavour: entrepreneurs sometimes have to use their skills to dismantle as well as to assemble corporate packages.

Under Alastair Down and after 1983 under his successor, John Maltby, who in the following years sold off over forty further subsidiaries, the Burmah group was gradually restructured. By its centenary year of 1986 it was no longer the integrated oil company it had been until lately; instead it was becoming a financially strong and compact group, concentrated around the manufacture and marketing, on an international scale, of specialised oil and chemical products and the transportation of liquefied natural gas.

'To celebrate a hundred years in business does not make the Burmah group unique,' John Maltby told his stockholders at the 1986 annual general meeting, 'but I can think of few, if any, other companies that have had to weather the sorts of challenges this company has faced and have come through them as successfully. We can build on a century's experience of good times and bad, of successful strategies and disastrous ones, to chart our future growth.'

Biographical Notes

Abbreviations: AFPFL = Anti-Fascist People's Freedom League; AOC = Assam Oil Company; BOC = Burmah Oil Company; APOC = Anglo-Persian Oil Company – to 1935; AIOC = Anglo-Iranian Oil company – 1935 to 1954; BP = British Petroleum – since 1954; FF & Co. = Finlay Fleming & Co., Rangoon; DBB = Dictionary of Business Biography; DNB = Dictionary of National Biography; DSBB = Dictionary of Scottish Business Biography; PPL = Pakistan Petroleum Ltd; WW = Who's Who; WWW = Who Was Who, under year of death.

ABRAHAM, Sir William Ernest Victor – WEVA – (1897–1980) CBE 1942, Kt 1977. Geologist, BOC 1920–37; London Office 1937–40; army 1940–5; rose to major-general; director BOC 1945–55; managing director 1948–55; director AIOC 1953–5. (WWW)

ASHTON, Sir Hubert (1898–1979) MC, KBE 1959. Assistant, FF & Co. 1922–30; London office 1930–45; MP, Chelmsford 1950–64; PPS to Chancellor of Exchequer 1951–5; to Lord Privy Seal 1955–7; Second Church Estates Commissioner 1957–62. (WWW)

AUNG SAN, Major-General (Bogyoke) (1916–47). Led oilfields strikes 1938–9; Commander, Burma Independence Army, 1942; later led anti-Japanese resistance movements in

389

Burma; president, AFPFL, 1945-7; Member of Constituent Assembly; led Burmese delegation to London, 1947; assassinated, 1947.

BERTHOUD, Sir Eric Alfred (b. 1900) KCMG 1954. With APOC/AIOC 1926-39; Assistant Secretary (later Under-Secretary) Petroleum Department, 1942-4; Foreign Office 1948-60. (WW)

BILSLAND, Lord (Alexander Steven Bilsland, 1892-1970) Bart. 1921; baron 1950; chairman Bilsland Bros Ltd, governor of Bank of Scotland, etc; director BOC 1947-66. (WWW)

BOWRING, Frederick C. (1897-1965). Director of Lobitos Oilfields Ltd, Anglo-Ecuadorian Oilfields Ltd 1934-65; chairman 1954-65; director BOC 1962-5.

BRIDGEMAN, Sir Maurice Richard (1904-80) KBE 1964. APOC from 1926; Assistant Secretary and Principal Assistant Secretary, Petroleum Department 1940-6; chairman BP 1960-1969. (DBB, WWW)

CADMAN, Sir John (1877-1941) KCMG 1918; Lord Cadman 1937. Professor of Mining, Birmingham University 1908-20; petroleum adviser, Colonial Office; member, Slade delegation to Persia 1913-14; director, Petroleum Executive 1917-21; joined APOC 1921; director 1923; deputy chairman 1925; chairman 1927-41. (DBB, DNB, WWW)

CAREY, Rupert Sausmarez (1905-1981) OBE. Burma Oilfields Rehabilitation Unit, 1945; general manager in the East 1949-54.

CARGILL, Sir John Traill (1867-1954) Bart. 1920. Assistant FF & Co. 1890-3; BOC Glasgow Office 1893; liquidator in BOC's reconstruction 1902; director 1902; chairman 1904-43; director APOC 1909-43. (WWW, DBB, DSBB)

CONDON, Michael James (b. 1915) CBE 1954. Assistant, BOC 1938; served in Burma 1938-40; army 1940-5; general manager, Pakistan 1949-60; general manager, India 1960-2.

DETERDING, Sir Henri Wilhelm August (1866–1939) KBE 1920. Joined Royal Dutch Oil Company, 1896; managing director, Asiatic Petroleum Company 1903; general managing director, Royal Dutch and director, Shell Transport & Trading Company 1907–36. (WWW)

DEWHURST, John Desmond (b. 1917). Son of Thomas Dewhurst (q.v.). Geologist, BOC 1946; served in Burma, India and Pakistan; general manager, Burma 1961–3; representative of Burmah group in Australia 1963–5; London office 1965 onwards; exploration and production manager and later divisional director; director BOC 1970–5; assistant managing director 1973–5.

DEWHURST, Thomas (1881–1973). Geologist, BOC 1910; senior geologist in Rangoon 1916; first chief geologist of BOC, London office 1922–38; geological adviser to APOC: to BOC 1938–61.

DORMAN-SMITH, Sir Reginald (1899–1977) Kt 1937. MP, Petersfield 1935–41; Minister of Agriculture and Fisheries 1939–40; governor of Burma 1941–6. (WWW)

DOWN, Sir Alastair Frederick (b. 1914) OBE, MC; Kt 1978. Chartered accountant, Scotland; joined AIOC 1938; army 1940–4; rose to colonel; chief representative of BP, Canada 1954–62; managing director BP 1962–9; deputy chairman 1969–75; chairman, BOC 1975–83; chief executive 1975–80. (DBB, WW)

DRAKE, Sir Arthur Eric Courtney (b. 1910) CBE, Kt 1970. Joined AIOC 1935; managing director BP 1958–62; deputy chairman 1962–9; chairman BP 1969–75. (DBB, WW)

DRYSDALE, John Alexander (1908–86). Assistant, BOC, Rangoon 1931; army 1942–6; London office (exploration manager) 1946; director BOC 1961–9; assistant managing director 1967–8.

EADIE, William Ewing (1896–1976). Chartered accountant, Scotland. Joined BOC, Rangoon 1921; seconded to Burmah-Shell 1928–41; London office 1941 onwards; chief accountant 1948–50; director BOC 1950–67; assistant managing director 1951–5; managing director 1955–61; chairman 1957–64; director BP 1955–64. (WWW)

EVANS, Percy (1892–1974). Geologist, BOC 1915; India 1915–31; resident geologist, Digboi 1931–6; senior geologist, India 1936–9; chief geologist, London office 1938–55; consultant 1955–70.

FARROW, Leslie William (1888–1978) CBE 1947. Chartered accountant; chairman C. C. Wakefield & Co. (later Castrol Ltd) 1943–66; director BOC 1966–70. (WWW)

FINLAY, John (b. 1918). Grandson of Kirkman Finlay. Burma fields 1942–52; AOC representative, Digboi and Delhi 1952–55; manager PPL 1955–9; Rangoon 1960–1; chief representative, India 1962–76.

FLEMING, Richard Evelyn (1911–77) MC. Director, Robert Fleming & Co., bankers; chairman 1966–74; director BOC 1959–75. (WWW)

FORSTER, Walter Leslie (1903–85) CBE 1942. Civil engineer and geologist; Royal Dutch-Shell 1925–52; adviser regarding denial of oil to enemy, Middle East, Russia and Burma 1940–2. (WWW)

FRASER (see Strathalmond)

GRAY, William Anstruther (1885–1967). Assistant FF & Co. 1910–26; general manager in the East 1926–9; London office 1929–37; director BOC 1937–59.

GREENWAY, Sir Charles (1857–1934) Bart. 1919; Lord Greenway 1927. Assistant Shaw Wallace & Co. 1893; senior partner 1907; partner R. G. Shaw & Co. 1907; London director BOC 1907; director APOC 1909–34; managing director 1910–1919; chairman 1914–27; retired 1927. (DBB, WWW)

HARPER, Sir Kenneth Brand (1891–1961) Kt 1936. Assistant
FF & Co. 1913–36; London office 1936–7; director BOC
1937–57; chairman 1948–57; managing director 1948–51;
director AIOC/APOC 1947–57; director Shell 1948–61.
(WWW)

LEPPER, Gordon Willis (1889–1950). Geologist; joined BOC
1910; senior geologist in the East 1922–36; geological adviser to
Petroleum Department 1939–46.

LINGEMAN, Paul Donald McAlister (1899–1970). Assistant
FF & Co. 1921; served in Burma, India and Pakistan; general
manager in the East 1945–9.

LOUDON, John Hugo (b. 1905) Hon KBE 1960. Joined Royal
Dutch-Shell 1930; managing director, Royal Dutch 1947–52;
president 1952–65; chairman 1965–76. (WW)

LUMSDEN, James Alexander (b. 1915) MBE 1945. Partner
Maclay Murray & Spens, solicitors of Glasgow 1947; director
BOC 1957–76; chairman 1971–5. (WW)

MACLACHLAN, William Patrick Gawain (b. 1918) MBE
1945. Assistant BOC 1939; army 1941–6; served in Burma,
India and Pakistan; general manager AOC 1957–60; chairman
Oil India Ltd 1959–60; general manager BOC (Pakistan
Trading) 1960–2; London office 1962–8; director BOC
1968–75.

MARDALL, E. G. C. (1903–86). Manager Lobitos Oilfields
Ltd 1957; general manager 1958; Lobitos board 1959; director
BOC 1962–8.

MAXWELL-LEFROY, Cecil Anthony (b. 1907) CBE 1959.
Joined BOC 1928; served in Burma and India; Oilfields
Manager, Burma 1949–51; assistant general manager, Burma
1951–4; general manager 1954–9.

NE WIN, Lieut-General (b. 1911). Commander-in-Chief,
Burma National Army 1943–5; member AFPFL Central

Board of Leaders 1945; Minister of Defence and Home Affairs 1949–50; Commander-in-Chief, Burma from 1949; prime minister 1958–60; president of Union of Burma since 1962.

NU, Thakin (b. 1907). Foreign minister, Burma 1943–5; vice-president AFPFL 1945–7; prime minister 1947–56, 1957–8, 1960–2.

ROPER, Sir Harold (1891–1971) MC, CBE 1943, Kt 1945. Assistant FF & Co. 1919; general manager in the East 1936–45; MP, North Cornwall 1950–9. (WWW)

SMITH, Robert Paterson (1903–71). Chartered accountant, Scotland. Asiatic Petroleum Co, Calcutta, 1926; Burmah-Shell, India 1928; joined BOC London office 1952; director 1955; assistant managing director 1956; managing director 1957–68; chairman 1965–71; director BP 1958–71. (WWW)

SPENS, Hugh Baird (1885–1958) DSO 1918, CBE 1946. Partner, Maclay Murray & Spens, solicitors, Glasgow; director BOC 1937–57. (WWW)

STRAIN, John Francis (b. 1905). Chartered accountant, Scotland; joined BOC, Rangoon 1928; served in Burma, India and Pakistan; London office 1946; chief accountant 1950–7; director 1957–73; deputy chairman 1967–71.

STRATHALMOND, Lord; William Milligan Fraser (1888–1970) CBE 1918; Kt 1939. Managing director, Scottish Oils Ltd 1919; managing director APOC 1923–8; deputy chairman 1928–41; chairman 1941–56; director BOC 1939–64. (DBB, DNB, WWW)

TAINSH, Harold Robert (b. 1912). BOC geologist 1934; senior geologist, Burma, 1946; chief geologist, London office 1955; director BOC 1963; assistant managing director 1970–2; non-executive director 1972–9.

WATSON, Robert Irving (1878–1948). In London office BOC 1901–2 and 1912 onwards; assistant FF & Co. 1902–12;

director BOC 1918–47; managing director 1920–47; chairman 1943; director APOC 1918–47; director Shell Transport & Trading Company 1929–47. (DBB, DSBB)

WHIGHAM, Gilbert Campbell (1877–1950). Assistant FF & Co. 1904; BOC general manager in India 1912–14; joined BOC London office 1919; London director 1919; director 1920–46; assistant managing director 1923–45; director APOC 1925–46.

WILLIAMS, Nicholas James Donald (b. 1925). Senior partner, Surridge & Beecheno, solicitors, Karachi 1955; legal adviser BOC 1961; co-ordinator for Eastern Operations 1963; director 1965–74; assistant managing director 1967–9; managing director 1969; chief executive 1971–4. (WW)

Crude Oil Production and Refinery Throughput Data 1924–61

(000 barrels)

Year	Total crude oil production – Burma	Refinery throughput		
		Burma	India (Digboi)	Total
1924	6692	4951	na	na
1925	6510	4959	na	na
1926	6191	4945	na	na
1927	6095	4955	na	na
1928	6510	4960	na	na
1929	6300	4955	na	na
1930	6461	4952	1041	5993
1931	6175	4945	1317	6262
1932	6379	5083	1380	6463
1933	6419	5092	1303	6395
1934	6556	5070	1638	6708
1935	6479	4993	1644	6637
1936	6834	5036	1654	6690
1937	7099	5068	1621	6689
1938	6821	5074	1636	6710
1939	7147	5411	1265	6676
1940	6986	5070	1652	6722
1941	7046	5120	1653	6773

(000 barrels)

Refinery throughput

Year	Total crude oil production – Burma	Burma	India (Digboi)	Total
1942	771 (200) (a)	560	1635	2195
1943	(600) (a)	na	1828	na
1944	(1200) (a)	na	2081	na
1945	(200) (a)	na	1706	na
1946	na	na	1620	na
1947	83	na	1662	na
1948	317	(89) (b)	1695	1784
1949	247	86	1706	1792
1950	539	226	1663	1889
1951	770	389	1826	2215
1952	829	400	1705	2105
1953	997	502	1812	2314
1954	1293	707	2001	2708
1955	1342	792	2287 (c)	3079
1956	1510	866	2597	3463
1957	2475	1474	2845	4319
1958	2895	2179	2867	5046
1959	3325	2468	2950	5418
1960	3402	na	na	na
1961	3511	2893	na	na

Notes: (a) Estimated Japanese output during occupation
(b) Total refined products from 1948 onwards
(c) Throughput of Burmah-Shell refinery at Bombay, from 1955 onwards, not included

Burmah Oil Company – Financial Data 1924–66
(£000s)

Year	Issued ordinary shares	Issued preference shares	Debentures	Total assets	Trading profit (b)	Investment income	Total income	Net profit (c)
1924	5,151	4,000	—	15,482	2,493	387	2,880	2,257
1925	5,151	4,000	—	16,494	2,243	766	2,319	2,405
1926	6,868	4,000	—	17,495	2,478	689	3,167	2,503
1927	6,868	4,000	—	17,518	1,903	803	2,706	1,915
1928	6,868	4,000	4,000	20,584	1,559	561	2,120	1,480
1929	6,868	4,000	4,000	22,693	2,957	1,213	4,170	3,437
1930	6,868	4,000	4,000	22,831	2,033	1,430	3,463	2,736
1931	6,868	4,000	4,000	23,266	1,586	998	2,584	1,869
1932	6,868	4,000	4,000	23,553	1,103	1,076	2,179	1,525
1933	6,868	4,000	4,000	24,006	1,480	1,125	2,605	2,012
1934	9,158	4,000	—	19,928	1,345	841	2,186	1,657
1935	9,158	4,000	—	20,781	1,620	1,057	2,677	2,277
1936	9,158	4,000	—	21,973	2,262	1,471	2,733	3,324
1937	9,158	4,000	—	23,626	2,502	2,217	4,719	3,998
1938	13,737	4,000	—	26,864	2,150	2,657	4,807	3,850
1939	13,737	4,000	—	27,321 (a)	1,928	2,385	4,313	3,434
1940	13,737	4,000	—	28,061	2,768	1,000	3,768	2,546
1941	13,737	4,000	—	31,040	3,530	1,336	4,866	2,832
1942	13,737	4,000	—	32,792	3,444	1,745	5,189	2,550
1943	13,737	4,000	—	33,491	1,863	2,122	3,895	2,155

Year	Issued ordinary shares	Issued preference shares	Debentures	Total assets	Trading profit (b)	Investment income	Total income	Net profit (c)
1944	13,737	4,000	—	43,035	1,517	2,135	3,652	2,626
1945	13,737	4,000	—	48,792	1,726	2,298	4,024	2,945
1946	13,737	4,000	—	38,962	560	2,572	3,132	2,378
1947	13,737	4,000	—	34,464	1,603	2,571	4,174	2,263
1948	13,737	4,000	—	49,237	4,088	2,735	6,823	2,058
1949	13,737	4,000	—	49,753	5,617	2,638	8,255	2,682
1950	13,737	4,000	—	53,396	6,838	2,944	9,782	2,891
1951	13,737	4,000	—	53,920	7,483	3,227	10,710	3,361
1952	20,605	4,000	—	54,610	5,465	3,309	8,774	2,872
1953	20,605	4,000	—	54,299	5,331	3,582	8,913	3,252
1954	20,605	4,000	—	56,494	5,131	4,228	9,359	3,729
1955	41,210	4,000	—	82,542	6,018	9,251	15,269	5,853
1956	41,210	4,000	—	90,448	7,585	10,333	17,918	7,124
1957	41,210	4,000	—	93,507	6,241	11,158	17,399	7,056
1958	41,210	4,000	—	96,001	6,779	10,904	17,683	7,506
1959	82,419	4,000	880	123,151	6,880	12,722	19,602	8,684
1960	82,419	4,000	5,055	126,036	4,973	14,672	19,645	9,996
1961	82,419	4,000	4,325	129,616	4,550	16,447	20,997	11,086
1962	93,798	4,000	1,569	158,481	9,221	17,937	27,158	13,613
1963	94,062	4,000	13,532	179,708	9,231	18,093	27,324	13,906
1964	117,578	4,000	11,426	204,538	11,287	21,627	32,914	15,629
1965	117,578	4,000	10,066	205,118	10,615	21,328	31,943	16,799
1966	123,786	19,000	31,076	263,503	16,628	21,136	37,764	24,188

Notes: (a) Consolidated balance sheet introduced this year, after establishment of wholly-owned subsidiaries
(b) Before taxation and depreciation
(c) After taxation and depreciation

Turnover (net of taxes, etc.) 1966 = £119.6 million

Index